Theories of Case

Case, a system which marks the relationships between words in a sentence, is fundamental to every language. Looking at how different theories of syntax have accounted for the distribution of case across languages, this accessible textbook introduces the various approaches to case that have been proposed in modern linguistics. Clearly organised into topics, it provides beginning students with a solid understanding of the ideas behind the development of theories of case. For the more advanced reader, it presents theories that have been formulated about the interaction between case morphology, argument structure, grammatical relations and semantics, and offers a detailed cross-theoretical discussion of how these are motivated. Each chapter contains practical exercises, encouraging students to engage with the ideas discussed. Drawing on data from a wide range of languages and pooling together a variety of perspectives, *Theories of Case* is essential reading for all those studying this important area of linguistics.

MIRIAM BUTT is Professor of Theoretical and Computational Linguistics at the University of Konstanz. She has authored, co-authored and co-edited a variety of books on morphosyntax, semantics, historical linguistics and computational linguistics, including *The Structure of Complex Predicates in Urdu*, *A Grammar Writer's Cookbook*, *Theoretical Perspectives on Word Order Issues*, and *The Projection of Arguments*, as well as *Time over Matter*, *Argument Realization*, and *Nominals: Inside and Out*.

CAMBRIDGE TEXTBOOKS IN LINGUISTICS

General editors: P. AUSTIN, J. BRESNAN, B. COMRIE, S. CRAIN, W. DRESSLER, C. EWEN, R. LASS, D. LIGHTFOOT, K. RICE, I. ROBERTS, S. ROMAINE, N.V. SMITH.

Theories of Case

In this series:

R.M. KEMPSON *Semantic Theory*
T. BYNON *Historical Linguistics*
J. ALLWOOD, L.-G. ANDERSON and Ö. DAHL *Logic in Linguistics*
D.B. FRY *The Physics of Speech*
R.A. HUDSON *Sociolinguistics* Second Edition
A.J. ELLIOT *Child Language*
P.H. MATTHEWS *Syntax*
A. RADFORD *Transformational Syntax*
L. BAUER *English Word-Formation*
S.C. LEVINSON *Pragmatics*
G. BROWN and G. YULE *Discourse Analysis*
R. HUDDLESTON *Introduction to the Grammar of English*
R. LASS *Phonology*
B. COMRIE *Tense*
W. KLEIN *Second Language Acquisition*
A.J. WOODS, P. FLETCHER and A. HUGHES *Statistics in Language Studies*
D.A. CRUSE *Lexical Semantics*
A. RADFORD *Transformational Grammar*
M. GARMAN *Pycholinguistics*
C.G. CORBETT *Gender*
H.J. GIEGERICH *English Phonology*
R. CANN *Formal Semantics*
J. LAVER *Principles of Phonetics*
F.R. PALMER *Grammatical Roles and Relations*
M.A. JONES *Foundations of French Syntax*
A. RADFORD *Syntactic Theory and the Structure of English: A Minimalist Approach*
R.D. VAN VALIN, JR and R.J. LAPOLLA *Syntax: Structure, Meaning and Function*
A. DURANTI *Linguistic Anthropology*
A. CRUTTENDEN *Intonation* Second Edition
J.K. CHAMBERS and P. TRUDGILL *Dialectology* Second Edition
C. LYONS *Definiteness*
R. KAGER *Optimality Theory*
J.A. HOLM *An Introduction to Pidgins and Creoles*
C.G. CORBETT *Number*
C.J. EWEN and H. VAN DER HULST *The Phonological Structure of Words*
F.R. PALMER *Mood and Modality* Second Edition
B.J. BLAKE *Case* Second Edition
E. GUSSMAN *Phonology: Analysis and Theory*
M. YIP *Tone*
W. CROFT *Typology and Universals* Second Edition
F. COULMAS *Writing Systems: An Introduction to their Linguistic Analysis*
P.J. HOPPER and E.C. TRAUGOTT *Grammaticalization* Second Edition
L. WHITE *Second Language Acquisition and Universal Grammar*
I. PLAG *Word-Formation in English*
W. CROFT and A. CRUSE *Cognitive Linguistics*
A. SIEWIERSKA *Person*
A. RADFORD *Minimalist Syntax: Exploring the Structure of English*
D. BÜRING *Binding Theory*
M. BUTT *Theories of Case*
N. HORNSTEIN, J. NUNES and K. GROHMANN *Understanding Minimalism*
B.C. LUST *Child Language: Acquisition and Growth*

Theories of Case

MIRIAM BUTT
Universität Konstanz

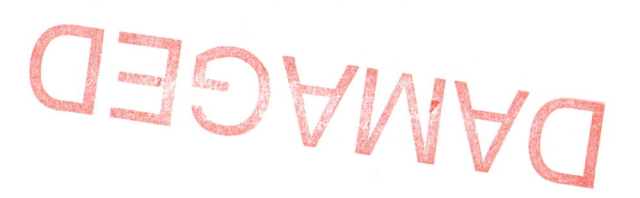

CAMBRIDGE UNIVERSITY PRESS

CAMBRIDGE UNIVERSITY PRESS
Cambridge, New York, Melbourne, Madrid, Cape Town, Singapore, São Paulo

Cambridge University Press
The Edinburgh Building, Cambridge CB2 2RU, UK

Published in the United States of America by Cambridge University Press, New York

www.cambridge.org
Information on this title: www.cambridge.org/9780521797313

© Miriam Butt 2006

This book is in copyright. Subject to statutory exception and to the provisions of relevant collective licensing agreements, no reproduction of any part may take place without the written permission of Cambridge University Press.

First published 2006

Printed in the United Kingdom at the University Press, Cambridge

A catalogue record for this book is available from the British Library

ISBN-13 978-0-521-79322-3   hardback
ISBN-10 0-521- 79322-X   hardback
ISBN-13 978-0-521-79731-3   paperback
ISBN-10 0-521-79731-4   paperback

Cambridge University Press has no responsibility for the persistence or accuracy of URLs for external or third-party internet websites referred to in this publication, and does not guarantee that any content on such websites is, or will remain, accurate or appropriate.

Contents

Acknowledgements   xi

Abbreviations   xiii

1 **Introduction**   1
   1.1   Overview   1
   1.2   What is Case?   3
         1.2.1   Head vs. Dependent Marking   5
         1.2.2   Is Everything Case? — Persian *ezafe*   6
         1.2.3   Adverbial Case   6
         1.2.4   Case and Finiteness   7
         1.2.5   Nominal Case   8
         1.2.6   Case Stacking   9
   1.3   Levels of Abstractness   11

2 **Foundational Perspectives**   12
   2.1   Introduction   12
   2.2   The Greek and Roman Tradition   13
   2.3   The Indian Tradition   15
   2.4   The Arabic Tradition   18
   2.5   Exercises   21

3 **Grammatical Relations**   23
   3.1   The Structure of Sentences   23
   3.2   Transformational Grammar, Case and the Passive   24
   3.3   Relational Grammar   26

3.4   The Notion of Grammatical Relations   28
3.5   Case Grammar and Thematic Roles   29
3.6   Core Ideas of Relational Grammar   33
    3.6.1   The Passive Revisited   33
    3.6.2   Case in Relational Grammar   36
3.7   The Unaccusative Hypothesis   38
3.8   The Universal Alignment Hypothesis   42
3.9   Summary   44
3.10   Exercises   44

4   Structural Case   46

4.1   The Structural View of Grammatical Relations   46
4.2   The Basic Architecture   46
4.3   Thematic Roles   48
4.4   Category Neutral Representations: X′-Syntax   51
4.5   The VP-internal subject hypothesis   53
4.6   Case and Agreement   55
4.7   D-Structure, θ-Theory, and Structural Case   55
    4.7.1   Unaccusatives and Unergatives   60
    4.7.2   Passivization   64
4.8   Structural vs. Inherent or Quirky Case   67
4.9   Taking Stock   71
4.10   Minimalism   73
    4.10.1   Phases, Merge and Features   73
    4.10.2   External Arguments   75
    4.10.3   Lexical Conceptual Structure   77
    4.10.4   Unergatives, Unaccusatives and Passives   79
4.11   English Double Objects   83
4.12   Discussion   87
4.13   Exercises   89

5   Linking Theories   91

5.1   Introduction   91
5.2   Representation of Predicate-Argument Structure   92
5.3   Lexical Decomposition and Linking   94
5.4   Proto-Roles   98
5.5   Kiparsky's Linking Theory   100

- 5.5.1 Semantic Form and Thematic Roles   101
- 5.5.2 The Feature System   103
- 5.5.3 Linking by Case, Position and Agreement   107
- 5.5.4 Passives, Unaccusatives and Unergatives   109
- 5.6 Lexical Decomposition Grammar   111
  - 5.6.1 Basic Analyses   113
  - 5.6.2 Unergatives, Unaccusatives and Semantics   114
  - 5.6.3 Quirky Case   116
- 5.7 Lexical-Functional Grammar   117
  - 5.7.1 LFG Basics   117
  - 5.7.2 Argument Structure and Thematic Roles   122
  - 5.7.3 Quirky Case and Early Association Principles   123
  - 5.7.4 The Introduction of Explicit Features   126
  - 5.7.5 Standard LFG Mapping Theory   127
  - 5.7.6 Argument Alternations   131
  - 5.7.7 Incorporation of Proto-Roles   135
- 5.8 Case Stacking   138
- 5.9 An Interactive Model of Case   142
  - 5.9.1 Linking   144
  - 5.9.2 Structural Case   145
  - 5.9.3 Quirky Case   146
  - 5.9.4 Semantic Case   146
- 5.10 Discussion   149
- 5.11 Exercises   150

6 The Ergative Dragon   153
- 6.1 Fighting Dragons   153
- 6.2 The Terminology   154
  - 6.2.1 Torres Straits and the Agentive Nominative   154
  - 6.2.2 A Misunderstanding with Georgian   156
- 6.3 Case Systems   158
- 6.4 Syntactic vs. Morphological Ergativity   161
- 6.5 Approaches to Morphological Ergativity   165
  - 6.5.1 The Ergative as an Inherent Case   165
  - 6.5.2 The Ergative as a Structural Case   169
  - 6.5.3 Linking theories revisited and more types of ergativity   173
- 6.6 Split Ergativity   175
- 6.7 Acquisition Issues   176

6.8 Historical Issues 179
6.9 Summary 183
6.10 Exercises 184

7 The Semantics of Case 188
7.1 Localist Theories 188
7.2 Agency vs. Experience 189
7.3 Object Alternations 191
7.4 Subject Alternations 197
7.5 Discussion 199
7.6 Exercises 200

8 More Theories Great and Small 202
8.1 Role and Reference Grammar 202
    8.1.1 Basic Linking 205
    8.1.2 Ditransitives and Dative Subjects 208
    8.1.3 Ergatives 211
8.2 Optimality Theory 212
    8.2.1 OT Basics 213
    8.2.2 Structural Case Revisited 216
    8.2.3 Harmonic Alignment 220
8.3 Discussion 224
8.4 Exercises 226

Language Index 250

Subject Index 252

Acknowledgements

This book is dedicated to Andrea Levitt and Anette Herskovits. They were my first linguistics teachers and were very bemused to discover that I had gone on to do syntax. Nevertheless, they set me on my current path and I would like to thank them for it.

This book has been with me for several years now, though for most of these years, it played more of a passive role than it deserved. This was partly due to the fact that it accompanied me to UMIST, Manchester in 2002, and then back to the University of Konstanz in 2003. This book is thus an English/German hybrid and I would like to thank both the Department of Linguistics at Konstanz and the Centre for Computational Linguistics at UMIST for providing a supportive and interesting working environment.

Thanks are also in order to a host of people, whose input and encouragement ultimately made this book possible. I would like to thank David Lightfoot and Paul Kiparsky for proposing that I take on this project and thus getting the ball rolling. At CUP, I would like to thank three editors for many helpful and cooperative exchanges. Andrew Winnard was the editor in charge when the ideas for the content of the book first took shape. Helen Barton is the editor who managed to impose deadlines politely, but firmly, and see the book to its completion. And, finally, the end production of the book was overseen by Annie Lovett in a very competent and professional manner. It was a pleasure to work with all of them.

David Adger, Judith Aissen, Mohamed Badawi, Josef Bayer, Ashwini Deo, Wilhelm Geuder, Helen de Hoop, Georg Kaiser, Ingrid Kaufmann, Tracy Holloway King, Paul Kiparsky, Carmen Kelling, Aditi Lahiri, Beth Levin, Andrej Malchukov, Judith Meinschäfer, Mahinnaz Mirdehghan, Rachel Nordlinger, Frans Plank, Gillian Ramchand, Christoph Schwarze, Peter Sells, Peter Svenonius, Robert D. Van Valin Jr., Connie de Vos, Björn Wiemer, Beate Wolke, Irene Wolke and Dieter Wunderlich have all given generously of their time, providing me with invaluable information, comments, feedback and criticism. Their input has helped shape the book from a gangly adolescent into something more mature. Thanks go to Katrin Schuhmann for careful proofreading and help with the index. Thanks also go to CUP, who had the manuscript proofread even more carefully. All remaining errors, misrepresentations and omissions are entirely my own responsibility.

Carmen Kelling in particular has been one of my most faithful and reliable readers. Ingrid Kaufmann had to put up with late-night discussions and complaints almost every day and managed to turn my musings into useful material that I could incorporate the next day. Special thanks are also due to Rajesh Bhatt, who visited during the last week of production and good-naturedly put up with late night discussions of case. Zhila Shah provided much needed moral sustenance during my stay in Lahore. Finally, very special thanks go to the Tequila Club, which is a truly most excellent institution!

Abbreviations

-	morpheme boundary	Part	Partitive
=	clitic boundary	Pass	Passive
Abl	Ablative	Past	Past
Abs	Absolutive	PastP	Past Participle
Acc	Accusative	Perf	Perfect
All	Allative	PerfP	Perfect Participle
Aor	Aorist	Pl	Plural
Asp	Aspect	Pres	Present
Caus	Causative	Prop	Proprietive
Dat	Dative	Ptcpl	Participle
Decl	Declarative	Purp	Purposive
Dem	Demonstrative	REC PAST	Recent Past
Des	Desiderative	SB	Subject
Dir	Direct (case)	Sg	Singular
Erg	Ergative	SUBJ	Subject
F	Feminine	Subj	Subject
Gd	Gerund	Tns	Tense
Gen	Genitive	Top	Topic
Imp	Imperative	TR	Transitive
Impf	Imperfect	VN	Verbal Noun
IND	Indicative		
Inf	Infinitive		
Inst	Instrumental		
INTR	Intransitive		
Loc	Locative		
M	Masculine		
N	Neuter		
Nfut	Nonfuture		
Nom	Nominative		
OAgr	Object Agreement		
Obj	Object		

1

Introduction

> So she began: 'O Mouse, do you know the way out of this pool? I am very tired of swimming about here, O Mouse!' (Alice thought this must be the right way of speaking to a mouse: she had never done such a thing before, but she remembered having seen in her brother's Latin Grammar, 'A mouse – of a mouse – to a mouse – a mouse – O mouse!')
> [Lewis Carroll, *Alice's Adventures in Wonderland*, p. 28]

1.1 Overview

This book is meant to serve as an introduction to various notions of case within modern theoretical linguistics. In order to tackle such an undertaking, several issues must be dealt with. One is the issue of what "case" really means. Another is the question as to which historically motivated assumptions have served to form our current notion of case. This book is written primarily from a syntactic point of view and therefore surveys a treatment of case as proposed within various theories of syntax, unavoidably, however, it also touches on semantic and morphological issues along the way.

Modern syntactic theories did not appear out of thin air (though that may appear to be the case to some, given the tremendous impact of the Chomskyan revolution in the 50s and 60s within theoretical linguistics). Rather, modern linguistic thought as practised in the Western world is informed directly by unbroken grammatical traditions which date back to the ancient Greek and Roman world. This is particularly true for case, as we are still using the nomenclature and the basic distinctions proposed by the Romans over 2000 years ago.

This book therefore includes a discussion of the treatment of case in the ancient Greek and Roman tradition, but then by way of comparison also includes a discussion of other theories that were on the market. A contemporary of the

Greek and Roman tradition was the Indian linguistic tradition, which dates back to at least Pāṇini's grammar of Sanskrit (about 600 BCE) and which remains current in much of Indian linguistic thought today.

Another tradition which developed a few centuries down the line and which had some interesting ideas with respect to the treatment of case is the Arabic tradition, which grew out of the formation of the Muslim Empire (about 700 CE). The book therefore includes a brief discussion of these foundational perspectives before moving on to a discussion of modern linguistic thinking.

One problem for any book on 'case' in modern syntactic theory is that a straightforward comparison across theories is doomed to fail. This is because the notion 'case' means different things to different people. Indeed, a survey of all the phenomena which have been described as 'case' leads one to the conclusion that one does not know what case really is. As such, this book focuses on a number of guiding themes which have been consistently associated with an analysis of case phenomena. Among these, the most central are the use of semantic or thematic roles and the role of grammatical relations in various theories of syntax. The book abstracts away from detailed considerations of the morphophonology; however, for each syntactic theory that is examined, I do ask the question: how well does it deal with the overt realization of case?[1]

Among the syntactic theories considered in this book are Relational Grammar (RG), Government and Binding (GB), the Minimalist Program (MP) or Minimalism, Lexical-Functional Grammar (LFG), and Role and Reference Grammar (RRG). This does not exhaust the number of different theories of syntax, but these are the theories which maintain an active research interest in case per se. A separate chapter is devoted to various types of *linking theories*, which seek to establish generalizations between overt case marking, argument structure and grammatical relations. I also discuss case within Optimality Theory (OT). Work in Optimality Theoretic Syntax has only really developed since Grimshaw's (1997) landmark article and as such OT represents a field of enquiry that is constantly shifting. The chapter on OT therefore runs the risk of being outdated almost as soon as the book is published; however, I have tried to concentrate on those approaches to case which will surely be thought of as "classic" or landmark papers in the time to come.

The book is organized as follows. The remainder of this chapter takes the reader through some phenomena that have been associated with the notion of case. This includes phenomena which everybody would agree that are indeed case, others which upon closer inspection must be rejected as being described as case and several others which certainly appear to be instances of case mark-

---

[1] A good bulk of the literature on case is devoted to a discussion of the morphophonological properties of case (see Blake 2001 for some references and discussion). This book does not do justice to this literature, but instead seeks to concentrate on the morphosyntactic and semantic issues that are connected with case phenomena.

ing, but which modern theories of syntax do not quite know how to deal with. Some of these phenomena will be encountered again in subsequent chapters. Others will never appear again. This book does not intend to provide an exhaustive discussion of the types of case phenomena—Barry Blake's book *Case* does a very good job of that already. This book instead concentrates on a few core phenomena which all theories must provide an account for, so as to keep some constant point of comparison across theories. Individual case marking phenomena are introduced along the way as needed for the illustration of particular theoretical considerations in the first part of the book, which deals with the ideas for case proposed in various syntactic theories. Once the foundational ideas of the various syntactic theories have been introduced, individual case marking phenomena which have received much attention in the syntactic literature are considered. This includes a discussion of quirky case and ergativity, but also of the semantics of case.

At the end of each chapter, I include a few exercises. These give the reader a chance to actively engage with the material that was introduced.

1.2   What is Case?

This section seeks to drive home the point that we do not have a well-defined understanding of the notion of case. There are some core notions which most linguists would agree on, but not every linguist will extend the label 'case' to the same range of phenomena. Going beyond just the linguistic community, most people who have gone to school and learned a foreign language will have encountered the notion of case in terms of a paradigm which they had to memorize. The classic example is Latin. The table in (1) shows the paradigm for Latin feminine nouns ending in *-a*.

(1)

Case Name	Singular	Plural
porta 'door'		
Nominative	porta	portae
Genitive	portae	portārum
Dative	portae	portīs
Accusative	portam	portās
Ablative	portā	portīs
Vocative	porta	portae

If you know anything about Latin, you will also know that other types of nouns (e.g., masculine nouns ending in *-us*) have a different set of endings than the ones shown above. You will also know that Latin adjectives have to agree in number, gender and case with the noun they modify. This makes for quite a complex system and for quite a bit of memorization that generations of schoolchildren have endured in the Western world. Note also that some of the forms in the cells of the table in (1) are the same. This is a sign of an incipient collapse of the case system: the modern descendants of Latin, e.g., French, Spanish or Italian, have not maintained the distinctions Latin made. Some historical processes with respect to case are discussed in section 6.8.

What could such a complicated case system be good for? After all, the modern Romance languages abandoned the Latin system due to a series of sound changes and English also does not make much use of case (see Hudson 1995 for the claim that English has no case whatsoever). One good hypothesis is that explicit case marking is useful for the establishment of the *semantic roles* of nouns (and pronouns) and their *syntactic* relationship to the verb. Blake (2001), for example, begins his book on case with the following definition.

> Case is a system of marking dependent nouns for the type of relationship they bear to their heads. [Blake 2001:1]

Compare this with Fillmore's (1968) understanding in his landmark paper *The case for case*.

> In the past, research on 'case' has amounted to an examination of the variety of semantic relationships which can hold between nouns and other portions of sentences; ...
> [Fillmore 1968:2]

Take the Latin examples in (2). Here we have a transitive verb 'see', which is the head of the sentence. Because this verb is transitive, it has two dependent noun phrases: 'girl' and 'door'. The noun *puella* 'girl' is marked with nominative case, while the noun *porta* 'door' has accusative case. The case marking allows us to conclude that in both (2a) and (2b) the girl sees the door, and not the other way around (which would be semantically odd).

(2) a. puella   portam   videt
     girl.F.Nom door.F.Acc see.Pres.3.Sg
     'The girl sees the door.'   Latin
   b. portam   puella   videt
     door.F.Acc girl.F.Nom see.Pres.3.Sg
     'The girl sees the door.'   Latin

English does not allow the same freedom in word order as Latin. Instead of overt marking on the noun, it makes use of the position of the noun in the sentence in order to indicate the seer vs. the thing being seen.

The generalization which emerges from this perspective is that case is a handy tool for marking semantic relationships between nouns and verbs, or, more generally between dependents and a head. Languages may choose to encode this relationship either structurally in terms of designated positions (e.g., English) or via overt morphological markers. Languages like Icelandic or Bulgarian, however, are somewhat of a problem for this view. Icelandic employs both strategies simultaneously in that it combines a rather rigid word order with a fairly rich and complex case marking system (Zaenen, Maling and Thráinsson 1985). This would appear to be a case of overkill and is something that has not been adequately explained by syntactic theories to date. The opposite is true of Bulgarian, which has about as much case marking as English does (i.e., virtually none), but which allows quite some freedom in word order, unlike English. The word order in Bulgarian is governed by *discourse configurational* factors (see Kiss 1995 for a discussion with respect to Hungarian). Common discourse configurational factors have effects like placing topics first in the sentence, or placing focused constituents immediately preverbally. Again, the interaction of discourse related factors with case marking remains poorly understood, even though there is a clear link (chapter 7).

Indeed, case is an area of morphosyntax which continues to receive quite a bit of attention in syntactic theories because no theory can honestly claim to have "the answer" as to why case works the way it does crosslinguistically. However, the approaches worked out for individual case marking phenomena have furthered our understanding of case and its interaction with other (morpho)syntactic phenomena considerably. Before going on to discuss these syntactic hypotheses in the rest of the book, I use the remainder of this section to introduce some phenomena which continue to be problematic and therefore of interest to syntactic theories of case.

1.2.1 Head vs. Dependent Marking

The core notion of case describes instances like the Latin paradigm in (1), which involves marking a noun via inflectional endings. In *dependent marking* languages such as Latin, the nouns bear some form of special marking which indicates their relationship to the head (the verb in the examples above). However, instances of *head marking* could also be seen as a type of case. In head marking languages the head of the phrase bears information about participants in the clause. An example from Navajo is shown in (3).

(3) At'ééd ashkii yiyiiłtsą
    girl boy 3Acc.3Nom.saw
    'The girl saw the boy.' (Jelinek 1987:89)   Navajo

These two types of marking strategies can be represented schematically as in (4) (taken from Nordlinger 1998:46).

(4) a. *Dependent-marked:* (as in Latin)
       Noun+Case Noun+Case Noun+Case Verb
    b. *Head-marked:* (as in Navajo)
       Noun$_1$ Noun$_2$ Noun$_3$ Verb+Aff$_1$+Aff$_2$+Aff$_3$

Not all linguists would be happy with classifying the method of crossreferencing a head and its arguments in (4b) as a phenomenon parallel to the marking of nouns in (4a). However, as case-bearing affixes are often historically derived from the incorporation of pronouns (e.g., Jelinek 1987 for Navajo), the two crossreferencing strategies could in fact reasonably be taken as instances of essentially the same phenomenon: case.

1.2.2 Is Everything Case? — Persian *ezafe*

Conversely, some phenomena may look like they should be classed as instances of case marking, but upon closer inspection of the language in question, this may not turn out to be quite right. Mel'čuk (1986), for example, considers the Persian *ezafe* construction in his search for a definition of case. An example is given in (5). Mel'čuk sees the *ezafe* construction as an inverse of his case 1, which is used to mark dependent nominals. In contrast, Mel'čuk analyses the *ezafe* morpheme in Persian as marking a certain noun to be the governing member of the construction, i.e., the non-dependent member.

(5) otâq-e   Ali
    room-Ezafe Ali
    'Ali's room' (Ghomeshi 1997:735)   Persian

Ghomeshi (1997), on the other hand, concludes that the actual function of the *ezafe* morpheme is to keep a running record of which nouns and adjectives have been 'linked' into the NP constituent. That is, the *ezafe* morpheme is a linker of some kind, which serves to indicate that the marked items all belong to the same constituent and in a particular order. This becomes particularly relevant when a large constituent as in (6) must be dealt with. While an argument could be made that this is a type of NP-internal case marking, this would involve stretching the understanding of case quite a bit.

(6) otâq-e   kuchik-e   zir-e   shirvuni-e Ali
    room-Ezafe small-Ezafe under-Ezafe roof-Ezafe Ali
    'Ali's small room under the roof' (Ghomeshi 1997:743)   Persian

The *ezafe* phenomenon is meant to serve as an example for how difficult it may be to judge prima facie whether a given phenemenon should even be included in a discussion of case or not. I would agree with Ghomeshi that the Persian *ezafe* construction does not belong in a discussion of case. However, there are other phenomena which are unexpected under Blake's or Fillmore's definitions of case, but which one would nevertheless want to include.

1.2.3 Adverbial Case

One such example is the occurrence of case markers on adjuncts. This has been termed *adverbial case* or *semantic case* (see also section 4.9). According to Blake's definition above, case markers should only occur on nouns which are dependent on a predicational head. This entails that case should be used to mark arguments of a verb, but not adjuncts. In fact, this is how most modern syntactic theories view the use of case as well. However, many languages use case to mark adjuncts. This section provides one example from German, and another from Korean, though examples from Latin or several other languages could also have been included. In both Korean and German, optional non-argument measure phrases appear in the accusative. The German verb *arbeiten* 'work' in (7) is generally intransitive (takes only one argument), as shown in (7a). In (7b) there is an additional accusative noun phrase; however, this accusative cannot be analysed as the object of the verb because the day has not been worked at or on. Rather, the accusative phrase is an adverbial of duration.

(7) a. Ich habe gearbeitet.
I.Nom have.Pres.1.Sg work.PastP
'I worked.' German

b. Ich habe [den ganzen Tag] gearbeitet.
I.Nom have.Pres.1.Sg the.M.Acc whole.M.Acc day work.PastP
'I worked the whole day.' German

Another example comes from Korean (e.g., Maling 1989). Here the adverbials can optionally be marked with the accusative case, as in (8), but unlike the German example above, the adverbials need not necessarily be accusative.[2] Again, as in German, the adverbial can be marked with accusative even when there is no object of the clause, as in (9).

(8) Suna-nŭn kŭ chaek-ŭl tu pŏn-(ŭl) ilk-ŏss-ta
Suna-Top the book-Acc two times-(Acc) read-Past-Decl
'Suna read the book twice.' Korean

(9) Suna-nŭn onŭl ilkop sikan tongan(-ŭl) cha-ass-ta
Suna-Top today seven hour for(-Acc) sleep-Past-Decl
'Suna slept for 7 hours today.' Korean

Given the basic assumption that the primary purpose of case is to mark the arguments of a predicate, this type of data remains an issue which has not as yet received a good/standard solution within modern syntactic theories.

1.2.4 Case and Finiteness

Another common assumption made in syntactic theories, and which has been formally articulated as the *Case Resistance Principle* (Stowell 1981), is that finiteness and case marking are in complementary distribution. While non-finite embedded clauses such as the Urdu infinitive in (10a) can be case marked, the corresponding embedded finite clause in (10b) bears no case marking.

[2]Thanks go to Shin-Sook Kim for supplying these examples.

(10) a. anjʊm=ne [gʰar a-ne]=ko kah-a
Anjum.F=Erg home.M.Loc come-Inf.Obl=Acc say-Perf.M.Sg
'Anjum said to come home.' Urdu

b. anjʊm=ne dekʰ-a [ke vo gʰar
Anjum.F=Erg see-Perf.M.Sg that Pron.3.Sg home.M.Loc
a-yi]
come-Perf.F.Sg
'Anjum saw that she came home.' Urdu

In many of the instances where an embedded predicate may be overtly case marked, it turns out to be a nominalization of some kind. This is true for Urdu as well, where the infinitive can be regarded as some kind of deverbal noun. Thus, because the verb has some nominal properties, it follows naturally that there should be the possibility of marking it with case. The verbs in embedded finite clauses are usually not nominalizations, but finite verbs. As such, they cannot be marked for case. Of course, there are counterexamples to this generalization (e.g., see Nordlinger and Saulwick 2002, ex. (32) for a dative (purpose) marked future), as there are counterexamples to a related generalization involving the case marking of dependents of nonfinite heads, discussed in the next section.

1.2.5 Nominal Case

A further issue to which quite a lot of attention has been devoted, but which will not figure much in this book is the treatment of the case marking on nominals which are licensed by other nominals. The standard case for this situation is the genitive, as in *John's hat*[3] or *The destruction of the city*. The genitive has therefore often been referred to as a *nominal case* and a distinction is made between verbal predicates which license *verbal case* such as nominative and accusative, and nominal predicates which license genitive case.

However, in some languages verbal nouns allow arguments with either a nominal case or a verbal case. A famous example comes from Japanese noun-verb complex predicates with *suru* 'do' (Grimshaw and Mester 1988), whereby the arguments of the noun-verb complex can be either marked with the genitive or with verbal cases such as the dative or accusative. The Urdu examples in (11) illustrate the same type of case marking alternation in conjunction with a verbal noun (infinitive).

The expected pattern is as in (11a), where the nominalization of the verb 'crackle' causes its object 'lightning' to appear in the genitive case, i.e., in a

---
[3]There is some discussion in the literature as to whether the English *'s* should be treated as case (e.g., Zwicky 1975), but this is irrelevant for our purposes, as many other languages use the genitive in just this configuration.

nominal case. The unexpected case is illustrated in (11b), where the embedded subject appears in the unmarked nominative case.

(11) a. adnan=ko [bıjli=ka   karak-na]   acc^{h}a
         Adnan=Dat lightning.F=Gen.M crackle-Inf.M.Sg good.M.Sg
         lag-ta
         seem-Impf.M.Sg
         'Adnan likes the crackling of lightning.'   Urdu

    b. adnan=ko [bıjli   karak-ni]   acc^{h}i
       Adnan=Dat lightning.F.Nom crackle-Inf.F.Sg good.F.Sg
       lag-ti
       seem-Impf.F.Sg
       'Adnan likes lightning crackling.'   Urdu

A related example from Latin, dubbed the narrative infinitive is shown in (12). Here there is no finite head of the sentence as the verb 'resist' is infinitive (nonfinite). In many theories of case, nominative case is associated with finite verb agreement and examples like this Latin one (similar examples can be found in French and Russian) are therefore unexpected.

(12) prīmō resistere macedōnēs
     first resist.Inf Macedonian.Nom.Pl
     'At first, the Macedonians resisted.'   Latin

The factors governing the appearance of verbal vs. nominal case in such environments remain the subject of investigation. I do not take up the issue of nominal case in any serious way in this book. I instead confine myself to a discussion of verbal case marking patterns, given that even within this more limited domain, the relevant phenomena, theories and issues encompass enough material for a multivolume tome.

The example in (11) does illustrate an issue which is taken up later in the book: the notion of quirky subjects. In (11), the subject is 'Adnan' and it is marked with a dative. This is contrary to the expectations of earlier versions of modern syntactic theories, which assumed that subjects should always be nominative. The existence of non-nominative subjects was first conclusively established for Icelandic (Zaenen, Maling and Thráinsson 1985) and such subjects have since been dubbed quirky (as the existence of this type of case marking was completely unexpected).

1.2.6 Case Stacking

Another fundamental belief about case, which is based on standard definitions and ideas handed down from the Romans, is that each nominal should only bear one case. However, this belief has been shattered by work on Australian languages, which allow *case stacking*.[4] An example from Kayardild is shown in (13). It illustrates the most extreme documented instance of case stacking.

The suffix glossed as C.OBL (complementizing oblique) indicates that this item is part of the embedded complement clause. The suffix glossed as M.ABL is a modal ablative and marks the clause as having past tense (together with the finite verb). Both of these suffixes can be argued to be case markers (Evans 1995b) as their distribution and morphosyntactic properties do not set them apart from other morphemes which would be considered to be standard case.

(13) Ngada mungurru, [maku-ntha   yalawu-jarra-ntha yakuri-naa-ntha
    I   know   [woman-C.OBL catch-PST-C.OBL fish-M.ABL-C.OBL
    thabuju-karra-nguni-naa-ntha   mijil-nguni-naa-nth].
    brother-GEN-INST-M.ABL-C.OBL net-INST-M.ABL-C.OBL]
    'I know that the woman caught the fish with brother's net.'   Kayardild
    (Evans 1995b:406)

As already hinted at by the modal ablative in (13), case markers are also put to work as tense/mood/aspect markers in Australian languages. The examples in (14) come from Kayardild (Evans 1995a:107–108).

(14) a. ngada   warra-ja ngarn-kir
        1.Sg.Nom go-Act beach-All
        'I am going/have gone to the beach.'   Kayardild

    b. ngada   warra-ju ngarn-kiring-ku
        1.Sg.Nom go-Pot   beach-All-MProp
        'I will go to the beach.'   Kayardild

    c. ngada   warra-jarra ngarn-kiring-kina
        1.Sg.Nom go-Pst   beach-All-MAbl
        'I went to the beach.'   Kayardild

    d. ngada   warra-da ngarn-kiring-inj
        1.Sg.Nom go-Des beach-All-MObl
        'I would like to go to the beach.'   Kayardild

The allative, modal proprietive, modal ablative and modal oblique all serve to express tense/aspect/mood distinctions. Note that this phenomenon is not confined to Australian languages, but that languages like Finnish have also been implicated in this type of case usage.

The phenomenon of case stacking is discussed again from the perspective of a formal analysis in chapter 8. The use of case as a marker of tense, aspect, or mood, however, is left aside within the scope of this book as this issue remains to be tackled properly within formal syntax and semantics (but see Nordlinger and Sadler 2004a,b for some recent, clear work on this issue).

---

[4]Case stacking has also been known as *Suffixaufnahme*, a term which has a long and venerable tradition (Plank 1995a).

1.3 Levels of Abstractness

In the process of introducing a number of standard ideas about case and some of the problematic phenomena for these standard ideas, we have encountered several different overt types of case marking. The Latin, German and Australian case markers are examples of case which is expressed via inflections on a noun. The case markers in the Urdu examples, on the other hand, are case *clitics*. This means that they are independent entities to the extent that they can be separated from their nominal hosts by other elements such as focus clitics. Furthermore, the English *to* as in *I gave milk to the cat* is generally interpreted as a dative case marker. This *to* is neither an inflection, nor a clitic, but has the syntactic status of preposition.

A great deal could be said about the differing realizational possibilities for case markers and one could argue about whether all of these different morphosyntactic creatures should all be lumped together under the label *case*. A great deal has in fact been said about this issue, however, in terms of syntactic approaches to case, these questions are rather uninteresting. The notion of case employed in theories of syntax is an abstract notion which is used to characterize the interaction between verbal lexical semantics, grammatical relations and word order. The overt realization of case must be dealt with by some component of the theory, however, that component is often left underspecified.

In what follows, for each syntactic theory surveyed, I will nevertheless pose the question whether the theory has anything to say about a typology of cases or case systems, and examine whether the theory worries about the determination of the overt form of case markers. However, since this is not the most interesting point of comparison (because most of the theories have not given these issues much thought), the book mainly focuses on two other guiding themes, namely the use of *semantic* or *thematic roles* and the postulation of grammatical relations. For each theory, I ask the following questions: Does the theory contain a notion of semantic roles and/or grammatical relations? If so, how are they expressed or encoded and what role do they play?

The intention is that the three guiding themes of semantic roles, grammatical relations and the overt appearance of case should allow for a good basis of comparison across theories. Establishing such a baseline for comparison is no trivial matter, as each theory has found differing sets of phenomena of interest by virtue of the theory-particular assumptions and argumentations. However, a general point of agreement seems to be that all theories should be able to account for the following basic constructions: basic transitives, ditransitives, unaccusatives vs. unergatives (section 3.7), passivization, quirky case (section 4.8) and ergativity (chapter 6). As such, the book focuses on these phenomena after a discussion of some of the foundational ideas with respect to case.

2

Foundational Perspectives

Before he died, Daddy taught me to read ancient syntax.
[Mel (aka Xena), *The Xena Scrolls*, Xena: Warrior Princess]

2.1 Introduction

Much of the terminology and some of the preconceptions governing modern syntactic thought find their roots in ancient times. Latin, Ancient Greek and Sanskrit are still taught as school subjects and many of us were put through declension tables which featured various forms of the noun for nominative, dative or accusative case. In my case (which is fairly typical), learning the declension tables took the form of rote memorization, but there were several questions I could have stopped to ask. For example, I could have paused to wonder what the word 'case' really meant, or why the declension tables are set up so that nominative always comes first, then genitive, etc. In fact, I did wonder about these questions, but only after I became a linguist.

It turns out that *case* is related to the Latin verb *cadere* 'to fall':

> The term case is from Latin *cāsus*, which is in turn a translation of the Greek *ptōsis* 'fall'. The term originally referred to verbs as well as nouns and the idea seems to have been of falling away from an assumed standard form . . .
> [Blake 2001:18]

The modern term *case* is thus directly attributable to ancient Greece via the Romans. This is also true for the standard case names employed in syntactic analyses today. Terms such as *nominative, genitive, dative, accusative, vocative* or *ablative* are the orginal Latin names, as they were translated by the Romans from Greek. Based on information found in Arens (1969:23–34, 32), Aroux, Koerner, Niederehe and Versteegh (2000) and Blake (2001), the next section briefly discusses the Greek and Roman foundational perspectives.

However, Greece and Rome were not the only ancient cultures which took an interest in linguistics. The earliest grammar available to us today is on Sanskrit. It dates from around the 6th century BCE and is generally attributed to Pāṇini. The ideas formulated in that grammar continue to shape Indian linguistic thinking today and have found their way into modern formal syntactic theories by way of work done by scholars such as Paul Kiparsky (e.g., the *Elsewhere Condition* in Kiparsky 1973). Particularly relevant for this book are the ideas on the relationship between semantic roles and case found in Pāṇini's grammar. These are discussed in section 2.3 and are followed by a short discussion of the Arabic linguistic tradition (section 2.4), which had firm ideas about the relationship between verbs and the nouns they govern.

The three ancient traditions introduced in this chapter provide the starting point for a discussion of three basic elements which will wend their way throughout the book: 1) the role of overt case marking; 2) the idea that semantic roles play an important part in the determination of case marking; 3) the realization that a more abstract level of analysis is needed—some notion of *grammatical relations*.

There are, of course, other notable linguistic traditions which go back to previous millenia. To name just two, there are the Hebrew and the Chinese traditions. However, unlike the traditions discussed here, as far as I could determine, the linguistic theorizing in these traditions did not include perspectives which are directly relevant to a discussion of modern theories of case.

2.2 The Greek and Roman Tradition

The tradition which recognizes the five cases shown in (1) as core cases of linguistic expression goes back to a school of philosophy propounded by Aristarchos of Samothrake (217–145 BCE) who lived in Alexandria and thought about grammar and grammatical terminology. One of his students, a certain Dionysios Thrax (ca. 170–90 BCE), wrote a grammar of Greek. Elements of his work have been preserved in an elementary grammatical treatise referred to as Tékhnē.

(1)
Greek	Modern (Roman)	Semantic Motivation
ορϑη 'orthe'	nominative	naming or straight case
γενικη 'genike'	genitive	of the genus, father's case
δοτικη 'dotike'	dative	giving/addressing
αιτιατικη 'aitiatike'	accusative	affected (Roman: accused)
κλητικη 'kletike'	vocative	calling

The Roman names for the cases are due to Remmius Palaemon who composed the *Ars Grammatica* (1st century CE). This work took over much of Thrax's work but was presumably also influenced by Varro's (116–27 BCE)

De Lingua Latina. Remmius Palaemon's grammar is not preserved, but as subsequent grammars over the centuries took the form of either minor reworkings or outright copies of this grammar, quite a substantial amount of knowledge can be amassed about Remmius Palaemon's original grammar.

While the Romans must be credited with preserving and transmitting the Greek school of thought, a mistake in translation remains with us to this day. The Greek word *aitiatike* had several meanings. The meaning intended by Thrax was that of affectedness, but the Roman translation picked up on the meaning of 'accused', hence the modern term *accusative*.

This mistake in translation illustrates an important point about the assumptions underlying the perception of case. In both Greek and Latin, case was marked via differing sets of morphological affixes on nouns. The appearance of these morphological affixes was tied to particular semantic functions. These perceived semantic functions were in turn encoded directly via case names which were deemed representative. The term dative is related to Latin *dare* 'to give' and is meant to reflect a participant who is a recipient, either of an object or of a more abstract entity. The *vocative* case denotes the form a person is addressed by. This case name is related to Latin *vocāre* 'to call, summon'.

The tight connection between case marking and semantics is mirrored by the Stoic school of thought. This line of philosophy was founded by Zeno of Citium (d. 261 BCE) and developed essentially independently from the school of thought that gave rise to Thrax's tradition of grammar. In both lines of thinking, case is associated directly with semantic notions. This differs markedly from the Sanskrit tradition (section 2.3), where the case markers were simply numbered, rather than associated directly with some kind of semantic import.

Given that modern linguistics continues to use the classificatory naming scheme of the ancient Greeks and Romans, a strong expectation as to the kinds of functions a given case should fulfil continues to exist. This is particularly true for fieldwork done on previously undescribed languages. If a given morphological form corresponds to what we think of as a dative or an instrumental in language X, then researchers become uncomfortable if this form is also used for various other 'non-dative' or 'non-instrumental' purposes.

As discussed in this book, modern syntactic theorizing with respect to case does not officially take into account very many semantic considerations. However, the ultimate classification and analysis of case marking patterns in modern syntax is strongly conditioned by the need to find meaning behind the distribution of case. As such, while it may seem that only the terminology has come down to us from the ancient Greeks and Romans, the fundamental assumption that case must be tied directly to semantics is still implicit in much of the work that is carried out.

This assumption is made explicit in modern Localist Theories of case and semantic roles (see section 7.1 for some discussion), which go back to Gruber

(1965). These theories hold that spatial notions are fundamental to our conceptualization of events and therefore also to the participants in events. Event participants are marked explicitly by case in order to identify their particular roles, e.g., a dative marks a recipient.

Modern localist theories appear to echo the Greek and Roman concerns with respect to case and semantics quite closely. The Tékhnē dealt with locative associations of three cases: genitive of origin, dative of location and accusative of direction. In Byzantine times, the grammarian Maximus Planudes (ca. 1300) dealt with this subject matter in some depth, causing researchers such as Hjelmslev (1935:10–12) to see Planudes as the first propounder of a truly localist theory of case (Robins 2000:420).

Some effects of localist theories have found their way into mainstream syntax via the work of Jackendoff (1972, 1990) in the form of *lexical decomposition*, discussed in chapter 5. With respect to this section, it suffices to say that the Greek and Roman linguistic tradition has not only furnished modern linguistics with the basic case terminology — it also colours modern views on case in that the type of case marking in Greek and Latin is taken to be basic and in that case is (pretheoretically) often associated with the type of semantics established by the Greeks and Romans. The precise import of the (often unquestioned) assumptions transmitted to us from the Greeks via the Romans is the subject of recurring discussion in the chapters to come.

2.3   The Indian Tradition

Grammars in the Indian tradition are set up quite differently in that a more complicated relationship between case and semantics is assumed. The most famous grammar in the Indian tradition, on which all subsequent grammars have built on down to modern times, is Pāṇini's grammar of Sanskrit (approximately 6th century BCE). Pāṇini was said to reside in northern India (what is now Pakistan) and it is not clear whether one person wrote the grammar, or whether it was a product of a school. Pāṇini's grammar did not arise out of nowhere — the mention of 10 grammarians who preceded Pāṇini shows that linguistic exploration of Sanskrit had a long and steady tradition.

Pāṇini's grammar, known as the *Aṣṭādhyāyī*, is a study in compactness and clever coding. The grammar consists of 4000 interdependent rules, ordered mostly by the type of topic addressed and the level of generality. The more general or default rules are couched so that they may be overridden by sets of more specific rules or statements of exceptions. Without any commentary, the rules come to about 30 printed pages. However, an extensive commentary is needed to understand the rules as each rule is couched extremely compactly in a linguistic metalanguage.

In order to avoid straying too far afield, this section concentrates on the analysis of case. As already mentioned, cases are simply numbered in this grammar. This avoids the prejudicial association of semantics directly with case forms. The following table is adapted from Blake (2001:64). It illustrates the declination of Sanskrit *deva-* 'god'.

(2)

Number	Declination	Western name
1	devas	nominative
2	devam	accusative
3	devena	instrumental
4	devāya	dative
5	devāt	ablative
6	devasya	genitive
7	deve	locative

The cases are given in the order they are introduced by Pāṇini in the grammar. For ease of exposition, I have included a column which lists the Western case name that corresponds most closely to the Pāṇinian classification. These correspondences should only be taken as a very rough guide to filtering the Pāṇinian system through Western eyes.

Pāṇini was aware of a number of semantic factors which played a role in the determination of morphological case. The semantic regularities he observed are couched in terms of an interaction between verbal lexical semantics and a theory of semantic roles, known as the *Kāraka Theory* (*kṛ* means 'to do', the form *kāraka* is a nominal stem derived from the base verb and means 'doer', so this is a theory of participants in an action or event). The semantic roles are defined explicitly as part of the grammar.[1] The rules defining the two most central roles, namely agent and patient are shown in (3).

(3) a. **Rule 1,4,49:** kartur īpsitatamaṃ karma

'*karman* is the thing most desired by the agent.'

b. **Rule 1,4,54:** svatantraḥ kartā

'The agent (*kartṛ*) is the independently acting one.'

These are also the last two roles introduced. Table (4) provides an overview of the kāraka roles defined by Pāṇini. They are given in the order mentioned in the grammar. Again, the Western name that is most closely equivalent is also provided in the interests of expositional ease.

---

[1]The editions of Pāṇini's *Aṣṭādhyāyī* consulted in the writing of this section are Böhtlingk (1839) and Katre (1987). The material presented here is based primarily on the more detailed discussion in Kiparsky and Staal (1969). Further sources are Itkonen (1991) and Bekkum, Houben, Sluiter and Versteegh (1997).

(4) **Kāraka Roles and Prototypical Definitions**

apādāna	the fixed point from which something recedes (ablative)
sampradāna	the item in view through the *karman* (goal)
karaṇa	the most effective means (instrument)
adhikaraṇa	locus, location (locative)
karman	the thing desired by the agent (patient)
kartṛ	the independent one (agent)

The definitions in (4) are only the prototypical ones. The roles in fact encompass a greater range of usage. The possible lexical semantic environments are specified in the grammar by means of reference to particular verb classes or a simple listing of the verbs which exceptionally require a particular semantic role, as illustrated by the rules in (5).

(5) a. **Rule 1,4,33:** rucyarthānām prīyamāṇaḥ

'With verbs of pleasing the one who is pleased is the *sampradāna* (goal). Example: Devadatta likes sweetmeats.'

b. **Rule 1,4,46:** adhiśīṁsthāsāṁ karma

'The locus is *karman* (patient) with the verbs *śīN* 'lie', *sthā* 'stand', *ās* 'sit', when preceded by *adhi* (preverb meaning roughly 'above', 'over', 'on', 'on to').'

The rules which define the semantic roles associated with differing verbs and verb classes interact with a set of other rules which govern the overt realization of case. Again, there is a set of default rules as in (6) which apply generally unless they are overridden by more specific rules (occurring later in the grammar) as in (7).

(6) **Rule 2,3,2:** karmaṇi dvitīyā

'Case 2 (accusative) is used when a *karman* (patient) is expressed.'

(7) **Rule 2,3,3:** tritīyā ca hoś chandasi

'Case 3 (instrumental) is also used for the *karman* (patient) of *hu* 'sacrifice' in the Chandas (Vedic Verse).'

The overall effect of this interacting system of rules is that there is no simple one-to-one correspondence between semantic roles and case marking. This is unlike what is assumed in much of standard linguistic theory today (see discussions in chapters to come). The following picture based on Itkonen (1991:49) illustrates the various case assignment possibilities for the two central semantic roles. The instrumental is taken to be the default realization of an agent, the accusative the default of the patient. In other contexts, e.g., in contexts in which a verb is marked active via another piece of morphology, the agent is realized as nominative. Or, given the right lexical semantics, the genitive is also possible. The case of the patient is furthermore dependent on voice and the particular lexical semantics of the verb involved.

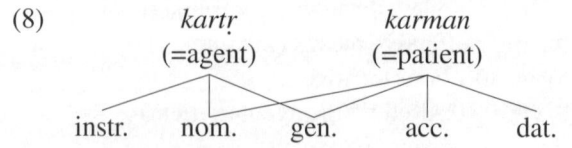

(8)   *kartṛ*   *karman*
               (=agent)   (=patient)

instr.   nom.   gen.   acc.   dat.

In contrast to the Ancient Greek and Roman tradition, there are no terminological classifications such as the *accusative of direction* or the *genitive of origin* in order to describe patterns which are seen as deviating from a norm. Rather, Pāṇini embeds the treatment of case in the general system of the grammar by which default rules are formulated which can then be overridden by more specific rules.

2.4 The Arabic Tradition

Another old linguistic tradition which has persisted to this day is a school of thought founded in the 8th century CE in the context of an expanding Islamic world.[2] Sībawaihi (d. 793 CE) is credited with having developed the first comprehensive analysis of the Arabic language on the basis of general linguistic principles. His grammar is known as *Al-Kitāb* (the book) and functioned as a model for all subsequent grammars, just as was the case in the Greek/Roman and Indian traditions. Sībawaihi's *Al-Kitāb* indeed continues to be looked to as an authority on Arabic.

The interest in grammar arose as part of larger religious concerns. The language of the Qur'ān, the holy book, is Arabic. To this day every Muslim reads the Qur'ān in Arabic.[3] Given the large amount of dialectal variation even at the time of the Prophet Mohammed (d. 632 CE) and the subsequent pressures of language change, establishing a study of the language of the Qur'ān was a priority. As Bekkum et al. put it:

> Since, as any revealed text, the *Qur'ān* is not always open to immediate understanding, be it only because it was revealed in a Bedouin society no longer extant in the first centuries of Islam, professional help was needed to explain its meaning. [Bekkum, Houben, Sluiter and Versteegh 1997:233–234]

Sībawaihi's predecessors thus mainly worked within an exegetical tradition, which turned into a real interest in the structure of the language around the time

---

[2] The material in this section is based on Owens (1990), Itkonen (1991), Versteegh (1997) and Bekkum, Houben, Sluiter and Versteegh (1997).

[3] This stands in stark contrast to Christianity, which has put a considerable effort into Bible translations.

of Sībawaihi. The structure of his grammar differs quite markedly from those of the Greek/Roman or Indian traditions: syntactic questions are followed by derivational morphology and finally, phonology and phonetics. The grammatical tradition includes a discussion of case marking, the formulation of a theory of government, and a concomitant notion of reconstruction which is somewhat reminiscent of ideas in modern linguistic theory (e.g., Lechner 1998).

Arabic is a VSO language, i.e., a language in which the verb is sentence initial, followed by the subject and then the object. Arabic had three of what we would recognize as case markers: accusative (*naṣb*), genitive (*jarr*) and nominative (*rafʿ*), associated with the underlying vowels /a/, /i/ and /u/, respectively. Case is not treated as such in the Arabic tradition, but is embedded within a larger theory of government in which governors (*ʿāmil*) such as verbs, prepositions or nominals determine the form of a governed element (*maʿmūl*).

(9) a. qāla zayd-un
said Zayd-Nom
'Zayd said.' Arabic

b. ra'ā zayd-an
saw.3.Sg Zayd-Acc
'He saw Zayd.' Arabic

c. min zayd-in
from Zayd-Gen
'from Zayd.' Arabic

The relationship between governor and the governed element is strict and tight. An element cannot have more than one governor and no phrasal element may intervene between the governor and the governed element. The verb 'say' thus governs the nominative Zayd in (9a) and the preposition *min* 'from' governs the genitive Zayd in (9c). Example (9b) further shows that grammatical relations like subject and object do not always have to be expressed by an overt NP, they can also be realized as part of the verbal morphology. In (9b) the subject is represented by the 3rd singular morphology on the verb 'see'.

The strict views on governance led to a differentiation between an underlying and a surface level of speech. In (10), for example, there are two accusative elements, whereby the preposed *Zayd* is functioning as a topic.

(10) zayd-an ḍaraba-hu rajul-un
Zayd-Acc hit-3.Sg.Acc man-Nom
'Zayd, a man hit. (A man hit Zayd)' Arabic

Only one of these accusatives is licensed by the verb 'hit'. In order to be able to license the other one, the Arabic grammarians posited an underlying level of representation which included a copy of the verb. (10) would thus be derived from (11).

(11) [ḍaraba zayd-an] [ḍaraba-hu] rajul-un
    hit   Zayd-Acc hit-3.Sg.Acc man-Nom
    'A man hit Zayd.'   Arabic

Note that the theory of government included a far more complex rule system than has been presented here. The examples in (10) and (11) merely serve to illustrate the basic ideas.

An example of further complexities which also needed to be dealt with within the theory of government is the relation between active sentences, passivization, and causativization. The passive and causative of (11) are shown in (12) and (13), respectively.

(12) ḍuriba zayd-un
     hit.Pass Zayd-Nom
     'Zayd was hit.'   Arabic

(13) 'a-ḍraba rajul-un   ʿamr-an   zayd-an
     Caus-hit man-Nom Amr-Acc Zayd-Acc
     'A man made Amr hit Zayd.'   Arabic

Sībawaihi held that the active and passive forms of a predicate were to be treated as equals in the sense that neither could be seen as being derived from the other. However, this turned out to be the minority view. The majority of Arabic grammarians (after Sībawaihi) held that the passive was to be derived from an underlying active form and that the causative could be seen as standing in a complementary relation to the passive, as shown in (14).

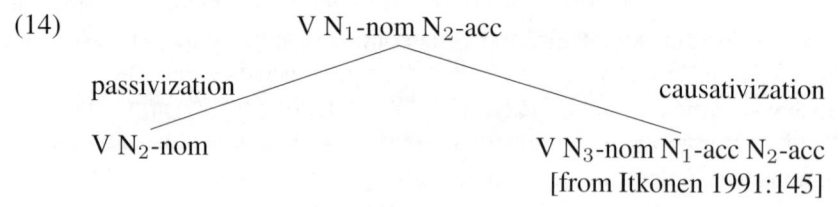

(14)   V N$_1$-nom N$_2$-acc

     passivization   causativization

     V N$_2$-nom   V N$_3$-nom N$_1$-acc N$_2$-acc
                                            [from Itkonen 1991:145]

For those readers familiar with Transformational Grammar (see section 3.2 for some discussion), the derivations of a causative or passive from an underlying active should feel familiar. The next chapter fast forwards on to the development of modern syntactic theory (1950s onwards) and takes up theoretical approaches to case in modern times. The discussion continues to pursue the three leading themes of the book: the overt realization of case markers, the coding of grammatical functions and semantic roles, and the relationship between case, semantic roles and grammatical functions. An occasional dip into theoretical ideas of the last few centuries constitutes part of the discussion to come, but we will not look back again quite so far as in this chapter.

2.5 Exercises

Exercise 1

The prototypical use of the Latin accusative was to mark the object, as in (1).

(1) puella   portam   videt
    girl.F.Nom door.F.Acc see.Pres.3.Sg
    'The girl sees the door.'   Latin

However, there were also other uses of the accusative. One of these is known as the *accusative of direction*, because the accusative rather than the locative is used for expressions of direction, as shown in (2).

(2) ībit   rōmam
    go.Fut.3.Sg Rome.Acc.F.Sg
    'He will go to Rome.'   Latin

Similarly, the prototypical use of the dative case in Latin is to mark the receiver or beneficiary of an action, as in (3), where the girls are the receivers of roses and therefore appear as the indirect dative object.

(3) claudia   puellae   rosās   dat
    Claudia.Nom girl.Dat.Sg rose.Acc.Pl give.Pres.3.Sg
    'Claudia is giving roses to the girl.'   Latin

In addition to this crosslinguistically prototypical use, the dative is also found in other environments in Latin. Two examples are in (4) and (5).[4]

(4) a. hoc   est   faciendum   mihi
       this.Nom.N.Sg be.Pres.3.Sg make.Gd.Nom.N.Sg I.Dat
       'This ought to be done by me.'
       'I ought to do this, must do this.'   Latin
    b. haec   Caesarī   facienda   erant
       this.Nom.N.Pl Caesar.Dat make.Gd.Nom.N.Pl be.Past.3.Pl
       'These things had to be done by Caesar.'
       'Caesar had to do these things.'   Latin

(5) a. crēdō   tibi
       believe.Pres.1.Sg you.Dat
       'I believe you.'   Latin
    b. placeō   tibi
       please.Pres.1.Sg you.Dat
       'I please you.'   Latin

How would the datives in (4) and (5) be dealt with in a Latin grammar? (You can try looking this up.) How would these datives be dealt with under a Pāṇinian approach? How do the two approaches differ?

---

[4]These and other examples are taken from Wheelock (1963).

Exercise 2

There is no overt case marking on nouns in English. However, subjects are generally sentence initial and objects must occur to the immediate right of the verb. The verb thus governs the object in the sense of the Arabic tradition. Following the Arabic tradition, propose an underlying structure for (6).

(6) Beans, I like.

Exercise 3

Like Arabic, the South Asian language Urdu has a morphological causative. In the style of the Arabic grammatical tradition, propose an underlying structure for the sentences in (7).

(7) a. anjʊm   nadya=se   paode=ko   kaṭ-a-ti
       Anjum.F.Nom Nadya.F=Inst plant.M=Acc cut-Caus-Impf.F.Sg
       'Anjum has Nadya cut the plants.'   Urdu

    b. anjʊm   nadya=ko   bʰag-a-ti
       Anjum.F.Nom Nadya.F=Acc run-Caus-Impf.F.Sg
       'Anjum chases Nadya away (makes her run).'   Urdu

3

Grammatical Relations

> The talk had covered the state of the Union, the state of the feminine mind, whether any cooked oyster can be fit to eat, structural linguistics, and the prices of books. [Rex Stout, *The Doorbell Rang* (A Nero Wolfe Mystery), p. 14]

3.1 The Structure of Sentences

Linguistics up until the middle of the 20th century had produced a wealth of descriptions for previously unexplored languages and had developed a good understanding of phonological and morphosyntactic phenomena, especially with respect to language change. However, there was no enterprise that worried about *syntactic structure* per se. That is, although there was work on the relative placement of individual elements (e.g., clitics, subject-object-verb order, pre- vs. postpositions), there was no investigation into deeper questions of syntax, such as the complex syntactic interplay between negation, question words and auxiliaries, or the identification of syntactic effects due to elements not visible at the surface (in parallel to phonological effects of underlying, but invisible phonemes). With the realization that much work needed to be done in this area, the linguistic game in the 20th century changed.

The change in linguistic awareness did not come about unreflectedly, as the following quote from Zellig Harris' book *Structural Linguistics* shows.

> 2. Transformations: The basic approach of structural linguistics (in this book) is to characterize each linguistic entity (element or construction) as composed out of specified ordered entities at a lower level. A different linguistic analysis can be obtained if we try to characterize each sentence as derived, in accordance with a set of transformational rules, from one or more (generally simpler) sentences, i.e. from other entities on the same level. A language is then described as consisting of specified sets of kernel sentences

and a set of transformations. The transformations operating on the kernels yield the sentences of the language, either by modifying the kernel sentences of a given set (with the same modification for all kernels in the set) or by combining them (in fixed ways) with other kernel sentences. [Harris 1951:vi]

Zellig Harris was one of the main players who got the modern syntactic ball rolling. This pursuit of a deeper understanding of syntax was taken up by Noam Chomsky, whose 1957 book *Syntactic Structures* had a huge impact on the field. Noam Chomsky went on to inspire generations of students.

The new found pursuit of a proper understanding of syntactic structure was also in part driven by computational concerns. In the wake of World War II, one prevalent idea was that one should be able to use the vast experience gathered with code cracking in order to help monitor communications of the Cold War enemies. The primary target was, of course, the USSR. The idea was that one should be able to harness the power of computers in order to build a machine translation system which would use mathematically well understood principles in order to 'crack' Russian and automatically translate it to English.

Indeed, the basic ideas articulated in *Syntactic Structures* (Chomsky 1957) formed the basis of much of computational linguistic research. In particular, the formulation of recursive context-free phrase structure rules provided an elegant way of dealing with some of the fundamental properties of natural language: 1) that language is potentially capable of producing strings of infinite length; 2) that context does not always matter. The latter property was convincingly illustrated by Chomsky with the (now) famous example *Colorless green ideas sleep furiously*. The syntax of this sentence is impeccable, despite the fact that the semantics are nonsensical in any imaginable context.

Within theoretical linguistics, the basic ideas around the notion of *derivations* via a series of *transformations* as formulated by Chomsky (1957) continue to permeate much of current linguistic thinking, including ideas about case, argument structure and grammatical relations.

3.2 Transformational Grammar, Case and the Passive

The precise nature of transformations was initially explored in work such as Harris (1957) and Chomsky (1957). When this work was taken up by the first generation of Chomsky's students at MIT, the influential theory of *Transformational Grammar* (TG) truly began to take off.

As stated in the quote from Harris (1951) above, the idea was to derive all possible sentences of a given language from a set of basic structures. That is, language was thought to consist of a basic *kernel* from which all other constructions could be derived via a set of *transformations*. One central transformation was one which derived a passive structure from an active kernel sentence. An early (and therefore fairly simple) statement of the relationship between active and passive in English can be found in Chomsky (1957:43).

(1) If S_1 is a grammatical sentence of the form
$NP_1 - Aux - V - NP_2$,
then the corresponding string of the form
$NP_2 - Aux + be + en - V - by + NP_1$
is also a grammatical sentence.

This generalization accounts for the relationship between the active sentence in (2a) and the passive version in (2b).

(2) a. The farmer has killed the duckling.
b. The duckling has been killed by the farmer.

This active-to-passive transformation subsequently was stated in a more sophisticated manner; however, in the context of our discussion, there are several points to note about the generalization in (1) which also hold for the later, more sophisticated formulations. One is that the transformation is very specific to English, including references to the precise position and form of the NPs, the verbs and the auxiliaries. Another is that there is absolutely no mention of case. Given that English does not have very much case marking, this may perhaps not be so surprising. However, if one replaced the NPs in (2) by pronouns, the question of overt case marking does arise because the *he* must be realized as *him* in the context of the *by*-phrase.

(3) a. He has killed it.
b. It has been killed by him.

It is interesting to draw a comparison between this approach and the view within Arabic linguistics sketched in (14) in section 2.4. The Arabic tradition also assumed that the passive was derived from a basic active clause. However, unlike Chomsky's early work on English, the Arabic tradition included an explicit statement about case: the passivization of an active nominative-accusative subject-object pattern included the transformation of an accusative object into a nominative subject.

The Arabic and the TG approach to passivization share the characteristic that they were designed specifically for a particular language: a universal application of the type of transformation articulated by Chomsky in (1) was not possible. Concerns about this language specific character of many of the transformations proposed within TG as well as their unconstrained nature prompted extensive debates in the 1970s. Researchers such as Lakoff (1971) and McCawley (1972) showed that the use of disjunctive possibilites within transformations resulted in a loss of generalization and that the kinds of (very complex) transformations being worked out within TG in principle permitted an application to arbitrary sets of categories which had nothing much in common (see

Bresnan 1977 for a good discussion of the issues at stake). Another deep concern was prompted by efforts to interface the syntactic generalizations with the newly developing field of formal semantics, based on Montague's work (Montague 1973). The question was: If certain things were shown to pattern together semantically, but were being treated syntactically via several different transformations, then did the syntactic theory not need fixing?

These criticisms led to important and lasting developments like the formulation of X′-theory (Chomsky 1970, Bresnan 1976; see section 4.4) and eventually resulted in a more constrained and very successful theory of syntax which became known as *Government-Binding* or GB (see chapter 4).

3.3 Relational Grammar

A very important impulse which was eventually incorporated into GB, and which is of central relevance in the context of this book, was the work done within *Relational Grammar* (RG). RG came into existence in the 1970s and was spearheaded by David Perlmutter and Paul Postal. The idea was to set up a viable alternative theory to TG, one which did greater justice to the interaction between grammatical relations, case and thematic roles across languages.

In one of the founding papers of RG, for example, Perlmutter and Postal (1983b) laid out some of the problems they saw with the transformational (TG) approach to passivization.[1] They first pointed out that since most languages of the world contain active-passive relations, one goal of linguistic theory should be to formulate a language independent characterization of passivization. They went on to point out that a characterization which presupposed an English word order as in the transformation in (1) did not do justice to verb final languages like Turkish or verb initial languages like Malagasy or Arabic. A useful characterization of passivization therefore clearly had to involve a level of description which was able to abstract away from the particular surface order of elements.

Perlmutter and Postal next considered case marking as a more general method of stating the relationship between actives and passives crosslinguistically. An initial hypothesis they explored is given in (4).

(4) The nominal that is in the accusative case in an active clause is in the nominative in the 'corresponding' passive clause.
(Perlmutter and Postal 1983:7)

This generalization works for English as well as several other languages like Arabic ((14) in section 2.4), Latin (5) and German (6).

(5) a. magister pueros laudat
teacher.Nom boy.Acc.Pl praise.3Sg
'The teacher praises the boys.' Latin

---

[1] Although this work was carried out in the 1970s, it took relatively long to be published.

b. puerī   ā magistrō   laudantur
   boy.Nom.Pl by teacher.Abl praise.Pass.3.Pl
   'The boys are praised by the teacher.'   Latin

(6) a. Die   Lehrerin   lobt
      the.F.Sg.Nom teacher.F.Sg.Nom praise.Pres.3.Sg
      den   Jungen.
      the.M.Sg.Acc boy.M.Sg.Acc
      'The teacher praises the boy.'   German

   b. Der   Junge   wird
      the.M.Sg.Nom boy.M.Sg.Nom become.Pres.3.Sg
      von der   Lehrerin   gelobt.
      of the.F.Sg.Dat teacher.F.Sg.Dat praise.PerfP
      'The boy was praised by the teacher.'   German

However, the generalization again does not seem to be valid crosslinguistically. One example comes from West Greenlandic, where subjects of transitives are in the *ergative* case (for more on the ergative case, see chapter 6), while the object is not overtly marked, as in (7a). This lack of overt marking is often referred to as *absolutive* case in the literature. The passivized version of (6a) is shown in (6b). The former absolutive object 'child' is now an absolutive subject, so no change in overt case marking can be observed.

(7) a. gimmi-p miiraq   kii-va-a
      dog-Erg child.Abs bite-3Sg-3Sg
      'The dog bit the child.'   West Greenlandic

   b. miiraq   gimmi-mik kii-tsip-puq
      child.Abs dog-Instr bite-Pass-3Sg
      'A child has been bitten by the/a dog.'   West Greenlandic

Perlmutter and Postal next tried to state the generalization in terms of the kind of verbal morphology that is used for passivization, but again found exceptions. On the basis of the crosslinguistic data they amassed, they went on to argue that if one was willing to adopt the assumption in (8), then a valid universal characterization of the passive could be as in (9).

(8) A clause consists of a network of grammatical relations. Among these relations are 'subject of', 'direct object of', and 'indirect object of'.

(9) a. A direct object of an active clause is the (superficial) subject of the 'corresponding' passive.

   b. The subject of an active clause is neither the (superficial) subject nor the (superficial) direct object of the 'corresponding' passive.

This characterization of passivization has entered linguistic theory as a basic fact about language and is now accepted across different theoretic persuasions.

In effect, Perlmutter and Postal argued that one needed to abstract away from the surface properties such as word order, case marking or verbal morphology via an abstract system of relations. That is, properties like word order, case marking, and verbal morphology were held to be superficial reflections of a more abstract system of grammatical relations. These relations held between noun phrases and the clause and between verbs (and other predicational elements) and the clause. A basic clause consisted of a network of abstract *grammatical relations* such as 'subject of', 'direct object of' and 'indirect object of'. The terms subject, object and indirect object were not new: this terminology had been in use for centuries, but had never been formally defined. While RG did not define these notions formally either, it did integrate them into a formal theory, which constrained their crosslinguistic distribution.

3.4 The Notion of Grammatical Relations

The terms subject, object and indirect object were familiar from grammars and language descriptions. The Oxford English Dictionary, for example, defines them as in (10) along with citations from standard grammar books of the 18th and 19th centuries.

(10) *Subject:* The member or part of a sentence denoting that concerning which something is predicated.

Object: A substantive word, phrase or clause, immediately dependent on, or 'governed by', a verb, as expressing, in the case of a verb of action, the person or thing to which the action is directed, or on which it is exerted.

Indirect Object: The Indirect Object of a verb denotes that which is indirectly affected by an action, but is not the immediate object or product of it, as 'Give *him* the book.' 'Make *me* a coat.'

These intuitive notions, which had standardly been used in grammatical descriptions of languages such as English, Latin, Greek, or Sanskrit, turned out to be too useful to be discarded within modern linguistics.

In articulating a revised version of the original TG, Chomsky (1965:71) includes a structural definition of the grammatical relations 'subject of' and 'direct object of', as shown in (11), assuming a tree as in (12).

(11) i. Subject-of: [NP, S]
    ii. Predicate-of: [VP, S]
    iii. Direct-Object-of: [NP, VP]
    iv. Main-Verb-of: [V, VP]

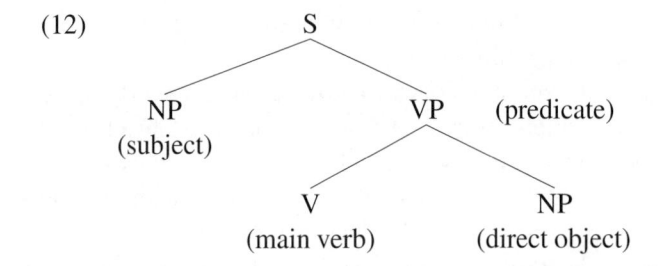

(12)
```
              S
            /   \
          NP     VP  (predicate)
       (subject) / \
                V   NP
          (main verb) (direct object)
```

This basic structural categorization remains a part of the modern descendants of TG, as is discussed in chapter 4. Note that there is no mention of case, nor is there room for an indirect object. To date, the indirect object remains somewhat of an anomaly within this theoretical tradition, requiring an extra VP layer to accommodate it structurally (cf. Larson 1988, see section 4.11). This contrasts with the basic assumption of RG in (8), which takes the notion of indirect object to be one of the basic grammatical relations.

The structure in (12) also does not constitute a theory of how case marking interacts with grammatical relations. Chomsky (1965:221–222, footnote 35) does note that he assumes case marking to be assigned at the level of phonological realization. That is: case is marked incidentally and language specifically as part of the pronunciation of a sentence and therefore does not play a significant role in the structural workings of a language. As discussed in section 3.6, this position stands in marked contrast with the basic assumptions of RG. Due mainly to the work done within RG on the systematic crosslinguistic interaction between case and grammatical relations, *Case Theory* emerged in the revised version of the theory known as Government-Binding (chapter 4).

3.5 Case Grammar and Thematic Roles

Fillmore's (1968) paper on *The case for case* was situated squarely within the vibrant discussions surrounding the emergence of TG. Fillmore saw himself as proposing a variant of TG; however, his *Case Grammar* turned out to be less of a variant of TG and more of an independent theoretical persuasion which shares some fundamental ideas with Tesnière's (1959) *Dependency Grammar*. Nonetheless, many of the basic ideas in this seminal paper provoked a fruitful debate[2] and were subsequently incorporated in some form or another across differing theoretical approaches, including GB, the successor of TG.

One of the fundamental ideas was that *case roles* or *case frames* should be acknowledged as one of the common universal bases of language, i.e., that some form of case plays a role in all languages. However, the relevant form of case is not its overt manifestation via some type of case marking (e.g., *he*

---

[2]Indeed, the debate was so intense that Fillmore published *The Case for Case Reopened* in 1977 in order to clarify (and sometimes revise) his basic ideas.

vs. *him* in English or *-p* for the ergative and *-mik* for the instrumental in West Greenlandic, cf. (7)), but a more *abstract* notion.

Fillmore proposes the notion of a *deep structure* at which underlying syntactic relations are coded which are distinct from notions like 'object of' and 'subject of' (as discussed in section 3.4), and which are also distinct from the overt realization of case. That is, the basic part of a sentence contains a proposition P which contains a tenseless set of relationships involving verbs and nouns. These are taken to be *case relationships* (C), as realized in (13).

(13) $P + V + C_1 + \ldots + C_n$

Fillmore argues that the case relationships needed for crosslinguistic analysis include at the very least: *Agentive, Instrumental, Dative, Factitive, Locative, Objective*. A first cut at a definition is shown in (14) (Fillmore 1968:24–25).

(14) **Agentive (A)** The case of the typically animate perceived instigator of the action identified by the verb.
Instrumental (I) The case of the inanimate force or object causally involved in the action or state identified by the verb.
Dative (D) The case of the animate being affected by the state or action identified by the verb.
Factitive (F) The case of the object or being resulting from the action or state identified by the verb, or understood as part of the meaning of the verb.
Locative (L) The case which identifies the location or spatial orientation of the state or action identified by the verb.
Objective (O) The semantically most neutral case, the case of anything representable by a noun whose role in the action or state identified by the verb is identified by the semantic interpretation of the verb itself; conceivably the concept should be limited to things which are affected by the action or state identified by the verb. The term is not to be confused with the notion of direct object, nor with the name of the surface case synonymous with accusative.

Given the basic formula in (13), languages are predicted to contain sets of formulas as in (15), which correspond to the basic kinds of sentences. An intransitive clause, for example, might consist of a verb and an agentive or objective case relation, depending on how 'active' the subject was (see section 3.7). A transitive clause would consist of a verb and an agentive and an objective.

(15) V + A   (intransitive, active subject)
V + O   (intransitive, inactive subject)
V + O + A   (transitive)
V + O + D + A (ditransitive)

A ditransitive adds a dative case relation as in *John* (A) *gave the books* (O) *to my brother* (D). Note that the underlying order of case relations as specified by (15) does not match the surface order for English. Fillmore's idea was that the *deep structure* (V+O+D+A) would be made to correspond to the surface string (or structure) via a series of transformations of the type available in TG.

While adopting the notion of deep structure per se, Chomsky (1965:64–71) argued quite forcefully that an integration of notions such as O, A, D or Subject into the categorical structure of a tree was mistaken. Syntactic trees should manipulate syntactic objects such as noun phrases or verb phrases, but not functional notions such as agentive or subject.

Fillmore's proposal of Case Grammar as a variant of TG was thus not accepted. However, the notion of a deep structure which licensed certain *thematic roles* became an integral part of linguistic theory. The concept of thematic roles was derivative of Fillmore's original case relations in that it emerged as part of the discussion around Fillmore's proposals. While the definitions provided by Fillmore in (14) would seem to be quite precise, it turned out that the determination of case relations or thematic roles was not always easy. For example, are the subjects in (16) (*dollars, smell, accident*) all the same kind of instrumental? Should instrumentals in general be allowed to surface as subjects when a more usual realization is in terms of a prepositional phrase as in (17)?

(16) a. Fifty dollars will buy you a second-hand car.
b. The smell sickened me.
c. The accident killed the woman.
[Fillmore 1977:61]

(17) John opened the door with a key.

The debate on the semantic definition or grounding of thematic roles is far from resolved. Most linguists agree that thematic roles are a problematic concept, but no consensus has been reached on how to do without the notion. One idea which has gained much attention is Dowty's (1991) notion of *proto-roles*. Dowty defines an agent or patient proto-role by means of a collection of semantic entailments (not all of which necessarily need to be met) and is thus able to abstract away from the niggling semantic problems which beset the precise definition of a thematic role (see section 5.4).

Some linguists have adopted proto-roles, others attempt to avoid the use of thematic roles altogether, but most end up making reference to thematic roles in some form or another. The thematic roles that are generally used include *agent, patient, theme, goal, beneficiary, experiencer, instrument*, and *location*. Some theories arrange these roles in *thematic hierarchies* and use the hierarchical arrangement to derive results about case marking and the licensing of grammatical relations as part of a *Mapping* or *Linking Theory* (see chapter 8).

Thematic roles played some part in the formulation of relationships between grammatical relations and case within RG. Before turning to a closer examination of this, it is worth detailing a few of the other lasting effects Fillmore's paper had on linguistic theory. One of his proposals was that each case relationship should occur only once in a simple clause (Fillmore 1968:21). This idea has found its way into GB/Minimalism as the θ-*criterion* in (18), which states that for each argument of a clause (typically an NP), there can be only one thematic or θ-role and that the same thematic role cannot be assigned to more than one argument (see chapter 4 for more discussion).

(18) **The θ-Criterion**
Each argument bears one and only one θ-role, and each θ-role is assigned to one and only one argument.

The proposal that a clause should not be able to duplicate case relations (thematic roles) demonstrates that Fillmore's discussion of case actually had nothing to do with the surface manifestation of case. In (19), for example, both the object (*me*) and the secondary object (*fear*) are in the accusative case.

(19) Der   Drache   lehrte   mich
the.M.Sg.Nom dragon.M teach.Past.3.Sg I.Sg.Acc
das   Fürchten.
the.N.Sg.Acc fearing.N.Acc
'The dragon taught me fear.'   German

Another influential idea which arose out of Fillmore's paper is the classification of languages by the case marking patterns. Because Fillmore defines *case frames* as in (15), it is possible to classify languages according to how they mark the agentive (A) of a transitive clause. For example, *ergative* languages tend to mark the agent with an ergative and the objective (O) with a nominative or absolutive. This nominative or absolutive tends to be exactly the same marker that is used for subjects of intransitives. In contrast, *accusative* languages such as English or German distinguish the object via an accusative case and generally group subjects together by marking subjects of both transitive and intransitive clauses consistently with the nominative. The classification of languages via case marking patterns is discussed in chapter 6.

Note that the systematic classification of languages via case frames differs markedly from previous approaches, which tended to concentrate on finding a unifying semantics for individual case morphemes, as in the work of Jakobson (1936) or the localist tradition (e.g., Hjelmslev 1935), see section 7.1.

In sum, although Fillmore's paper *The case for case* is not about the distribution of overt case, but about the definition of semantically motivated thematic roles, many of the core ideas have entered linguistic theory and have played a significant role in exploring the interaction between case, grammatical relations and thematic roles. RG was one of the first theories to deal with all of these notions seriously. The next section therefore introduces some core concepts of RG. This is followed by a section on the Unaccusative Hypothesis, which has played an important role in theories of lexical semantics and case.

3.6 Core Ideas of Relational Grammar

As already mentioned, RG was proposed in the 1970s as an alternative theory to TG. RG sought to do justice to the interaction between grammatical relations, case and thematic roles across languages. As part of this effort, work within RG analysed a large and diverse set of languages. A representative collection of work within RG can be found in Perlmutter (1980), Perlmutter (1983), Perlmutter and Rosen (1984) and Perlmutter and Joseph (1990).[3]

3.6.1 The Passive Revisited

A core idea of RG is that the grammatical relations subject, direct object, and indirect object (the so-called 'term' relations, see below) must be taken as primitives of theory. In particular, they cannot be defined in terms of other properties such as word order, phrase structure configurations or case marking.

The *term* grammatical relations are named by integers, and occupy the upper range of a hierarchy of nominal relations, as shown in (20). The lower ranked *non-term* relations include both oblique relations (corresponding roughly to adjuncts) and the 'chômeur' relation (see below). The correspondence of the integers to pretheoretical names for grammatical relations is shown in (21).

(20) Hierarchy of Grammatical Relations
$1 > 2 > 3 >$ Nonterm relations

(21) Correlations/Naming
1 subject
2 direct object
3 indirect object

The relationship between predicates (mainly verbs) and terms (grammatical relations) was represented by Relational Networks. With time, a simplified notation for these relational networks emerged. This simplified notation for the formal representation/analysis of a standard transitive clause is shown in (22). A network consists of basic elements such as *arcs*, which represent the relations between *nodes*, which are elements represented by integers. In (22), the P arc denotes the relation between a predicate and the clause. The 1 arc describes the relation between the clause and *the farmer* (a 'subject' relation). Similarly, the 2 arc denotes a relation between the clause and *the duckling* (an 'object' relation).

[3]These references are not meant to be exhaustive, especially as work within RG continues.

(22)

```
         P
        / \    1   2
       /   \  / \ / \
      ↓     ↓   ↓
    killed  the farmer  the duckling
```

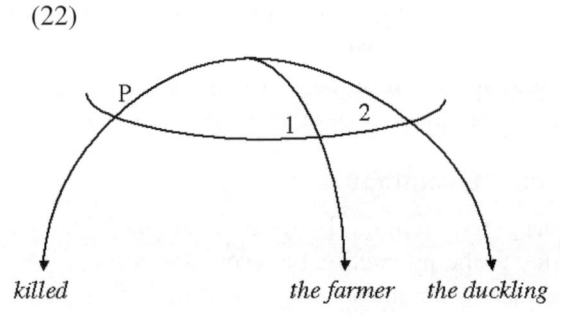

Like in TG, some kinds of clauses are considered to be more basic than other kinds. For example, passivization is considered to apply universally (see section 3.3) to a relational network which contains a 1 and a 2 arc (i.e., a subject and an object). The network in (22) is thus a potential candidate for passivization, the effects of which are rendered in (23).

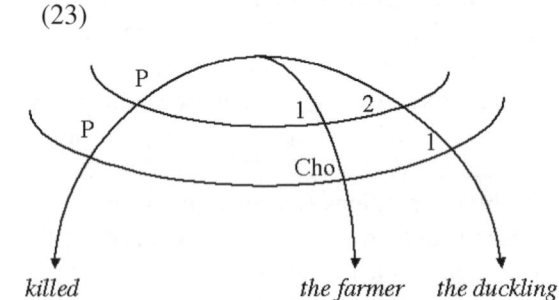

(23)

```
            P
          /   \   1   2
         P   /     \   1
          \ /  Cho  \ /
           ↓         ↓         ↓
        killed   the farmer   the duckling
```

The representation in (23) contains two *strata*. The initial stratum is identical to the analysis of the active sentence in (22). In the second stratum, the status of the terms has changed: the former 1 (subject) is now something called a *Cho* (chômeur),[4] while the former 2 (object) is now a 1 (subject).

Relational networks are governed by a number of laws and rules. The laws are formulated as universal and inviolable constraints. The rules could be language particular and allow for operations on relational networks. As RG was developed, the system grew to be quite large and intricate, as many laws interacted with one another. This section discusses only some of the basic ones.

For example, take the general 1-Advancement Exclusiveness Law in (24). This law places constraints on the possibilities of *advancement* within a given network. Advancement rules allow a 2 or 3 node in an initial stratum to advance

---

[4] For those wondering about this terminology, here is the explanation.

> The term 'chômeur' is a French word meaning 'unemployed' or 'idle'. ... The choice of terminology is meant to reflect the idea that a nominal that is en chômage in a given stratum does not bear the term relation in that stratum that it bears in a higher stratum. [Perlmutter and Postal 1983:21]

to a higher integer in a subsequent stratum. Possible common advancement rules are 2-1, 3-1 or 3-2 advancement.

(24) **The 1-Advancement Exclusiveness Law:**
A given clause can have at most one advancement to 1.

The advancement rules are relevant for the discussion at hand because a common characteristic of passivization is 2-1 advancement. In the passive representation in (23), the effect of 2-1 advancement advances the initial 2 (*the duckling*) to a 1. After 2-1 advancement has taken place, there are two 1s in the relational network. This situation is outlawed by another crosslinguistically applicable law, namely the *Stratal Uniqueness Law* in (25), which prohibits the co-occurrence of more than one subject, object or indirect object per clause within a single stratum. Crosslinguistically, this generalization is bolstered by a solid amount of evidence.

(25) **The Stratal Uniqueness Law:**
No more than one nominal can head an arc with a given term in a given stratum.

Something must therefore be done with the 1 corresponding to *the farmer*. There are several possibilities, but the one which applies here is the concept of *Chômeur* (Cho) or Argument Demotion.

(26) **Chômeur Condition:**
If a nominal$_i$ assumes the term relation borne by nominal$_j$, nominal$_j$ becomes a chômeur.

The initial term 1 (the farmer) thus becomes a chômeur and cannot be realized as a term (core grammatical relation) anymore: it must be realized as a non-term (adjunct) *by*-phrase. The Final 1 Law in (27) ensures that each clause must contain a subject in the final analysis. This idea of a *subject requirement* is echoed in most theories of syntax.

(27) **The Final 1 Law:**
Every basic clause must have a 1-arc in the final stratum.

The *duckling* corresponds to a 1 in the final stratum in (21), so the Final 1 Law is satisfied and the relational network represents a licit RG analysis. The effect of the analysis is that the duckling functions as the subject in the passive, whereby the farmer node was put en chômeur and can only be expressed as an non-term in (28).

(28) The duckling was killed by the farmer.

The simple example of passivization shows that Relational Grammar is a *multistratal* theory of grammar, with a stratum corresponding roughly to a stage in a transformational derivation. It was thus relatively straightforward for transformational/derivational frameworks which built on TG to adopt some of the central ideas of RG, like the Unaccusative Hypothesis (section 3.7).

3.6.2 Case in Relational Grammar

Case as such is not accorded a formal role within RG, though much of the discussion does revolve around analysing overt case marking patterns in a wide array of languages. RG implicitly assumes a relationship between overt case marking and grammatical relations. For European languages, for example, the correlation is something as in (29).

(29)
Case	Grammatical Relation
nominative	subject (Final 1)
accusative	object (Final 2)
dative	indirect object (Final 3)

The possible correlation between thematic roles and grammatical relations, on the other hand, is addressed more explicitly (see section 3.8). Before moving on to that issue, it is instructive to take a look at a language with a complicated case marking system in order to understand how case and grammatical relations interact in a typical RG analysis.

The language in question is Georgian, which has been analysed in great detail by Alice Harris (e.g., Harris 1981). The discussion in this section is based on Harris (1984). One feature of Georgian is that case patterns differ according to the tense/mood/aspect of the clause. In particular, in something that has come to be dubbed *dative inversion*, the subject is marked in the dative when the verb carries evidential marking. The object *bracelet* is dative in (30a), but nominative in (30b). The indirect object *mother* is also dative in (30a), but is marked by a postposition in (30b).

(30) a. rezo   samajurs   ačkebs   dedas.
Rezo.Nom bracelet.Dat he-gives-her-it-Ind mother.Dat
'Rezo is giving Mother a bracelet.'   Georgian

b. turne   rezos   samajuri   učukebia   dedastvis.
apparently Rezo.Dat bracelet.Nom he-gave-it-Ev mother-for
'Apparently Rezo gave a bracelet to Mother.'   Georgian

The question is how this rather complex case alternation can be explained, especially in light of the fact that the underlying predicate argument structure of the sentence has not changed: in both sentences it is Rezo who gives a bracelet to his mother, regardless of the overt case.

The RG analysis therefore begins by postulating the same *underlying* structure for both sentences, i.e., both sentences are based on the same initial stratum. The initial grammatical relations are shown in (31). This analysis is supported by a host of phenomena in Georgian, as Harris (1984) demonstrates.

(31) | Initial Grammatical Relations | | Overt Case Marking |
|---|---|---|
| Rezo | 1 (subject) | Nominative |
| samajuri 'bracelet' | 2 (direct object) | Dative |
| deda 'mother' | 3 (indirect object) | Dative |

In (30a), the subject is nominative; however, both the direct and indirect object are dative. This is because the dative and accusative in Georgian are not distinguished (a common crosslinguistic phenomenon). In light of the Georgian data, one could stop to ask oneself why one would expect an object to be accusative? Is that the definition of a direct object? How are accusatives in general defined, i.e., what is the *function* of an accusative as opposed to a dative? The answers tend to be as follows: we have distinct accusative marking on direct objects in many languages, therefore we expect direct objects to be marked with an accusative. In languages where this is not the case, we assume that the dative and the accusative have collapsed into one form as part of historical change. For some languages this historical change can indeed be documented, so the assumption for other languages seems warranted.

To return to the RG analysis of (30): the version in (30b) involves demotion of the initial 3. This is effected by another general rule, shown in (32), which demotes a 1 to a 3. The rule is commonly referred to as *Inversion*.

(32) **Inversion:** Subject ⟶ Indirect Object
(1 ⟶ 3)

The initial stratum for both (30a) and (30b) is shown in (33). This initial stratum is also the final stratum for (30a). But the Inversion rule is involved in (30b) and this results in a multistratal analysis.

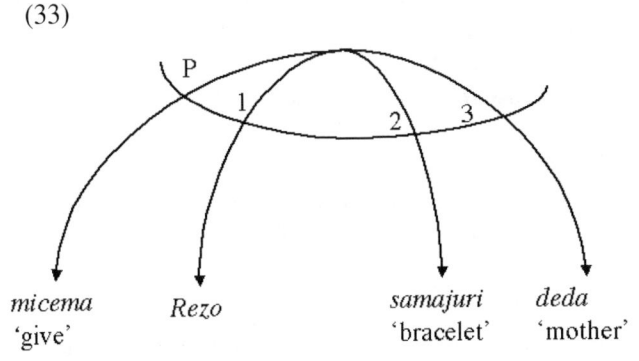

(33)

```
           P
         1   2   3
       ↓   ↓   ↓   ↓
    micema  Rezo  samajuri  deda
    'give'        'bracelet' 'mother'
```

The Inversion rule demotes the 1 (*Rezo*) to a 3, as shown in (34). Since there is already a 3 in the clause (*mother*), this 3 must become a chômeur by the Stratal Uniqueness Law. We would now be done except for the Final 1 Law, which states that there must be a 1 in the final stratum. Since the 1 became a 3, a new 1 must be found. The initial 2 is allowed to advance to a 1 via the 2-1 Advancement rule that played a crucial role in passivization.

(34)

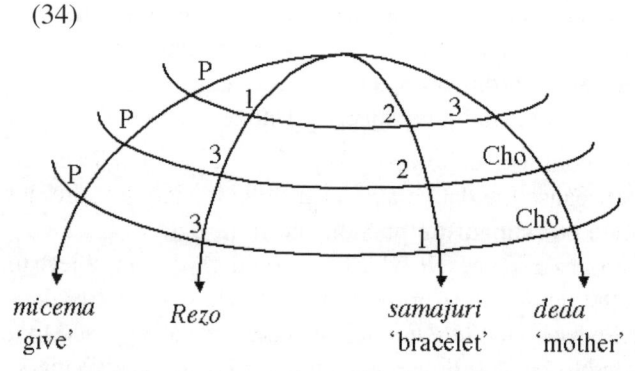

```
        P
    P   1    2  3
  P     3      2   Cho
        3      1   Cho
```

micema   Rezo   samajuri   deda
'give'   'bracelet' 'mother'

The final analysis thus gets the case marking exactly right, if one assumes a correlation between 3 and dative case and 1 and nominative case: *Rezo* as the final 3 is marked with the dative case, the chômeur *mother* must be marked postpositionally (like the English *by*-phrase in the passive), and the final 1, the subject *bracelet*, has nominative case.

(35)

Final Grammatical Relations		Overt Case
Rezo	3 (indirect object)	Dative
samajuri 'bracelet'	1 (subject)	Nominative
deda 'mother'	Cho (indirect object)	Postpositional

This Georgian example illustrates that some correlation between grammatical relations and case marking is assumed to hold. However, although case patterns are one of the core subjects of investigation within RG, the precise interplay between case and grammatical relations is not defined formally. This is partly because the relationship between grammatical relations and case marking is not straightforward and does involve semantic and further morphosyntactic factors, which go beyond representations of grammatical relations. The lack of generalizations about overt case marking continues to be true for some syntactic theories (e.g., GB/Minimalism, Head-Driven Phrase Structure Grammar, Combinatory Categorial Grammar), whereas others have formulated explicit theories of *linking* to determine the interrelationship between case, grammatical relations, thematic roles and clausal semantics (chapter 5).

3.7 The Unaccusative Hypothesis

That verbs come in different flavours is well known: one can distinguish between intransitive verbs such as *fall*, transitive verbs such as *kick* and ditransitives such as *give*. In addition, some verbs are known to be associated with dative arguments and these tend to denote some kind of psychological experience, like the Latin *placēre* 'please' (see chapter 2, exercise 1).

In addition, intransitive verbs can be divided into two major classes crosslinguistically. The fact that not all intransitive verbs behave alike had, of course, been noted on a language-by-language basis, but it did not become clear until the 1970s that a universally valid generalization could be made about the two different types of intransitive verbs.

Fillmore was a pioneer in this area as well. Fillmore (1968) posited two general formulas to derive intransitive case frames (cf. the discussion in section 3.5). According to these formulas, intransitives come in two versions: in one the single argument is an agent and the subject is therefore more 'active'. In the other, the argument is objective and therefore less 'active'.

(36) V + A   (intransitive, active subject)
      V + O   (intransitive, inactive subject)

Perlmutter and Postal (1984:98–99) provide a list of examples for both types of predicates, which were dubbed *unergative* (the agentive ones) and *unaccusative* (the objective ones) for reasons which should become clear by the end of this chapter.

(37) **Unergative Verbs**

Willed or Volitional Acts	*speak, laugh, walk, cry* ...
Manner of Speaking	*whisper, mumble, bellow* ...
Animal Sounds	*bark, neigh, roar* ...
Involuntary Bodily Processes	*cough, sneeze, belch* ...

(38) **Unaccusative Verbs**

Affected Argument	*burn, fall, dry* ...
Inchoatives	*melt, die, grow* ...
Existing and Happening	*exist, happen, arise* ...
Involuntary Emission of Stimuli	*shine, clink, stink* ...

A substantial body of work in RG is related to the *Unaccusative Hypothesis*, which states that some intransitives act as if they have an underlying 2, i.e., an object/theme (Perlmutter 1978). These are the unaccusatives. The Unaccusative Hypothesis goes hand in hand with assumptions about what constitutes basic clause structure types, shown in (39).

(39) **The Unaccusative Hypothesis**
    Certain intransitive clauses have an initial 2 but no initial 1.

(40) Basic Clause Structures
    A *transitive* stratum is one that contains a 1-arc and a 2-arc.
    An *unergative* stratum is one that contains a 1-arc and no 2-arc.
    An *unaccusative* is one that contains a 2-arc and no 1-arc.

While RG is not a theory that is widely practised, the terms *unaccusative* and *unergative* have become well established and tend to be difficult to remember when first encountered, especially when one is not aware of the original reasoning that led to their coinage.

The terms themselves are due to Geoffrey Pullum (Perlmutter and Postal 1984:95) and he proposed them on the following basis: 'if a 1 in a stratum with a 2 is an ergative, a 1 in a stratum with no 2 should be called an *unergative* 1, and likewise, if a 2 in a stratum with a 1 is an accusative, a 2 in a stratum with no 1 should be called an *unaccusative* 2' (Pullum 1991:151). That is, let us assume that 2s (objects) are usually marked with the accusative case and can therefore be thought of as 'accusatives'. Now, in a clause with only an initial 2 argument, this argument must eventually advance to a 1 (due to the Final 1 Law). That is, the underlying 'object' must be realized as a subject eventually. If one thinks of objects as being named by the label accusative, then what one has in this situation is an *unaccusative*. Let us further assume that because in many languages the agent argument is marked with an *ergative* case (see chapter 6), the 1 in basic transitive clauses can be thought of as ergative. Then, if this is the case, in a situation where there is an agent(=1) argument with no patient(=2) argument, this situation can be thought of as *unergative*.

Note that although the above passage has tried to state things as clearly as possible, the reader may still be confused. The terminological confusion surrounding the classification of verb types became even worse with the advent of Burzio (1986) (PhD thesis dated to 1981), who decided to call unaccusatives 'ergative verbs' (without providing any particular reasoning). It seems that since then the field of theoretical linguistics has lived in a permanent state of confusion, with papers published on German 'ergative verbs' even though German does not employ an ergative case marker. Furthermore, in languages like Urdu, it is precisely the unergative class of verbs which allow an overt ergative case marker (cf. Davison 1999).

(41) a. nadya=ne kʰãs-a
     Nadya=Erg cough-Perf.M.Sg
     'Nadya coughed.'   Urdu

   b. nadya=ne nɑha-ya
     Nadya=Erg bathe-Perf.M.Sg
     'Nadya bathed.'   Urdu

Despite this terminological confusion (see Pullum 1998 for a nice discussion), the division of intransitive verbs into unaccusatives vs. unergatives has proved to be extremely useful in understanding a number of linguistic phenomena, such as auxiliary selection in Romance and Germanic languages, the use of impersonal passives, and *ne*-cliticization in Italian (Rosen 1984, Burzio 1986). In what follows, the data with respect to auxiliary selection is discussed.

In Italian, some intransitive verbs co-occur with the perfect auxiliary *avere* 'have' while others require *essere* 'be'. This contrast is illustrated in (42). The discussion here is based on Perlmutter (1980), from where all of the examples have been taken (close glosses have been added).

(42) a. Giorgio ha   lavorato   tutta la   giornata.
       Giorgio have.Pres.3.Sg work.Part.M.Sg all the.F.Sg day.F.Sg
       'Giorgio has worked all day.'   Italian
    b. Giorgio è   arrivato   alle cinque.
       Giorgio be.Pres.3.Sg arrive.Part.M.Sg at.the five
       'Giorgio arrived at five o'clock.'   Italian

Transitive sentences always use 'have' unless they contain a reflexive verb, as in (43b).

(43) a. Giorgio ha   ucciso   Guido.
       Giorgio have.Pres.3.Sg kill.Part.M.Sg Guido
       'Giorgio (has) killed Guido.'   Italian
    b. Giorgio si è   ucciso.
       Giorgio self be.Pres.3.Sg kill.Part.M.Sg
       'Giorgio (has) killed himself.'   Italian

The distribution of these auxiliaries can be accounted for very simply by the following generalization within RG.

(44) Auxiliary Selection in Italian
     Select *essere* 'be' in any clause that contains a 1-arc and an object-arc with the same head. Otherwise, select *avere* 'have'.

If we analyse *lavorare* 'work' as an unergative verb and *arrivare* 'arrive' as a typical unaccusative verb (which is reasonable, given the description of typical unergative and unaccusative verbs in the previous section), then the unaccusative intransitive in (42b) represents a situation in which the clause has a nominal which heads an arc that contains both a 1 and a 2 (the 2 must advance to a 1 due to the Final 1 Law) This is illustrated in (45).

Similarly, in the reflexive example in (43b), the nominal is analysed as heading both a 1-arc and a 2-arc in (46). This analysis represents the fact that the same individual, *Giorgio* is interpreted as both agent and patient. This situation thus also falls under the generalization in (44): reflexives are predicted to select for *essere* 'be'. The reflexive clitic *si* is taken to be a superficial reflex of the unaccusative configuration.

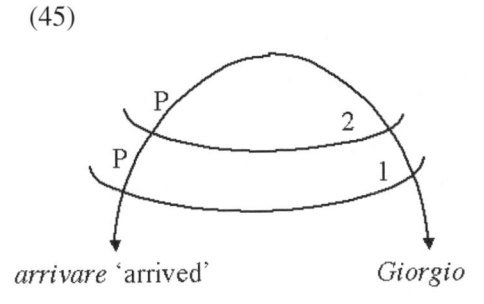

(45)

arrivare 'arrived'   *Giorgio*

(46)

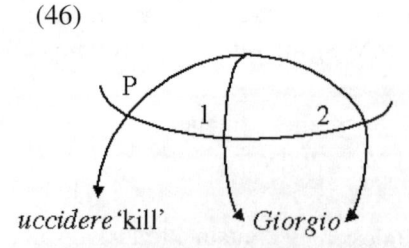

uccidere 'kill'   *Giorgio*

The transitive and the intransitive unergative, on the other hand, default to selecting *avere* 'have' since they do not fit the description in (44).

The data from auxiliary selection in Italian thus provides support for the Unaccusative Hypothesis. A similar pattern of auxiliary selection holds for languages like German and Dutch, though in these languages semantic factors such as telicity play a role. A nice discussion of the Dutch facts can be found in Zaenen (1993). Zaenen's analysis is based on the Unaccusative Hypothesis, though her approach is not couched within RG. Like the general approach to passivization that was first formulated within RG, the Unaccusative Hypothesis has become part of standard linguistic thinking.

3.8 The Universal Alignment Hypothesis

Given that the syntactic differences between unaccusatives and unergatives seem to be rooted in semantic differences, and given Fillmore's work on case roles, one could imagine a straightforward one-to-one correspondence between thematic roles and grammatical relations. RG explored this hypothesis by formulating the Universal Alignment Hypothesis (UAH).

(47) **The Universal Alignment Hypothesis** (Rosen 1984)
There exists some set of universal principles on the basis of which, given the semantic representation of a clause, one can predict which initial grammatical relation each nominal bears.

A (simplified) correspondence that could be assumed to hold between thematic roles and grammatical relations is shown in (48). Indeed, this correspondence is implicitly assumed in a number of syntactic theories.

(48)   **A Simplified Correspondence**

Thematic Role	**Grammatical Relation**
Agent	Subject
Experiencer	Subject
Patient	Object
Theme	Object
Goal/Beneficiary	Indirect Object
Location	Oblique
Instrument	Oblique/Adjunct

Rosen (1984) surveyed a number of differing languages with respect to the Unaccusative Hypothesis. One central tenet of RG is that the initial stratum of grammatical relations is connected to verbal semantics. With respect to the Unaccusative Hypothesis, the identification of semantic factors governing the distinction between unergatives and unaccusatives suggested that this distinction was not random, but was due to the underlying verbal semantics.

However, the verbal semantic classification does not seem to hold crosslinguistically. Examples such as the ones below from Choctaw and Italian show that the same verbal semantics can give rise to different initial grammatical relations in different languages (the examples are from Rosen 1984:61–62). The verb for 'die' in Choctaw, in (49a), for example, acts like an unergative, as evidenced by nominative subject (initial 1s are marked with the nominative). In the Italian example in (49b), on the other hand, the verb for 'die' selects the *essere* 'be' auxiliary, which shows that it behaves like an unaccusative.

(49) a. illi-li-tok   kiyo (Initial Term 1)
     die-1st.Nom-Pst not
     'I did not die.'   Choctaw
   b. Non sono morto (Initial Term 2)
     not I.am died
     'I did not die.'   Italian

Similarly, the Choctaw verb for 'sweat' in (50a) looks like an unaccusative because its only argument is marked with accusative case (unaccusative verbs have initial 2s, which are often marked with accusative case crosslinguistically). The Italian verb for 'sweat', on the other hand, behaves like an unergative because it selects for the *avere* 'have' auxiliary.

(50) a. sa-laksha   (Term 2)
     1st.Acc-sweat
     'I sweated.'   Choctaw
   b. Ho   sudato   (Term 1)
     I.Nom sweated
     'I sweated.'   Italian

One is forced to the conclusion that while the unaccusative/unergative distinction provides an extremely useful understanding of the behaviour of intransitives both within a language and crosslinguistically, not all verbs behave alike across languages, or even within a language (see Legendre 1989, 1990 for a detailed study of French). There are at least two ways to account for these crosslinguistic differences. One explanation is that while the underlying verbal semantics are always the same crosslinguistically, the unaccusative/unergative distinction is not based on exclusively semantic factors. In contrast, a different explanation could argue that not all verbs can be assumed to have exactly the same lexical semantics in all languages. For example, one could interpret the above data as showing that in some languages 'die' is treated more like an 'active' verb (you can go and actively die), whereas in others, it is something which happens to you. While this scenario may seem plausible to some readers, and indeed, serve to save the UAH, others may find it ludicrous. To date, there is no hard evidence which could decide definitively between the two options. Within RG, Rosen (1984) concluded that the evidence for the UAH was not convincing. However, a closely related idea, namely Baker's (1988) Uniformity of Theta Assignment Hypothesis (UTAH), see chapter 4, has established itself as a core part of syntactic theorizing. The precise nature of the interface between lexical semantics, thematic roles, case marking and grammatical relations thus continues to be the topic of active research.

3.9 Summary

This chapter has introduced the idea that abstract syntactic concepts mediate between the lexical semantics of a verb and the expression of case. In particular, *grammatical relations* were identified as one of these abstract syntactic concepts. Grammatical relations have formed a part of the descriptive grammatical tradition and have found their way into modern theories of syntax. This chapter discussed some of the founding ideas leading to the current understanding and use of grammatical relations and also introduced the notion of thematic roles in interaction with grammatical relations. The next chapter goes on to examine the fundamental ideas guiding a purely structural approach to grammatical relations, thematic roles, and case.

3.10 Exercises

Exercise 1

The two sentences in (1) are an active and a passive in German, respectively.

(1) a. Der   Lehrer   lobt
       the.M.Sg.Nom teacher.M.Sg praise.Pres.3.Sg
       den   Hund.
       the.M.Sg.Acc dog.M.Sg.Acc
       'The teacher praises the dog.'   German

   b. Der   Hund   wird
      the.M.Sg.Nom dog.M.Sg become.Pres.3.Sg
      vom   Lehrer   gelobt.
      by.the.Dat.M.Sg teacher.M.Sg praise.Part
      'The dog is praised by the teacher.'   German

Give stratal Relational Grammar analyses for the two sentences in (1) and say which laws were needed in the construction of the analysis.

Exercise 2

Recall the Georgian case alternation (section 3.6.2). Another case alternation involving the dative occurs with 'affective' verbs as in (2) (Harris 1984).

(2) gelas   uqvars   nino.
Gela.Dat he-loves-her-Ind Nino.Nom
'Gela loves Nino.'   Georgian

Under the assumption that the initial and final grammatical relations are as sketched below and that the analysis involves Inversion, as it did for the dative alternation in section 3.6.2, give a stratal analysis of (2).

Initial Terms		Final Terms	
Gela	1 (subject)	Gela	3 (indirect object)
Nino	2 (direct object)	Nino	1 (subject)

Exercise 3

The following two Old English sentences are from Allen (1995:133–135).

(3) ... swa heo maran læcedom   behofað
     so it greater leechcraft.Acc needs
'... so it requires greater medicine'
(COE), ÆCHom I, 33 496.30   Old English

(4) Micel   wund   behofað micles   læcedomes
great.Nom wound.Nom needs   great.Gen leechcraft.Gen
'A great wound requires great medicine.'   Old English
(COE) Bede 4 26.350.19

Provide RG analyses for these sentences. Each sentence should start out with the underlying terms 1 (*it/wound*) and 2 (*leechcraft*). Assume that you always want to treat a nominative as a subject and an accusative as an object, but that the genitive in (5) is analysed as a chômeur (like the instrumental in the passive).

4

Structural Case

Words dissemble	Plant them
Words be quick	They will grow
Words resemble walking sticks	Watch them waver so
[Jim Morrison, An American Prayer]

4.1 The Structural View of Grammatical Relations

This chapter introduces the basic approach to case and valency within the linguistic tradition represented by Government-Binding (GB) and the more recent versions of the theory, namely the Minimalist Program (MP). This chapter, as well as chapter 6 on ergativity, were difficult to write because the majority of generative linguists work within the GB/MP framework and hence the available literature is vast. The consensus on any particular analysis, however, is minimal. It is therefore a challenge to illustrate the basic ideas and assumptions comprehensively without also introducing the complete formal machinery and the various discussions which argue for or against a particular solution. In what follows, I rely mainly on Haegeman (1991), Carnie (2002) and Adger (2003).

A fundamental assumption is that the grammatical relations as well as the thematic roles discussed in chapter 3 should be encoded structurally. Case marking per se does not play a large role in the theory, as it is relegated to the morphophonological component whose job it is to 'spell out' the structural relations which are at the heart of the theoretical investigations. In order to understand where this intuition comes from, and how it plays out, the next sections go through some of the pertinent historical developments.

4.2 The Basic Architecture

The Minimalist Program is one of a succession of frameworks articulated by Noam Chomsky. The earliest framework was *Transformational Grammar*, which grew directly out of Chomsky's thesis work and enjoyed wide circulation in the form of *Syntactic Structures* (1957), as discussed in chapter 3. Basic ideas about case were first articulated in Government and Binding (Chomsky 1981) in terms of a *Case Theory*. The Minimalist Program is the most current version (Chomsky 1995), though the ideas proposed there have already been extended, e.g., by *Derivation by Phase* (Chomsky 2001).

The basic architectural assumptions of GB are as follows: a grammar is a system of rules which relates several subcomponents to one another. There is a lexicon, which lists all the arbitrary and stipulative knowledge and provides the language particular word forms (i.e., English *talk* vs. French *parler*). The component of crucial interest is the syntax, which consists of a categorial component that provides basic information about syntactic categories and about the relations between syntactic elements. A set of phrase structure rules (the PS component) creates D(eep)-structures from the lexical information. A transformational component further operates on this basic or 'deep' component and transforms the underlying abstract structures to a representation that is closer to the actual *surface form*. The Phonological Form (PF) component operates on this representation and 'spells it out', that is, it provides the morphophonological and prosodic rules needed to realize an abstract form that consists of something like 'talk' plus featural specifications of third person and singular number as *talks*. Over time, this component has also been given more and more responsibility for ensuring the correct surface word order of the clause. In classic GB, however, this fell squarely within the domain of the transformational component.

Logical Form (LF) is the final stage of a syntactic representation created by the transformational component operating on S-Structure. LF is a level of syntactic representation which is assumed to interface with the conceptual-intentional systems of the human brain. Semantic rules operate at the interface between syntax and concepts. This branch of syntactic representation is the one that is most directly geared towards a subsequent formal semantic analysis of the sentence. The resulting architecture can be pictured via the now famous inverted 'T-model' in (1).[1]

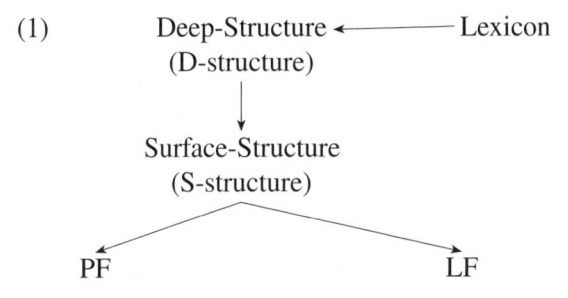

(1)   Deep-Structure ←——— Lexicon
       (D-structure)
              ↓
       Surface-Structure
        (S-structure)
         ↙   ↘
       PF   LF

[1] The terms Deep Structure and Surface Structure were used in earlier versions of the theory. They were replaced by the more abstract terms D-Structure and S-structure.

In this model, the lexicon feeds into the first level of syntactic analysis, the D-structure. The D-structure provides the underlying analysis of the clause, similar to the initial stratum proposed by RG (section 3.6). A number of transformations may then operate on the underlying representation, resulting in the S-structure, which is pronounced appropriately by the PF component and readied for semantic interpretation at LF. Note that no direct connection between phonology and semantics is anticipated in this architecture, a point which has given rise to some discussion, as there are linguistic phenomena such as focus, which require an interaction between prosodic PF factors and semantic LF interpretation (e.g., Cinque 1993, Reinhart 1996, Zubizarreta 1998).

The following sections chart the development and motivation of this architecture and provide detailed sample analyses of the basic types of phenomena already encountered in the previous chapters: unergatives, unaccusatives, transitives, ditransitives, passivization, and dative subjects.

4.3 Thematic Roles

In his *Remarks on Nominalization* paper, Chomsky (1970) argued that verbs and the nominals derived from them must share a common representation in the form of lexical entries which are neutral with respect to syntactic category. The evidence for this is provided by a comparison of the complements required by a verb and those required by its corresponding derived noun. As can be seen in (2) and (3), the verb and its corresponding nominalized form do not differ in the number and type of complements. The transitive verb *destroy* requires an agent and a patient, the ditransitive verb *present* requires an agent, a patient and a goal/beneficiary. While these complements or *arguments* are not necessarily realized in exactly the same surface form when the verbs are nominalized, the overall valency and type of argument remains the same: there is still an agent (expressed by the genitive or via a *by*-phrase), a patient (expressed via an *of*-phrase) and a goal (in (3) only, no change in surface form). [2]

(2) a. The army destroyed the city.
    b. The destruction of the city by the army.
    c. The army's destruction of the city.

(3) a. John presented the medal to Mary.
    b. John's presentation of the medal to Mary.
    c. The presentation of the medal to Mary by John.

The evidence from nominalizations thus suggests a level or type of representation at which there is shared information between verbs and their corre-

---

[2]There is a difference between the arguments of nominalizations and the arguments of verbs in that the former are optional. However, this difference is immaterial to Chomsky's basic argument. For a standardly recognized in-depth discussion of the arguments of nouns, see Grimshaw (1990).

sponding nouns. In time, this came to be referred to as *argument structure*. The argument structure of a predicate (predicates include verbs, nouns, adjectives, or prepositions) specifies the number and type of arguments a predicate subcategorizes for. Argument structures were also invested with hierarchical relationships which held between arguments, so that an agent, for example, is generally taken to be the 'highest' argument in the hierarchy and thus the most likely to be realized as a subject. The labels for the individual members of an argument structure differ from theory to theory and, within theories, from author to author (see chapter 5). Fillmore's (1968) proposals for the naming of case roles were not taken up (see Jackendoff 1972 for a discussion of shortcomings), instead a convention based on initial ideas by Gruber (1965) and Jackendoff (1972) has prevailed. Common argument role labels are: *agent, theme/patient, goal/beneficiary/recipient, source, location*. First due to Gruber and Jackendoff, the term *thematic relations* or *thematic role* gained currency as a cover term. In order to make clear that this term was intended as a primarily syntactic concept, Chomsky (1981) used the term θ-*role* and formulated a θ-*theory* to account for the licensing of a predicate's arguments.

Fillmore's (1968) proposals made a very explicit connection between semantics, case marking and syntactic structure. However, this architecture was incompatible with a number of ideas within generative grammar. One problem was that Fillmore encoded notions like 'Subject', 'Object' and 'Predicate' directly as part of the syntactic representation (see (7)). This was argued to be theoretically incoherent (e.g., see Chomsky 1965:68). Fillmore's approach also faced problems when confronted with further empirical evidence.

One problem has to do with *argument alternations*. The direct connection between semantically grounded case roles such as *locative* or *instrumental* and syntactic representations postulated by Fillmore turned out to be too direct for cases of argument alternation such as the now famous *spray/load* constructions illustrated in (4) and (5) (S. Anderson 1971). Given that the case roles of each of the participants must be identical in both the a and b sentences, then how could the difference in surface structure be explained? Why did a theme like *paint* surface as an object in one case, and as a prepositional phrase in another?

(4) a. John sprayed paint on the canvas.
b. John sprayed the canvas with paint.

(5) a. John loaded the wagon (with hay).
b. John loaded hay (on the wagon).

Another concrete illustration of the problem is based on the *swarm* alternation in (6). There is general agreement that both of these sentences have the same underlying case roles, namely an objective (or theme), the *bees*, and a locative or location, the *garden*. However, a close examination of the sentences shows that they must be interpreted differently at the semantic level. In

(6b) the entire garden must be full of bees, whereas in (6a) only some part of the garden need have bees in it.

(6) a. Bees are swarming in the garden.
b. The garden is swarming with bees.

Now, if one took Fillmore's ideas on the interaction between case roles and syntax seriously, then the case roles would have to appear as a direct part of the syntactic structure and from there on be subject to transformational rules. That is, the two sentences in (6) would have to be derived from the same underlying syntactic representation, namely something similar to what is depicted in (7). Here, K represents the case morpheme, which is zero for *bees*. In Fillmore's case grammar, prepositions were considered to be case markers on a par with morphological case.

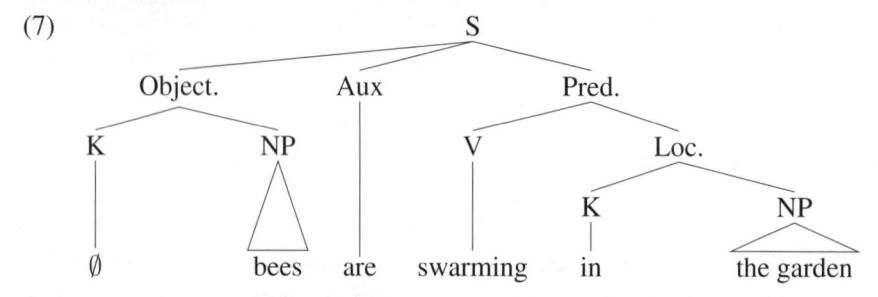

(7)
```
                        S
        ┌───────────────┼───────────────┐
      Object.          Aux            Pred.
      ┌──┴──┐           │          ┌────┴────┐
      K    NP           V              Loc.
      │    △                       ┌────┴────┐
                                   K         NP
                                   │         △
      ∅   bees        are   swarming   in   the garden
```

The basic problem with this sort of analysis was posed by the *Katz-Postal Hypothesis* (Katz and Postal 1964), which sought to integrate principled rules for deriving semantic interpretations from syntactic structures. The hypothesis basically states that rules for semantic interpretation should operate exclusively on underlying phrase structures. Or, to put it slightly differently: transformations do not change meanings (formulation based on Jackendoff 1972:7). Now, given that the underlying structure is the same for both of the sentences in (6), the problem is that no application of transformational rules, however elegantly and cleverly formulated, could hope to yield the two different semantic interpretations that are necessary in order to capture the semantic differences between the two sentences in (6) (Anderson 1971).

Based on a range of further data, Anderson (1971) instead proposed that the generalization needed to account for the semantic alternation in (6) could be best captured by referring to syntactic notions, such as 'object-of', by establishing that only underlying direct objects can be interpreted 'holistically', that is, as signifying that *all* of the garden is full of bees (6b). The argument was that the case roles (Objective and Predicative) could not make the right kinds of distinctions to allow for the correct semantic interpretation of the sentences, because the correct semantic interpretation depends on the syntactic configuration, and not the particular case roles, to guide it. Thus, lexical semantics had to be mediated via structural relations, which then fed into a semantic component for clausal interpretation. Note that this is also the conclusion arrived at by Perlmutter and Postal (1983) in the context of Relational Grammar, which prompted them to adopt abstract entities such as 1, 2 and 3, rather than semantically based labels such as agent, patient or goal.

While a direct syntactic encoding of semantically grounded case roles clearly does not provide the right results, Jackendoff (1972) also contended that semantic information should not be neglected in the construction of an underlying level of representation. Therefore, an underlying representation was needed that could mediate between lexical semantics and the syntactic structure. The next sections chart the development of *deep structure*, which encoded the necessary information in a suitably abstract, yet semantically grounded manner.

4.4 Category Neutral Representations: X′-Syntax

Recall that Chomsky's (1970) paper on nominalization concluded that verbs and nouns must share a category neutral argument structure. While many theories are content with using representations of the kind shown in (8), the highly structuralized assumptions of Chomsky's transformational tradition demanded a representation which tied the argument relations intimately to syntactic trees.

(8) *destroy*< agent, theme >

In order to achieve a representation with the desired initial neutrality between nouns (N) and verbs (V), the notion of $\overline{\overline{X}}$-syntax (or X′-syntax) was put to use. $\overline{X}$-syntax provides a category neutral general schema for syntactic representations. The basic structure that was (and is) assumed to hold is the simple binary branching tree shown in (9).

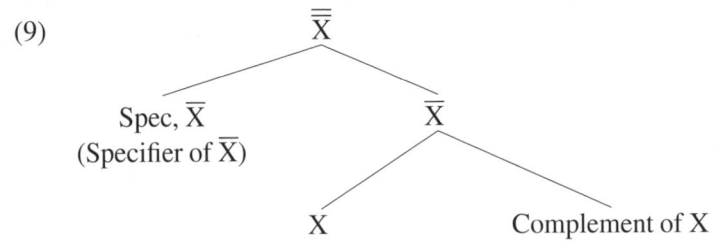

(9)
```
                    X̿
                   / \
          Spec, X̄      X̄
       (Specifier of X̄)  / \
                        X   Complement of X
```

The specifier of a category X generally works out to be the syntactic subject if X is instantiated as a verb. If X is instantiated as a noun, then the specifier often works out to be a genitive possessor. This basic pattern is illustrated in (11) for the data in (10b) (based on Chomsky 1970:53).

(10) a. John proved the theorem.
 b. John's proof of the theorem.

The category neutral lexical entry for *prove* only states that an agent phrase (the specifier) and a further complement (the patient) are required, i.e., the category-neutral representation would be as in (9). If realized as a noun, then the structure in (11) is appropriate. Note that by convention a 'double-bar' category is referred to by its more traditional name, i.e., $\overline{\overline{N}}$ is NP, $\overline{\overline{V}}$ is VP, etc.

The structure in (11) does not yet match the desired surface form, namely *John's proof of the theorem*. Under Chomsky's model it was assumed that the PF component contains a general rule for English by which the specifier of a noun is realized via the genitive, possessive *'s*. Similarly, the complement of a noun must be properly pronounced with an *of*. Thus, the precise morphological case or surface form of an argument is a matter of PF realization, as already mentioned, and therefore relatively uninteresting from a theoretical point of view. In contrast, the *structural* relationships that can be articulated are taken to be of great theoretical interest.

(11) [tree diagram: $\overline{\overline{N}}$ branching to John and $\overline{N}$; $\overline{N}$ branching to N (proof) and $\overline{\overline{N}}$ (the theorem)]

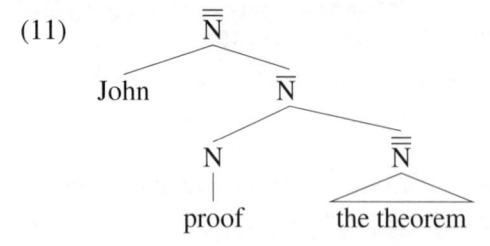

If *prove* is realized as a verb, then in principle the same basic configuration between specifier, complement and predicate (the X, i.e., the verb or noun) is assumed. In (12) the complement of V is again *the theorem* and the specifier is *John*. Note, however, that the subject *John* does not actually occupy the specifier position of VP, but a position outside of the VP, namely the canonical subject position in English. Further assumptions about basic transformations are necessary in order to arrive at this structure and indeed, as discussed in the next section (section 4.5) the theory was changed subsequently to allow for a cleaner solution.

(12) [tree diagram: S branching to NP (John) and VP; VP branching to PAST and $\overline{V}$; $\overline{V}$ branching to V (prove) and NP (the theorem)]

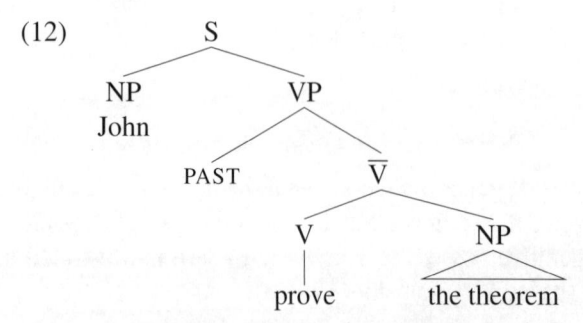

Also note that the actual specifier position contains information about tense. The verb is assumed to combine with this abstract tense information and then the PF component applies a general rule which pronounces *prove*+PAST as *proved*. The positioning of tense information in what generally functions as a type of subject or possessive position is not a happy solution, to say the least, and further work on tense subsequently produced a theoretical consensus that one should assume *functional* categories above the VP level. The functional categories project according to the general X'-schema and are assumed to be responsible for information such as tense, aspect, agreement and also case.

4.5 The VP-internal subject hypothesis

English is a language whose basic word order is subject-verb-object (SVO). This pattern matches the general specifier-head-complement pattern established via X'-syntax. This general schema is also supported by evidence involving auxiliaries in verb-subject-object (VSO) languages such as Irish or Welsh. Example (13) provides a sentence with basic VSO word order in Irish. At first glance this would not appear to support the basic specifier-verb-complement schema. However, when an auxiliary is added, the word order after the auxiliary is exactly SVO. Furthermore, there is some evidence that in Irish the subject, the verb and the object are contained within a constituent in (13b) (McCloskey 1983). The most natural category to assume for this constituent would be a VP, thus bolstering the idea that all of the arguments of a verb are initially contained within a VP that follows the specifier-verb-complement schema.

(13) a. Phóg Máire an lucharachán
kissed Mary the leprechaun
'Mary kissed the leprechaun.' (Carnie 2002:202) Irish

b. Tá Máire ag pógáil an lucharachán
is Mary Asp kiss the leprechaun
'Mary is kissing the leprechaun.' (Carnie 2002:202) Irish

The problem now is how the different surface word orders of English and Irish can be derived, based on one and the same underlying specifier-verb-complement pattern. The solution proposed by Koopman and Sportiche (1991) came to be known as the VP-internal subject hypothesis because they argued that in all languages, be they SVO or VSO, the subject was initially placed in the specifier of VP (also see Lamontagne and Travis 1986). In English, this subject had to raise to a higher position, but could remain in the lower position in Irish. The reasons for this difference involve data from agreement and quantifiers and are too complex to be summarized here. Important is that languages were assumed to be parametrized according to where nominative case could be assigned. Assuming a general structure for finite clauses as in (14), based on Carnie (2002:241), the idea is that English only licenses the nominative subject case in the Spec, IP (specifier of IP) position, whereby Irish or Welsh license it in the Spec, VP position. The IP stands for inflectional phrase and contains the finite features (often instantiated via auxiliaries) of a clause.

(14)

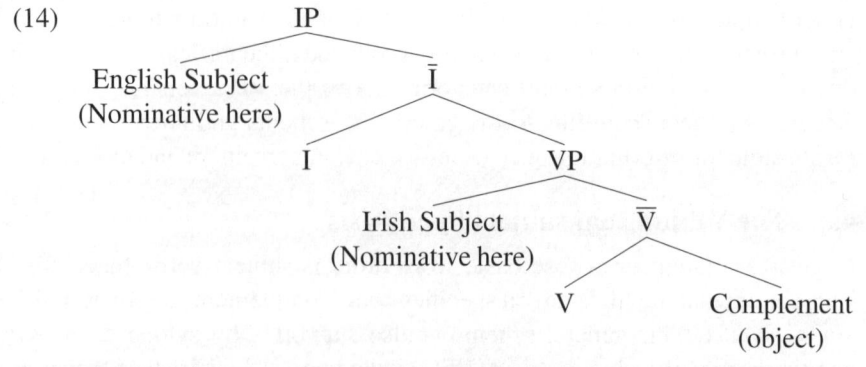

```
              IP
         ╱         ╲
English Subject     Ī
(Nominative here) ╱   ╲
                 I    VP
                   ╱     ╲
            Irish Subject  V̄
           (Nominative here) ╱  ╲
                            V   Complement
                               (object)
```

The differences between Irish and English can now be accounted for as follows. In both English and Irish, the underlying structure for *Mary is kissing the leprechaun* is as in (15). However, in English, the subject *Mary* must move to the specifier of IP in order to receive nominative case. The resulting word orders are thus exactly right for both English and Irish.[3]

(15)

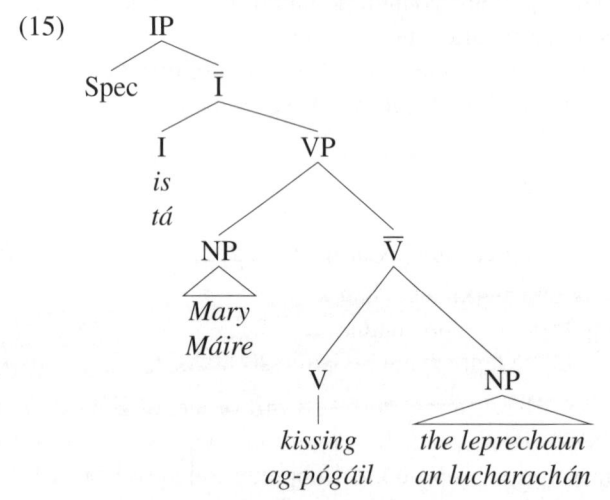

```
            IP
         ╱     ╲
       Spec     Ī
              ╱   ╲
             I    VP
             is  ╱   ╲
             tá NP    V̄
               Mary  ╱   ╲
               Máire V    NP
                     │
                  kissing  the leprechaun
                  ag-pógáil an lucharachán
```

The NP-movement in English is linked to the need for the subject to agree with the finite element in the clause (Koopman and Sportiche 1991). The agreement patterns in VSO languages like Irish, Welsh or Arabic differ from that of English. In Arabic, for example, the verb does not have to agree with its subject, but may display a default agreement form. The same holds in Welsh for nouns (but not pronouns). Welsh also has asymmetric agreement in conjuncts, something which is not found in English (e.g., Sadler 2003). The connection

---

[3]The analysis for Irish has to be more complicated as it turns out that the *ag* on the verb is an aspectual marker which thus must interact with the Asp(ectual) functional category. See Ramchand (1997) for some discussion. The same naturally applies to the English progressive *-ing*, whose treatment is also simplified here.

drawn by Koopman and Sportiche between agreement and the position of subjects therefore seems a reasonable hypothesis.

4.6 Case and Agreement

Though not discussed at any length in this book, the *head* of IP, i.e. the I, is a finite element which is responsible for tense and verb agreement in the clause. Following the consequences of the VP-internal hypothesis (and other thoughts that were formulated around this time), a close interaction between case and agreement that is mediated by finiteness must be assumed. The precise assumption is that nominative case is primarily assigned in the specifier of IP.

The close relationship between nominative case and finiteness is borne out by the fact that most languages do not allow the arguments of non-finite clauses to contain a nominative subject argument. This is illustrated in (16) for English, where the non-finite embedded clause *to sleep* cannot have a nominative subject (*he*), but has Exceptional Case Marking (ECM), see section 4.12. In contrast, the embedded finite clause *that he slept* allows the nominative *he*.

(16) a. Nadya wanted him/*he to sleep.
     b. Nadya thought that he slept.

However, the assumption that there is a close relationship between agreement and case is not borne out crosslinguistically. South Asian languages provide a broad range of agreement patterns, which demonstrate that nominative and agreement are not as tightly connected as predicted.[4] Faced with a wide variety of crosslinguistic data, the IP has grown in complexity. The complex or 'exploded' IP originally goes back to arguments by Pollock (1989) on differences between English and French. It is now often assumed to contain nodes governing agreement that are separate from nodes which regulate tense (TP).

The correlation that nominative subject case and tense are related appears to hold true in a majority of the world's languages. In European languages, the agreement facts fall in line with nominative case and tense, and so a close relationship between all three factors was assumed, with agreement being postulated as the governing force behind case assignment. More recent accounts distinguish more carefully between the various factors that are involved and link nominative case to the presence of the head of TP (T) and its features.

4.7 D-Structure, θ-Theory, and Structural Case

At this point, enough background information has been amassed to allow an introduction of the basics of θ-theory as introduced by Chomsky (1981) and as practised for many years by a broad array of researchers. For one, the idea of

---

[4]Subbarao (2001), for example, concludes that a notion of 'null agreement' is needed to be able to cover all the phenomena surveyed in his typological look at the interaction between case and agreement in South Asian languages.

thematic relations or roles had been firmly established as being of relevance to the licensing and case marking of arguments. For another, X'-theory allowed a clear definition of a *structural* relationship between arguments. Finally, nominative case had been linked to the functional element I (or T for tense), which was responsible for clausal tense and agreement.

The basic architecture was articulated as shown in (1). The semantic dimension underlying the participants of an action were encoded in terms of thematic roles such as *agent, patient,* or *theme,* as discussed in section 4.3. These thematic or θ-roles, as they were dubbed by Chomsky, were encoded in the lexicon and from there were *projected* to the D-structure. This was governed by the Projection Principle in (17).

(17) **Projection Principle** (simple form)
Lexical Information is syntactically represented.

Verbs carried specifications as to the type and number of their arguments in the lexicon, perhaps as in (18). The assumption was that this information was structurally represented. The syntactic projection of the verb *destroy*, for example, would therefore be the VP constituent in (19).

(18)

Verb	Thematic Roles	Verb	Thematic Roles
destroy	agent theme	*sneeze*	agent
give	agent theme beneficiary	*fall*	theme

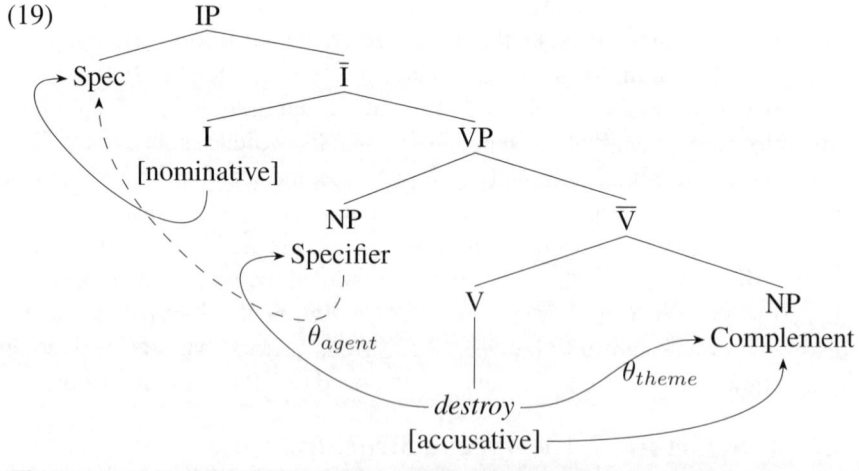

(19)

There are several things happening in this D-structure tree. The by now familiar X'-schema gives rise to the basic blueprint of the clause: the verb *destroy* heads the VP projection which contains a specifier and a complement position. Since we are assuming a finite clause, the I projection is licensed. This I could contain either an abstract tense feature such as PAST or PRESENT, which would combine with the verb at surface structure (S-Structure) so that *destroy* would be realized as *destroyed* or *destroys*. Alternatively, the I could host an auxiliary, giving rise to a periphrastic construction such as *was destroying*.

The verb also assigns θ-roles to the available structural argument positions. The number and type of θ-roles it can assign are specified lexically. However, the position and type of arguments that are available for θ-role assignment are determined structurally. The verb *destroy* has two θ-roles to assign, the theme is assigned to the complement of the verb, the agent to the specifier of VP. In principle, it would be possible to project the lexically specified information in any which way. For example, one could decide to assign *both* the agent and the theme to the specifier. The θ-criterion in (20) serves to rule out this possibility by legislating that each structural argument position can receive no more than one θ-role, and vice versa. This is particularly important when NP-movement is involved. Theoretically, NPs could pick up extra θ-roles as they move to different positions in the tree. The θ-criterion legislates against this possibility.

(20) **The θ-Criterion**
Each argument bears one and only one θ-role, and each θ-role is assigned to one and only one argument.

One also cannot project the lexical information so that the agent is assigned to the complement and the theme to the specifier. While not explicitly stated in the formulation in (17), this restriction is part of the more complex version of the Projection Principle (cf. Chomsky 1981:38). A stronger version of the θ-criterion and the Projection Principle is the UTAH (Baker 1988:46) in (21). This requires that thematic roles and structural positions always stand in a one-to-one relationship.

(21) **The Uniformity of Theta Assignment Hypothesis** (UTAH)
Identical thematic relationships between items are represented by identical structural relationships between those items at the level of D-structure.

The UTAH allows a clear formulation of the underlying properties of the alternation in (22). Here the *ice cream* must be a theme in both (22a) and (22b) and therefore appears as the complement of the verb in both cases at D-structure, even though at S-structure it surfaces as an object in (22a) and as a subject in (22b) (see section 4.7.1 on unaccusatives). Furthermore, even though there is no agent in (22b), the relationship between *ice cream* and *mush* remains the same in both versions. The thematic relationship between *ice cream* and *mush* is identical and this is mirrored at the structural level.

(22) a. Julia melted the ice cream into mush.
b. The ice cream melted into mush.

Finally, as also indicated in (19), case is assigned structurally. The assignment of nominative case has already been discussed: it is licensed or assigned by I to the specifier of IP. The accusative case, which has not been mentioned so far, is assigned structurally to the VP complement by the verbal head. The intuition at the heart of these assignments expresses the empirical observation that in many languages the nominative subject is generally situated in the near vicinity of the inflected, tensed verb or auxiliary. The accusative object, on the other hand, is generally found close to the verb and generally forms a VP constituent together with the verb. It thus seems natural to assume that I on the one hand, and V on the other, are responsible for the assignment of case.

Under this treatment, case is closely associated with structural position. Nominative and accusative are therefore commonly referred to as *structural* or *abstract Case*. The capital letter on *Case* is meant to signal that the term 'case' is being used in a theoretically special manner. The term *abstract* makes note of the fact that these are the two cases which are often unmarked or phonologically null crosslinguistically. In the Irish in (13), for example, neither of the participants are overtly case marked for nominative or accusative case. English also only shows case differences in the pronominal system. One reasonable strategy in the face of such evidence might be to conclude that English or Irish have no case marking system (cf. Hudson's 1995 conclusion for English). Another strategy would be to decide that Irish and English do indeed function like German or Latin, which have overt nominative and accusative case marking, but that because these cases signal primarily *structural* rather than primarily semantic relationships, these case relations are indeed primarily structural. As such, overt case marking is not a necessity, but a matter of language particular pronunciation. This latter strategy is the one adopted within GB.

Structural Case is independent of thematic roles. For example, in (22), the *ice cream* is a theme/patient in both sentences. This does not preclude it from being assigned accusative structural Case in (22a) and nominative structural Case in (22b). The same point can be illustrated with another class of transitive verbs. These *psych verbs* have an argument structure which consists of an experiencer and a stimulus or theme which provides the experience.

(23) Xena enjoyed the show.

In (23), *Xena* is the experiencer and *the show* is the stimulus or theme. These thematic relations are assigned lexically by the verb *enjoy*, as shown in (24). Despite this marked difference in thematic roles, the assignment of structural Case works exactly as in (19). This independence of thematic roles and structural Case assignment allows the flexibility needed to deal with various types of transitive verbs (e.g., agentive *destroy* vs. experiential *enjoy*), unaccusatives, passivization and a range of other phenomena.

Structural Case assignment to NPs is strictly regulated by the *Case Filter* in (25). The Case Filter ensures that every structurally realized NP is case marked (originally proposed by Rouveret and Vergnaud 1980).

(24)

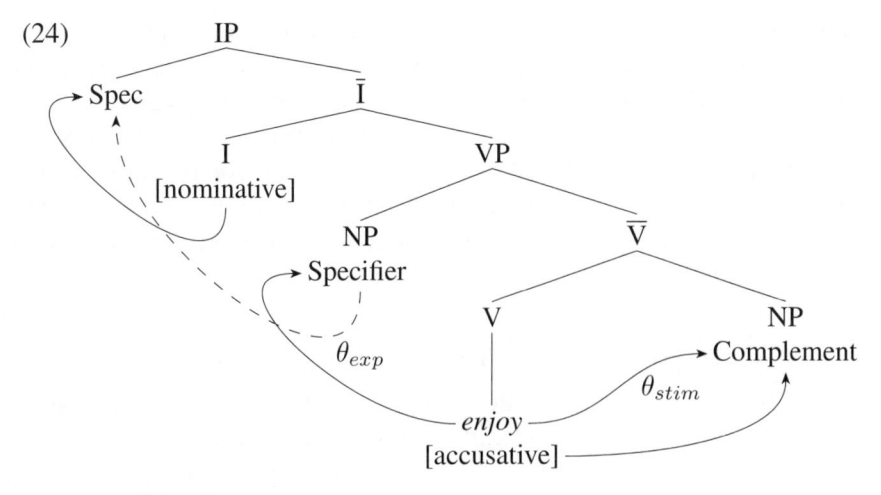

```
           IP
      ╱        ╲
   Spec         Ī
               ╱  ╲
              I    VP
        [nominative]
                  ╱    ╲
                 NP     V̄
              Specifier
                 │      ╱    ╲
                θ_exp  V      NP
                       │   Complement
                     enjoy    θ_stim
                   [accusative]
```

(25) **The Case Filter**
Every overt NP must be assigned Case

As already mentioned, structural Case does not necessarily translate into overt morphology on the NP. The NPs in the sentences in (26) and (27) are both considered to have structural nominative and accusative Case. However, only in languages like Latin is this case marking realized morphologically. The overt realization of case marking is merely a matter of language-particular pronunciation in the PF component and is of no deep theoretical interest.

(26) Insincerity destroys truth.

(27) simulātiō   dēlet   vēritātem
     insincerity.F.Sg.Nom destroy.Pres.3.Sg truth.F.Sg.Acc
     'Insincerity destroys truth.' (based on Cicero)   Latin

The effect of this model is that there is a single underlying representation, namely the lexical argument structure, which specifies the number and type of possible θ-roles. This lexical information can be projected into the syntax in various ways. One way is via the verbal projection, as shown above. Another way is via the nominal projection (section 4.4). In nominalizations, the lexical information projects to an NP, but because this projection is headed by a noun and not a verb, accusative case cannot be assigned to the complement. Neither is nominative case possible in the specifier, because there is no link to tense and inflection via the I projection. Instead, as discussed in section 4.4, the arguments of the noun are marked by the genitive and prepositions (e.g., *of*).

The other important consideration for this model was that while the lexical semantic generalizations carefully established by Gruber (1965), Jackendoff (1972) and others needed to be taken into account, the available evidence indicated that lexical semantics could not flow directly into the semantic interpretation of the clause, but needed to be mediated by the syntax (section 4.3). This mediating effect is realized by the interaction of θ-roles and structural position. Lexical semantic relations are not directly encoded in the syntax, as originally proposed by Fillmore (1968), but the pertinent information enters the syntax via θ-assignment. As shown in the next sections, this consistently associated NPs with a certain θ-role, but allowed for syntactic variation. That is, a theme NP could be realized variously as an object ((28a)), or as a subject ((28b)), without precluding a correct clausal semantic interpretation. The same is true for the *swarm* examples discussed in section 4.3.

(28) a. The army destroyed the city.
b. The city was destroyed by the army.

In what follows, examples are given for the treatment of unaccusatives, unergatives and passives and so-called 'quirky case', because these have been established as core phenomena that any theory of case must be able to deal with. Nothing so far has been said about ditransitives or other kinds of possible verbal arguments. These phenomena continue to be problematic within the GB/MP approach and are addressed in separate sections (and chapters).

4.7.1 Unaccusatives and Unergatives

The Unaccusative Hypothesis introduced in chapter 3.6 established a crosslinguistically relevant difference between two types of intransitive verbs: unaccusative and unergatives. Roughly, unergatives are agentive while unaccusatives are non-agentive. A typical example for an unergative is *sneeze* or *cough*, typical examples of unaccusatives are *fall*, *roll* or *melt*.

The blueprint for a D-structure of a typical transitive verb was given in (19). This D-structure conforms to the X'-schema and provides the basis for an analysis of unergatives and unaccusatives. It is therefore instructive to recall the D-structure and to understand the resulting S-structure.

In the S-structure in (29) (based on transitive *melt* rather than on *destroy*), movement is again indicated via a dashed line. In addition, (29) includes several *t*s, which stand for the *trace* of a moved element. Every moved element is coindexed with its trace. Movement is licensed by a very general Move-α rule. In principle, therefore, anything can move. In practice, however, Move-α is motivated by constraints such as the Case Filter, so only certain items move.

The traces are a means of recording the transformations that have taken place from D-structure to S-structure. They also allow the recovery of pertinent information across derivational levels. An immediate example where the recovery of information becomes relevant is provided by the agent phrase. This has moved from the underlying position in SpecVP (Specifier or VP) to the SpecIP in order to receive nominative case. This movement was forced by the Case Filter, which requires that every NP must be assigned structural Case. In its S-structure position, there is no indication of the θ-role assigned to the NP.

However, since it is coindexed with the trace in the specifier of VP, we know that this NP was assigned the agent θ-role at D-structure. Thus, *Julia* has been identified as a nominative agent, and *the ice cream* as an accusative theme via an interaction of several different aspects of the grammar.

(29) Julia melted the ice cream. (S-structure)

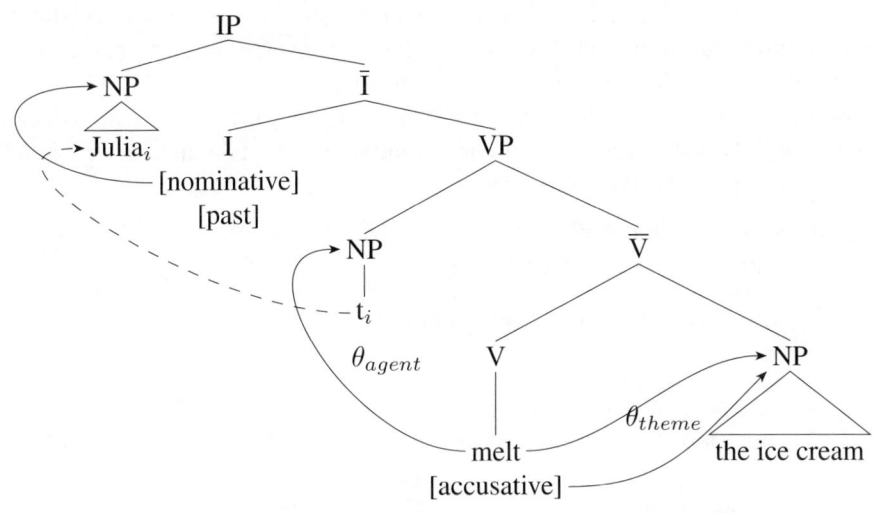

Now consider the D-structure analysis for the unaccusative version of *melt* in (30). The verb is lexically specified for only one argument, a theme. The theme projects into a D-structure with a complement, but nothing in SpecVP.

(30) The ice cream melted. (D-structure)

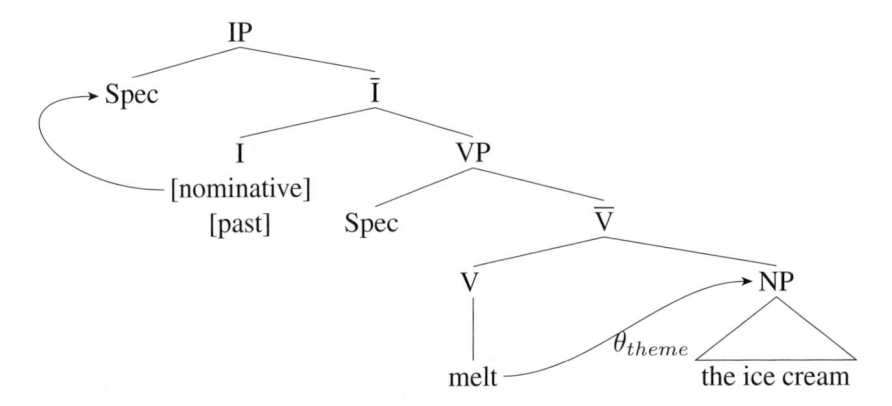

A comparison with (29) shows that in both cases the *ice cream* is analysed as the theme. In (29) the *ice-cream* remained in the complement position, but it cannot do so in (30). The reason for this is the Case Filter, which states that every NP must be assigned case. However, as shown in (30), the verb cannot assign accusative case to its complement, as it did in (29).

The reason for this is not clear within GB/MP, though what has become known as *Burzio's Generalization* in (31) seems to be crosslinguistically valid. Burzio (1986:178–179) observed that only verbs which are capable of assigning a θ-role to the 'external' argument (see section 4.10.2) in SpecVP can assign accusative Case. This observation has so far eluded further understanding, despite rounds of lively conferences and debates. One strategy has been to attempt to recast the generalization in terms of a dependence of the accusative case on the nominative (e.g., the discussion in section 6.5.2). However, this does not really allow for a deeper understanding of the phenomenon either and so the Generalization remains a source of investigation and debate.

(31) **Burzio's Generalization:** A verb which lacks an external argument fails to assign accusative Case.

(32) The ice cream melted. (S-structure)

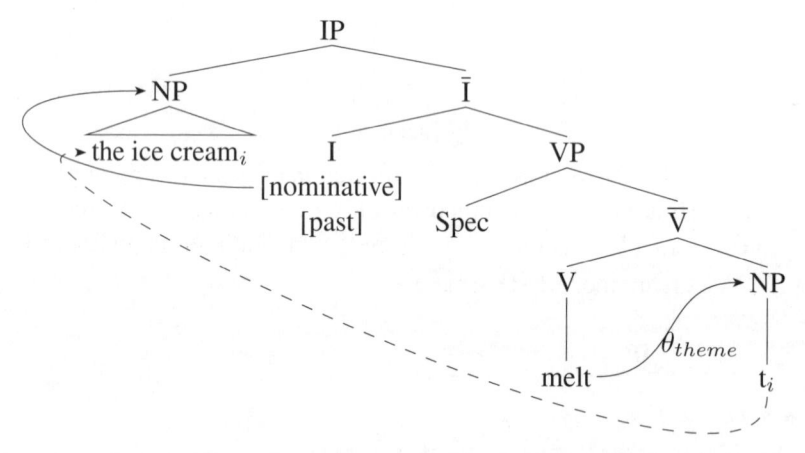

Given Burzio's Generalization, the analysis of the unaccusative version of *melt* proceeds as follows. Because *melt* has no agent θ-role, it cannot assign structural accusative Case. This leaves *ice cream* with a θ-role, but without Case. The only available position in the clause where it could receive Case is SpecIP. As a result, the *ice cream* moves to SpecIP, as shown in (32). This satisfies the Case Filter and the sentence is now also in the right order.

Another reason for the verbal complement to move is the Extended Projection Principle (EPP), whose precise formulation is quite complicated. Its effect is to ensure that the specifiers of functional projections, in our case the IP, are filled. This principle is needed for sentences with impersonal subjects, such as in (33). In (33a) there is no agent, patient or theme, which could fruitfully be argued to be an argument of *rain*. Rather, there is some semantically undefined 'it' which is raining. In the German impersonal passive in (33b), there is nothing in the sentence that could be identified as a subject. However, German requires *something* in the immediately preverbal (or pre-auxiliary) position. In this case, the 'here' does the trick and is licensed by the EPP.

(33) a. It rained.
    b. Hier wird getanzt.
       here become.Pres.3.Sg dance.PastP
       'It is danced here.'   German

In languages like English, which do not allow subjectless sentences (the *it* in (33a) is the syntactic subject), the EPP translates to a requirement that every clause have a subject. One simplified formulation along these lines is given in (34) (this formulation does not account for the German subjectless pattern in (33b)). As the name implies, the EPP extends the basic Projection Principle discussed in (17). Note also that as formulated in (34), the EPP has exactly the same effect as RG's Final 1 Law (section 3.6). The basic intuition is that all well-formed clauses should contain a syntactic subject.

(34) **Extended Projection Principle** (simple form)
     All clauses must have subjects. Lexical Information is syntactically represented. (Carnie 2002:175)

The other major class of intransitive verbs is formed by unergatives. A D-structure for a typical unergative is shown in (35).

(35) Kim sneezed. (D-structure)

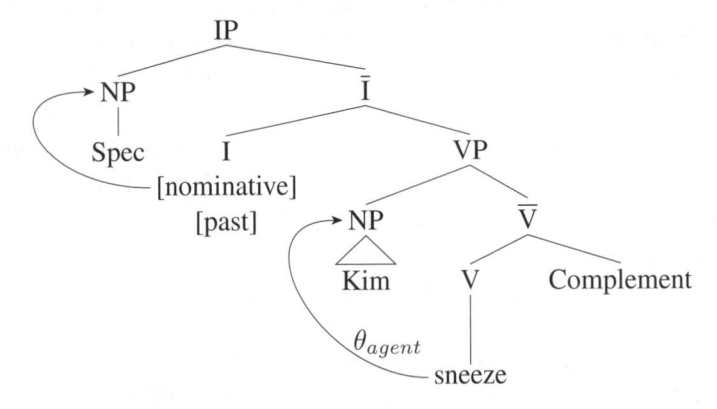

This time there is no complement to the verb. Unergative verbs only have an agent θ-role to assign and the corresponding argument is projected into SpecVP. Because the verb has an external argument in SpecVP, it could in principle assign accusative Case to the complement (cf. Burzio's generalization in (31)), but there is no complement, so accusative is not assigned. The agent must move to SpecIP for nominative case, as is shown in (36).

(36) Kim sneezed. (S-structure)

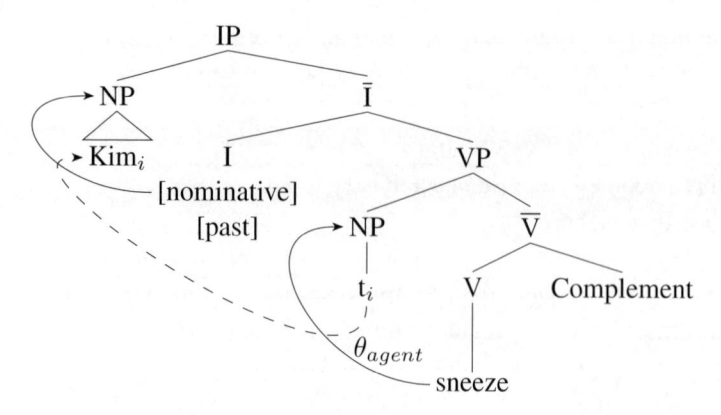

```
                        IP
                   ┌────┴────┐
                  NP         Ī
                   △     ┌───┴───┐
                 Kimᵢ    I       VP
                      [nominative] ┌──┴──┐
                       [past]      NP     V̄
                                    |   ┌─┴──────┐
                                    tᵢ   V   Complement
                                    |    |
                                  θ_agent sneeze
```

The basic X′-schema in conjunction with assumptions about the Case Filter and an interaction between case, tense and agreement thus allows for an elegant treament of basic active clause types. The next sections discuss passivization and instances of non-structural Case.

4.7.2 Passivization

The pioneering work by practitioners of RG served to establish universal characteristics of passivization (section 3.6). The analysis abstracted away from language-particular surface properties. RG argued that the relevant generalizations could be captured most efficiently and elegantly by assuming an abstract syntactic interface between thematic roles and grammatical relations (e.g., subject, object) independent of an argument's particular syntactic position.

This general perspective on the passive was imported into GB. The relevant properties of the passive within GB are taken to be as in (37). However, it should be noted (37i) is actually a language particular property, as not all languages reflect passivization through a change in verbal morphology.

(37) **Properties of Passivization** (Haegeman 1991:185)
   i. the verb morphology is affected;
   ii. the external theta role of the verb is absorbed;
   iii. the structural Case of the verb is absorbed;
   iv. the NP which is assigned the internal theta role of the passive verb moves to a position where it can be assigned Case;
   v. the movement of the NP is obligatory in view of the Case Filter;
   vi. the movement of the NP is allowed because the subject position is empty.

Besides the obvious theory-specific differences in *how* the generalizations with respect to passivization are stated, there is a crucial difference between the

RG and the GB perspective. In RG, passivization was seen as being driven by the advancement or *promotion* of a 2 to a 1. Because this resulted in two 1s, one of the 1s needed to be demoted (Cho). Further work suggested passivization was better understood as being about the *demotion* of the agent, namely the 'external' θ-role (see section 4.10.2 for some discussion of this term). This demotion then necessarily has to be followed by a promotion of the theme argument, because the demotion or suppression of the external argument goes hand in hand with the *absorption* of the structural Case the verb can assign and the theme must move to another position to receive Case. This understanding of the passive is now generally adopted across differing theories.

As can be seen in the D-structure in (38) for a typical passive, the suppression of the external argument means that the agent θ-role cannot be projected.

(38) The city was destroyed. (D-structure)

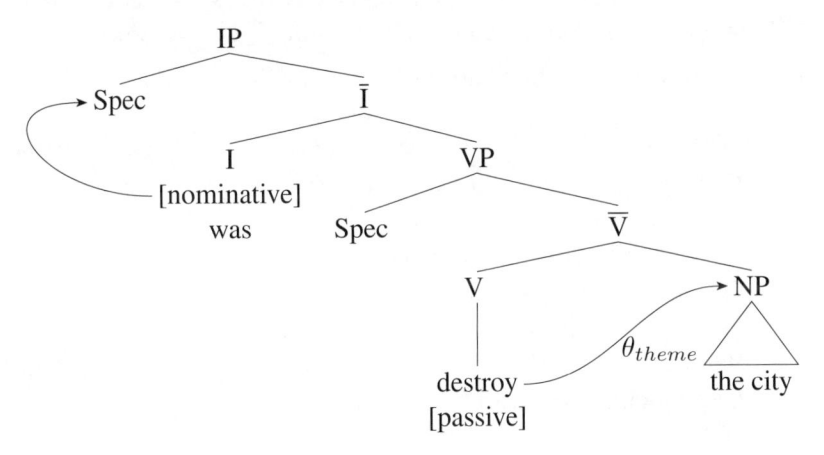

(39) The city was destroyed. (S-structure)

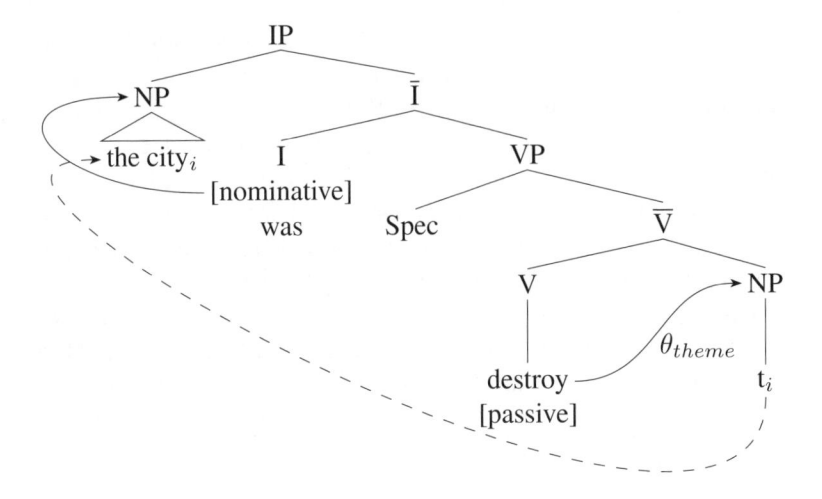

This has the effect that the accusative Case cannot be assigned to the complement of the verb. The D-structure of a passive thus bears a striking resemblance to the D-structure of an unaccusative. Just as with the unaccusative, the NP in the verbal complement must move in order to receive structural Case. As shown in (40), it moves to the SpecIP position because that is the only position where structural Case can be assigned.

The parallelism between unacccusatives and passives is warranted, as already observed by Perlmutter (1978) in the context of RG, because many linguistic phenomena group passives and unaccusatives together. One relevant example comes from Italian auxiliary selection. This was already discussed in section 3.7, but is repeated here for ease of exposition. Both passives (40b) and unaccusatives (40c) select the *essere* 'be' auxiliary, whereas transitives (40a) and unergatives (40d) select the *avere* 'have' auxiliary. Further well known data come from Dutch auxiliary selection (*hebben* 'have' vs. *zijn* 'be', see Zaenen 1993 for a recent discussion) and *ne*-cliticization (Burzio 1986).

(40) a. L'artiglieria ha affondato due navi nemiche.
   the artillery has sunk two ships enemy
   'The artillery has sunk two enemy ships.' Italian

b. Due navi nemiche sono affondate.
   two ships enemy are sunk
   'Two enemy ships have been sunk.' Italian

c. Giovanni è arrivato.
   Giovanni is arrived
   'Giovanni has arrived.' Italian

d. Giovanni ha telefonato.
   Giovanni has telephoned
   'Giovanni has telephoned.' Italian

The overall effect of the GB analysis is thus identical to that of the RG analysis. However, the GB analysis assumes a very strict positional representation of thematic roles and grammatical relations. Such positional or structural assumptions are absent in RG. The fruitfulness underlying the structural assumptions of GB remains a matter of debate. On the one hand, the rigorous representation in terms of structural positions allows the formulation of strong and interesting crosslinguistic predictions. On the other hand, languages with richer case marking, complex agreement, and freer word order than English pose an immediate problem and despite a growing body of work on a diverse number of languages (e.g., Bayer 2004, Bobaljik 1993, Bok-Bennema 1991, Harley 1995, Mahajan 1990, Massam 1985, McGinnis 1998a,b,c), the analyses with respect to case marking are far from providing an account that is generally valid and that has received broad consensus. Some relevant data and analyses are discussed in chapters 6 and 7.

4.8 Structural vs. Inherent or Quirky Case

The discussion so far has focused on *structural Case*. This is defined as a property of a structural configuration and generally assigns *nominative* and *accusative* case. However, as is well known, and as already has been discussed in this book, a range of further cases exist which need to be accounted for as well. An immediate example is the dative argument of ditransitive verbs in languages such as German. Marking the goal/beneficiary argument of a ditransitive verb with the dative as in (41a) is a very common crosslinguistic option. However, it just so happens that English, Italian and French, the languages which initially provided the bulk of the data for transformational analyses, do not have a morphological dative case,[5] but mark the goal/beneficiary argument with a preposition, as shown in (41b) for English.[6]

(41) a. Gabi   gab   dem   Hund einen   Knochen.
       Gaby.Nom give.Past the.M.Sg.Dat dog   a.M.Sg.Acc bone
       'Gaby gave a bone to the dog.'   German
     b. John gave a bone to the dog.

The solution to the problem of morphological datives was based on the further observation that cases which go beyond nominative and accusative tend to be associated with some semantic content. That is, while nominative and accusative can mark a variety of θ-roles, the other cases tend to be restricted to a subset of the possible semantic meanings (cf. the discussion of case labels in chapter 2). Datives tend to mark goals or beneficiaries, the instrumental marks instruments ((42a)) or agents by whose means something can be done ((42b)), and vocatives as in Latin are used to call or address somebody.

(42) a. darvaza   cabi=se   kʰʊl-a
       door.M.Sg.Nom key.F.Sg=Inst open-Perf.M.Sg
       'The door opened by means of the key.'   Urdu
     b. nadya=se   cal-a   nahĩ ja-ega
        Nadya=Inst walk-Perf.M.Sg not go-3.Sg.Fut.M.Sg
        'Nadya cannot possibly walk.'   Urdu
        'Walking will not be done by Nadya.'

A distinction is thus drawn between structural and *inherent* Case. Predicates are assumed to be marked lexically as inherent Case assigners. Inherent Case is further assumed to be licensed by the θ-role of the Case assigner (see also Chomsky 1986:186–204).

---

[5]Though Romance pronouns do show a dative inflection.
[6]English displays a *dative alternation* by which most ditransitives not derived from Latinate roots (e.g., *donate* has a Latinate root) allow an alternative in which the goal/beneficiary becomes the structural object. No prepositional marking is necessary: *John gave the dog a bone*. An initial analysis involved a small clause construction (Chomsky 1981:171–172), which allowed the assignment of structural Case to *bone*. A more recent approach is discussed in section 4.11.

(43) **Inherent Case** (Chomsky 1981:171)
Structural Case in general is dissociated from θ-role; it is a structural property of a formal configuration. Inherent Case is presumably closely linked to θ-role.

A goal θ-role thus might give rise to overt dative case in some languages. The analysis of the German ditransitive in (41), for example, would now proceed as follows. The subject *Gabi* receives structural nominative Case in SpecIP and the object 'bone' is structurally marked with accusative Case as the complement of the verb at D-structure. Note that the accusative is not next to the verb in (41). The assumption for German is that the verb has moved away from its complement to pick up tense. The indirect object 'dog' cannot receive structural Case, but must be case marked in some other way to pass the Case Filter. The assumption is that the ditransitive German verb 'give' is marked lexically as an inherent Case assigner and that it can assign inherent dative Case to 'dog' because it also θ-marks that NP argument with the goal θ-role.

However, the idea that any non-nominative or non-accusative case must necessarily be analysed as inherent Case could be disputed on the grounds of a different linguistic intuition. Based on the Greek/Latin tradition (chapter 2), one could argue that datives on indirect objects are just as 'regular' as nominatives on subjects and accusatives on objects. Indeed, a quick investigation into case systems crosslinguistically suggests (44) as a first generalization for the assignment of dative case (cf. Maling's 2001 discussion on datives).

(44) **Generalization for Dative Case**
Goals/Beneficiaries are realized as datives by default.

On the other hand, there are further instances of case marking which would seem to be less 'regular' and therefore rather more exceptional than indirect dative objects. Some German examples are provided in (45). In (45a) the direct object is not accusative, but dative, in (45b) there is an extra accusative object, and in (45c) the direct object is marked by the genitive.

(45) a. Gabi half dem Hund.
Gaby.F.Sg.Nom help.Past.3.Sg the.M.Sg.Dat dog.M.Sg
'Gaby helped the dog.' German

b. Der Drache lehrte mich
the.M.Sg.Nom dragon.M teach.Past.3.Sg I.Sg.Acc
das Feuerspeien.
the.N.Sg.Acc fire-breathing.N.Acc
'The dragon taught me how to breathe fire.' German

c. Gabi gedachte vergangener Freuden.
Gaby.F.Sg.Nom recall.Past past.F.Pl.Gen joy.F.Pl
'Gaby recalled past joys.' German

Such 'irregular' case markings tend to be the result of an interaction of regular verb semantics with quirks of historical change. That is, the verbal semantics or thematic roles alone cannot motivate the case assignment. This stands in clear contrast to the dative case on indirect objects, which could be motivated by something as in (44). For example, one could argue that the dative case in (45a) is regular because 'dog' is clearly the beneficiary of the helping action. However, why then is *mich* 'me' in (45b) not marked with a dative case when this is also clearly a beneficiary?

Another consideration which separates accusative objects from other kinds of objects is based on evidence with respect to passivization. Recall that one of the characteristics of passivization is that the accusative object of the active clause is realized as a nominative subject in the corresponding passive. Or to put it in another way, accusative case is not *preserved* under passivization.

Now consider the passive form of (45a), shown in (46). As expected, the active subject *Gabi* is demoted and is optionally realized as an adjunct. The 'dog' occupies what looks to be a subject position, but unlike what is usual for passivization, 'dog' is not nominative. Instead, it has retained or *preserved* the dative case. This follows from the distinction between structural and inherent Case in that inherent Case is taken to be just that: 'inherent'. It is a lexically stipulated property and therefore does not interact with purely structural processes, such as passivization.

(46) Dem   Hund   wurde   (von Gabi) geholfen.
     the.M.Sg.Dat dog.M.Sg become.Past.3.Sg by Gaby   help.PastP
     'The dog was helped (by Gaby).'   German

Recall also from (37) that passivization is assumed to absorb the structural Case assigned by a verb. However, in (46) no structural Case is assigned to the complement because the verb assigns the goal θ-role to the complement 'dog' and therefore assigns an inherent dative Case, thus satisfying the Case Filter.

Dative arguments are never subjects in German and because German is a language with fairly free word order, there is no readily identifiable 'subject position', like in English. In (46), the 'dog' has nevertheless moved from the complement position to a clause initial position because of the German requirement that *something* should appear in clause initial position before the finite verb. Within GB, this requirement is taken care of by the EPP, which demands that the extended projection be filled. One possible landing site for 'dog' is SpecIP. This position is generally associated with nominative Case and subjecthood, but 'dog' in (46) is neither nominative nor a subject. One possible analysis is to assume that if 'dog' moves here, it nevertheless does not receive nominative Case, because it is already inherently Case marked. Another possible analysis is to assume that 'dog' does not move to SpecIP, but instead moves to another position in the extended projection. The common assumption for German is a SpecCP position, where CP stands for complementizer phrase. Yet another possible analysis would assume that an NP can bear *both* structural and inherent Case. The 'dog' would thus have inherent dative Case and structural nominative Case (cf. Mahajan 1990 on Hindi).

The linguistic evidence for German points to an analysis of dative passives as instances of subjectless sentences along the lines of the impersonal passive in (33). That is, subjects in German are assumed to be associated strictly with nominative case. Icelandic, however, is another matter altogether. Icelandic is also a Germanic language and one that became famous for what is now known as 'quirky case'. Quirky case is essentially another name for inherent Case, though not as theory specific. In a now classic paper, Zaenen, Maling and Thráinsson (1985) very carefully and thoroughly established that like German, Icelandic allowed various types of non-canonical case marking on objects, but that unlike in German, these dative or genitive objects had to be analysed as syntactic subjects in the corresponding passive clauses. An example parallel to what has been discussed for German is shown in (47). Again, there is a nominative subject and a dative direct object in the active (47a) and again the dative case is preserved under passivization in (47b).

(47) a. Ég hjálpaði honum.
I helped he.Dat
'I helped him.' Icelandic

b. Honum var hjálpað.
he.Dat was helped
'He was helped.' Icelandic

Zaenen, Maling and Thráinsson (ZMT) established a number of *subject tests* for Icelandic. These included reflexivization, subject-verb inversion, extraction from complement clauses, and subject ellipsis. Their work left no doubt that core verbal arguments did not have to conform to the subject=nominative, object=accusative and direct object=dative pattern that had been assumed on the basis of inherited expectations from the Greek/Roman grammatical tradition. Rather, subjects can be nominative, dative or genitive (but they rarely seem to be accusative) and indirect as well as direct objects can be accusative, dative or genitive (for a discussion of nominative objects, see chapter 6). Despite this gamut of possible case markings, accusative objects in Icelandic still behave differently from the other objects, because accusative case is absorbed under passivization. This would seem to support the basic distinction between structural (nominative and accusative) and inherent (all other kinds) Case.

ZMT themselves worked within Lexical-Functional Grammar (LFG) and presented an analysis in terms of *default* vs. idiosyncratic lexical properties. In particular, as an early part of *linking theory*, they formulated crosslinguistic association principles, which governed the relationship between overt case marking, thematic roles and grammatical functions. Such linking theories are discussed in the next chapter (chapter 5). Before moving on to that discussion, however, this chapter rounds out the discussion of structural Case by taking stock of the theoretical ideas introduced so far, and by surveying more recent developments within the derivational tradition in section 4.10.

4.9 Taking Stock

The central thrust of GB's Case Theory is the formulation of structural licensing conditions on noun phrases. An NP can only appear as part of an analysis if it has Case. The licensing conditions related to structural Case are abstract in the sense that they cut across various kinds of lexical semantic verb classes: structural Case can be assigned to a variety of different thematic roles. Inherent or quirky case, in contrast, is stipulated as part of the lexical entry of the verb.

There is a third type of Case that is generally acknowledged, but which has not been discussed so far. It is well known that case can be used to mark directional/locational or temporal NPs in a clause. These NPs tend to be adjuncts, as already discussed in section 1.2.3, but can also function as locative, directional or temporal arguments of a verb. The temporal uses generally measure out a given span of time in which the action occurred (see example (7) in section 1.2.3). This type of case is often referred to as *semantic case*. Very little work has been done on semantic case, primarily because it tends to be associated with adjuncts, and the theoretical concern is with licensing and constraining the appearance of core verbal arguments. However, in some cases the spatial and temporal NPs may function as arguments of the verb. Even in instances where they are not arguments, the case marking patterns show parallels to the distribution of structural Case on core verbal arguments (e.g., Maling 1989).

Widespread agreement on case is restricted to a small subset of the crosslinguistic patterns: genitive for possessors in NPs, accusative for objects, nominative in subject position of a finite clause, and datives for secondary objects of ditransitives. The case on spatial and temporal adjuncts or arguments is connected to their semantics, something which is taken to be straightforward and of no great theoretical interest (semantic case is assigned at D-structure, like inherent Case). Every NP in a clause, however, must pass the Case Filter and therefore be assigned Case somehow, be it structural, inherent or semantic.

The heart of Case Theory in GB actually revolves around several constructions that I have not discussed. Analyses of expletives, Exceptional Case Marking (ECM) and control verbs via an empty PRO were used to motivate some of the central principles of Case Theory as presented above. Expletives such as *it* in *It is raining* are argued to have no thematic role, but still need to receive nominative Case (see section 5.5.1 for further discussion). This was taken as one piece of evidence that Case and thematic roles are not identical and have to be handled via different parts of the analysis. Another central piece of evidence for the disassociation of Case and thematic roles (contra Fillmore's approach, for example, see section 3.5) comes from ECM constructions as in (48).

(48) John believes [him to play the harp].

The verb *believe* subcategorizes for an agent and a proposition, i.e., a sentence. In (48) this proposition is non-finite. Since the *him* is the subject of the embedded clause and not the object of the matrix clause, the accusative case on *him* is unexpected. ECM constructions show that the argument of one verb (*to play*) can receive structural Case from another verb (*believe*). The assignment of thematic roles is therefore not identical to the assignment of structural Case.

Closely related to ECM constructions are control verbs. Examples with *persuade* and *promise* are shown in (49), whereby *persuade* is an *object control verb*, while *promise* is a *subject control verb*. In each case, the subject of the embedded non-finite verb (*vote*) is null and is *controlled* by either the matrix subject or object. The empty embedded subject is known as PRO.

(49) a. Kim persuaded Sandy$_i$ [PRO$_i$ to vote].
      b. Kim$_i$ promised Sandy [PRO$_i$ to vote].

The control/raising facts play a central role in Case Theory. They are theoretically interesting, because the inability of the embedded subject to appear overtly is tied to an analysis in which it cannot receive structural Case (Chomsky 1981) and so must be realized as an empty PRO (i.e., not be pronounced).

It is remarkable that the heart of Case Theory should be based on elements that are either invisible, or are not typical thematic arguments of a clause (expletives and ECM). It should therefore also not come as a surprise to find that core predictions of Case Theory do not hold up once a larger range of crosslinguistic data is taken into account, particularly from languages which actually have functioning case systems. For example, Case Theory predicts that exceptionally case marked arguments should only ever be able to receive structural Case, and that PRO should never be able to receive Case. Both of these predictions are contradicted by data from Icelandic. This has prompted revisions of Case Theory and has given rise to several individual solutions, but as far as I am aware, there is no one standard and coherent analysis for the range of crosslinguistic phenomena.

Many of the revisions of Case Theory took place in the 1990s, which is also the time when a new version of the theory was developed, namely Minimalism. The introduction of Minimalism sought to effect a paradigmatic change and so the remainder of this chapter discusses some of the basics of Minimalism. The issues that are surveyed are confined to those which are relevant to the preceding material, or which foreshadow material discussed in the next chapters.

4.10 Minimalism

The ideas described in the preceding sections were part and parcel of GB, whose most productive time was in the 1980s and whose clear structural assumptions and predictions entrenched themselves firmly in the linguistic landscape. However, with time various improvements and advancements combined to form a relatively unwieldy theoretical apparatus. As had already been the case several times since the inception of Transformational Grammar, the founder of the theory decided to clear away the dead wood and focus on the basic linguistic intuitions that underlie the framework. The result in the early 1990s was the Minimalist Program (MP), which has since undergone further extensions.

Within MP, a linguistic expression is defined as a pair (π, λ) that is generated by an optimal derivation satisfying given interface conditions (Chomsky 1995:212). We have met the members of this pair before under the labels of PF (π) and LF (λ), respectively. PF and LF are assumed to interface via syntactic conditions. The job of a syntactic theory thus became to formulate interface conditions which express properties of these representational levels, rather than to do syntax for the sake of syntax itself. Syntax is seen as a computational system whose properties (combination and projection of information, recursion, and feature checking) are there to ensure an analysis that allows the correct semantic interpretation and pronunciation of a clause.

The Universal Grammar (UG) component continues to be assumed. This crosslinguistically valid component provides a unique computational system for derivations. The derivations are of the general type seen so far in this chapter, but are now explicitly motivated and triggered by morphosyntactic properties. Some of the relevant morphosyntactic properties such as tense and verb inflection have already been encountered in this chapter, but there are assumed to be many more. Crosslinguistic syntactic variation is motivated by differences in these morphological properties at the language particular level.

4.10.1 Phases, Merge and Features

MP rejects purely syntactic notions such as D-Structure and S-Structure. As MP developed, the different stages of transformations/derivations were modelled via *phases* (Chomsky 2001). The derivation of a sentence thus occurs in several phases. The equivalent of S-structure is spell-out, which is the stage of the derivation at which the representation that has been built is fed into the PF interface. The equivalent of D-structure is the *first merge* of a head with the item it selects, for example, a V with an NP. Phases do not have to apply in a strict order. Thus, the first merge of an item into the derivation could happen at any stage. Phases are not in any sense representational levels. They are just moments in the build up of the structure where what has been created becomes opaque to what is subsequently being built. This opacity models a range of syntactic phenomena that had previously been dealt with via a set of independent constraints (e.g., barriers to movement), none of which are relevant here.

Structurally, the derivations generally continue to follow the X′-schema, though the rules for building up trees have been broken down into smaller steps. In a manner very reminiscent of Aravind Joshi's Tree-Adjoining Grammar (TAG Abeillé and Rambow 2000), basic binary branching trees are combined via a *merge* operation. This merge also reincarnates the *Generalized Transformation* proposed in Chomsky (1957).

For example, the two basic trees in (50) could be combined as in (51) to yield the fundamental specifier-head-complement schema. Here XP, YP and ZP stand for any possible category and provide the points of possible merger. In the merged tree in (51), the VP's YP has been replaced by the $\overline{V}$ projection. A double-bar (VP, IP, NP, etc.) projection is still considered to be maximal.

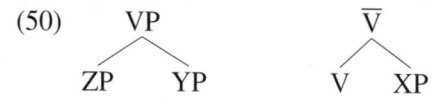

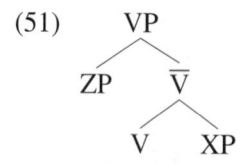

(50)   VP $\overline{V}$
       / \   / \
      ZP   YP   V   XP

(51)   VP
       / \
      ZP $\overline{V}$
           / \
          V   XP

The two subtrees could merge in any order. This, together with the idea that a head selects exactly one item, models the strong binary branching and antisymmetry ideas of Kayne (1994). The combinatory system is very flexible and allows for a large variety of combinatory possibilities. In current analyses, trees nevertheless tend to end up in the familiar X′-schema, and functional (e.g., I) categories always appear above the lexical (e.g., V) categories, as was the case in GB. These restrictions follow from a separate set of constraints.

Within GB, the X′-schema imposed a strict template on lexical and functional projections. The effect was that some analyses contained a large number of unfilled positions: the existence of these positions was required by X′-syntax, but otherwise not necessarily motivated. Also, functional projections such as IP were assumed to be part and parcel of any given clause. Within MP, any given partial tree must be evoked by a lexical item or a morphosyntactic feature. This potentially allows clauses without an IP (if there is nothing that licenses tense), or without the full X′ projection. In practice, the resulting trees look much like what we have seen before. In principle, however, there is a possibility for more elegant analyses and greater room for analytic manoeuvring.

Features play a large role in this approach. The notion of abstract features was already encountered with respect to abstract designations such as [PAST] or [NOMINATIVE]. These designations are passed on to the PF component to be pronounced according to the specific phonology of a language. The MP assumes that every lexical or functional item carries such abstract features and that these features come in two varieties: *interpretable* and *uninterpretable*. The uninterpretable features are responsible for the bulk of the morphosyntactic analysis of a sentence. These features need to be *checked* as part of the derivation of a sentence, because they cannot be interpreted by the semantic component. That is, if all derivations in all the phases that can take place have taken place, and if at the end of the last phase there is still an uninterpretable feature somewhere in the tree, then the derivation is said to *crash*. The features are assumed to come in feature-value pairs. This bears some similarity to the attribute-value matrices assumed by unification based theories like HPSG or LFG (see section 5.7), but the use and interpretation is not equivalent. The values for the features are not always specified and no examples of feature-value pairings are included in this discussion.

Case features are generally taken to be uninterpretable (see section 4.10.4), though some newer work is exploring the possibilities of interpretable case features as well (e.g., Svenonius 2002, see section 7.4). Uninterpretable case features model syntactic wellformedness in terms of structural Case. Interpretable case features add a semantic dimension to the analysis.

Feature checking is governed by structural considerations whose precise formulation can become quite complex. For our purposes, it is sufficient to know that features can be checked among sisters within a tree, as well as between a specifier or a head and a head. The specifier or head and the other head need not be in the same local X' configuration, but could in principle be at some distance from another. This latter relationship is termed *Agree*. If an NP contains an uninterpretable feature that cannot be checked in its local X'-configuration, then the NP must move in order to have its feature checked in some other part of the tree. Features have a further property: they can be either *strong* or *weak*. A strong feature must be checked in a local configuration and is therefore likely to trigger movement. A weak feature never triggers movement.

The designation of particular features as strong vs. weak is subject to crosslinguistic variation. Syntactic variation in languages is thus motivated primarily by a difference in the type and content of the abstract features carried by lexical and functional items. In essence, crosslinguistic variation boils down to trivial differences at the morphological level, something which has been a basic tenet of the transformational tradition from the outset, and which has now been very clearly articulated within MP.

4.10.2 External Arguments

Before moving on to sample Minimalist analyses of case, another major development in the representation of arguments needs to be addressed. Recall that under the VP-internal hypothesis (section 4.5), the agent argument was placed in SpecVP, squarely within the VP projection. However, this hypothesis conflicted with other intuitions in the literature. Williams (1981) coined the term *external argument* because it seemed that the 'highest' argument of a verb (e.g., the agent of a transitive verb) had special properties with respect to derivational morphology. The highest argument is special in the sense that it does not interact with derivational morphological processes such as adjectival formation with *-able*. This is illustrated by (52), where only the underlying theme is retained as the argument predicated over by *understandable*.

(52) a. Kim understands her reasoning.
b. Her reasoning is understandable.

This evidence points to a close relationship between a verb and its *internal* argument, namely the theme, and one which excludes the agent. Hence, the agent could be thought of as being 'external' to the core predication of the verb. Marantz (1984) articulates a theory of grammatical relations based on this premise. In his approach, for example, a verb like *give* only lexically encodes the argument roles *theme* and *goal*. The presence of the agent is licensed structurally as part of the syntactic tree. Based on evidence from semantics and morphosyntax, Kratzer (1994, 1996) also advocated separating the highest (usually the agent) argument from the basic argument projection of the verb. Kratzer argued that the external argument is introduced by a separate head in a configuration that is separate from, and external to, the VP. In particular, she motivated this idea with respect to *voice* morphemes in Malagasy.

Chomsky himself had already assumed in 1981 that the highest argument was determined structurally, rather than by the verb. This intuition was bolstered by argumentation such as Williams' and Kratzer's. The ultimate consequence is that external arguments generally are not lexically specified. Rather, their presence follows from structural syntactic requirements.

> This account presupposes that the θ-role of a subject (where it has one) is determined by the VP of S rather than by the verbal head of this VP ... [Chomsky 1981:37]

External arguments are licensed by a vP projection and are situated in Spec$v$ (pronounced 'little v', Chomsky 1995:315). The first phase representation of a typically transitive clause is as in (53) (based on Adger 2003:205). There are several things to note about (53). One is that there is no SpecVP position. Since this partial tree is not licensed or motivated by any lexical item or morphosyntactic feature, it is not merged into the tree. Another is the notation with angle brackets ($<$ $>$). In the first phase of derivation, the subject is situated in Spec$v$P. However, in subsequent phases, this subject must move to SpecIP to have its case feature (nominative) checked and to satisfy the EPP (section 4.7).

(53)
```
            IP
           /  \
      Subject  Ī
              / \
             I   vP
                /  \
         <Subject>  v̄
                   / \
                  v   VP
                     /  \
                    V    complement
```

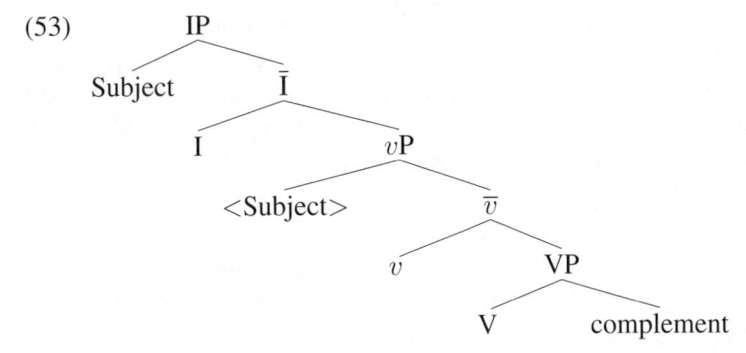

In GB, movement was registered via traces. MP instead introduces a *copy-theory of movement*. That is, the moved item is copied from its original position and then merged back into a higher position. In Adger's system, which is the one adopted here, the original place from where the item was copied/moved is marked via angle brackets and is referred to as a 'ghost'. This ghost is not eligible for pronunciation by the phonological component by default. Only the highest version of the moved/copied item is pronounced by default. Lower copies can be pronounced when the phonology would otherwise crash the derivation (clitics are a good example, see Franks and King 2000:343).

Since partial trees have to be motivated by overt lexical items, morphemes, or abstract features, one might ask what licenses the *v*P projection in a basic transitive sentence like *The dog chased the cat*. The verb *chase* licenses the VP projection via the V. The information that the clause should be past tense is situated in I. So what is the role of *v*? One of Kratzer's motivations for *v* was voice morphology in languages such as Malagasy. In other languages, an overt transitive, causative or other type of verbal morpheme provides evidence for *v* (see McGinnis 1998b,c for an analysis of Georgian, for example).

Another strand of research which informed the assumption of a *v*P in English (and crosslinguistically) is work by Hale and Keyser (1993), who built on the notion of VP-shells as introduced by Larson (1988) for the double object construction (section 4.11). VP-shells allow for a complex internal structure, i.e., a VP could be contained within another VP. Once a complex VP internal structure had been introduced, the internal structure of the verbal projection could be rethought and reshaped in quite fundamental ways.

4.10.3 Lexical Conceptual Structure

Hale and Keyser (1993, 2002) argue for a complex structural representation of Lexical Conceptual Structure (LCS). This complex structural representation encodes fundamental semantic notions such as CAUSE, by which one event is seen to lead to or cause another event, and CHANGE, by which an event results in a changed state of affairs. They maintained that θ-roles such as *agent* or *patient* must be seen as derivative notions of such fundamental event semantics.

The Hale and Keyser type of approach to lexical semantics is known more generally as *lexical decomposition* and is practised across differing types of theoretical frameworks. The common ground for most frameworks is the classic work on lexical semantics by Dowty (1979) or Jackendoff (1972, 1990). The work on lexical semantic decomposition grew out of *Generative Semantics* (e.g., Lakoff 1971), an approach which attempted to link semantic representations to the tree structures assumed within generative syntax. This theory was abandoned largely because of the perceived unrestricted nature of its analyses. Subsequent formulations of lexical decomposition strove towards a relatively small inventory of possible lexical semantic building blocks. Some approaches are heavily influenced by Dowty's (1979) work, which assumes just three basic operators for the representation of lexical semantics: CAUSE, DO and BECOME. The CAUSE represents the cause or instigation of an event, the DO characterizes the event in progress, and the BECOME denotes the result state. Any given event can thus be thought of as consisting of several subevents: a causing subevent, a process subevent, and a result subevent. While most approaches agree on some kind of lexical decomposition, the precise details differ. A typical representation, taken from Rappaport Hovav and Levin (1998), is shown in (54).

(54) [[x ACT y] CAUSE [BECOME [y $< STATE >$]]]

Here there is a generic action (ACT) which involves two participants, an x and y, and which causes a certain state of affairs, namely that the y participant comes to be in a certain state. If the generic action were *melt*, for example, then (54) could be the abstract representation for (55). That is, the variable x would be instantiated by *sun*, the variable y by *ice cream*, and the resulting interpretation of (54) would be that the *sun* acted upon the *ice cream* and caused the *ice cream* to come to be in a state of being melted.

(55) The sun melted the ice cream.

Representations like the ones in (54) link event semantics closely to the realization of argument positions. That is, event participants which initiate or cause change occupy a different part of the subevental representation than event participants who are affected or changed by the action that was caused. Given the rigid structural assumptions of GB/MP, it is natural to map the representation of subevents onto tree structures.

The CAUSE subevent generally involves an agent/causer and a subevent that is caused or instigated. This translates naturally to the vP projection, whereby the causer/agent is situated in Spec$v$P and the complement is the VP sister of v (cf. (53)). Some approaches, like Hale and Keyser's, assume that this VP encodes a RESULT or CHANGE subevent. Other approaches, like that of Ramchand (2002), assume that the VP encodes the *process* (DO) subevent, and that a further RP (result phrase, BECOME) can be merged as a sister of the verb.

A basic blueprint is shown in (56).[7] For a basic transitive verb like *melt*, the process participant is identical to the result participant and is coindexed in the syntax. This corresponds to using the same variable twice in representations like Rappaport Hovav and Levin's (54).

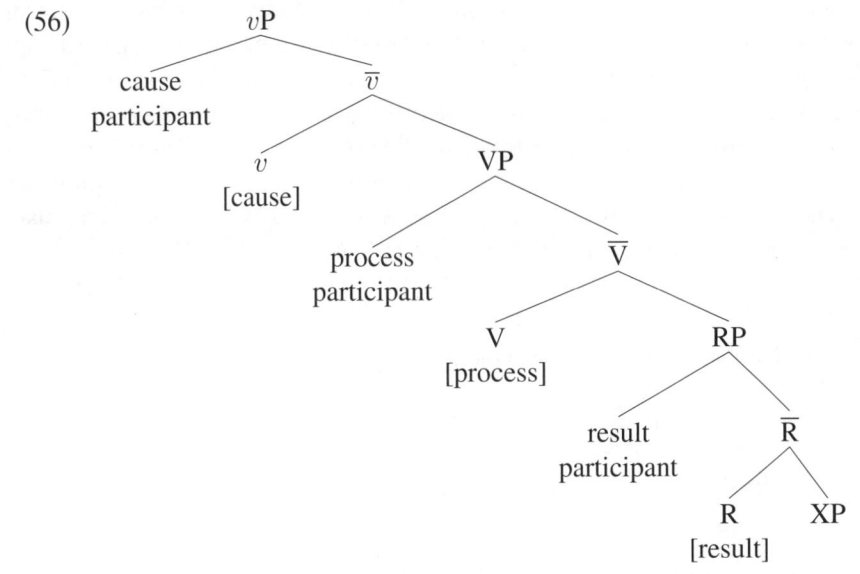

(56)
```
              vP
         /         \
      cause         v̄
   participant    /    \
                 v      VP
              [cause]  /   \
                    process  V̄
                   participant  /  \
                              V    RP
                          [process]  /  \
                                  result  R̄
                                participant /  \
                                           R   XP
                                        [result]
```

This section and the preceding sections have introduced some core concepts assumed within MP. There are more issues and ideas which could have been introduced, but the concepts discussed so far are of particular interest as they are not purely theory internal, but have become part of standard linguistic knowledge and terminology. The notion *external argument*, for example, is recognized by a wide variety of frameworks, even if there is no structural analysis that places this argument (e.g., the agent) into a structurally external position. In MP, external arguments are in a position that is *external* to the core VP predication. The precise internal structure of the VP continues to be the subject of debate in MP. In what follows, I assume a simple VP for purposes of illustration (based on Adger 2003) and address the issue of a more complex VP again in section 4.11 on double objects.

4.10.4 Unergatives, Unaccusatives and Passives

This section presents sample analyses for unaccusatives, unergatives and passives in parallel to those presented in sections 4.7.1 and 4.7.2. An analysis of a sentence involving an unergative verb is shown in (57). At this phase in the

---

[7]There are further differences between the two types of approaches. One line of thinking, represented here by Hale and Keyser (1993), assumes that representations as in (56) are part of the lexicon. Other approaches, represented here by Ramchand (2002), assume that this representation is situated in the syntax and that there is no syntactic structure in the lexicon (Borer 2003).

derivation, several partial trees have already been merged and the analysis has moved beyond the first phase (essentially the vP).

The agent of *sneeze* was structurally realized in Spec$v$P in the first phase of syntactic analysis. This entity, *Kim*, bears a case feature which is as yet unspecified. The valuation and checking of case feature essentially implements the Case Filter, which states that each NP must receive case (see Pesetsky and Torrego 2001, 2004 for a discussion of this correlation). The idea is that the unspecified case feature must be *valued* or specified by information coming from a different place. This could be the finite/inflectional element I, which is assumed to bear a nominative feature, similar to what was assumed within GB.

The v also carries inflectional features which need to be valued. The place for this is again I, which specifies a [past] feature in (57). The V feature on the verb *sneeze* indicates which partial trees it can be merged with. In (57), the verb has merged as a complement of v.

(57) Kim sneezed. (Features Unchecked)

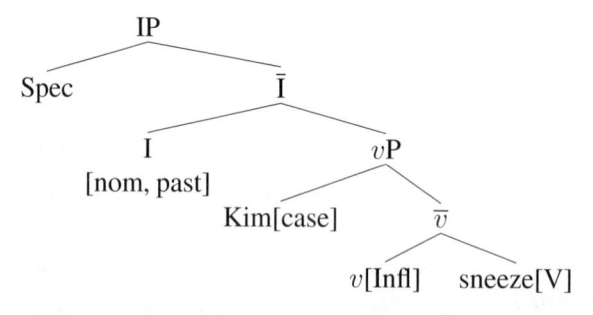

```
                IP
              /    \
           Spec     Ī
                  /   \
                 I     vP
             [nom,past] / \
                    Kim[case] v̄
                             /   \
                         v[Infl]  sneeze[V]
```

(58) Kim sneezed. (Features Checked)

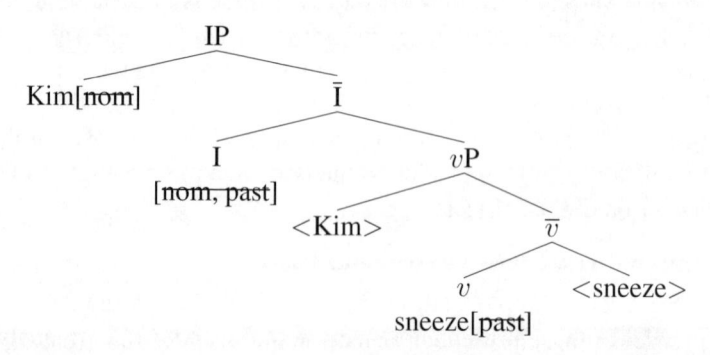

```
                    IP
                  /    \
            Kim[nom]    Ī
                      /    \
                     I      vP
                 [nom,past] /  \
                        <Kim>   v̄
                               /   \
                              v    <sneeze>
                         sneeze[past]
```

In (58), *Kim* has been copied and moved to SpecIP in order to have its case feature valued as [nom] and then checked by I. The verb *sneeze* moves to v by assumption (see Adger 2003 for discussion and motivation of this analysis). This v head carries an unspecified inflectional feature which must be valued and checked somewhere. The responsible location again is I, which carries a specific inflectional value, namely [past]. I can value and check the unspecified feature [Infl] on v via the Agree relation, which can hold at some distance.

At this point, all the uninterpretable features have been checked, all the items of the clause are in the right order, and the derivation succeeds. Now consider the analysis of an unaccusative clause in (59). The theme is realized as a sister to the verb. This NP carries an underspecified case feature which must be valued and checked as with unergatives.

In a transitive clause, the v is assumed to carry an [acc] case feature, which is responsible for checking the case feature of the theme. Accusative case assignment is associated with v because of Burzio's Generalization (section 4.7.1), which states that only configurations which include an external argument can assign accusative Case. In a transitive clause, the agent argument is situated in Spec$v$P and the v is therefore assumed to be responsible for the assignment of structural accusative Case to the complement of V. An alternative way of motivating the association of v with accusative case is presented by Pesetsky and Torrego (2001, 2004), who seek to tie case features to the expression of tense in TP. As part of this, they assume that parts of the TP projection are responsible for relating the cause component expressed by vP to the result component expressed by the VP, giving rise to well known aspectual effects such as telicity (section 5.7.7). These aspectual effects are tied to the TP projection by Pesetsky and Torrego. In other approaches, a special Asp(ectual)P is assumed. In either case, the responsibility for accusative case is seen to lie with the vP.

(59) The ice cream melted. (Features Unchecked)

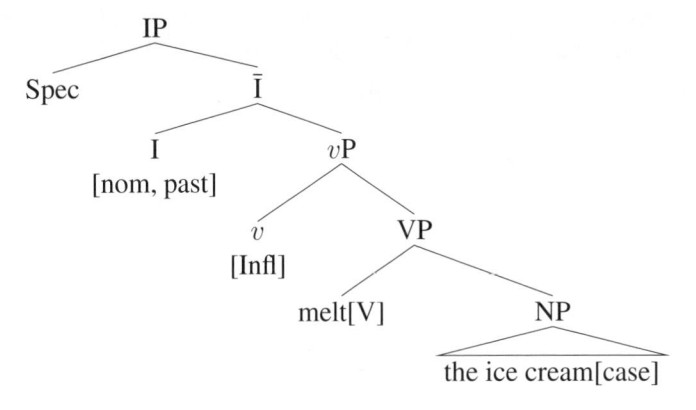

```
                    IP
                   /  \
               Spec    Ī
                      / \
                     I   vP
                [nom, past] / \
                           v   VP
                         [Infl] / \
                           melt[V]  NP
                                    |
                            the ice cream[case]
```

To return to the unaccusative configuration in (59), here the accusative feature cannot come into play because there is no external argument in the vP projection. The only place that can value the case feature of the NP is SpecIP, and that is where the NP is moved to in (60).

Recall that unaccusative verbs are by definition non-agentive verbs. As such, it seems odd that the vP projection appears as part of an unaccusative analysis.

However, McGinnis (1998a,b), for example, motivates the vP projection for unaccusatives by assuming that another role of the v is to model aspectual information. This seems like a reasonable idea since unaccusatives are generally associated with a change of state (e.g., *fall, melt*) of the theme.

Since this and various ideas on unaccusatives continue to be the subject of debate, I follow the basic analysis provided by Adger (2003) for the purposes of this book. By this, *ice cream* moves to SpecIP in (60) to satisfy the EPP.

(60) The ice cream melted. (Features Checked)

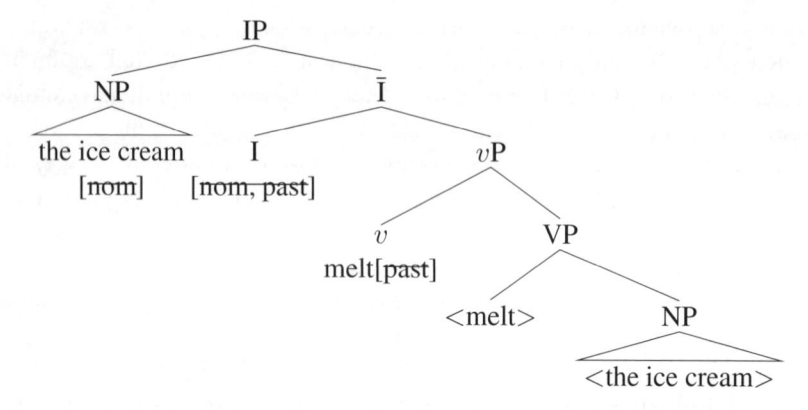

[Tree diagram: IP dominates NP "the ice cream [nom]" and Ī; Ī dominates I "[nom, past]" and vP; vP dominates v "melt[past]" and VP; VP dominates <melt> and NP <the ice cream>]

Finally, (61) illustrates a basic passive, which is parallel to the unaccusative case, as discussed in section 4.7.1. The I now contains the passive *be* auxiliary, which carries a passive feature ([pass]). In our example, this will be overtly realized (pronounced) as *was*. The passive feature is connected to inflection, as such it is checked like the past participle feature.

(61) The city was destroyed. (Features Checked)

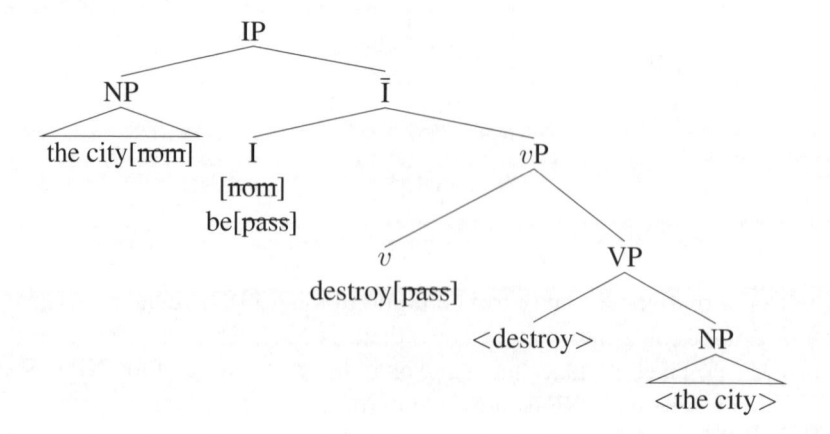

[Tree diagram: IP dominates NP "the city[nom]" and Ī; Ī dominates I "[nom] be[pass]" and vP; vP dominates v "destroy[pass]" and VP; VP dominates <destroy> and NP <the city>]

This concludes the illustration of basic analyses within MP. No analyses of quirky or inherent Case (section 4.8) are provided because there is no standard analysis of inherent Case within MP. However, there are some sophisticated and thoughtful analyses of non-structural Case. Some of these individual proposals are discussed as part of chapter 7.

4.11 English Double Objects

A very recent analysis of the English double object construction by Beck and Johnson (2004) involves structural lexical decomposition of the type introduced in section 4.10.2. As such, this analysis fits in well with the discussion at hand. Recall that the alternation shown in (62) is known as the *dative alternation* (section 4.8). The variant in (62b) is known as the *double object* construction, because there are two structural objects: neither one is semantic in the sense that it is introduced by a preposition.

(62) a. Kim gave a bone to the dog.
b. Kim gave the dog a bone.

Double object constructions occur in other languages as well, where they tend to be licensed by an extra *applicative* morpheme on the verb (e.g., for Bantu see Bresnan and Moshi 1990). No such overt morphology exists in English. As such, this construction has been discussed for several decades and continues to be problematic (see Marantz 1984 for an early comparative discussion of Bantu and English double objects).

One possible standard analysis is based on the small clause idea (Chomsky 1981:171, Kayne 1984), by which two arguments are assumed to be connected via an empty head. A small clause is a minimal predication, i.e., it contains a subject and a property of which something is predicated. In contrast to a proper copula construction as in (63), where the *is* establishes the connection between the subject and the property predicated of it, small clauses have a hidden or empty head. Standard examples which are used to motivate small clauses are resultatives as in (64), where *door* and *green* are analysed as forming a minimal predication in which *door* is the subject of predication and the *green* is the property predicated of the subject. The idea is that (63) and (64) are essentially parallel, but that the relationship which holds between *green* and *door* is not expressed by an overt copula in (64).

(63) The door is green.

(64) Kim painted the door green.

The analysis of (62b) shown in (65) is a modern combination of the small clause analysis and Larson's (1988) original proposal of VP-shells. (65) is based on Beck and Johnson 2004:101, which follows a standard analysis by which Larson's VP-shell analysis is reinterpreted as vP. In (65) the verb *give* will eventually raise to v, as was seen in section 4.10.4, and *Kim* will raise to a higher SpecIP position for nominative Case. The direct object *dog* has its accusative case valued and checked by v. Under the small clause analysis, the empty head X checks the case of the secondary object *bone*. The X stands for a generic X′ head for which no particular category has been determined as yet.

(65) Kim gave the dog a bone. (First Phase)

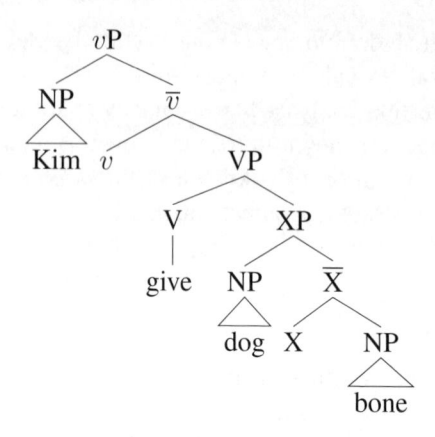

```
            vP
           /  \
         NP    v̄
         △   / \
        Kim v   VP
              /   \
             V     XP
             |    /  \
           give  NP   X̄
                 △  / \
                dog X  NP
                       △
                      bone
```

(66) Kim gave a bone to the dog. (First Phase)

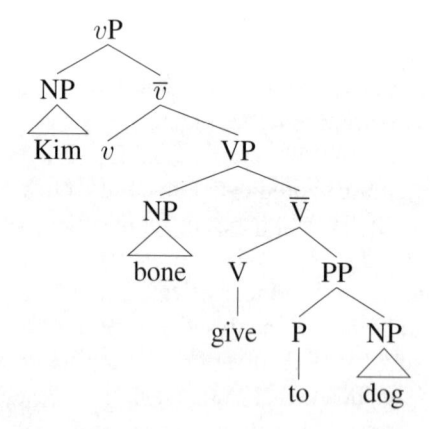

```
            vP
           /  \
         NP    v̄
         △   / \
        Kim v   VP
              /   \
             NP    V̄
             △   /  \
           bone V    PP
                |   /  \
              give P    NP
                   |    △
                   to  dog
```

Beck and Johnson make a very specific proposal about the nature of the XP in (65). Before moving on to a discussion of their proposal, an analysis of the version with the *to* indirect object (62a) is presented in (66) (based on Beck and Johnson 2004:100). Versions of this analysis are standardly assumed within the GB/MP tradition. It is provided here as a point of comparison and reference. The analysis in (66) contains a prepositional phrase which is merged as a complement to the verb. The preposition *to* in turn structurally licenses the indirect object *dog*. The theme, which was so far encountered as the verbal complement is now realized in SpecVP.

Recall that a basic tenet of the GB/MP tradition is that identical thematic relations should be represented as identical structural relations. The strong formulation of this is the UTAH (section 4.7). An immediate question is whether the standard analysis of English ditransitives indeed conforms to the UTAH. Adger (2003) answers this question in the affirmative by formulating the consequences of the UTAH within MP as shown in (67).

(67) **Consequences of the UTAH:** (Adger 2003:139)
   a. NP daughter of vP →interpreted as agent
   b. NP daughter of VP →interpreted as theme
   c. PP daughter of $\overline{\text{V}}$→interpreted as goal

At the first phase of syntax, the agent is situated in vP, as has already been demonstrated several times. This is unproblematic given the discussion on external arguments in section 4.10.2. In the analyses presented so far, the theme has been represented as the complement of the verb. In (66), it is situated in SpecVP. Adger's formulation in (67b) allows for both of these possibilities: the theme may appear in either SpecVP or as complement of the verb, as long as it is an immediate daughter of the VP constituent. This flexible interpretation of structural requirements is entirely in line with Minimalist principles, because the basic building blocks of structures are the simple binary branching mother-daughter configurations seen in (50). The precise location of specifier vs. complement is not crucial, what is important is the projection in which arguments appear. Note that this is also in line with Hale and Keyser's (1993) structural interpretation of subevental event semantics (section 4.10.2).

Having established an analysis for the *to* indirect object, the discussion with respect to the English double object construction can now be completed. Recall that the analysis in (65) included a mysterious XP. Beck and Johnson (2004:103) argue on semantic grounds that the double object construction must be interpreted along the lexical decompositional lines shown in (68).

(68) [[x ACT$_{give}$ y] CAUSE [BECOME [z HAVE y]]]

Under this analysis, there is a giving action which involves two participants, an agent (x) and a theme (y). This action causes a certain state to hold in which a third participant (z) comes to possess or *have* the theme involved in the giving action. Within the assumptions of MP, this lexically decomposed representation translates directly and naturally to the structural representation in (69).

The agent is situated in vP, which is identified with the causing subevent. This subevent causes a 'having' subevent, which is headed by a HAVE relation and which projects to a HAVEP in Beck and Johnson's analysis. The HAVE subevent contains two participants, one in SpecHAVEP and the other in the HAVE complement position. In analogy to the small clause construction in (64), the HAVE relation expresses the idea that the SpecVP (*dog*) has the property of being in possession of a bone (complement of HAVE). Languages differ as to whether they allow double object constructions or not. Harley (2002), for example, explicitly ties this to the presence versus absence of the HAVE head (P$_{HAVE}$ in her approach) in the lexical inventory of a language.

(69) Kim gave the dog a bone. (First Phase)

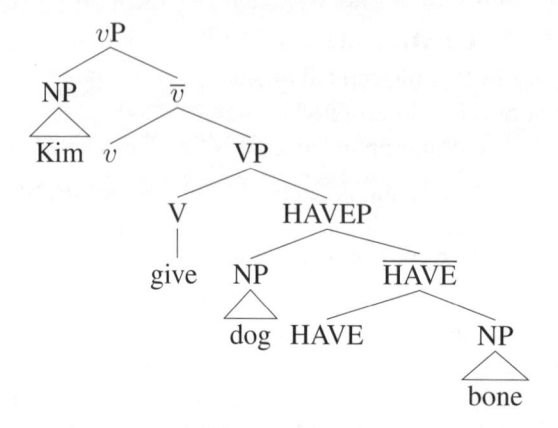

A final point to make is that the structures assumed by Beck and Johnson do not assume that there is one identical underlying argument structure for the *to* and the double object variant. This analysis and other recent analyses like that of Pesetsky (1995) and Harley (2002), follow Oehrle's (1976) arguments that the constructions should not be derived from the same underlying argument structure. Pesetsky's and Harley's analyses are similar to Beck and Johnson's in that both the *to* variant and the double object construction are analysed via a version of the small clause analysis. In the *to* variant, the preposition *to* licenses the goal argument, in the double object construction an empy possessive or HAVE head licenses the object.

In contrast, the assumption of a single underlying structure guided Larson's (1988) original proposal: the *to* variant was taken as basic and the double object variant was derived from the *to* variant. Given this fundamental assumption, there are different possibilities of deriving the dative alternation. Baker (1996), for example, seeks to tie the dative alternation to aspectual factors and realizes this in terms of an interaction with the functional projection AspP (cf. the discussion on affectedness in section 5.3). Many of the linking theories introduced in chapter 5 also assume an identical underlying argument structure, but rather than trying to derive one variant from another, as was done by Larson, alternative methods of *linking* or projecting the argument structure into the syntax are explored.

4.12 Discussion

The above consideration of the dative alternation leads nicely into the discussion of linking theories presented in the next chapter. Before moving on to that, a few concluding observations as to the material in this chapter are in order.

The relative merits of the various approaches and proposals within MP remain subject to ongoing discussion in the field. The discussion is lively and there is little consensus on any one analysis as 'standard'. There are, however, a number of guiding principles, which are accepted by all researchers within MP. This should be evident from a comparison of the discussions with respect to GB and MP in this chapter. While the technical apparatus and some of the guiding ideas have changed, many of the fundamental principles established within GB with respect to the licensing of case, the interaction between case and agreement and the representation of thematic roles and grammatical relations continue to be accepted and have been reimplemented within MP. In some cases, the reimplementation can lead to new insights, in other cases, it turns out to be just a different way of saying the same thing.

In both GB and MP, overt case marking plays next to no role. The realization of case morphology is considered to be the domain of PF, i.e., a matter of spell out or pronunciation of abstract case features. These abstract case features are divided into structural and inherent Case, whereby structural Case is essentially equivalent to grammatical relations in other syntactic approaches. Nominative Case is strictly correlated with subjects of finite clauses, and accusative Case is correlated with objects. Any deviation is considered exceptional.

There is no independent notion of grammatical relations in this approach. Grammatical relations are represented structurally, but structural positions do not define grammatical relations. That is, the SpecVP position does not define an object or a subject (cf. section 4.11). Rather, grammatical relations are correlated with the assignment of structural Case. As the discussion in section 4.11 showed, indirect objects are somewhat problematic in that they become exceptional when not licensed by a preposition. This means that for languages like Icelandic, Georgian, or Latin, which mark indirect objects morphologically on a par with subjects and direct objects, indirect objects are assumed to be a separate kind of syntactic creature from subjects and direct objects.

This tension has given rise to interesting debates. In German, for example, subject, objects and indirect objects are all marked morphologically. However, nominative and accusative morphology are only distinct in the masculine singular. Without other clausal or discoursal clues, nominative and accusative nouns can therefore often not be told apart. This contrasts with the morphology of genitives and datives, which allow a more definitive identification because of their distinct forms. Bayer, Bader and Meng (2001) use this observation and a battery of syntactic tests to argue that dative indirect objects should indeed be differentiated from subjects and objects, as is predicted by the fundamental assumptions of GB/MP (cf. also Fanselow 2000, Vogel and Steinbach 1998). Other scholars do not admit this evidence and instead point to other evidence which puts dative indirect objects in the same class as nominative subjects and accusative objects (e.g., Fanselow 1987, Wegener 1991 and Wunderlich and Lakämper 2001).

As the sections on external arguments and double objects (sections 4.10.2 and 4.11) show, there is a general trend towards incorporating ever more precise lexical semantic information into the structural representations. That is, the focus of the theoretical work tends to be more on the representation of lexical semantics, than on different systems of case or the crosslinguistic distribution of overt case marking. Like in Pāṇini's Sanskrit grammar, lexical semantics are mediated via a syntactic structure, namely argument structure. The arguments or thematic roles of a given verb follow from lexical decompositional analyses of the type seen in the previous sections, and they are assumed to map onto a structural representation. A difference between Pāṇini's grammar and the approach introduced here is that Pāṇini did not hold rigid structural beliefs. This is partly motivated by the fact that Sanskrit is a free word order language, so that rigid structural representations are not the first hypothesis one would entertain, in contrast to English, which has very rigid word order constraints.

In the next chapter, several different types of linking theories are introduced. One of these was formulated by Paul Kiparsky, who is a Sanskrit scholar (among many other things), and whose linguistic thinking is influenced by Pāṇini's analyses for Sanskrit. The discussion in the next chapter thus provides a contrast to this chapter and illustrates how different theoretical assumptions may be applied to the same basic data.

Several ideas which are considered to be fundamental to GB/MP Case Theory have not been discussed in this chapter. These have not been included here for various reasons. The so-called *psych verbs* are not discussed here, but are left for the chapter on semantically motivated case marking (chapter 7).

The use of AgrP to regulate case assignment is representative of about a decade-long line of investigation within GB/MP (approximately spanning the 1990s). Many phenomena and languages were explored under the assumption that case marking was directly related to agreement. This line of research has not been discussed in this chapter, because the theoretical assumptions involved are often quite complex, and because they have been largely abandoned in more recent work (Chomsky 1995 explicitly abolishes AgrP). However, examples of this line of investigation become relevant with respect to ergativity and are therefore discussed in section 6.5.1.

4.13 Exercises

Exercise 1: Basic Concepts

Briefly answer the following questions. They are intended to help you get your bearings with some basic concepts of GB.

1. What is the difference between structural and inherent Case?
2. How is morphological (overt) case handled within GB?
3. Does GB make use of the concept of thematic roles? If so, how?
4. How are grammatical relations encoded in GB?

Exercise 2: Crosstheoretical Comparison

1. Does GB represent an improvement over what RG had to offer with respect to case?
2. Chomsky (1981:170) gives the following set of correspondences:

   (1) i. NP is nominative if governed by AGR
      ii. NP is objective if governed by [a transitive] V
      iii. NP is oblique if governed by P
      iv. NP is genitive in [$_{NP}$ ___ $\bar{X}$]
      v. NP is inherently Case-marked as determined by properties of its [−N] governor.

   In (1), names of cases, grammatical relations and structures are all interwoven. Is this desirable?

Exercise 3: Passive

1. Explain why *Kim worked* cannot be passivized by using the GB assumptions about the properties of the passive construction.
2. Give an analysis (i.e., draw some trees) for the Icelandic sentences in (2), which involve the use of inherent Case.

   (2) a. Ég hjálpaði honum.
         I helped he.Dat
         'I helped him.'
      b. Honum var hjálpað.
         he.Dat was helped
         'He was helped.'

Exercise 4: Old English

The Old English sentences in (3) and (4) have already been encountered in Exercise 3 of the previous chapter, where an RG analysis was required. Now provide an analysis for these sentences in Minimalist terms.

(3) ... swa heo maran læcedom behofað
     so it greater leechcraft.Acc needs
'... so it requires greater medicine' (Allen 1995:135)   Old English
(COE), ÆCHom I, 33 496.30

(4) Micel wund behofað micles læcedomes
    great.Nom wound.Nom needs great.Gen leechcraft.Gen
'A great wound requires great medicine.' (Allen 1995:135)
(COE) Bede 4 26.350.19   Old English

Assume that in both sentences the *it/wound* is initially merged in the Spec$v$P position and that in (3) *leechcraft* is merged as complement to V.

For (4), there are several possibilites. This argument bears genitive case marking and since datives and genitives shared some characteristics in Old English, a more complex analysis along the lines of ditransitive clauses might be conceivable. Another possibility is a more basic analysis in terms of inherent Case. On the other hand, the genitive is not retained under passivization and thus bears some resemblance to the structural accusative. Justify whatever analysis you develop.

5
Linking Theories

dekʰo,	cʰor	ke	kis	rɑste	vo	jate	hẽ
see	leave	having	which	road	they	go	PRES

sare	rɑste	vapıs	mere	dıl	ko	atẽ	hẽ
all	roads	back	my	heart	ACC	come	PRES

See, whichever road you take, all roads come back to my heart.
[Song *nahin samne tu* from the Hindi movie *Taal*]

5.1 Introduction

This chapter is about *argument linking* or the 'linking problem', as Maling (2001) calls it. Linking is a term used for generalizations which are involved in mapping predicate-argument structures to a syntactic representation. Linking theories are concerned with the relationship between lexical semantics, argument structure, case marking, grammatical relations and syntactic structure. Linking theories differ with respect to the particulars of each of these dimensions; however, the basic domain of inquiry is similar enough to warrant discussing a number of different theories within one chapter.

This chapter begins with some fundamental ideas about predicate-argument structure in relation to thematic relations, lexical decomposition and proto-roles. These ideas provide some of the basic building blocks for linking theories. The next sections then introduce differing linking theories, beginning with Kiparsky's theory of case, continuing with Wunderlich's Lexical-Decomposition Grammar, and closing with LFG's Mapping Theory. Another approach that falls under the definition of linking theories is not discussed in this chapter, but in chapter 8. This has been done for ease of exposition, as a discussion of Role and Reference Grammar without a reference to ergativity (chapter 6) is very difficult (this is also true of some of the linking theories introduced in this chapter and so some ergative examples have already crept into this chapter).

5.2 Representation of Predicate-Argument Structure

The notation for the representation of predicate-argument structures has its roots in logical formulae. In formal logic, a basic way to express a relationship between individuals is through a *predicate* (cf. the term *predicate* for verbs and other items which place elements in relation to one another). One way of representing a relationship between an x and a y is by a predicate P as in (1).

(1) P(x,y)

With respect to a *proposition*, that is a sentence, a basic transitive clause like (2) might be represented as in (3). Here, X and Y stand for some individuals which are related by the predicate 'like'. In (2), these variables X and Y have been instantiated by 'Kim' and 'Sandy'.

(2) Kim likes Sandy.

(3) Like(k,s)

When it became clear that a representation was needed, which was neutral with respect to syntactic category (part of speech), a logic-based notation came to be used. Recall from chapter 4 that Chomsky's (1970) *Remarks on Nominalization* established that a shared representation for both nouns and verbs was necessary in order to be able to account for nominalization patterns as in (4).

(4) a. John presented the medal to Mary.
    b. John's presentation of the medal to Mary.

In both the verbal predication in (4a) and the nominal predication in (4b), the number and type of arguments that are expressed are the same: in both cases there is an agent (John), a theme (medal), and a goal/beneficiary (Mary). This shared information came to be called *argument structure* or *predicate-argument structure*. As discussed in chapter 4, the arguments or θ-roles, are represented structurally within the transformational tradition.

However, while the idea of argument structure and thematic roles as a level of representation which mediated between syntax and semantics generated a large body of interest, not all practitioners of generative syntax were ready to follow Chomsky's reasoning. Rappaport (1983), for example, was instrumental in showing that deep structure (D-structure) could not be equivalent to argument structure. She demonstrated that argument structure is not just category neutral, it has to be structurally neutral as well.

Her general line of argumentation can be illustrated with respect to examples like those in (4). These types of nominalizations are particularly interesting because they can potentially participate in the dative alternation discussed in section 4.11, which already presents problems for a rigidly structural theory of argument representation. One particular problem thematized by Rappaport was the pattern in (5) and (6). The verb *command* takes an agent (general), a goal (troops) and a theme/proposition (to leave) as arguments (5a). Unlike other ditransitive verbs in English, however, the goal argument of *command* cannot be expressed via a *to* indirect object (5b). This fact by itself does not necessarily pose a problem. The real problem only becomes apparent once the corresponding derived nominalizations are taken into account.

(5) a. The general commanded the troops to leave.
    b. *The general commanded to leave to the troops.

(6) a. *The general's command of the troops to leave.
    b. *The general's command the troops to leave.
    c. The general's command to the troops to leave.

The only good nominalization is the version in (6c). However, given the transformational and structural assumptions of the time, there was no natural way of deriving (6c) from (5a). That is, given that both (5a) and (6c) have to be derived from the same underlying structural representation of arguments, it is not clear how the *to* can be licensed on *troops* in (6c) without also assuming it in the underlying representation for (5a). Rappaport therefore concluded that while it was correct to assume a single underlying argument structure for both (5a) and (6c), namely something as in (7), it was not correct to represent these arguments structurally in the same way for both verbs and nouns.

(7) *command*:   (agent goal theme)

Instead, these thematic roles could be listed in the lexicon and then *linked* via linking rules to verbal and nominal expressions, respectively. This linking idea is shown schematically in (8). Rappaport worked within Lexical-Functional Grammar (LFG), which assumes a number of grammatical relations, called *grammatical functions*. Besides the usual subject and object functions, there are also obliques (OBL), which generally correspond to PPs in English, and the XCOMP for non-finite embedded complements.

(8) a. The general commanded the troops to leave.
      argument structure: *command*: (agent goal theme)
      gram. func. assignment: SUBJ OBJ XCOMP
      syntactic expression: NP   NP   VP

    b. The general's command to the troops to leave.
      argument structure: *command*: (agent   goal   theme)
      gram. func. assignment: POSS OBL$_{GOAL}$ XCOMP
      syntactic expression: NP   PP [to___]   VP

In (8a) the goal argument of the verb is linked to the object and the nonfinite complement *to leave* is linked to an XCOMP. In (8b), in contrast, the goal is linked to an oblique (PP). The connection to a goal argument is notated as a subscript on the oblique (OBL) grammatical function. This specification requires that the goal be realized as a *to* PP in the syntax. Note that this model of syntax assumes several independent, but interactive, levels of representation. For one there is the predicate-argument structure, which encodes the number and type of participants in a category neutral and structurally independent manner. Then there are the grammatical relations, which interact with, but are not wholly determined by the argument structure. These grammatical relations can be realized in the syntax in various ways. In English, the subject is realized as a preverbal NP. The subject of the same predication in Irish (section 4.5), for example, would be realized postverbally. The overt syntactic realization is thus considered to be a language particular matter, which is unlike the transformational model presented in chapter 4. That model assumes a language universal structural representation at the initial stages of syntax, but allows language particular variation in the later stages of derivation.

The idea that argument structure should be seen as a structurally neutral level of representation was supported early on by a flurry of papers on nominalization, adjective formation, passivization, resultatives, polyadicity and unaccusative verbs (e.g., Bresnan 1982a,b, Simpson 1983, Zaenen and Maling 1983) and remains a central tenet of theories like LFG and the linking theories discussed in this chapter.

5.3 Lexical Decomposition and Linking

The term *linking* gained currency in linguistic theories due to the work of Ostler (1979) on the rules governing case realization in Sanskrit. Ostler in turn credits Carter (1977) with first using the term, and indeed builds on his ideas, but it was Ostler's formulations which informed the further development of linking theories around that time. Ostler worked broadly within Fillmore's Case Grammar (section 3.5) and used Jackendoff's (1972, 1976) ideas on lexical decomposition to formulate correlations between case and thematic relations in Sanskrit. Since many approaches assume some form of lexical decomposition in their analyses, including analyses within MP, it is worth revisiting the basic ideas here (see section 4.10.2 for previous discussion), particularly since Jackendoff (1990) also explicitly formulates a linking theory.

Jackendoff (1976) argues that the rather vague use of thematic role labels such as *agent, patient, location, recipient*, or *instrument* needed to be given more substance in order to be truly useful for linguistic analysis. This is a concern that was shared by many linguists, since Fillmore's (1968) original proposals were not satisfactory enough. Jackendoff's solution, based on Gruber (1965), was to define thematic roles in terms of positions in a semantic analysis that *decomposed* the basic predication via semantic *primitives* such as GO, BE and CAUSE. An example of a Lexical Conceptual Structure (LCS) representation based on later work (Jackendoff 1990) is shown in (9).

(9)
$$\left[\begin{array}{l} \text{give} \\ \left[\begin{array}{l} \text{CAUSE}([\alpha], \text{GO}_{Poss}([\beta], \text{TO}[\ ])) \\ \text{AFF}([\ ]^{\alpha}, [\ ]^{\beta}) \end{array} \right] \end{array} \right]$$

In this lexical entry the event denoted by the English verb *give* is lexically decomposed into several primitives, namely CAUSE, GO and TO. The representation expresses that there is an event in which a participant (first argument of CAUSE) caused something (first argument of GO) to go to another participant (argument of TO). The verb *give* thus has exactly three arguments which need to be linked into the syntax. In addition to this *Thematic Tier*, Jackendoff includes an *Action Tier* with the AFF(ectedness) relation in the LCS representation. In (9), the two participants on the Action Tier are the causer of the event (coindexed with an α) and the theme/patient (coindexed with a β). The Action Tier privileges two event participants, the actor and the patient/beneficiary of the action. This is in accordance with a much cited insight that the typical verbal event is transitive and involves two participants, an actor and a thing or person acted upon (Hopper and Thompson's 1980 notion of transitivity). Notice also the correlation with the postulation of exactly two structural Cases, namely nominative and accusative, in chapter 4.

Within Jackendoff's system, there is no direct reference to thematic roles. Thematic roles do not form primitive notions in his approach, rather they are defined structurally in terms of positions within the LCS. A rough correspondence between LCS positions and thematic roles is shown in (10).

(10)
Position at LCS	**Corresponding Thematic Role**
First argument of AFF	actor
Second argument of AFF$^-$	patient
Second argument of AFF$^+$	beneficiary
First argument of CAUSE	agent (usually simultaneously actor)
First argument of Location and Motion functions	theme
Argument of TO	goal
Argument of FROM	source

Based on the LCS representations, Jackendoff (1990) goes on to formulate a linking theory which places the thematic relations at LCS in relationship with a syntactic structure. Because Jackendoff's primary language of investigation is English, his theory has little to say about case and the syntactic representations he assumes are akin to those of GB/MP seen in chapter 4. A minimal syntactic hierarchy (Jackendoff 1990:258) is given in (11), whereby (11a) represents the external argument (usually the subject), (11b) the direct (first) object and (11c) the secondary (indirect) object.

(11) a. [_S NP* ...]
      b. [_VP V NP* ...]
      c. [_VP V ... NP* ...]

This syntactic hierarchy is placed into correspondence with the LCS via a linking principle which aligns a *thematic hierarchy* with the syntactic hierarchy in (11). The thematic hierarchy is a listing of thematic roles, structured from 'highest' to 'lowest', whereby the thematic roles are read off of the LCS from left to right, and beginning with the Action Tier. The linking of the information in the LCS representation for *give*, for example, would work out as follows. First the arguments on the Action Tier are read off from left to right: actor and patient. Then the remaining argument on the Thematic Tier, a goal argument, is added to the hierarchy as the lowest argument. This results in the list in (12). These three arguments are then aligned with the syntactic hierarchy in (11) to express a ditransitive with an indirect *to* object.

(12) *give*: actor patient goal

(13) Kim gave a bone to the dog.

The dual representation in terms of the Action and Thematic Tiers, provides the flexibility needed to account for argument alternations like the English dative alternation. The analysis is based on the well known observation that there is a semantic difference between the two alternatives (cf. S. Anderson 1971, section 4.3). The semantic difference is loosely described as involving a notion of 'affectedness' in that the most affected argument is realized as the direct object. In (13), the *bone* is the direct object and is considered to be more 'affected' than the dog, who is just the location where the object ends up being. In the double object alternative in (14), on the other hand, the *dog* as the direct object of the action is more affected than the bone.

(14) Kim gave the dog a bone.

This semantic effect is not very clear with the use of *give* above, but consider the difference between *Kim gave me a headache* (*me* is affected) and **Kim gave a headache to me*.

The semantic difference can also be illustrated via other well known argument alternations, such as the one involving the verb *teach* in (15) and the *spray/load alternation*, illustrated in (16) with the verb *load*. In (15a) the version with the *to* indirect object does not entail that the *agents* indeed received a knowledge of Urdu. That is, there is no guarantee that they were indeed 'affected' by the teaching in the way that was intended. When the *agents* are realized as a direct object in (15b), on the other hand, they must have been successfully taught Urdu and any indication to the contrary is ungrammatical. In (15b) the agents are thus definitely affected by the action.

(15) a. The CIA taught Urdu to the agents (but they didn't learn any).
   b. The CIA taught the agents Urdu (*but they didn't learn any).

(16) a. The women loaded the boxes into the truck.
   b. The women loaded the truck with the boxes.

Similarly, in (16a), the semantic entailment is that *all* of the boxes have been loaded into the truck. This is not true of (16b), where some of the boxes may have not been loaded into the truck. Furthermore, (16b) entails that the truck is fully loaded. This is not the case in (16a), where there could still be room in the truck, even if all the boxes have been loaded. Thus the boxes are the most affected entity in (16a), but the truck is the most affected entity in (16b).[1]

In Jackendoff's system, this difference between more and less affected is modelled at the Action Tier. The double object alternative of the dative alternation, for example, is realized via an LCS in which the argument of TO and the second argument of AFF are coindexed. This signals that the first argument of GO, the beneficiary, should be interpreted as the affected participant in (17).

(17)
$$\left[\begin{array}{l} \text{give} \\ \left[\begin{array}{l} \text{CAUSE}([\alpha], \text{GO}_{Poss}([\ ], \text{TO}[\beta])) \\ \text{AFF}([\ ]^\alpha, [\ ]^\beta) \end{array} \right] \end{array} \right]$$

(18) *give*: actor beneficiary theme

The thematic roles extracted from this LCS are shown in (19). This corresponds to the double object construction in (14). Thus, even though the lexical semantic representation of the verb *give* has not changed (cf. (9)), the separation of thematic role labels from lexically decomposed semantics allows the right kind of syntactic variation for the right kind of semantic alternation.

Jackendoff's approach assumes no strict one-to-one mapping between syntactic positions and thematic roles. This stands in contrast to the assumption of the UTAH in GB/MP (chapter 4). The possible mappings allowed by Jackendoff's linking are quite complex, as shown in (19) (Jackendoff 1990:268).

(19) **Linking Hierarchy**

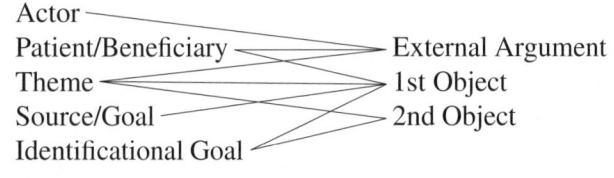

Actor ——————————— External Argument
Patient/Beneficiary ————— 1st Object
Theme ————————— 2nd Object
Source/Goal
Identificational Goal

---

[1] Another observation is that discourse may play a role so that the direct object is placed more in focus than the secondary object or the PP (e.g., Erteschik-Shir 1979, Givón 1984, Thompson 1995, Arnold, Wasow, Losongco and Ginstrom 2000). Discourse factors remain to be properly explored by theories of case and are therefore not discussed any further here.

Despite Jackendoff's very explicit and detailed lexical semantic analyses, his approach has not found a large following. Part of the problem seems to be that despite the very careful formulations, the definitions are not systematic enough to allow a development of the ideas and analyses by an independent linguistic community. The problem underlying the use of thematic role labels therefore continues to be a thorn in the side of linguistic thinking, leading to the formulation of several alternative solutions. One popular solution is briefly described in the next section.

5.4 Proto-Roles

In a very influential article, Dowty (1991) took on the unsatisfactory situation with respect to thematic roles and proposed the notion of *Proto-Roles*.[2] Rather than working with an unspecified number of ill-defined thematic role labels, he proposed just two roles, *Proto-Agent* and *Proto-Patient*. Each of these roles is characterized by a list of entailments (Dowty 1991:572), shown in (20). For an argument to qualify as a Proto-Agent or Proto-Patient it does not have to entail all of the properties, but only some of them (at least one). The [e] properties are enclosed in brackets because Dowty only included them on a tentative basis.

Because only some of the properties need to apply for a participant to be classified as a Proto-Agent or Proto-Patient, the difference between a Proto-Agent and a Proto-Patient does not always have to involve the same properties and therefore makes for a *fuzzy* boundary between Proto-Agents and Proto-Patients in any given situation. The distinction is context sensitive because it is drawn on a clause by clause basis by *comparing* the number of typical Proto-Patient vs. typical Proto-Agent properties of any given argument, and then basing the *argument selection* decision on that.

(20) **Proto-Role Entailments**

Proto-Agent
  a. volitional involvement in the event or state
     (Ex.: Kim in *Kim is ignoring Sandy.*)
  b. sentience (and/or perception)
     (Ex.: Kim in *Kim sees/fears Sandy.*)
  c. causing an event or change of state in another participant
     (Ex.: loneliness in *Loneliness causes unhappiness.*)
  d. movement (relative to the position of another participant)
     (Ex.: tumbleweed in *The tumbleweed passed the rock.*)
  e. (exists independently of the event named by the verb)
     (Ex.: Kim in *Kim needs a new car.*)

---

[2] A very similar idea was proposed much earlier by Van Valin (1977b), see section 8.1, and Dowty's ideas were inspired by the earlier work.

Proto-Patient
  a. undergoes change of state
     (Ex.: cake in *Kim baked a cake.*, error in *Kim erased the error.*)
  b. incremental theme
     (Ex.: apple in *Kim ate the apple.*)
  c. causally affected by another participant
     (Ex.: Sandy in *Kim kicked Sandy.*)
  d. stationary relative to movement of another participant
     (Ex.: rock in *The tumbleweed passed the rock.*)
  e. (does not exist independently of the event, or not at all)
     (Ex.: house in *Kim built a house.*)

A simple example is provided by the pinching event in (21). A consideration of the properties of the participants involved in a pinching event identifies *Kim* as the Proto-Agent (P-A) and *Sandy* as the Proto-Patient (P-P). The P-A properties a, c, and e apply to *Kim*, but none of the P-P properties are relevant. In contrast, the P-P property c applies to *Sandy*, but none of the P-A properties. Given the Argument Selection Principle in (21), *Kim* can therefore be identified as the subject and *Sandy* as the object.

(21) Kim pinched Sandy.

(22) **Argument Selection Principle**
In predicates with grammatical subject and object, the argument for which the predicate entails the greatest number of Proto-Agent properties will be lexicalized as the subject of the predicate: the argument having the greatest number of Proto-Patient entailments will be lexicalized as the direct object. [Dowty 1991:576]

This Argument Selection Principle comes with several corollaries. One is that in a situation in which two arguments have about equal P-A and P-P properties, either one could be realized as a subject or an object. This corollary is useful for a number of phenomena in which such subject-object alternations are indeed observed. Another corollary is that in events involving three participants, the non-subject argument which has more P-P properties is realized as the direct object. If they have about the same number of P-P properties, then either one could be realized as the direct object. This is the case for the by now familiar English dative alternation (section 5.3), for example.

Another property of Dowty's Proto-Role theory is that a given argument could have either no role, or more than one Proto-Role associated with it. Again, this allows more flexibility in argument expression than the UTAH introduced in chapter 4, something which is needed in order to account for the full range of argument realization possibilities crosslinguistically.

Dowty also takes up the notoriously difficult boundary between unaccusative verbs (e.g., *die*) and unergative verbs (e.g., *sneeze*). As Rosen (1984) (section 3.8) showed, the same verbs could be classified as unaccusative (e.g., Italian 'die') in one language and unergative (e.g., Choctaw 'die') in another. Dowty proposes that this fuzzy crosslinguistic boundary is due to the fact that the notions 'unaccusative' and 'unergative' are not monolithic concepts, but make reference to the Proto-Agent and Proto-Patient properties. That is, the Italian verb for 'die' may entail more P-P properties for its argument than the Choctaw expression for 'die'. This causes the Italian verb 'die' to be classified as a non-agentive, i.e., unaccusative verb for syntactic purposes, while the Choctaw version is classified as more agentive, i.e., unergative.

Despite the inherent flexibility and intuitive appeal of Dowty's system, it falls short of being able to account for argument realization and argument alternations crosslinguistically. Like Jackendoff, Dowty primarily focuses on English and therefore does not take case into account. Primus (1999, 2002), for example, works on languages with overt case and reformulates the Proto-Role entailments in order to be able to take case assignment into account.[3]

Primus is not the only one to have adopted a version of Dowty's Proto-Roles. The idea found great resonance among the linguistic community and even though Dowty himself explicitly did not intend the Proto-Roles to be used for the 'linking up' of different levels of representation (Dowty 1991:576), as he saw no sense in such an approach in the first place,[4] several linguists working with linking theories have integrated Dowty's Proto-Roles into their approach. Some examples of such integration will be discussed as part of this book. An example discussed in this chapter in particular is Zaenen's (1993) LFG analysis of Dutch unaccusativity (section 5.7.7) (also see RRG, section 8.1). But first, the next two sections discuss linking theories which rely more heavily on the type of lexical decomposition discussed in section 5.3.

5.5 Kiparsky's Linking Theory

Kiparsky's theory of linking and case is a combination of insights from generative grammar and Pāṇini's ancient ideas about the relationship between case and thematic roles. Kiparsky's initial linking ideas built on the analyses of Ostler (1979), but have developed far beyond those initial proposals into quite a complex and elegant system (Kiparsky 1987, 1988, 1997, 2001).

The theory postulates that there are three equally privileged components which determine the syntactic function of an argument: case, agreement and

---

[3] Also see Primus (1997) for the introduction of a *Proto-Recipient* role.

[4] In this respect, Dowty aligns himself with the derivational approach presented in chapter 4, as he sees no need for a separate representation involving thematic roles. Rather, following standard notions of Montague grammar, he sees his Proto-Role entailments as applying directly to an architecture which closely intertwines syntactic and semantic representations.

position. Kiparsky's theory focuses explicitly on the role of case marking in identifying grammatical relations and thus stands in stark contrast to the generative tradition (RG in chapter 3, GB/MP in chapter 4, and Jackendoff's and Dowty's contributions) in that case is taken to inform syntactic function, rather than the other way around. In the theories discussed so far, case was seen as an expression of syntactic function, and one whose 'spell out' or overt realization was a matter of secondary interest. In Kiparsky's approach, case is of primary interest, but the approach is by no means confined to an investigation of case.

5.5.1 Semantic Form and Thematic Roles

The theory presupposes the distinction between lexical semantics and thematic roles that was argued for by Jackendoff (section 5.3). In particular, Kiparsky assumes Bierwisch's (Bierwisch 1983, 1986, Bierwisch and Schreuder 1992) two-tiered lexical decomposition. The Semantic Form (SF) represents that subset of conceptual knowledge which is relevant for the linguistic system. SF is distinct from our conceptual and world knowledge, but does interact with it. Though not discussed in section 5.3, this idea is in line with Jackendoff's assumptions, as is the idea that thematic roles can be read off the lexically decomposed SF. The thematic roles are the subset of SF information which interacts with the syntax of a language. They are extracted from the SF representation via *lambda abstraction*, a device employed within formal semantics for the binding of variables in logic formulae. As in Jackendoff's approach, thematic role labels like *agent* or *patient* have no formal status within the theory, but they can be used as informal and convenient designations for positions at SF. Sample lexical entries for the verbs *show* and *put* are given in (23).

(23) a. *show*: $\lambda z \lambda y \lambda x$ [x CAUSE [CAN [y SEE z]]]
 b. *put*: $\lambda z \lambda y \lambda x$ [x CAUSE [BECOME [y AT z]]]

The entry for *show*, for example, says that this is an event by which an x causes another event. The causation of this event in turn makes a seeing event possible. In this seeing event a y sees a z. The variables x, y, and z are made available as thematic roles via lambda abstraction. Lambda abstraction is denoted by the Greek λ symbol. The resulting argument structure under this approach is the material to the left of the square brackets, namely $\lambda z \lambda y \lambda x$.

The order of the thematic roles is important. A variable's depth of embedding at SF determines the thematic role's position in the thematic hierarchy. In (23), the x is the 'highest' thematic role and therefore the argument that tends to be linked to the most prominent syntactic function, the subject. The z is the 'lowest' thematic role and is thus likely to be linked to an oblique prepositional phrase as in *on the floor* in (24b), or a secondary object in (24a).

(24) a. The real estate agent showed the customers the house.
 b. Kim put the bone on the floor.

The linking principles by which thematic roles are related to syntactic functions like subject or object are regulated by the assignment and unification of feature spaces which are themselves very simple, but whose relational and crossmodular nature allows for a complex interplay of relationships. The feature system is introduced in the next section (section 5.5.2).

One point to make about the relationship between SF and thematic roles, i.e., the information that interacts with the syntax, is that it need not be one-to-one. This is an assumption made by most theories of syntax and case. The notion adopted by Kiparsky allows a relatively straightforward illustration, so the discussion occurs here even though it could theoretically occur at any point.

English, like other languages, has a so-called *middle* construction, which is like the passive in that the agent is suppressed, but is unlike the passive because the morphology and the semantic interpretation differs. An example is shown in (25). The SF for the middle use of *show* is assumed to be the same as that of the active use in (24a). That is, any action of showing necessarily involves an agent (the shower), an object (the thing shown) and a goal (the person shown to). However, in the middle construction, only one of these participants is expressed in the syntax. As such, the SF and the argument structure show a mismatch: the SF includes three participants, but only one of these participants, the z, is represented at argument structure and only that one is linked to a syntactic function, in this case a subject (Kiparsky 1997:474).

(25) This house shows well.
   show: λz [x CAUSE [CAN [y SEE z]]]

The converse point can be made with weather verbs like *rain* in (26) or verbs of existence like the use of *come* in (27). In these cases, the SF either contains no semantically motivated or *thematic* arguments ((26)), as they are called in other theories, or less participants than at argument structure ((27)).

(26) It rained.
   rain: λx [RAIN]

(27) There came a war.
   come: $\lambda y \lambda x$ [y COME]

As already mentioned, this mismatch is acknowledged across theoretical frameworks. It has been shown that weather verbs like *rain* do not act like they have a semantically motivated argument. The constructions are therefore known as *impersonal*. There is no agent or theme which rains, there is only the event of raining. However, because languages like English require that each clause should contain a syntactic subject, an (English *it, there*), a semantically empty pronoun, fulfils this requirement. In languages like Urdu, which do not have expletives, but which do have verbs of simple 'happening' or existence, the situation is described as an agentless (impersonal) happening.[5]

(28) barıʃ   hui
rain.F.Sg.Nom become.Past.F.Sg
'It rained (lit. rain happened).'   Urdu

Having introduced the basic ideas with respect to the representation of arguments, the next sections introduce the actual linking theory, beginning with the two simple linking features that carry the bulk of the analysis.

5.5.2 The Feature System

Thematic roles are linked to the (morpho)syntax via two features: [± H(ighest) R(ole)], [± L(owest) R(ole)]. These features refer to the position of the thematic roles with respect to one another. For example, [+HR] denotes that this is the highest role, [−HR] expresses that this argument is not the highest role. The arguments of the verb *show*, for example, are specified as in (29).

(29) *show*:   λz   λy   λx   [x CAUSE [CAN [y SEE z]]]
             [+LR] [   ] [+HR]

The z argument is the most embedded at SF, is therefore the lowest, and is thus assigned the [+LR] feature. The x argument is the least embedded at SF, therefore the highest argument and therefore is assigned the [+HR] feature. The y argument is neither the highest nor the lowest role and it is not assigned any featural specifications. An alternative to assigning no features would be to assign it the feature bundle [−HR, −LR], however because Kiparsky works with a subtle *feature unification* system, the option in (29) turns out to be preferable.

The [± HR], [± LR] are called *case features*. Besides specifying thematic roles, they also provide a classification of cases. Kiparsky distinguishes between *abstract case* and *morphosyntactic case*. The abstract cases correspond to grammatical relations in other theories. The basic crosslinguistic inventory of abstract cases along with their featural specifications is shown in (30). Note that Kiparsky assumes four basic abstract cases, not two like the GB/MP tradition (Kiparsky 2001:326).[6]

(30) **Abstract Case**: grammatical relations
     Transitive Subject   [+HR, −LR]
     Intransitive Subject   [+HR, +LR]
     Higher (Indirect Object) [−HR, −LR]
     Lower (Direct) Object   [−HR, +LR]

---

[5]See Bolinger (1972) for an argument that *it* is not semantically empty in English, but is so semantically general, as to give the impression of emptiness (also see Ruwet 1991).

[6]His classification corresponds to Dixon's (1979) classification of basic grammatical relations in terms of A (agent, subject of transitive clauses), S (subject of intransitive clauses), D (dative) and O (object). See chapter 6 on ergativity for some further discussion.

Thematic roles and grammatical relations are thus classified by exactly the same featural system. This allows an interaction between them, more precisely, thematic roles and grammatical relations can be *linked* to one another via the feature specifications. Kiparsky assumes a number of principles which constrain this linking relation. Some of the very basic ones are given in (31) (Kiparsky 1997, 1998).

(31) a. **Uniqueness:** A predicate has at most one [+HR] role (defined as the *subject*) and at most one [+LR] role.
   b. **Unification:** Associated feature matrices must be non-distinct (one must not have a plus value where the other has a minus value).
   c. **Specificity (Blocking, 'Elsewhere'):** Specific rules and morphemes block general rules and morphemes in the shared contexts.

The Uniqueness Principle ensures that an argument structure is basically well formed: labelling more than one thematic role as highest or lowest makes no sense. The Unification Principle allows the featural specification of the x argument in (29) to unify with that of a transitive subject in (30), for example. Basically, if two entities have incompatible featural specifications like [+HR] and [−HR], then no unification is possible and the two entities cannot be linked.

The Specificity Principle is a version of the more general *Elsewhere Principle* familiar from phonology (and ultimately based on Pāṇini's grammar of Sanskrit) (Kiparsky 1973). This condition allows more specific information to apply before general principles. Thus, if an argument is assigned the feature [−LR] by a language or construction specific rule, for example, and if by a general or universal principle it should be assigned the [+LR] feature, then the more specific designation *blocks* the application of the universal rule.

Returning to the verb *show*, note that this verb participates in the dative alternation, as shown in (32). As in Jackendoff's approach, this alternation is based on the same underlying argument structure, namely, (29).

(32) a. The real estate agent showed the house to the customers.
   b. The real estate agent showed the customers the house.

In the argument structure of *show* the x argument is assigned the [+HR] feature by the universal rule that the highest argument should bear this feature (recall that the highest argument is the least semantically embedded argument). Its featural specification is compatible with the specifications of a subject and it is therefore linked to a subject in the syntax, namely the *real estate agent* in both (32a) and (32b). The z argument is compatible with the specifications of a direct object, as such it may surface as a direct object in (32a) and as secondary direct object in the double object construction in (32b). The y argument bears no specifications whatsoever and is therefore in principle compatible with any argument. It cannot be linked to a subject because that grammatical relation has already been linked and Uniqueness would be violated. It can, however, be linked to either an indirect object (*to the customers*) in (32a) or to the direct object (*the customers*) in (32b).

Crosslinguistically, the case features do not just classify thematic roles and grammatical relations, they also, and perhaps most importantly, classify morphosyntactic cases. Since English does not have overt morphosyntactic case (except on pronouns), consider the German example in (33).

(33) Der   Affe   gibt dem   Hund
    the.M.Sg.Nom Affe.M.Sg gives the.M.Sg.Dat dog
    einen   Kuchen.
    a.M.Sg.Acc cake.M.Sg.Acc
    'The monkey is giving the dog a cake.'   German

This is a normal ditransitive clause whose main predicate is *geben* 'give'. The argument structure is shown in (34). Note that this representation differs from the one for *show* in (29), but encodes the same information. For one, the lexically decomposed SF has been left out in favour of representing only the relevant arguments. For another, the arguments are shown in order from highest to lowest, an order that is the general rule in linguistic discussions of argument structure. Kiparsky himself adopts this representation (Kiparsky 1997) for ease of exposition and I follow him.

(34) *geben* 'give':   λx   λy   λz
                     [+HR] [ ] [+LR]

The arguments of *geben* 'give' have been assigned exactly those features one would expect from the discussion above. In German, case marking is sometimes of greater relevance than grammatical relations. Some clauses are subjectless in German and many of the relevant syntactic generalizations need to be stated in terms of the *nominative* argument rather than the subject argument. German is also a language with fairly free word order, so position is not a reliable indicator. Kiparsky therefore links arguments to morphosyntactic case for those languages in which morphosyntactic case plays a role, in addition to linking arguments to grammatical relations, as discussed above. Morphosyntactic cases are also classified via the [± HR], [± LR] case features, as shown in (35) (Kiparsky 1997, 2001). This classification is taken to be universally valid, though individual languages may allow for exceptional specifications (cf. the Specificity Principle).

(35) **Morphosyntactic Case**:
    nominative [ ]
    accusative [−HR]
    genitive   [−LR]
    dative   [−HR, −LR]

The nominative is in principle compatible with any argument. This reflects the fact that crosslinguistically the nominative is not fussy about what kind of thematic role it is linked to. Recall from chapter 4 that this is one reason why the nominative is identified as an abstract structural Case within GB/MP. The accusative is only excluded from the highest role in an argument structure. This again reflects the crosslinguistic tendency for accusatives to be associated with objects, i.e., accusatives are almost never used to mark agents, the highest argument of an argument structure. The genitive is a complicated case which is not discussed much in this book. It is compatible with a range of thematic roles and a range of grammatical relations, but it generally appears in argument structure configurations which have a lower thematic role than it. The default realization of the dative is on arguments that are neither the highest nor the lowest role in an argument structure.

This classification of morphosyntactic cases works out exactly right for the German pattern in (33) in combination with the Specificity Principle. The Principle states that each thematic role should be associated with the most specific case feature bundle possible. That is, Kiparsky's system relies on the relative *markedness* of feature specifications. Markedness is a concept familiar from phonological analyses: an element is considered the more marked the more featural specifications are associated with it. The more marked an element is, the more specific the information it bears. The Specificity Principle prefers the association of more specific information before more general information and therefore the nominative is not associated with the z argument, event though in principle the nominative is compatible with all three arguments.

The more specific feature specification compatible with the z argument is the accusative specification. It selects an argument that is definitely not the highest role and as such is compatible with an argument specified as the lowest argument. The y argument is only compatible with the dative, since it is neither the highest, nor the lowest role. So, the dative is linked to the y argument. This leaves the x argument, for which the remaining compatible case is the nominative and this yields exactly the right result. The association of the genitive with the x argument is ruled out due to a constraint on verb agreement, see below.

The morphosyntactic case inventory in (35) reflects only a subset of the world's possible cases. Case inventories differ from language to language. For one, languages may contain more or less cases than those listed in (35). Finnish is famous for having 15 cases, for example. For another, a language may specify a given case, e.g., the genitive or accusative with a different feature bundle. In practice, as Kiparsky's investigations to date have shown, this is rarely the case. However, languages often do differ on the alignment of cases with thematic roles and with grammatical relations. These subtle crosslinguistic differences can be accounted for by postulating differences in terms of the assignment and interaction of the [±HR,±LR] features.

Kiparsky further distinguishes between *morphosyntactic* and *morphological* case. The latter is the overt realization (or 'spell out') of abstract morphosyntactic case over which relevant linguistic generalizations can be stated. That is, morphosyntactic cases can in principle have differing morphophonological realizations, as is shown for the Urdu dative in (36), where the overt dative form for a pronoun can alternate between an inflectional *-e* and the clitic *ko*. A system which failed to recognize that the *-e* and *ko* are expressions of the same abstract *function* would represent a failed linguistic analysis.

(36) ʊs-e/=ko   bukʰ   lɑg-i   hɛ
     Pron-Dat/=Dat hunger.F.Sg.Nom be.attached-F.Sg be.Pres.3.Sg
     'She/he is hungry (lit. to him/her hunger is attached/stuck).'   Urdu

This Urdu example also serves to illustrate another point. Recall from section 4.8 that not all case marking patterns follow the default associations which are generally assumed: that agents are nominative subjects, themes/patients are accusative objects and goals/beneficiaries are dative indirect objects. For Icelandic, for example, it was established conclusively that some datives have to be analysed as subjects. The same is true for the Urdu example in (36).

Kiparsky assumes along with the GB/MP analyses that these examples are instances of language specific patterns, i.e., of exceptional or *quirky* case marking. In Urdu, goals are generally linked to datives, including such abstract goals/locations as the dative in (36). The relevant lexical entry for the Urdu 'be attached' in (37) thus carries a different feature specification from the [+HR] that would be assigned to it according to the universal rule.

(37) *lag* 'be attached': λx λy
                            [−HR]
                            [−LR]

This feature specification is compatible with the dative case for the x argument. The y argument could in principle be linked to the nominative or the accusative. It is linked to the nominative and not the accusative because of another factor that comes into play: linking by agreement. Note that the verb agrees with the y argument, not the dative x argument. In Kiparsky's system, linking by agreement interacts with case and positional linking. This interaction is discussed in the next section.

5.5.3 Linking by Case, Position and Agreement

Kiparsky's theory does justice to the time honoured observation that there is a correlation between freedom of word order and richness of morphology. This observation goes back to linguistic giants such as Wilhelm von Humboldt and Otto Jespersen, who are responsible for much of the solid ground which modern generative theories find themselves on today.

> Typologically oriented grammatical theorizing at least since Humboldt has assumed that word order and inflectional morphology are alternative means of expressing grammatical relations. From this premise, Boas, Sapir, and Jespersen explicity derive the interesting crosslinguistic prediction that richness of inflection should be correlated with freedom of word order. [Kiparsky 1997:473]

Kiparsky notes that the correlation between morphology and word order holds only in one direction: languages without much morphology have little word order freedom, but languages with morphology could still have a fairly rigid word order (Icelandic is an example). Furthermore, there is a correlation between the syntactic licensing of arguments and position, case, and agreement. Languages which have no or little case morphology tend to make heavy use of agreement morphology to identify the subject vs. the object in a clause (American Indian languages fall under this category). Languages with a complex morphological case system may make little use of verb agreement (Australian languages are an example). And languages like English or Chinese, which have little to no morphology, rely on positional clues (the subject in English is generally sentence initial, while the direct object in simple declaratives is always immediately adjacent and to the right of the verb).

However, Kiparsky sees these crosslinguistic generalizations as finding no echo in purely syntactic approaches like those of GB/MP. While that tradition recognizes a close interaction between case assignment and agreement, the postulated interaction is so closely intertwined as to be almost identical. This close identification of case and agreement does not do justice to the variety of documented crosslinguistic patterns. Moreover, Kiparsky sees the relegation of morphosyntactic case to PF (Phonological Form) as theoretically deficient, because it cannot properly account for crosslinguistic differences.

> The upshot is that nothing in this theory [broadly the GB/MP tradition] precludes a language with the morphology of English or Chinese from having the syntax of German or Japanese.
> [Kiparsky 1997:473]

That is, there is no good way of accounting for the fact that English and Chinese, which have next to no morphology, are structurally rigid languages, while languages like German and Japanese, which allow relatively free word order, have a reasonable amount of morphology. Kiparsky therefore gives morphology a central place in his theory. One central piece of linking theory is formed by case, as was discussed in the previous section. The other two central linkers are *agreement* (morphology) and *position* (syntax). The linking of thematic relations to grammatical relations thus depends on an interaction of case morphology, agreement relations and positional constraints.

Since English is a language with very little morphology, but strong positional requirements and subject agreement, the main linkers for English are positional, mediated by subject agreement. As such, the discussion in the previous section (section 5.5.2) for English *show* was not quite right. Rather than directly linking to abstract case (grammatical relations), the linking is mediated by the general positional constraints in (38).

(38) a. Complement positions are [−HR]
  b. Non-final complement positions are [−LR]

That is, the abstract case classification in (30) informs the first assignment of features to an argument structure, as shown in (39) for the transitive verb *pinch*. These featural specifications must now be unified with the positional and agreement specifications for English.

(39) *pinch*: λx λy
       [+HR] [+LR]

One analysis for English could assume that [−HR] complement position is associated with the complement of the verb. The [−LR] feature could be associated with SpecIP. Additionally, subject agreement is assumed to be associated with the [+HR] feature, which also interacts with the SpecIP position in English. Taking together the feature specifications in (39) with these positional and agreement specifications, the x argument is linked to the subject in SpecIP and the y argument is linked to the complement of V position (object).

Kiparsky observes that a corollary of this system is that if a language has neither case nor agreement, like Chinese, for example, it must obey very fixed word order constraints, because in these languages only the positional linkers are available, allowing for no word order variability that could be licensed by an interaction with case or agreement linkers.

5.5.4 Passives, Unaccusatives and Unergatives

This section briefly presents the analysis of passives, unaccusatives and unergatives in Kiparsky's linking theory. The analyses are not spectacular and are presented mainly in order to maintain a presentational parallelism across theories.

The passive is assumed to be a morphosyntactic operation which *demotes* the [+HR] argument. For the example with *pinch* in (40) this means that the x argument is no longer available for linking and must be realized as an adjunct.

(40) *pinch*:   [λx]   λy
           [+HR] [+LR]
             |
    (agreement)   [+HR]

The linking theory includes a preference for a [+HR] feature in the final specification. This is a structural requirement and can be satisfied by subject-verb agreement ([+HR]) in English. The y argument is therefore linked by agreement to SpecIP and is realized as a subject.

For a language like German, where case is more important, the nominative is the only compatible case, as a quick look at the morphosyntactic case specifications in (35) shows. The accusative is ruled out because then there could be no [+HR] specification, which is independently required in Kiparsky's system. The [−LR] of the genitive and the dative are incompatible with the [+LR] specification of the y argument and as German has no other cases in its case inventory, the nominative is the only compatible case. In addition, nominative goes together with subject agreement in German, so the required [+HR] is explicitly licensed by the subject agreement linker for a sentence like (41). Note that the subject appears at the beginning of the sentence here, though it could also have been placed elsewhere. German allows relatively free word order and position plays no role in the linking of the y argument.

(41) Der   Hund   wurde   (von Affen)   gekniffen.
     the.M.Sg.Nom dog.M.Sg was.3.Sg by monkey.M.Pl pinched
     'The dog was pinched (by monkeys).'   German

The analyses of unaccusative and unergative verbs are identical in Kiparsky's approach. This differs from the assumptions in RG and GB/MP (chapters 3, 4). The syntactic differences between unergatives and unaccusatives (auxiliary selection, *ne*-cliticization, etc.) fall out from other principles of the grammar, but not from the relationship between thematic roles, position, and case.

(42) *fall* (unaccusative):   λx   *sneeze* (unergative):   λx
                              [+HR]   [+HR]
                              [+LR]   [+LR]

The single argument of both unaccusative *fall* and unergative *sneeze* is assigned the feature specification [+HR,+LR], namely that of an intransitive subject (cf. (30)). In languages like German, Italian and Dutch, this feature specification is compatible only with the nominative case and this is indeed the case marking found on subjects of both unaccusatives and unergatives. For languages like Urdu, which distinguish unaccusatives and unergatives in terms of case marking, additional assumptions must be made.

In developing his linking theory, Kiparsky focused primarily on difficult issues within case and agreement, such as data from ergative languages (see chapter 6) and dative case in Germanic (i.e., 'quirky' case). Just as the discussions in the previous chapters could not do justice to the amount of work done in each of the frameworks, the brief discussion in this chapter cannot do justice to the range of data accounted for by Kiparsky, nor can it do justice to examining those phenomena not easily accounted for under this linking conception. One example is the Urdu/Hindi case system, which is also problematic for GB/MP. A closer look at this system is provided as part of section 5.7.

In sum, Kiparsky's linking theory defines a complex interaction between case, agreement and syntactic position for the syntactic realization (licensing) of semantic arguments. While case, agreement and position interact, they are not identified with one another via structural positions, as is the case in the GB/MP approach. Indeed, the concept of a 'linking theory' is not possible within the structural GB/MP tradition, because thematic roles are always initially identified with particular structural positions. There is no 'linking' because the question of variable linking possibilities does not arise. Language specific variation in the realization of arguments is analysed in terms of movements which are driven by featural checking requirements (feature checking), among them case and agreement checking. However, case and agreement do not license variable argument realization: arguments are always initially realized in the same structural position, be it in Japanese, German or English.

The next section introduces a closely related linking approach, namely Wunderlich's Lexical Decomposition Grammar. This is followed by a relatively long section introducing the basics of LFG and its linking theory, along with approaches to case which do not necessarily assume a linking theory.

5.6 Lexical Decomposition Grammar

Wunderlich (1997) introduces *Lexical Decomposition Grammar* (LDG), whose primary purpose is to account for argument and case patterns and argument alternations crosslinguistically. LDG is primarily a theory of linking and was inspired by Kiparsky's linking theory (section 5.5). As LDG grew, it in turn informed the further development of Kiparsky's linking theory. In particular, Kiparsky adopted the Semantic Form (SF) representation for argument structure from the work done by Wunderlich (ultimately based on Bierwisch's 1983 ideas). Kiparsky worked with explicit thematic role hierarchies in the first versions of his theory (see section 5.7.2), but abandoned them later in favour of SF-based argument structure representations as in (43).

(43) *pinch*: $\lambda y \quad \lambda x \quad \lambda s \ \{\text{PINCH}(x,y)\}(s)$
　　　　　+hr　−hr
　　　　　−lr　+lr

Note that the representations in LDG always include the SF and the lambda arguments. The arguments are ordered from right to left, i.e., the x argument in (43) is the 'highest' and the y argument is the 'lowest'. Also note that this representation includes a situation variable s. This binds the event denoted by the verb, but has no further relevance to argument linking. Features are rendered in lower case, not upper case as in Kiparsky's system. The reason for this is discussed below.

The features used in LDG are cross-classificational, just as in Kiparsky's system. Arguments are classified via these features (43), as are cases, agreement linkers and positions, when applicable (e.g., Wunderlich 1996, Wunderlich and Lakämper 2001, Stiebels 2000, 2002). A representative case inventory is given in (44) (Wunderlich 1997, Wunderlich and Lakämper 2001, Wunderlich 2003). This case inventory includes the *ergative* case, which is briefly discussed further on (see chapter 6 for general discussions on the ergative). These cases are considered to be *structural cases* in that they are responsible for marking the core arguments of a clause and are only indirectly related to semantic factors, if at all. The system is expanded to include a notion of *semantic case* in Wunderlich and Lakämper (2001). Semantic case is used to analyse case marking on locational, directional or temporal arguments in languages like German or Finnish.

(44) **Structural Cases**
Dative [+hr, +lr]
Accusative [+hr]
Ergative [+lr]
Nominative/Absolutive [ ]

LDG assumes that a clause could in principle have any number of structurally case marked arguments. In practice, however, constraints on distinctiveness of case marking work out so that a clause containing more than three arguments can only have maximally three structural cases. Further case marked constituents must be licensed via semantic case. In contrast, GB/MP postulates the existence of just two structurally case marked arguments.

One substantial difference between Wunderlich's LDG and Kiparsky's linking theory is the interpretation of the features. The observant reader will have noticed that in (43) and (44), the features are lowercased, whereas they are uppercased in Kiparsky's representations. This reflects a slightly different use of the feature space. The [±h(igher)r(ole)] and [±l(ower)r(ole)] stand for 'there is a/no higher role' and 'there is a/no lower role'.

The main reason behind Wunderlich's deviant use of the features is a different conception of markedness. Whereas Kiparsky defines and uses his feature space in a way that is familiar from phonology, Wunderlich pursues a different theory of markedness. In Kiparsky's sytem, the less features there are, the less marked a given element is. In Wunderlich's system, the more plus marked features there are, the more marked a given element is. Wunderlich's linking theory is part of a more general approach to morphological and syntactic markedness by which elements are considered to be more marked when they bear '+' features, less marked when they are associated with '−' features and even less marked when they are not specified for any features. The dative in (44) is thus a highly marked case: it bears two '+' features. The nominative is the least marked case, because it is specified for no features whatsoever. This fits in with the crosslinguistic observation that the nominative appears in a variety of structural contexts and can be associated with different thematic roles, while the dative generally appears in semantically marked contexts.

5.6.1 Basic Analyses

This section goes through a few basic analyses in order to illustrate the basic principles of LDG. A canonical transitive as in (45), for example, is analysed as in (46) and is associated with nominative and accusative via the case linkers in (44).

(45) Die   Affen   kneifen   den   Hund.
     the.M.Pl.Nom monkey.M.Pl pinch.3.Pl.Pres the.M.Sg.Acc dog.M.Sg
     'The monkeys are pinching the dog.'   German

(46) *kneifen* 'pinch': λy λx λs {PINCH(x,y)}(s)
                         +hr   −hr
                         −lr   +lr
     case: acc   nom

The linking proceeds according to the following logic. The nominative is in principle compatible with both x and y, the dative is not compatible with anything, and the accusative is only compatible with y. The ergative is not part of the case inventory of German (or English), so it is not applicable here. The nominative is considered to be the default structural case, so it must be used at least once as a linker. According to the Uniqueness constraint in (47), no linker should be used more than once, so since the accusative can only apply to the y argument, it is used to link the y, and the nominative links the x argument.

(47) **Uniqueness Constraint**
     For a given thematic structure, each linker applies only once.

Passivization is assumed to existentially bind the highest argument (marked by the logical quantifier ∃), as shown in (49). This renders the x argument unavailable for linking in the syntax. But the x argument is still contained within the lexical semantics of the verb and can therefore be expressed via an adjunct, as in (48). The feature specifications of all the other arguments are not affected, as shown in (49). Because the nominative is the least marked case, it is the preferred case linker by default and the y argument is now marked with the nominative instead of the accusative.

(48) Der   Hund   wurde   (von Affen)   gekniffen.
     the.M.Sg.Nom dog.M.Sg was.3.Sg by monkey.M.Pl   pinched
     'The dog was pinched (by monkeys).'   German

(49) *kneifen* 'pinch': λy ∃x λs {PINCH(x,y)} (s)
 +hr
 −lr
case: nom

The linking pattern for a typical ditransitive as in (50a) is shown in (50b). The specifications for the highest role (x) and the lowest role (z) have not changed. The intermediate role is specified as being part of an argument structure in which there is both a lower and a higher role. The case linking follows as described above, with the addition that the dative is now compatible with the y argument.

(50) a. Der Affe gab dem Hund
 the.M.Sg.Nom Affe.M.Sg gave the.M.Sg.Dat dog
 einen Kuchen.
 a.M.Sg.Acc cake.M.Sg.Acc
 'The monkey gave the dog a cake.' German

 b. *geben* 'give': λz λy λx λs {ACT(x) & BECOME POSS(y,z)}(s)
 +hr +hr −hr
 −lr +lr +lr
 case: acc dat nom

The passive version of (50a) is shown in (51a). This is analysed as in (51b). Again, the highest argument (x) is existentially bound, rendering it unavailable for linking. The nominative is in principle compatible with both the y and the z arguments, but it can only be used to link an argument once, due to the Uniqueness Constraint in (47). The dative is only compatible with the y argument, so it is linked with the dative. The nominative as default linker takes care of the z argument, providing exactly the right case pattern for (51a).

(51) a. Dem Hund wurde ein Kuchen gegeben.
 the.M.Sg.Dat dog was.3.Sg a.M.Sg.Nom cake.M. give.PastP
 'The dog was given a cake.' German

 b. *geben* 'give': λz λy ∃x λs {ACT(x) & BECOME POSS(y,z)}(s)
 +hr +hr
 −lr +lr
 case: nom dat

5.6.2 Unergatives, Unaccusatives and Semantics

Like in Kiparsky's system, no structural difference is made between unaccusative verbs such as *fall* and unergatives such as *sneeze*. Both argument structures consist of only one argument, which is specified as having neither a lower argument nor a higher argument alongside it ([−hr, −lr]). By default, this is linked to the nominative case in languages such as German, English or Italian. The syntactic differences between unaccusatives and unergatives in terms of auxiliary selection, etc. are analysed as being grounded directly in the lexical semantics of a verb, rather than being mediated by the linking of arguments into the syntax (see Kaufmann 1995a,b for detailed argumentation that the supposedly syntactic differences can all be accounted for directly in terms of semantics, also see Maling 2001 for similar argumentation with respect to datives in Icelandic and German).

This works out well for languages which do not distinguish unaccusatives and unergatives in terms of case marking. However, for a language like Basque or Urdu, something extra must be assumed. As shown in (52) for Urdu, unaccusative verbs like 'fall' have a nominative subject, while unergatives like 'cough' can select for an ergative subject. I have so far avoided discussions of ergativity and for the present discussion it is enough to understand the ergative as a (rough) marker of agentive subjects.

(52) a. yassin gır-a
Yassin.M.Nom fall-Perf.M.Sg
'Yassin fell.' Urdu

b. yassin=ne kʰãs-a
Yassin.M=Erg cough-Perf.M.Sg
'Yassin coughed (purposefully).' Urdu

For Basque, Joppen-Hellwig (2001) argues that the supposedly intransitive unergatives are actually syntactically transitive because they contain an argument which is linked via an agreement linker as part of the verbal morphology (see section 6.5.2.1 for an example). The linking pattern for Basque unergatives thus works like that of a transitive verb, i.e., the analysis as for 'pinch' in (46). Since Basque contains an ergative marker in its inventory, the highest (x) argument is linked via the ergative case linker, and not the nominative.

This type of analysis does not cover the Urdu data in (52), since the constructions are syntactically intransitive. Instead, a postulated link between the positive [+lr] and [+hr] features comes into play (Joppen and Wunderlich 1995, Wunderlich 1997, Wunderlich and Lakämper 2001, Wunderlich 2003). The idea is that the positive marked features can be associated with semantic connotations. The [+lr] feature is associated with a degree of *control* over the action (roughly, agentivity). The [+hr] tends to indicate a degree of affectedness. The logic is as follows: if there is a higher role ([+hr]) in the argument structure, this higher role is likely to be the one manipulating or causally affecting the lower one, thus leading to a semantic entailment of affectedness. By the same logic, the [+lr] tends to indicate control or agentivity: if there is a lower role, the higher role usually will be controlling the action in some way.

Applying this semantically based interpretation of the positive features yields an analysis as in (53b) for (52b) and the analysis in (53a) for (52a).

(53) a. *gırna* 'fall': λx λs {FALL(x)}(s)
      inherent: −lr
      default: −hr
      case: nom

  b. *kʰāsna* 'cough': λx λs {COUGH(x)}(s)
      inherent: +lr
      default: −hr
      case: erg

This analysis yields the right case marking patterns under the assumption that control over an action is related to ergative case and that this is lexically specified. There are further complications with the ergative in Urdu, discussed as part of section 5.7, but I leave those aside here, focusing instead on the aspect of *lexical* feature assignment.

5.6.3 Quirky Case

Recall from section 4.8 that Icelandic allows for dative subjects, a phenomenon which has become known as quirky case. As in the GB/MP tradition and similar to what happens in Kiparsky's linking theory, such quirky case is assumed to be exceptionally specified as part of the verb's entry. This exceptional or *lexical* specification could be semantically grounded, as proposed for Urdu in (53), but it need not be.

The German verb 'help' in (54) takes a quirky dative object. The LDG analysis is shown in (54b). The y argument is lexically specified with the [+lr] feature, thus blocking the default assignment of [−lr] (there is no lower role), which would have otherwise applied. Since German has no ergative case in its case inventory and since the nominative applies to the x argument by default, the only possible case linker for the y argument is the dative, giving exactly the right case pattern.

(54) a. Gabi   half   dem   Hund.
      Gaby.F.Sg.Nom help.Past.3.Sg the.M.Sg.Dat dog.M.Sg
      'Gaby helped the dog.'   German

  b. *helfen* 'help': λy λx λs HELP(y)(x)(s)
      lexical: +lr
      default: −lr
               +hr −hr
      case: dat nom

The analysis in (54b) extends to the Icelandic dative patterns as well. However, recall that Icelandic datives were shown to be able to be subjects in general, whereas this is not true of German. Since Wunderlich's LDG grammar does not include an explicit linking to grammatical relations, this difference between the two languages cannot be accounted for directly in terms of factors involving grammatical relations. This stands in contrast to Kiparsky's approach, which does include grammatical relations as part of the basic inventory.

The differences between German and Icelandic are accounted for via an integration of Optimality Theory (OT) into LDG (Wunderlich 2003). Even though Kiparsky's newer work on linking also makes use of OT (e.g., Kiparsky 2001, but see Asudeh 2003 for arguments that the adoption of OT is unneccessary for Kiparsky's analysis), this theoretical framework has deliberately not been introduced as part of this chapter. Rather, because it is an approach which is compatible with a variety of syntactic approaches, a more general introduction to OT in relation to case is provided in section 8.2.

This section has sought to provide a basic understanding of feature-based linking theories. Only a few basic examples have been discussed, but LDG can account for a large range of crosslinguistic argument alternation patterns in terms of case marking and agreement (e.g., Stiebels 2000, 2002, Wunderlich 2003). The next section introduces yet another linking theory which is based on just two features. However, this theory is embedded in a larger theory of syntax, so the primary focus is not always case per se, as is true of both Kiparsky's and Wunderlich's linking theories. Rather, more direct importance is accorded to grammatical relations. Case, as well as agreement and position, play a role in the linking of thematic roles to grammatical relations, but the generalizations are not encoded as directly as in Kiparsky's or Wunderlich's approaches.

5.7 Lexical-Functional Grammar

Lexical-Functional Grammar (LFG) took shape in the late 1970s when Joan Bresnan's linguistic concerns about the continued viability of Transformational Grammar met up with Ron Kaplan's ideas about psycholinguistics and computational modelling. The collection of papers in Bresnan (1982b) sets out the fundamental ideas of LFG. The theory has since been extended to include new ideas and cover more data from a wide array of languages, but the fundamental ideas put forth in the late 1970s and early 1980s continue to be valid. This theoretical stability is fairly unique within generative syntax. LFG has the goal of combining linguistic sophistication with computational implementability (Dalrymple et al. 1995). A broad range of both theoretical and computational linguists work within LFG, with a few individuals who do both. Several current textbooks are available (Falk 2001, Bresnan 2001, Dalrymple 2001), as is a description of a major computational grammar development effort (Butt, King, Niño and Segond 1999).

5.7.1 LFG Basics

LFG separates facts about linear word order and constituency from the 'functional' analysis of a clause. Word order and constituency are represented at c(onstituent)-structure via the familiar tree representations, as shown in (55). LFG assumes a version of X'-theory that goes back to Bresnan (1977). For current assumptions about c-structural representations, see Bresnan (2001).

The f(unctional)-structure is represented in terms of an attribute-value matrix (AVM) and encodes functional syntactic information about grammatical relations, tense/aspect, case, number, person, etc. An f-structure for (55) is shown in (56).

(55) Peter drinks coffee.

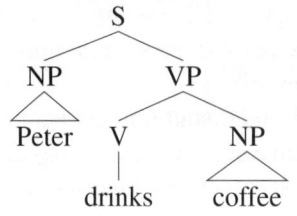

```
        S
       / \
      NP   VP
      /\   /\
   Peter  V   NP
          |   /\
        drinks coffee
```

(56) Peter drinks coffee.

$$\begin{bmatrix} \text{PRED} & \text{'DRINK<SUBJ,OBJ>'} \\ \text{SUBJ} & \begin{bmatrix} \text{PRED} & \text{'PETER'} \\ \text{NUM} & \text{SG} \\ \text{PERS} & 3 \\ \text{CASE} & \text{NOM} \end{bmatrix} \\ \text{OBJ} & \begin{bmatrix} \text{PRED} & \text{'COFFEE'} \\ \text{PERS} & 3 \\ \text{CASE} & \text{ACC} \end{bmatrix} \\ \text{TENSE} & \text{PRES} \end{bmatrix}$$

F-structures are a *projection* from the c-structure because they are related to the c-structure via a formal system of annotations. A typical (simplified) example for a fragment of English is shown in (57). The c-structure is built up on the basis of phrase structure *rewrite* rules. The rule in (57a), for example, says that a sentence consists of two major constituents, an NP and a VP. In effect, the S (sentence) is rewritten as an NP and a VP. Rewrite rules are part of the common heritage of modern generative syntactic theories (cf. Chomsky 1965) and continue to be a standard part of computational linguistics.

(57) a. S ⟶ NP VP
          (↑SUBJ)=↓ ↑=↓

   b. VP ⟶ V NP
           ↑=↓ (↑OBJ)=↓

The phrase structure rules in (57) are *annotated* with functional equations. These equations provide the basis for computing the f-structure (information about number, person, tense, etc. is part of the lexical entries of the nouns and the verb in our example). The up arrow refers to the mother node, i.e., VP in (57b), the down arrow references the current node, i.e., V or NP in (57b). These annotations relate the c-structure in (55) and the f-structure in (56) via a formal mathematical projection ϕ.

The effect of the projection architecture is that the levels of representation *constrain* each other mutually. That is, an analysis can only be successful if the f-structure information is complete and consistent, and if the phrase structure rules license the structure. Information at f-structure may flow together from different sources (not illustrated here). The pieces of information are combined with one another via *unification*, the same process that is assumed in Kiparsky's and Wunderlich's linking theories. Finally, because the relation between c-structure and f-structure is stated in terms of a mathematical projection, its *inverse* can also be computed. That is, not only can one 'see' into the f-structure from the c-structure, but the f-structure can refer back to the c-structure. No level is truly primary and no information is ever lost via derivations. LFG thus falls under the label of unification-based declarative theories of syntax (Head-driven Phrase Structure Grammar also falls under this category). In contrast to the fundamental derivational assumptions of GB/MP (chapter 4), LFG assumes no derivations from one structure to another. Indeed, this is one of the characteristics which makes LFG computationally tractable.

The f-structure is an abstract level of representation which is not tied to the particular word order or surface form of a language. Crosslinguistic generalizations about passivization, for example, are formulated with respect to f-structure. The c-structures, in contrast, encode language specific requirements on word order and constituency. The idea is that an SVO language like English and an SOV language like Urdu may differ wildly on the surface, but are similar at the basic predicational level. Urdu is a language with relatively free word order that shows no convincing evidence for a VP constituent in main clauses (Butt 1995), but the verbal complex is quite complicated. These properties are encoded at c-structure (59), where the two NPs and the verbal complex are represented as sisters to one another: the object NP and the verb do not form a constituent. The structure of the verbal complex is not elaborated on any further here, it is simply abbreviated under a $\overline{V}$ (see Mohanan 1994).

(58) yassin dud^h pi-t-a hɛ
Yassin.M.Sg.Nom milk.F.Sg.Nom drink-Impf-M.Sg be.Pres.3.Sg
'Yassin drinks milk.' Urdu

(59)
```
         S
        /|\
      NP NP V
      /\ /\ /\
   yassin dudʰ pita hɛ
```

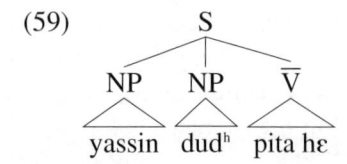

In contrast to the c-structure, the f-structure for (58) in (60) is almost identical to the English one. The Urdu sentence has a present tense auxiliary, but the English sentence does not. This difference is reflected at c-structure, but not at f-structure, since the sentence is in the present tense in both cases, irrespective of the language particular morphosyntactic expression. Note that the Urdu f-structure contains gender information, which the English f-structure does not. This is because gender is syntactically relevant in Urdu, but not in English. Another difference is the information about case. The sentence in (58) is a *double nominative* sentence, a pattern which is considered to be unusual, but which is run-of-the-mill in Urdu (see section 5.9). Finally, the values of the PREDs differ. Despite these differences, the f-structures are *structurally* identical to one another. This is not true for the c-structures. F-structure is considered to be the appropriate level for machine translation, because this level of representation abstracts away from information that is too language particular, but still contains enough syntactic information to be useful (e.g., Frank 1999).

(60)
$$\begin{bmatrix} \text{PRED} & \text{'PINA<SUBJ,OBJ>'} \\ \text{SUBJ} & \begin{bmatrix} \text{PRED} & \text{'YASSIN'} \\ \text{NUM} & \text{SG} \\ \text{PERS} & 3 \\ \text{GEND} & \text{MASC} \\ \text{CASE} & \text{NOM} \end{bmatrix} \\ \text{OBJ} & \begin{bmatrix} \text{PRED} & \text{'DUD}^{h}\text{'} \\ \text{GEND} & \text{FEM} \\ \text{PERS} & 3 \\ \text{CASE} & \text{NOM} \end{bmatrix} \\ \text{TENSE} & \text{PRES} \end{bmatrix}$$

The f-structure in (60) includes two basic grammatical relations: SUBJ(ect) and OBJ(ect). Grammatical relations are assumed as part of the syntactic inventory of every language and are referred to as *grammatical functions* (GF) to indicate their functional status, which is the relation of arguments and predicational elements to one another. Because grammatical functions are not subject to crosslinguistic variation, but are a basic part of the syntactic description language for every language, they are represented at f-structure (and only at f-structure). LFG assumes the GFs in (61).

(61) **Grammatical Functions**
SUBJ OBJ OBJ$_\theta$ OBL(ique)$_\theta$ COMP(lement) XCOMP(lement) ADJUNCT

Dalrymple (2001:11–27) provides a useful discussion of the GFs as well as several syntactic tests by which they can be identified (also see Mohanan 1994 for a battery of subject tests for Hindi). COMP and XCOMP represent clausal arguments. Canonically, the COMP is used for finite clauses (e.g., the English *that*-clause), the XCOMP encodes nonfinite 'open' embedded clauses. An example is the *to win* in *John wants to win*. Here, the embedded verb *win* does not have an overt subject, rather, its subject is 'controlled' by the matrix subject *John* (see Bresnan 1982a for the classic discussion on control and complementation). Finite clauses like the English *that*-clause are considered to be 'closed' because all of the arguments are realized internal to the clause (no control from the matrix clause).

The canonical example for OBJ$_\theta$ is the indirect dative object in languages like German (33) and the second object in the English double object construction (62b). The OBL is used for prepositional phrases which are arguments of the verb. A classic example is the English indirect *to* object (62a). Other instances of OBL occur with verbs of motion as in (64), where the location is subcategorized for by the verb.

(62) a. Kim gave a bone to the dog.
b. Kim gave the dog a bone.

(63) Chris went to/in/behind the house.

The OBJ and OBL are subscripted with a θ to indicate that these GFs are sensitive to thematic role information. That is, PP arguments as in (63) generally reflect a very specific semantics. Similarly, indirect objects are generally tied to goals. Evidence from Bantu secondary objects (Bresnan and Moshi 1990) shows that their syntactic realization is closely related to thematic role information. This is in contrast to SUBJ and OBJ, which are not as selective about thematic roles. This classification of grammatical relations is more similar to GB/MP's assumption that there are exactly two structural Cases, namely nominative (subject) and accusative (object), than to Kiparsky's and Wunderlich's specification of at least four structural cases.

The GFs in (61) are arranged in a hierarchy, just like the thematic roles are. Linking is assumed to prefer a mapping between highest thematic role and highest GF (SUBJ). The default mapping is therefore straightforward: agents should map to subjects, themes should map to objects, etc. However, because languages exhibit many phenomena where this default mapping does not apply, an explicit linking or *Mapping Theory* was formulated to account for deviations and argument alternations. The next few sections first introduce some basic ideas about the representation of argument structure (section 5.7.2) and then chart the development of linking theory via the classic investigation into Icelandic quirky case (section 5.7.3), before presenting LFG's standard Mapping Theory in section 5.7.5.

5.7.2 Argument Structure and Thematic Roles

In addition to the basic c- and f-structural representations, LFG's projection architecture potentially allows for several other projections. One standard additional projection is the s(emantic)-projection (e.g., Halvorsen and Kaplan 1988, Dalrymple 1999), which encodes the semantic analysis of the clause. Another standard projection is the a(rgument)-structure, which encodes thematic role information. A-structure in LFG is generally represented as in (64). This is very much like the representations of argument structure seen so far. The a-structure can be formally represented as an AVM, just like the f-structure (e.g., Butt 1998), but for ease of exposition and in keeping with the bulk of the literature on argument structure, representations as in (64) are used here.

(64) *pound* $<$ agent theme $>$

The a-structure encodes predicate-argument relationships in terms of thematic roles. These thematic roles are arranged in a thematic hierarchy, shown in (65) (based on Bresnan and Kanerva 1989). The agent is the highest role on this hierarchy, followed by beneficiaries, followed by recipient/experiencers, instrumentals, then themes/patients. The locative role is lowest on the hierarchy. It has been pointed out that current work on linking in LFG makes no crucial reference to the thematic role hierarchy (Beth Levin, p.c. summer 2002); however, as it has not been officially abolished and has a role in the standard version of LFG's linking theory, I discuss it as part of this chapter.

(65) **Thematic Role Hierarchy**
$ag > beneficiary > recipient/experiencer > inst > th/pt > loc$

The hierarchy in (65) differs from the one assumed by Jackendoff (section 5.3), Grimshaw (1990) and others. LFG assumes this particular ordering of thematic roles because of arguments put forward by Kiparsky (1987), and because of further evidence adduced from Bantu languages. Kiparsky's argumentation was based on a number of phenomena, among them facts about idiom formation. He observed that the 'inner' arguments of a verb (the arguments closest to the verb within a VP) tend to be lexicalised as idioms before outer arguments. The English idioms in (66) illustrate this: idioms with themes and locatives are easy to identify, but idioms with other arguments become rarer as one moves up the thematic hierarchy. Idioms involving agents are very rare.[7]

---

[7] See Nunberg, Sag and Wasow 1994 for a critical discussion of the idiom evidence.

(66) Verb+Locative (*put X to shame*)
Verb+Theme (*give X a hand, ring a bell*)
Verb+Theme+Locative (*let the cat out of the bag*).

Further evidence for the thematic hierarchy comes from historical change and the unmarked word order of languages. Crosslinguistically, agreement morphemes are often derived from pronouns which have been incorporated into the verb. This historical process applies preferentially to the highest thematic role, namely the agent, thus resulting in subject agreement, and then proceeds on down the hierarchy. As to word order facts, the thematic role hierarchy tends to reflect the unmarked word order in language after language.

All of these pieces of evidence indicate that there is *something* to a thematic hierarchy, despite the general dissatisfaction in the linguistic community with thematic roles as theoretical constructs. Standard LFG linking theory assumes the thematic roles in the thematic hierarchy. But since the linking between thematic roles and grammatical functions is achieved by means of a feature system, the thematic roles are generally classified and referred to via these features. That is, once the feature system has been put in place, no explicit formal reference needs to be made to the individual thematic roles.

Another alternative to the use of thematic role labels is to adopt Dowty's Proto-Roles (section 5.4) into the linking system. This alternative has been pursued by several researchers within LFG (e.g., Alsina 1996, Zaenen 1993, Kelling 2003). Since Zaenen (1993) specifically addresses unaccusativity in Dutch, this approach is discussed in section 5.7.7.

5.7.3 Quirky Case and Early Association Principles

Recall that the classic paper on inherent or quirky case in Icelandic (Zaenen, Maling and Thráinsson 1985) used LFG as its investigative framework. In order to account for the diverse set of case marking patterns in Icelandic, Zaenen, Maling and Thráinsson (ZMT) formulated some principles which governed the relationship between thematic roles, case and grammatical functions. The association principles for Icelandic are shown in (67).

(67) **Icelandic Association Principles**
   1. AGENTS are linked to SUBJ (Universal)
   2. Casemarked THEMES are assigned to the lowest available GF. (Language Specific)
   3. If there is only one thematic role, it is assigned to SUBJ; if there are two, they are assigned to SUBJ and OBJ; if there are three, they are assigned to SUBJ, OBJ, 2OBJ. This principle applies after principle 2 and after the assignment of restricted GFs. (Universal)
   4. Default Case-Marking: the highest available GF is assigned NOM case, the next highest ACC. (Universal)

The association principles are divided up into language specific and universally applicable ones. Crosslinguistically, it is assumed that agents will be linked to subjects (67.1) and that nominative and accusative case are the core cases which are preferably assigned before all others (67.4). Languages may differ, however, with respect to how they deal with some of the thematic arguments. For Icelandic, the rule in (67.2) is applicable. The effect of the association principles is best illustrated via a concrete example. The Icelandic verb *óska* 'to wish' can be used either transitively or as a ditransitive so that the goal 'her' in (68) is optional. When it is present, it is realized as the direct object (OBJ). When it is not present, the theme argument is instead linked to the direct object, as shown in (69).

(68) þú hefur óskað (henni) þess
you have wished her.Dat this.Gen
'You have wished this on/for her.' (ZMT 1985:470)   Icelandic

(69) *óska*: < agent theme (goal) >
              [+gen] [+dat]
   a.   SUBJ   2OBJ OBJ
   b.   SUBJ   OBJ

ZMT define inherent lexical case as being an idiosyncratic property of a lexical item, assigned by a verb, preposition or adjective. In (69), the theme 'this' is assigned inherent genitive case by the verb 'wish'. If the theme were not marked with the genitive feature, then it would be linked to an OBJ in both the transitive and the ditransitive scenario by the association principles in (67). But given the special marking in conjunction with the language specific principle in (67.2), it is assigned to a secondary object (the modern OBJ$_\theta$), rather than the direct object in (69a). In (69b), the theme is linked to the direct object because that is the lowest available GF, given that there are no further arguments to be accommodated.

This analysis fits the passivization facts perfectly. Based on RG's insights with respect to passivization (section 3.6), classic LFG assumes that passives are related to actives via a *lexical rule*. This rule demotes the SUBJ and promotes the original OBJ to the subject of the passive. As shown in section 5.7.5, the formulation of the passive changed with the introduction of a full-blown linking theory; however, for the discussion at hand, the classic formulation applies. For (69), LFG's analysis of the passive predicts that the theme could only surface as the subject of a passive in the transitive context. This is indeed the case, as is illustrated in (70): the *þess* 'this' can only be the subject of a passive in the transitive version, not in the ditransitive version. In the ditransitive version, it is the goal OBJ which undergoes passivization, and which surfaces as the passive subject (70c).

(70) a. þess   var óskað
       this.Gen was wished
       'This was wished.' (ZMT 1985:471)   Icelandic

   b. *þess   var óskað henni
       this.Gen was wished her.Dat
       'This was wished on her.' (ZMT 1985:471)   Icelandic

   c. Henni   var óskað þess
       her.Dat was wished this.Gen
       'On her was wished this.' (ZMT 1985:471)   Icelandic

As has already been discussed, ZMT's notion of inherent case came to be known as quirky case (see section 4.8). The term 'quirky' suggests a random lawlessness, but a close inspection of ZMT's original paper shows that inherent case assignment actually proceeds in a very regulated manner. The 'quirky' genitive or dative cases are always regularly associated with a given thematic role. Genitives regularly occur on themes (70) and datives mark goals as well as themes. There seem to be no instances of truly idiosyncratic case, rather case assignment seems to be principled and follows from lexical semantic factors. This view is confirmed by more recent work on Icelandic (Maling 2001, Svenonius 2002).

There are, of course, instances of truly exceptional or quirky case that cannot be explained on the basis of any generalizations; however, the famous Icelandic 'quirky' case does not seem to be an example of it. A truly idiosyncratic case pattern is presented in (71). The example comes from Urdu, which requires the agentive ergative case on subjects of transitive perfect verbs. The verb 'bring' in (71) is a transitive verb with perfect morphology and the bringer can be classified unproblematically as an agent. But the subject 'Nadya' is nominative and not ergative.

(71) nadya   kıtab   la-yi
     Nadya.F.Sg.Nom book.F.Sg.Nom bring-Perf.F.Sg
     'Nadya brought a book.'

The reasons for this aberrant case marking are not clear, but there is some speculation that it is due to a historical reanalysis of the verb for 'take' (*le*) in combination with the verb for 'come' (*a*) as the verb 'bring'. The verb for 'come' is unaccusative and therefore requires a nominative subject. It could be that this entirely regular requirement has carried over into this new context, where it is irregular. Whatever the reason, the verb 'bring' must stipulate that the subject is always nominative (the nominative on objects is regular in Urdu, see section 5.9).

(72) *la* 'bring' (↑PRED)='la< agent[−o] theme[−r] >'
                  (↑SUBJ CASE) = NOM

The lexical entry in (72) reflects a modern analysis of linking and case. The verb's argument structure is accessed via the f-structural PRED feature (cf. Alsina 1996). The thematic roles at a-structure are linked via the features [±o] and [±r] to grammatical relations (section 5.7.5). This linking can proceed regularly, but the stipulation about the subject's case marking ensures that default case association principles cannot apply.

5.7.4 The Introduction of Explicit Features

Today's standard Mapping Theory includes the use of the abstract linking features [±o] and [±r], briefly introduced above. Before moving on to a description of Mapping Theory, this section charts the development of these abstract features.

In classic LFG, grammatical functions were classified as either *semantically restricted* or *semantically unrestricted*, as shown in (73). This classification was based on data from control and complementation (Bresnan 1982a).

(73) **Semantically Unrestricted:** SUBJ, OBJ, OBJ2
     Semantically Restricted: OBL$_\theta$

Based on this classification, Levin (1987, 1988) postulated a [+unr(estricted)] feature, which she used for a cross-classification of thematic roles and grammatical functions in a manner that should be familiar from Kiparsky's and Wunderlich's work (note that Levin's investigations were carried out in part at Stanford, where Paul Kiparsky was developing his linking theory at around the same time). Levin formulated several *linking rules* for the assignment of grammatical functions to thematic roles, which made specific reference to the [+unr] feature. Representative linking rules are shown in (74), and an illustrative example is provided in (75).

(74) a. **The Agent Rule:** Assign SUBJ to agent.
      b. **The Goal Rule:** Assign OBL$_{goal}$ to goal.
      c. **The Passive Agent Rule:** Assign OBL$_{ag}$ or $\emptyset$ (the suppressed argument) to agent.
      d. **The Theme Rule:** Assign +unrestricted to theme.

(75) a. (↑PRED) = 'break < theme   >'
                              +unr.
                              SUBJ

      b. (↑PRED) = 'break < agent   theme >'
                             SUBJ   +unr.
                                     OBJ

The unrestricted theme in (75a) is in principle compatible with all of the unrestricted GFs in (73). However, the subject must be assigned to the theme because of the Subject Condition in (76) (originally due to Baker 1983). It has already been mentioned that this condition cannot hold for all languages, with German being a notable exception, but it does hold for English and a substantial number of other languages.

(76) **Subject Condition**
Every verbal predicate must have a SUBJ.

In (75b), the theme is again in principle compatible with all the unrestricted GFs; however, the SUBJ must be linked to the agent via the Agent Rule and because LFG, like other theories, assumes that there can be at most one GF of any type in a given clause, the SUBJ is out. The OBJ is linked to the theme because it is higher on the grammatical function hierarchy than the indirect object and is therefore preferred for linking.

5.7.5 Standard LFG Mapping Theory

LFG's *Lexical Mapping Theory* or *Mapping Theory* grew out of early work like ZMT's analysis of Icelandic and German and Levin's work on English. On the surface, the standard theory seems to differ substantially from the loosely formulated Association Principles of ZMT. However, the underlying spirit of the approach has not changed. Linking is primarily a relationship between thematic roles and grammatical functions, as formulated by Levin. This relationship can be mediated by information contributed by the case markers of a language. The lexical requirements of a predicate serve to block the universal default linking principles that would apply otherwise. This is similar to what is assumed in Kiparsky's and Wunderlich's linking theories. However, the pertinent information about case is not encoded in the same terms as that of grammatical functions or thematic roles: the feature space assumed for thematic roles and grammatical functions is kept separate from information about case. This is very much unlike Kiparsky's and Wunderlich's theories, which integrate case directly into the linking principles.

The discussion in this section is based on Bresnan and Zaenen (1990), Alsina and Mchombo (1993), Bresnan and Kanerva (1989) and Bresnan and Moshi (1990). Further reading and discussion can be found in Bresnan (1990, 1994). As in Levin's first formulation for linking, thematic roles and grammatical functions are cross-classified by features. Like in Kiparksy's linking theory, there are just two relevant features. One of these features follows directly from Levin's work: the feature [±restricted]. This is a semantically grounded feature, which indicates whether a given thematic role or grammatical function is sensitive to semantic restrictions.

The second feature is [±o(bjective)]. This feature is more difficult to justify. It marks whether thematic roles are likely to be linked to *objectlike* GFs. Alsina (1996:19) argues that the focus on objects is misguided because many crosslinguistic phenomena single out the subject in opposition to the other GFs. He therefore proposes two different features: [± subj(ect)] and [± obl(ique)]. However, this idea has found no resonance within LFG.

The [±r,±o] features classify GFs as shown in (77) and (78). Subjects and obliques are not objective functions, so they are [−o]. Subjects and objects tend not to be semantically restricted, so they are [−r]. The clausal COMP and XCOMP are not considered in this classification (see Berman 2003, Dalrymple and Lødrup 2000 on the status of clausal arguments).

(77)

$$
\begin{array}{ccc}
-r & \text{SUBJ} & -o \\
\text{OBJ} & & \text{OBL}_\theta \\
+o & \text{OBJ}_\theta & +r
\end{array}
$$

(78) **Features** **Grammatical Functions**
 [−o]   SUBJ, OBL
 [+o]   OBJ, OBJ$_\theta$
 [−r]   SUBJ, OBJ
 [+r]   OBJ$_\theta$, OBL$_\theta$

The thematic roles are classified by these same features, but there is not as exhaustive a classification as for the grammatical relations. Various papers have explored differing classifications, leading to the very general principles in (79) (Bresnan and Zaenen 1990).

(79) **Classification of Thematic Roles**
 Patientlike roles: [−r]
 Secondary patientlike roles: [+o]
 All others: [−o]

The general nature of the principles allows for some flexibility in classifying individual thematic roles. This flexibility is necessary for a crosslinguistic account of linking. Some examples of standard classifications and the possible linking spaces that they license are shown in (80) (Bresnan and Kanerva 1989, Bresnan and Moshi 1990). For example, an agent argument classified as [−o] can only be linked to subjects and obliques, a theme or patient argument classified as [−r] can only be linked to subjects or objects.

(80)   ag   th/pt   loc
      [−o]   [−r]   [−o]
       | | |
     SUBJ/OBL SUBJ/OBJ SUBJ/OBL   Possible Linkings

The possible correspondences between thematic roles and grammatical functions are regulated by *Mapping Principles*, shown in (81), and wellformedness conditions, some of which are shown in (82) (Bresnan and Zaenen 1990). The θ stands for thematic role and the $\hat{\theta}$ refers to the highest argument on the thematic role hierarchy.

(81) **Mapping Principles**
   a. Subject roles:
      (i) $\hat{\theta}$ is mapped onto SUBJ; otherwise:
            $[-o]$
      (ii) θ is mapped onto SUBJ
            $[-r]$
   b. Other roles are mapped onto the lowest compatible function on the markedness hierarchy, where the subject is the least marked.
      SUBJ < OBJ, OBL$_\theta$ < OBJ$_\theta$

(82) **Wellformedness Conditions**
   a. *Subject Condition:* Every (verbal) lexical form must have a subject.
   b. *Function-argument biuniqueness:* Each a-structure role must be associated with a unique grammatical function, and conversely.

The Function-argument biuniqueness condition in (82b) is reminiscent of GB's θ-Criterion. It has been challenged within LFG (Mohanan 1994, Alsina 1996) for not allowing the necessary flexibility to account for instances of *Argument Fusion* in complex predicates such as causatives (section 5.7.6).

The feature classifications together with the mapping and wellformedness principles constitute the essence of LFG's linking theory. Note that no direct reference is made to case as part of the core linking theory. This contrasts with Kiparsky's and Wunderlich's approaches. In LFG, case marking is assumed to interact with both thematic role information and grammatical functions (Alsina 1996; section 5.9). There are default case assignments such as the nominative on subjects, the accusative on objects and the dative on indirect objects. Deviating patterns can follow from either lexical stipulation, or from language particular case association rules (cf. the Icelandic and Urdu examples in section 5.7.3). For the most part, case marking is considered to follow from a generalizable interaction of structural and semantic factors. However, there is nothing inherently encoded in the formalism which would prevent an LFG researcher from adopting a Kiparsky style approach to linking theory.

This section closes with the usual basic examples, namely, a transitive, a passive, an unaccusative and an unergative (taken from Bresnan and Zaenen 1990). In (83), the transitive verb *pound* has two arguments, an agent and a patient/theme. These are featurally classified according to (79) and then mapped to SUBJ and OBJ straightforwardly according to the mapping principles.

(83) a-structure: *pound* < agent theme >
                         [−o]   [−r]
                          | |
     f-structure: SUBJ   OBJ

Passivization is assumed to suppress the highest thematic role, as shown in (84). This thematic role is no longer available for linking and can optionally be realized as an adjunct. The only argument available for linking into the syntax is the theme. This could potentially be linked either to a subject or an object, but because of the principle in (81), it is linked to the subject.

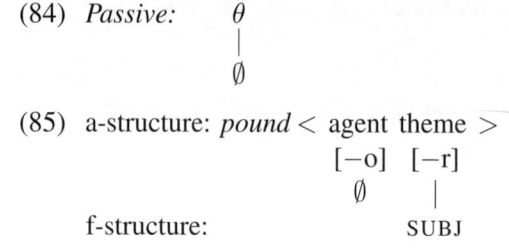

(84) *Passive:* $\hat{\theta}$
                   |
                   ∅

(85) a-structure: *pound* < agent theme >
                         [−o]   [−r]
                          ∅ |
     f-structure: SUBJ

The single argument of unaccusatives is a theme, as in (86). This is classified by the feature [−r] and is linked to a subject rather than an object because of the mapping principles in (81). The unaccusative situation is thus exactly parallel to the passive in (85). The analysis of passives and unaccusatives essentially follows the insights formulated by RG, and is parallel to the GB/MP analysis in many respects. One major difference between the GB/MP approach and this one, however, is that LFG allows for the mapping between thematic roles and grammatical functions to vary (e.g., section 5.7.6 on argument alternations). This possibility is not part of the architectural design of GB/MP because arguments are represented structurally in the same way as grammatical relations: the possibility of a mismatch, or of a variable *linking space* between thematic arguments and grammatical relations, is therefore precluded.

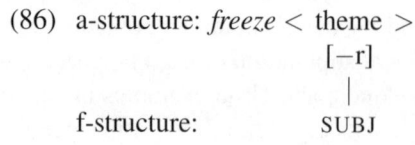

(86) a-structure: *freeze* < theme >
                            [−r]
                             |
     f-structure: SUBJ

The unergative analysis in (87) also works quite straightforwardly. The only argument of an unergative verb like *bark* is an agent. This is classified as a [−o] thematic role and links to a subject.

(87) a-structure: *bark* < agent >
                          [−o]
                           |
     f-structure: SUBJ

Unergatives and unaccusatives are thus analysed differently within LFG's linking theory. This is again broadly akin to GB/MP, but is very different from the analysis in Kiparsky's and Wunderlich's approaches, where unergatives and unaccusatives are not differentiated in terms of feature classification or linking. The case marking facts discussed in section 5.6, by which some languages differentiate between unergatives and unaccusatives via case marking (e.g., Urdu, where unergative subjects are ergative and unaccusative subjects are nominative) can be accounted for straightforwardly under LFG's analysis if case marking is assumed to be sensitive to thematic role information, as was proposed by ZMT for Icelandic. The ergative case can thus be correlated with agents (or the feature [−o] if one would like to avoid reference to thematic role names) and the nominative can be correlated with themes (or the feature [−r]).

5.7.6 Argument Alternations

One reason linking theories have resisted a one-to-one mapping from a-structure to grammatical relations in the syntax is the crosslinguistic recurrence of argument alternations. One very famous alternation investigated within LFG is *locative inversion* in Chicheŵa, shown in (88) (Bresnan and Kanerva 1989, Bresnan 1994).

(88) a. a-lendô-wo   a-na-bwér-á   ku-mu-dzi
   2-visitor-2 those 2 SB-REC PST-come-IND 17-3-village
   'Those visitors came to the village.'   Chicheŵa
   (visitors=subject)

   b. ku-mu-dzi   ku-na-bwér-á   a-lendô-wo
   17-3-village 17 SB-REC PST-come-IND 2-visitor-2 those
   'To the village came those visitors.'   Chicheŵa
   (village=subject)

Chicheŵa is a Bantu language, which does not mark arguments via case, but instead uses a complex noun class system. The noun classes have a rough semantic/cognitive basis, but this is only rough, so the different classes are usually indicated by numbers, e.g., 2 for visitors and 17 for village in (88).

Bresnan and Kanerva (1989) amass definitive evidence which shows that 'visitors' is the subject in (88a), but not in (88b). In (88b) the subject is 'village'. One piece of evidence for subject status is verb agreement: in (88a) the verb agrees with 'visitors' via the class 2 marker, in (88b), the verb agrees with 'village' via the class 17 marker. Locative inversion is triggered by focus, so that the location ('village') is focused in (88b).

The possibility for locative inversion follows very elegantly from the standard linking principles. The thematic roles are classified as shown in (89) via the general classification principles in (79). Both the theme and the locative could link to either SUBJ or OBL. In (89a) default linking occurs according to the mapping principles in (81): the theme is linked to the subject because it is higher on the thematic role hierarchy than the locative.

In (88b), the locative argument is linked to the subject due to the special focus context. In this context, locatives are associated with the [−r] feature, which means they can only be linked to a subject, thus preempting the theme. Since there cannot be two subjects in a clause, the theme is linked to the other compatible GF, the OBJ.

(89) a. a-structure: *come* < theme loc >
        [−r] [−o]
         | |
      f-structure: SUBJ OBL

   b. a-structure: *come* < theme loc >
        [−r] [−o]
              [−r]
         | |
      f-structure: OBJ SUBJ

Another instance of an argument alternation that follows elegantly from LFG's linking theory is provided by crosslinguistic patterns of causative formation.[8] In causatives, an event is caused by the action of a causer. In the Chicheŵa examples in (90) (Alsina and Joshi 1991, Alsina 1997), there is a cooking event which is caused or instigated by a causer external to the actual cooking event. There are three syntactic arguments in (90): a causer/agent (the porcupine); another agent (the owl), who is also the *causee*, i.e., the person/thing who is at the receiving end of the causing action; a theme/patient of the caused event (the pumpkins). Causativization in many languages is signalled by an explicit *causative morpheme*. In Chicheŵa, like in many languages, the causative morpheme is attached to the event that is caused ('cook').

(90) a. Nŭngu   i-na-phík-ítsa   kadzīdzi maûngu
       porcupine SUBJ-PAST-cook-CAUS owl   pumpkins
       'The porcupine made the owl cook the pumpkins.   Chicheŵa

   b. Nŭngu   i-na-phík-ítsa   maûngu kwá kádzīdzi
       porcupine SUBJ-PAST-cook-CAUS pumpkins by owl
       'The porcupine had the pumpkins cooked by the owl.   Chicheŵa

Causatives also show an argument alternation. As can be seen in (90) and in the French and Urdu examples in (91) and (92), respectively, the causee alter-

---

[8]For reasons of space, I do not include a discussion of the English dative alternation. One possible analysis is parallel to Jackendoff's approach (section 5.3). This analysis is based on the idea that the goal *to* argument in *Kim gave a bone to the dog* is a location, whereas in *Kim gave the dog a bone*, the goal is a recipient, i.e., more of a secondary patientlike object (in Jackendoff's analysis the goal in this situation is also represented on the Action Tier and is therefore a patient, i.e, an affected entity, see section 5.3). From here on the linking principles apply straightforwardly.

nates between a direct argument of the clause, or an oblique PP (Chicheŵa and French) and an instrumental (Urdu). Chicheŵa does not have case marking, but like in English, the direct object appears immediately adjacent to the verb. In (90a) the causee is the direct object, in (90b) the causee is an oblique PP.

(91) a. Jean a   fait   manger les gâteaux aux   enfants.
        Jean has made eat   the cakes   to the children
        'Jean made the children eat the cakes.' (Alsina 1996)   French

   b. Jean a   fait   manger les gâteaux par les enfants.
        Jean has made eat   the cakes   by the children
        'Jean had the cakes eaten by the children.' (Alsina 1996)   French

(92) a. anjʊm=ne   saddaf=ko   masala   cakʰ-va-ya
        Anjum.F=Erg Saddaf.F=Acc spice.M.Nom taste-Caus-Perf.M.Sg
        'Anjum had Saddaf taste the seasoning.'   Urdu

   b. anjʊm=ne   saddaf=se   masala   cakʰ-va-ya
        Anjum.F=Erg Saddaf.F=Inst spice.M.Nom taste-Caus-Perf.M.Sg
        'Anjum had the seasoning tasted by Saddaf.'   Urdu

Urdu is a language with fairly rich case marking and with few positional constraints, unlike English, French and Chicheŵa. The same type of causative alternation can nevertheless be observed (Butt 1998, Saksena 1980). The argument alternation coincides with a semantic difference. When the causee is realized as a direct argument, it must be interpreted as *affected* by the action. That is, in (90a) the focus is on the owl having to cook the pumpkins and how good or bad it might feel about that. In (90b), on the other hand, the focus is on the pumpkins and that they be cooked. It is not important who cooks them, or how they might feel about it, just that they become cooked.

This semantic difference holds for Urdu (Butt 1998) and Romance (Alsina 1996) as well. It is related to the affectedness issue with the dative alternation where the goal in *Kim gave the dog a bone* is considered to be a patient and therefore in a sense more affected by the action than in *Kim gave a bone to the dog* (cf. the discussion of affectedness in section 5.3).

Alsina and Joshi (1991) model this semantic difference via a difference in *Argument Fusion*. They examine causatives in Chicheŵa and Marathi (a South Asian language related to Urdu/Hindi), and propose an analysis by which two separate argument structures are combined and one of the arguments of each argument structure is identified with an argument in the other one. Causative morphemes or the French causative verb *faire* 'make' (91) are taken to have three arguments: a causer agent, a patient and a caused event. This is shown in (93). When a causative morpheme or verb is combined with another verb, it embeds this verb's argument structure in its own, as shown in (94).

(93) CAUSE < agent patient event >

(94) CAUSE < agent patient 'cook' < agent patient > >

There are four semantic arguments in (94). However, as is evident from the examples above, only three arguments are expressed in the syntax. The idea is that two of these arguments *fuse* at argument structure before being mapped into the syntax. After argument fusion there are only three arguments left to be linked. Alsina and Joshi (1991) posit parameters on Argument Fusion. The parameters allow fusion of the matrix patient argument with *either* the embedded agent or the embedded patient.

When the causee (the matrix patient) is fused with the embedded agent, the embedded agent is no longer available for linking, as shown in (95a). In this case the causee is considered to be the affected argument of the causation and is mapped to the direct object. The embedded patient is mapped to a secondary object (90a). When the matrix patient is fused with the embedded patient, then this argument is no longer available for linking and the agent of the embedded predicate is linked to an oblique (90b). In this case, the embedded patient (the pumpkins) is considered to be the object affected by the caused action, and not the embedded agent (the owl).

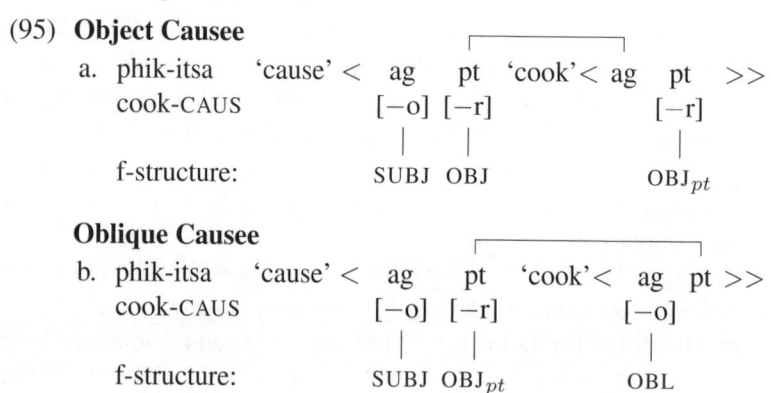

(95) **Object Causee**

    a. phik-itsa   'cause' <   ag   pt   'cook' < ag   pt >>
        cook-CAUS   [−o] [−r]   [−r]

        f-structure: SUBJ OBJ   OBJ$_{pt}$

Oblique Causee

    b. phik-itsa   'cause' <   ag   pt   'cook' < ag   pt >>
        cook-CAUS   [−o] [−r]   [−o]

        f-structure: SUBJ OBJ$_{pt}$ OBL

Alsina (1996, 1997) formulates a case assignment condition for Romance, which ensures that the dative is assigned to the higher object, the causee (children) in the context of (95a). For French this would be the *aux* in (91a). For Urdu, Butt (1998) proposes to instead make use of the [+r] feature to denote affectedness. That is, semantic affectedness is flagged by the feature which indicates that a semantic restriction is playing a role. In (95a), the causee (Saddaf) would be considered to be semantically affected and would therefore map to an OBJ$_\theta$, which is correlated with the accusative *ko*. In (95b), the embedded patient would be flagged as semantically affected via the [+r] classification. This leaves the causee to be realized as an OBL agent, which is correlated with the instrumental case in Urdu.

LFG's linking theory is thus primarily concerned with the relationship between argument structure and grammatical relations (f-structure). Case marking can enter the linking process directly (e.g., ZMT's approach to Icelandic in section 5.7.3; also see section 5.9), but case marking can also be regulated via assignment principles, both default and special, after linking has taken place. This is what is assumed in Alsina's (1996) treatment of Romance, for example.

A final point with respect to causatives and linking theories in general relates to the domain of linking. As the name already indicates, Lexical Mapping Theory assumed that the linking from thematic roles to grammatical functions was based on a single lexical entry, i.e., was taken care of entirely within the *lexical component*. However, the causatives show that argument alternations and complex argument structures can arise either in the lexicon, or in the syntax (see Alsina 1997 for an explicit comparison between Bantu and Romance). In Urdu and Chicheŵa causativization is accomplished via a causative morpheme. In French, however, the same causative is signalled via the verb *faire* 'make'. Alsina (1996) and Butt (1995) showed that the architecture underlying LFG's linking theory needed to be extended in order to be able to account for argument linking where the arguments are contributed by two distinct words in the syntax. That is, the basic principles of linking theory as presented in the last two sections continue to apply, but are allowed to operate on argument structures put together in the syntax. The analyses assume a complex interaction between c-structure, a-structure and f-structure, where one structure cannot be built up without information present at another structure. The argument structure is thus not primary, nor is the c-structure. There is no derivation from one level of representation to another one, as in the GB/MP tradition. To put it in another way, each of the levels of representation *constrain* one another within LFG's projection architecture.

To conclude the discussion of standard linking theory, the theory can account for a very wide range of crosslinguistic data, including argument alternations with reference to just two abstract features. Case marking can enter the linking process directly, or it can be regulated via assignment principles, both default and special, after linking has taken place. The next two sections introduce some further developments with respect to linking and case. These developments have not been integrated into standard linking theory; however, they have become part of the standard body of knowledge within LFG and are therefore discussed here.

5.7.7 Incorporation of Proto-Roles

Zaenen (1993) conducts a detailed study of the interaction between syntax and verbal lexical semantics in Dutch. As mentioned previously, auxiliary selection is one syntactic reflex of unaccusativity. Unaccusative verbs in Dutch select for *zijn* 'be' while unergatives select for *hebben* 'have'. Zaenen's study goes beyond intransitive verbs in showing that there are more general factors at play, which allow an explanation of auxiliary selection in some transitive constructions as well. One example comes from psych verbs. As shown in (96), the psych verbs 'please' and 'irritate' select for the 'be' and 'have' auxiliaries, respectively.

(96) a. Dat is me jarenlang goed bevallen. (with *zijn* 'be')
that is me yearlong good pleased
'That has pleased me well for years.'   Dutch
b. Dat heeft me jarenlang geirriteerd. (with *hebben* 'have')
that has   me yearlong irritated
'He has irritated me for years.'   Dutch

Zaenen shows that semantic factors are at the root of the auxiliary selection patterns. The 'have' auxiliary is associated with control over an action, whereas the 'be' auxiliary is selected when an argument is affected or changed (change of state). In this latter case, the relevant aspectual notion is *telicity*. An action is considered *telic* when the action is *completed* and when the relevant argument has undergone a change of state (i.e., when a cake has been baked, or an apple has been eaten). Recall from section 5.4 that Dowty's Proto-Role entailments include the notion of control (Proto-Agent property) and incremental theme and change of state (Proto-Patient properties). These latter two properties give rise to telicity effects and can therefore be analysed as triggering the selection of the 'be' auxiliary.

Zaenen incorporates Dowty's Proto-Role entailments into linking theory as shown in (97). The Proto-Agent and Proto-Patient properties are determined as discussed by Dowty (1991). If an argument has more patient than agent properties, it is classified as a [−r] thematic role. Conversely, if an argument has more agent than patient properties, it is classified as a [−o].

(97) **Association of Features with Participants** (Zaenen 1993:150,152)
1. If a participant has more patient properties than agent properties, it is marked −r.
2. If a participant has more agent properties than patient properties it is marked −o.
3. If a participant has an equal number of properties, it is marked −r.
4. If a participant has neither agent nor patient properties, it is marked −o.

A quick check with the formulations in section 5.7.5 show that this is entirely in keeping with the spirit of standard linking theory. However, the incorporation of Proto-Role information allows Zaenen to dispense with thematic roles and the thematic role hierarchy. Given the general dissatisfaction of the linguistic community with the status of thematic roles (section 5.4), this represents an improvement over the standard theory. Linking is instead accomplished via the default association of [±o,r] marked arguments with the grammatical function hierarchy, as shown in (98).

(98) **Association of Features with GFs** (Zaenen 1993:151)
Order the participants as follows according to their intrinsic markings:
$-o < -r < +o < +r$
order the GR [grammatical functions] as follows:
SUBJ < OBJ < OBJ$_\theta$ (< OBL)
Starting from the left, associate the leftmost participant with the leftmost GR it is compatible with.

Unaccusatives can now be analysed as follows: The single argument of unaccusatives such as 'fall' has more patient properties than agent properties, is thus classified as a [−r] role, and is therefore linked to the SUBJ grammatical function. In contrast, the single argument of an unergative such as 'dance' has more agent properties than patient properties, and is therefore classified as a [−o] role and is also linked to SUBJ. The difference in auxiliary selection is taken to be sensitive to the [−r] feature, as shown in (99). If the single argument is [−r], as is the case for unaccusatives, then the right auxiliary is 'be', otherwise the 'have' auxiliary must be selected.

(99) **Auxiliary Selection** (Zaenen 1993:149)
When an −r marked participant is realized as a subject, the auxiliary is *zijn* 'be'.

This more general analysis of unaccusatives in terms of Proto-Role properties extends to the psych verb pattern in (96). The verbs 'please' and 'irritate' both have two arguments. However, only in the 'irritate' case does the first argument ('that') have Proto-Agent properties and can thus be classified with a [−o]. In contrast, the first argument of 'please' has no Proto-Agent properties and ends up classified as a [−r] argument. This leads to its realization as a SUBJ, which in turn triggers the Auxiliary Selection Principle in (99). The example with 'please' thus contains a 'be' auxiliary, while the example with 'irritate', whose SUBJ is a [−o] argument, does not.

Zaenen's linking architecture remains true to the basic spirit of linking theory, but allows a better integration of relevant semantic factors. Her approach dispenses with extra levels of analysis, rather than relying on more (cf. Jackendoff's Action Tier in section 5.3, for example).

Kelling (2001, 2003) adopts Zaenen's architecture for an analysis of argument linking in French nominalizing suffixes and French psych verbs, respectively. Other approaches which have integrated Proto-Role properties into an analysis of the relationship between argument structure and grammatical functions are Alsina (1996), Ackerman (1992) and Ackerman and Moore (2001). In his treatment of Romance causatives, Alsina revises LFG's standard linking theory considerably. Ackerman's (1992) ideas are similar in spirit to Zaenen's analysis, but he offers a slightly different way of integrating Proto-Roles for a treatment of the locative alternation. Finally, Ackerman and Moore (2001) incorporate Proto-Role properties into the selection of arguments without making explicit reference to LFG's standard linking theory, though they assume their ideas are compatible with it.

This concludes the discussion of standard concepts within LFG and the role of linking theory. The next two sections expand the discussion of case within LFG to include perspectives on case which have not been encountered so far in this book. This includes a look at non-configurational languages (section 5.8) and a complex interaction between case marking, grammatical functions and thematic roles (section 5.9). The last section in particular brings together the three guiding themes of this book (case, thematic relations and grammatical relations) and serves to conclude this chapter.

5.8 Case Stacking

The previous section presented an analysis of unaccusativity in Dutch. Even though Dutch is a language with no case marking, unaccusative verbs are relevant within the larger context of this book. This section turns to some Australian languages, whose exuberant use of case marking more than compensates for languages such as Dutch or English.

Nordlinger (1998, 2000) takes on the phenomenon of *case stacking* that was briefly described in chapter 1. The example there was from the Australian language Kayardild. The example from Martuthunira in (100) is similar, but simpler. The word 'pouch' is marked with three cases: one to show that it is signalling a location, one to show that it is part of a possessive or accompanying relation to another word (the proprietive case), and one to show that it is part of (modifying) an accusative case marked noun. The word 'joey' (a baby euro — a euro is a type of kangaroo) has two cases. The proprietive shows that it stands in an accompanying relationship with another (it is with the euro), and the accusative to show that it is part of (modifying) an accusative case marked noun. Finally, the 'euro' is accusative as the direct object of the clause, while the 'I' is nominative (unmarked).

(100) Ngayu nhawu-lha ngurnu   tharnta-a mirtily-marta-a
      I   saw-Past   that.Acc euro-Acc joey-Prop-Acc
      thara-ngka-marta-a.
      pouch-Loc-Prop-Acc
      'I saw the euro with a joey in (its) pouch.'   Martuthunira
      (Dench 1995:60)

The f-structure analysis in (101) shows that the case markers indicate which functional layers of analysis the case marked word is embedded in. That is, the three case markers on 'pouch' signal that it is a locative adjunct embedded under a proprietive adjunct that in turn modifies an accusative direct object. It is well known that the order of the stacked case markers obeys an *iconicity principle* (Dench and Evans 1988). That is, the order of the case markers is directly reflective of (or iconic to) the level of embedding in the clause.

Case stacking is a completely unexpected phenomenon from the perspective of theories based on the Latin, Greek or Sanskrit paradigms. In these languages, and all of the languages surveyed so far as part of the book, a noun phrase carries only one case marker as a unique identifier of its role in the clause. Indeed, for a theory which assumes a clausal 'blueprint' as in the GB/MP tradition, the Australian case stacking data is disturbing. Recall from chapter 4, that case morphology is considered a mere surface ('spell out') manifestation of a bundle of syntactic features (e.g., Chomsky 1995). Case stacking is surprising from this perspective, because embedding relationships within the clause are assumed to follow from syntactic structure and thus do not necessarily have to be spelled out in terms of morphological case.

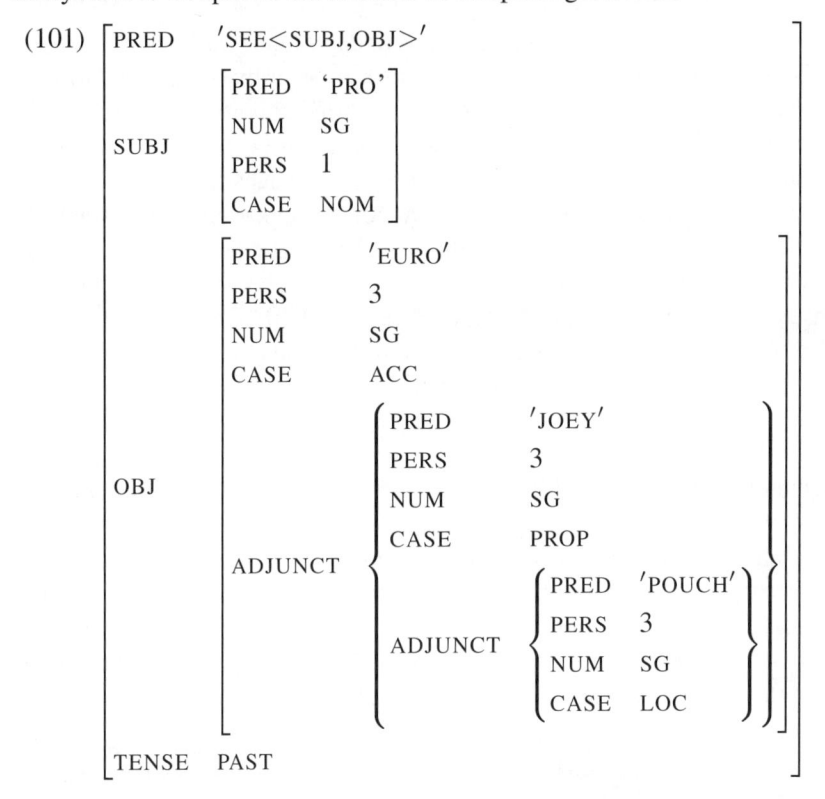

(101)
$$\begin{bmatrix} \text{PRED} & \text{'SEE}<\text{SUBJ},\text{OBJ}>\text{'} \\ \text{SUBJ} & \begin{bmatrix} \text{PRED} & \text{'PRO'} \\ \text{NUM} & \text{SG} \\ \text{PERS} & 1 \\ \text{CASE} & \text{NOM} \end{bmatrix} \\ \text{OBJ} & \begin{bmatrix} \text{PRED} & \text{'EURO'} \\ \text{PERS} & 3 \\ \text{NUM} & \text{SG} \\ \text{CASE} & \text{ACC} \\ \text{ADJUNCT} & \left\{ \begin{matrix} \text{PRED} & \text{'JOEY'} \\ \text{PERS} & 3 \\ \text{NUM} & \text{SG} \\ \text{CASE} & \text{PROP} \\ \text{ADJUNCT} & \left\{ \begin{matrix} \text{PRED} & \text{'POUCH'} \\ \text{PERS} & 3 \\ \text{NUM} & \text{SG} \\ \text{CASE} & \text{LOC} \end{matrix} \right\} \end{matrix} \right\} \end{bmatrix} \\ \text{TENSE} & \text{PAST} \end{bmatrix}$$

Besides case, another property relevant for argument linking is word order (cf. Kiparsky's idea from section 5.5 that there are three linkers: case, agreement and word order). Australian languages are well known for allowing extremely free word order.[9] The most famous case is Warlpiri (Hale 1983), but the Wambaya sentence from Nordlinger (1998:96) in (102) also illustrates the pertinent facts. Wambaya, like Warlpiri, allows for *discontinuous constituents*. In (102) the 'big' at the end of the clause modifies the 'dog' at the beginning of the clause. The way one can tell that these two pieces of the clause belong together is by the case marking: both are marked with the agentive ergative case. Note that the case marking and word order facts do not actually provide clues about whether the 'big' modifies the 'dog' or vice versa (see Simpson 1991 for a detailed discussion of these constructions in Warlpiri). However, it would be pragmatically odd for 'dog' to be the adjunct and 'big' the head (i.e., English 'dog big'), so the only reasonable interpretation of (102) is one which corresponds to 'big dog' in English.

(102) galalarrinyi-ni gini-ng-a dawu bugayini-ni
 dog.I-ERG 3SG.MASC.A-1.O-NFUT bite big.I-ERG
 'The big dog bit me.' Wambaya

The only word order requirement in Wambaya (and Warlpiri) is that the finite element, mostly an auxiliary, as in (102), be in the second position.[10] Otherwise, the elements of the clause may be ordered quite freely (subject to discoursal constraints). Australian languages have thus been referred to as *nonconfigurational*, as opposed to *configurational* languages like English. Non-configurational languages pose a problem for an approach like GB/MP, in which heads, complements and specifiers all have their preordained position and NPs and verbs move only for specific reasons such as having their case or tense and agreement features checked (section 4.10). The Australian facts are therefore interesting, and have given rise to quite some discussion (e.g., see Speas 1990 for a proposal of how Warlpiri can be thought of as configurational).

The free word order facts together with case stacking prompted Nordlinger (1998) to formulate quite a different perspective on the role of case. She sees morphology as playing a large role in *constructing* the syntax of the clause, rather than being a mere spell out of an underlying abstract representation. In the Wambaya sentence in (102), she views the ergative *ni* as carrying the following pieces of syntactic information: i) that there be a subject; ii) that it be ergative. These pieces of information are encoded as part of the lexical entry of the ergative, as shown in (103a). Similarly, the abstract entries for the

---

[9]This is an overgeneralization, as not all Australian languages function alike. There are major differences between languages and language families, none of which can be addressed in the space of this book. See Nordlinger (1998) for an overview and references to the pertinent literature.

[10]More familiar Indo-European languages such as Latin or the Slavic language family also allow the separation of a modifier from its head. However, the constraints on what can be separated and when are nowhere near as free as in Australian languages.

accusative, proprietive and locative in Martuthunira specify the grammatical function they indicate, as well as the case feature, as shown in (103b–d).

Note the special use of the ↑ in the lexical entries of the case markers. The specification of the case feature is standard: each case marker specifies that the attribute CASE is assigned a certain value (ergative, accusative, etc.). This ensures that whatever constituent carries the case marker will be analysed as ergative, or accusative, or locative, etc. The second line in each entry involves *inside-out functional designation* (Dalrymple 1993, 2001). The ↑ following the specification of a grammatical function formulates a requirement that, come what may, the constituent should be analysed as a subject in (103a), an object in (103b), and an adjunct in (103c–d).

(103) a. ERG: (↑CASE) = ERG
                          (SUBJ ↑)

      b. ACC: (↑CASE) = ACC
                          (OBJ ↑)

      c. LOC: (↑CASE) = LOC
                          (ADJUNCT ↑)

      b. PROPRIETIVE: (↑CASE) = PROP
                          (ADJUNCT ↑)

The case markers themselves thus specify quite a lot of information. Besides contributing a value for the case feature at f-structure, they also impose a well-formedness requirement on the analysis. The analysis can only be wellformed if any constituent marked by the ergative, for example, is analysed as part of the subject at f-structure.

The strong and active role ascribed to case morphology by Nordlinger allows an elegant treatment of discontinuous constituents as in the Wambaya example in (102), as well as an interesting wrinkle in Australian syntax. In Wambaya (and Warlpiri), it is next to impossible to distinguish between adjectives and nouns. Thus, the 'big' in (102) could very well have been analysed as the head noun of the subject, if there were no other suitable candidate available (e.g., Simpson 1991). Nordlinger therefore proposes that each word be specified for either constituting the head of the phrase, or for modifying another word as an adjunct.[11] Given this optionality, the problem of discontinuous constituents as in (102) is rendered unproblematic within LFG's unification based formalism.

Without going through the mechanics in detail, the effect of the analysis is this: the combination of information from the lexical entries of 'big', 'dog' and the ergative case in (103) results in the two partial f-structures shown in (104)

---

[11] This is accomplished by means of the *Principle of Morphological Composition* introduced by Nordlinger (1998).

and (105). Both the ergative 'dog' and the 'big' specify that they are parts of the subject. The 'dog' serves as the head of the phrase and the 'big' as an adjunct which modifies it.

(104) $\left[\text{SUBJ} \begin{bmatrix} \text{PRED} & \text{'DOG'} \\ \text{CASE} & \text{ERG} \end{bmatrix} \right]$

(105) $\left[\text{SUBJ} \begin{bmatrix} \text{CASE} & \text{ERG} \\ \text{ADJUNCT} & [\text{PRED} \quad \text{'BIG'}] \end{bmatrix} \right]$

These two sets of information are unified into the structure shown in (106) as a routine part of the clausal analysis within the LFG formalism. The problem of discontinuous constituents is solved by using the case morphology as a primary source of information about clausal structure. Again, this contrasts with a view which sees morphology as an uninteresting reflex of underlying structural relationships.

(106) $\left[\text{SUBJ} \begin{bmatrix} \text{CASE} & \text{ERG} \\ \text{PRED} & \text{'DOG'} \\ \text{ADJUNCT} & [\text{PRED} \quad \text{'BIG'}] \end{bmatrix} \right]$

In sum, Nordlinger's approach places prime importance on the actual case markers. The only other approaches seen so far which have incorporated case directly into syntactic analyses are the linking theories developed by Kiparsky and Wunderlich. In Kiparsky's approach, case, thematic roles and grammatical relations all interacted. In Wunderlich's approach, thematic relations and case, but not grammatical relations, were seen to interact. In Nordlinger's approach, case and grammatical relations interact directly; however, the status of argument structure and thematic roles is not clear. Although Nordlinger's analysis is consonant with LFG's linking theory, it is not discussed as part of her treatment of case.

The next section introduces a model of case within LFG that assumes an interaction between all the factors investigated as part of this book: argument structure, grammatical relations, overt case marking and syntactic position.

5.9 An Interactive Model of Case

Urdu exhibits alternations in which the only difference between two clauses is the case morphology on one of the noun phrases. This morphological difference signals a difference in semantic interpretation. Some examples are shown in (107) and (108). In (107a), the ergative subject indicates that the participant ('Nadya') has some control over the action, whereas the dative case in (107b) implies more of an obligation to perform the action (see Bashir 1999 for a more differentiated analysis). This is an example of case marking involving a *subject alternation*, or *differential subject marking* as it has come to be called in the Optimality Theoretic literature (section 8.2).

(107) a. nadya=ne   zu   ja-na   hɛ
Nadya.F.Sg=Erg zoo.M.Sg.Obl go-Inf.M.Sg be.Pres.3.Sg
'Nadya wants to go to the zoo.'   Urdu

b. nadya=ko   zu   ja-na   hɛ
Nadya.F.Sg=Dat zoo.M.Sg.Obl go-Inf.M.Sg be.Pres.3.Sg
'Nadya has to go to the zoo.'   Urdu

Example (108) involves an *object alternation*, or *differential object marking* in Optimality Theoretic terms. Here the only difference between the two sentences is the case marker on the object in (108b). In addition to marking dative case, as in (107b), the *ko* also functions as a marker of specificity/definiteness on direct objects in Urdu. Because it appears only on direct objects in this semantic context, and because it is not retained under passivization, this case marker can be analysed as an accusative.[12] The effect of *ko* in (108b) is that Nadya must be interpreted as having a particular giraffe in mind that she wants to go to see. In (108a), in contrast, it could be some generic giraffe or giraffes that Nadya would like to see (at the zoo, for example). The 'giraffe' in (108a) is glossed as nominative. This case has no overt morphophonological realization in Urdu, something which is crosslinguistically quite common.

(108) a. nadya=ne   jiraf   dekʰ-na   hɛ
Nadya.F.Sg=Erg giraffe.M.Sg.Nom see-Inf.M.Sg be.Pres.3.Sg
'Nadya wants to see a giraffe/giraffes.'   Urdu

b. nadya=ne   jiraf=ko   dekʰ-na   hɛ
Nadya.F.Sg=Erg giraffe.M.Sg=Acc see-Inf.M.Sg be.Pres.3.Sg
'Nadya wants to see the giraffe.'   Urdu

Parallels to this alternation between nominative and accusative can be found in Turkish (Enç 1991) and other South Asian languages. In this example, as in (107), the only difference between the a and b versions is the case marking. This, and the clear connection to a semantic difference prompted Butt and King (1991) to begin formulating an approach to case that included a notion of *semantic case*. This term has generally been used to refer to the case marking of adjuncts such as locatives or temporal expressions (e.g., see Zaenen, Maling and Thráinsson 1985). Butt and King used this term to apply to those case markers of core arguments which also contribute information that is relevant

---

[12] This analysis is not shared across all researchers. Mahajan (1990) and Davison (1999, 2000), for example, consistently gloss the *ko* only as a dative.

for the final semantic interpretation of the clause.[13] In order to allow the semantic information contributed by the case markers to flow directly into the analysis of the clause, Butt and King (1991) proposed explicit lexical entries for case markers. An example taken from later work (Butt and King 2003), is shown in (109) for the use of accusative *ko* in (108b).

(109) ko (↑ CASE) = ACC
  (OBJ ↑)
  (↑$_{sem-str}$ SPECIFICITY) = +

Butt and King's (1991) proposals for semantic case foreshadowed Nordlinger's ideas about *constructive case* (section 5.8) in that the case markers themselves are considered to be active components which contribute to the analysis of a clause. The lexical entry for the accusative use of *ko* states that: i) the case is accusative; ii) the relevant NP should be a direct object; iii) the NP should be interpreted as specific at the level of s(emantic)-structure.

Based on data mainly from Urdu, Georgian and Russian, Butt and King went on to develop their initial ideas on case in separate and joint work (Butt 1995, Butt 1998, King 1995, Butt and King 2002, 2003). Butt and King (2002) provides a comprehensive account of case in Urdu from both a diachronic and a synchronic perspective, Butt and King (2003) focuses on both Urdu and Georgian and represents the most recent formulation of the theoretical analysis.

The next few sections briefly present the essential points of the theory. Butt and King (2003) assume a version of linking theory (section 5.9.1), and postulate the existence of differing kinds of case: structural or default case (section 5.9.2), semantic case (section 5.9.4), and quirky case (section 5.9.3). The analysis makes full use of LFG's projection architecture, including the semantic projection, as seen in (109), and the argument projection (a-structure).

5.9.1 Linking

Butt and King (2003) assume the version of linking theory proposed in Butt (1998). In particular, this includes a treatment of the causative alternation discussed in section 5.7.6 and the existence of dative subjects as in (107b). In this version of linking theory, no explicit thematic hierarchy is assumed and the thematic roles are restricted to a very basic set: *agent, goal, theme, locative*. Beneficiaries, recipients, experiencers, etc. are all assumed to be an instance of a goal, more or less abstract. The relevant linking principles are shown in (110). An *affected* object participant like *apple* in *Nadya ate the apple* is linked from a semantically restricted [+r] theme. A non-affected object such as *dog*

---

[13] Adjuncts are also assumed to have a kind of semantic case. The assignment conditions for case on adjuncts are assumed to follow straightforwardly from purely semantic factors, not a complex interaction involving the analysis of core grammatical relations and clausal semantics.

as in *Nadya saw the dog* is linked from a [−r] theme (see Butt 1998 for details on integrating aspectual affectedness into linking theory).

(110) **Linking Principles**
  Theme: [−r] (neutral) or [+r] (semantically restricted)
  Goal: [+o] or [−r]
  Default: [−o]

Goals can be classified as either [+o], in which case they are linked to an objective function, or as [−r] to allow for dative subjects. As in standard linking theory (section 5.7.5), the default specification is [−o], so this is what locatives and agents will be classified as.

Again, as in standard linking theory, case as such is not integrated directly. Case marking becomes relevant for linking when different linking possibilities exist. The information provided by the case morphology can be used to select just one of the possibilities. Case can thus function as a type of secondary linker (cf. Kiparsky 1987, 1997, section 5.5). However, the function of case morphology is taken to go beyond just the determination of grammatical functions. As shown in the next sections, the specifications associated with case morphology are seen as actively interacting with the semantic and syntactic information specified in other parts of the grammar. The grammatical functions related to the predicate-argument structure via linking theory are a part of the grammar which case marking interacts with. Linking theory does not exclusively determine case marking, nor does case marking exclusively determine the choice of grammatical function.

5.9.2 Structural Case

Positional case is associated only with syntactic information. This case can be thought of as being 'assigned' as in the GB/MP tradition (chapter 4). That is, there is assumed to be a syntactic configuration which requires a particular case marking. Structural case can be correlated with grammatical function, or it may be associated with a particular phrase structure position. An example of purely positional case is the adnominal genitive in English (see King 1995 for examples from Russian). As shown in (111), the prenominal NP position is identified as genitive as part of the positional information in the syntax (the ↑=↓ notation indicates that the noun is the head of the phrase).

(111) English Adnominal Genitives (simplified structure)

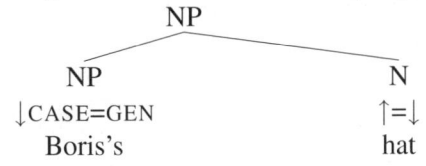

```
                NP
              /    \
            NP      N
         ↓CASE=GEN  ↑=↓
          Boris's   hat
```

Structural case is often an instance of default case and hence functions as the Elsewhere Case (cf. Zaenen, Maling, and Thráinsson's 1985 notion of default vs. lexically stipulated case in section 5.7.3 and Kiparsky's use of the Elsewhere condition in section 5.5.2). For languages which require that all NPs have case, this can be stated as in (112a), analogous to the Case Filter (Rouveret and Vergnaud 1980, chapter 4). If a given NP is not already associated with case due to some specification in some other part of the grammar, then default case assignment principles as in (112b–c) can apply. Default case only applies to the core grammatical relations subject and object. The other grammatical relations tend to involve some kind of specialized semantics and therefore do not involve defaults. Note that this is essentially the insight behind GB/MPs postulation of exactly two structurally Case marked arguments, which are associated with nominative and accusative case (chapter 4).

(112) a. Wellformedness principle: NP: (↑CASE)
    b. Default: ((↑SUBJ CASE)=NOM)
    c. Default: ((↑OBJ CASE)=ACC)

In Urdu, the nominative is the default case (Mohanan 1994:100). The default assignments in (112) are therefore inappropriate for Urdu and should instead be amended as shown in (113). The content of the default assignment principles may vary from language to language, however, the existence of a default case for subjects and objects is expected to hold crosslinguistically.

(113) c. Default: ((↑OBJ CASE)=NOM)

In a way, structural case is the most uninteresting type. If a theory of case were confined to this plus a list of exceptions to the rule, then no justice would be done to the full range of crosslinguistic case marking.

5.9.3 Quirky Case

As mentioned in section 5.7.3, the term 'quirky case' is used only for those situations in which there is no regularity to be captured: the case assignment is truly exceptional to the system and no syntactic or semantic regularities can be detected. Under the assumption that case morphology plays a large role in the fundamental organizing principles of language, quirky case is expected to be fairly rare. Instead, case morphology is likely to be part of a coherent system, with only a few exceptions along the way. These exceptions are generally due to historical reasons and have not been eradicated or reanalysed as part of a regularization of the case system (see section 6.8 on historical change).

5.9.4 Semantic Case

In Urdu and in most South Asian languages, semantic case is the most general type. The defining characteristics of semantic case in the sense of Butt and King are: i) semantic predictability; ii) subjection to syntactic restrictions, such as being confined to certain grammatical functions. Indeed, most cases cannot appear on just any grammatical function, but are restricted to one or two. As a concrete example, the table in (114) shows the distribution of case in Urdu.

(114) **Overview of Urdu Case Markers**

Case Morphology	Case Label	Grammatical Relation
∅	nominative	subj/object
ne	ergative	subject
ko	accusative	object
	dative	subject/indirect object
se	instrumental	subject/oblique/adjunct
k-	genitive	subject (infinitives)
		specifier/possessives
mẽ/par/tak	locative	oblique/adjunct

Under Butt and King's analysis, most instances of case will work out to be examples of semantic case. This is because the bulk of the crosslinguistic case marking phenomena involve an interaction between syntactic and semantic constraints. Take the ergative case in Urdu, for example. This case marker can only appear on subjects and so must obey a particular syntactic restriction. As an agentive case, the ergative does not just play a structural role, it also gives rise to some semantic effects. As is well known from a host of studies on Hindi/Urdu (just a few include Kachru 1978, 1987, Mohanan 1994, Davison 1999), the ergative alternates with the unmarked nominative on unergative intransitives (the most comprehensive study of the distribution of the ergative is Davison 1999). As shown in (115), this alternation correlates with an expression of control/volitionality.

(115) a. yassin kʰãs-a
 Yassin.M.Sg.Nom cough-Perf.M.Sg
 'Yassin coughed.' Urdu

 b. yassin=ne kʰãs-a
 Yassin.M.Sg=Erg cough-Perf.M.Sg
 'Yassin coughed (purposefully).' Urdu

Another example is the accusative/dative *ko* in Urdu. As was seen in connection with example (108), when it appears on direct objects, it signals specificity. Again, there is a combination of syntactic (direct objects only) and semantic factors (specificity) that are involved. The *ko* can also appear on subjects (107b) and on indirect objects, as in (116).

(116) nadya=ne bılli=ko dud di-ya hɛ
 Nadya.F=Erg cat.F.Sg=Dat milk.M.Nom give-Perf.M.Sg be.Pres.3.Sg
 'Nadya has given milk to the cat.' Urdu

In both cases, the dative is associated with a more or less abstract goal. In (116) the 'cat' is the goal of the giving. In *experiencer* constructions as in (107b), the experiencer of the event can be thought of as a kind of abstract goal. Experiencer subjects encompass modal contexts as in (107b) or (117a), and psych predicates as in (117b) or the subjects of noun-verb complex predicates, in (117c) (cf. Verma and K.P. Mohanan 1990 on experiencer subjects, and Mohanan 1994 and references therein).

(117) a. nadya=ko   skul   ja-na   par-a
        Nadya.F.Sg=Dat school.F.Sg.Obl go-Inf.M.Sg fall-Perf.M.Sg
        'Nadya had to go to school.'   Urdu

   b. nadya=ko   dar   lag-a
        Nadya.F.Sg=Dat fear.M.Sg.Nom be attached-Perf.M.Sg
        'Nadya was afraid.'   Urdu

   c. nadya=ko   kahani   yad   a-yi
        Nadya.F.Sg=Dat story.F.Sg.Nom memory come-Perf.F.Sg
        'Nadya remembered the story.'   Urdu

   d. nadya=ne   kahani   yad   k-i
        Nadya.F.Sg=Erg story.F.Sg.Nom memory do-Perf.F.Sg
        'Nadya remembered the story (actively).'   Urdu

With psych predicates as in (117c) there is again an alternation with the ergative, though in this case it correlates with the use of the agentive 'do' in (117d) vs. the non-agentive 'come' in (117c). The dative use of *ko* is also governed by a combination of syntactic and semantic factors. It is restricted to indirect objects and subjects, but cannot be relegated to the status of an unpredictable quirky case since there are coherent syntactic and semantic generalizations as to its distribution and use. Within Butt and King's system, the *ko* is therefore analysed as a semantic case. The final lexical entry for *ko* is shown in (118) (Butt and King 2003).

(118) ko
        Possibility 1 ($\uparrow$ CASE) = ACC
                     (OBJ $\uparrow$)
                     ($\uparrow_{sem-str}$ SPECIFICITY) = +

        Possibility 2 ($\uparrow$ CASE) = DAT
                     (GOAL $\uparrow_{arg-str}$)
                     (SUBJ $\uparrow$) $\vee$ (OBJ$_{go}$ $\uparrow$)

The entry for *ko* specifies that it can be used either as an accusative, or as a dative. As an accusative, it can only appear on a direct object and is associated with specificity in the semantic projection (Possibility 1). As a dative, it can only appear on either subjects or indirect objects (OBJ$_{go}$) and requires a goal argument at a-structure via the inside-out functional designation. This entry nicely illustrates that the information associated with case morphology is assumed to interact with information specified in other parts of the grammar at several levels of representation. In this case, the f-structure is involved as well as the semantic projection, and the argument structure. Case is thus recognized as being an extremely complicated and complex part of the morphosyntactic and semantic interface.

5.10 Discussion

This chapter has surveyed a number of different linking theories, has introduced concepts such as lexical decomposition and Proto-Roles, and has continued the discussion on the representation and nature of thematic roles. In particular, for each linking theory, the chapter looked at how it dealt with our three main ingredients: case morphology, argument structure and grammatical relations. Each linking theory turned out to have a different perspective on how these factors interact. In addition, some semantic factors connected with case morphology were introduced. The semantic underpinnings of case systems are discussed in more detail in chapter 7, but this chapter has served to introduce a few initial phenomena.

There are several topics which could and perhaps should have been included in this chapter, but which I have left for chapters to come in the interests of readability. One is a discussion of Role and Reference Grammar (RRG), which contains a well articulated linking theory. Another topic concerns Optimality Theory (OT). OT is not so much a single theory, as a metatheory. As such, it has been adopted by the practitioners of a wide variety of different frameworks, among them GB/MP and LFG. The newer formulations of Wunderlich's Lexical-Decomposition Grammar and Kiparsky's linking theory also both assume OT. In some ways, it is therefore not correct to present their theories without the OT component, as was done in this chapter. However, I felt it would be better to introduce the individual core ideas in their own right, and then to introduce the OT principles that are shared across a number of different frameworks in a different chapter (chapter 8).

The next chapter introduces a topic that has been carefully skirted up to now, but which has already been introduced to some extent in this chapter via Urdu. The next chapter takes on the theoretical concept of *ergativity*. Discussions surrounding ergativity are much more complex than the simplified description in this chapter would indicate, and are therefore best tackled in a separate chapter.

5.11 Exercises

Exercise 1: Basic Concepts

Answer the following questions briefly. They are intended to help you get your bearings with the basic concepts in the theories introduced in this chapter.

1. How are thematic roles encoded in:
   - Jackendoff's analysis
   - Wunderlich's LDG
   - Kiparsky's linking theory
   - LFG
2. Why did Dowty propose Proto-Roles?
3. How are grammatical relations encoded in:
   - Jackendoff's analysis
   - Wunderlich's LDG
   - Kiparsky's linking theory
   - LFG
4. What is the role of overt case morphology in:
   - Jackendoff's analysis
   - Wunderlich's LDG
   - Kiparsky's linking theory
   - LFG
5. How does Quirky Case enter into the picture in:
   - Jackendoff's analysis
   - Wunderlich's LDG
   - Kiparsky's linking theory
   - LFG

Exercise 2: Passives

1. **Transitives**
   Provide an analysis of the passivized German sentence in (1b) from the perspective of:
   - Wunderlich's LDG
   - Kiparsky's linking theory
   - LFG

(1) a. Die   Katze   jagt   den   Hund.
       the.F.Sg.Nom cat.F.Sg chases the.M.Sg.Acc dog.M.Sg
       'The cat is chasing the dog.'   German
    b. Der   Hund   wurde   gejagt.
       the.M.Sg.Nom dog.M.Sg become.Past.3.Sg chase.PerfP
       'The dog was chased.'   German

2. **Unergatives**
   Explain why a sentence such as *Kim worked* cannot be passivized under the assumptions of:
   - Wunderlich's LDG
   - Kiparsky's linking theory
   - LFG

3. **Unaccusatives**
   Show how the single argument in *Kim fell* is realized in the syntax in the framework of:
   - Wunderlich's LDG
   - Kiparsky's linking theory
   - LFG

Exercise 3: Datives

1. Provide an LFG analysis of the English dative alternation in (2) (note: there are several possible alternatives).
   (2) a. The dean gave a certificate of excellence to Kim.
       b. The dean gave Kim a certificate of excellence.
   Optional: Do both (2a) and (2b) sound equally good? If not, then why not?

2. Provide an analysis in terms of both Kiparsky's linking theory and LDG for the Urdu dative subject construction in (3).
   (3) nadya=ko   γʊssa   a-ya
       Nadya.F.Sg=Dat anger.M.Sg.Nom be come-Perf.M.Sg
       'Nadya got angry.'

Exercise 4: Case Alternations

The data in (4) and (5) are from Sanskrit and Vedic (an older form of Sanskrit). As in the modern languages (cf. section 5.7.6), there are case alternations which seem to signal semantic differences.

1. Provide an analysis of the case alternation in (4) (soma is a drink preferred by the gods) in terms of LDG, Kiparsky's linking theory and LFG. Compare and contrast the analysis in each approach.

    (4) a. pibā   somam
            drink.Imp soma.Acc
            'Drink soma.' (Ṛgveda VIII.36.1)   Vedic
       b. pibā   somasya
            drink.Imp soma.Gen
            'Drink (of) soma.' (Ṛgveda VIII.37.1)   Vedic

You may wish to be guided in your analysis by the following observation made by Jamison (1976:131,135):

> It is probably the case that the alternation between AC [accusative case] and GC [genitive case] with verbs of consumption originally signalled a semantic difference. A food or drink in AC [accusative case] was entirely consumed, while only part of one in the genitive was.

2. The two sentences in (5) are examples of a causative construction. Provide an analysis of the fact that the causee ('queen' and 'dogs', respectively) is accusative in (5a) and instrumental in (5b).

    (5) a. mantrapūtam   carum   rājñīm
            consecrated.Acc porridge.Acc queen.Sg.Acc
            praśayat   munisattamaḥ
            best-of-ascetic.Nom eat.Caus.Impf.3.Sg
            'the best of ascetics made the queen eat a consecrated porridge.' (Kathaāsaritsāgar 9.10)   Sanskrit
       b. tām   śvabhiḥ   khādayet   rājā
            Demon.F.Sg.Acc dog.Pl.Inst eat.Caus.Opt.3.Sg king.Nom
            'Her the king should order to be devoured by dogs.' Sanskrit
            (Mahābhārata 8.371)

You may wish to be guided in your analysis by the discussion of analogous facts in Urdu in section 5.7.6 and the following observation made by Speijer (1886:§49) about this data:

> If one wants to say *he causes me to do something, it is by his impulse I act*, there is room for the type [accusative causee], but if it be meant *he gets something done by me, I am only the agent or instrument through which he acts*, the instrumental is on its place.

6

The Ergative Dragon

kesariṇā kariṇam nihatya kutracidagami
lion.Inst elephant.Acc down.smite.Gerund somewhere.go.Aor.Pass.3.Sg
'The lion, having slain the elephant, disappeared.'
Daçak. 18, Vedic Sanskrit

(Possible ergative use of an instrumental in the accusative language Sanskrit.)

6.1 Fighting Dragons

Ergativity is one of the subjects I found very confusing when I was a student. The literature is huge and encompasses a truly diverse set of languages. It is also characterized by widely divergent opinions, assumptions and terminology. At some point, during the writing of my dissertation, I woke up after having dreamt of trying to capture a fiery, proud, and colourful dragon that was flying around, causing trouble. This was the Ergative Dragon.

One chapter cannot hope to do justice to the nightmarish complexity of the literature. However, it can provide a useful overview of the centrally relevant issues and discussions. This chapter first charts the origin of the term 'ergative' by way of a historical introduction. The history of the description and analysis of ergative languages is characterized by a misunderstanding which occurred early on. This first misunderstanding was then compounded by the further confusion introduced by Burzio (1986) in his equation of the *unaccusative* with the term *ergative*. This has led to books entitled *Ergativity in German* (Grewendorf 1989), for example, even though German contains no signs of an ergative case or even an *ergative system* (section 6.3). What is meant, of course, is that the book represents a study of *unaccusative* phenomena in German (cf. section 3.7). However, for an uninitiated non-German speaking reader, this may not be immediately obvious.

After an initial introduction to the terminology and the phenomenon, the chapter presents the standard conception of ergativity (section 6.3), including morphological vs. syntactic ergativity and split ergativity (section 6.6). Some space is devoted to discussing the ergative as an inherent vs. a structural case in GB/MP on the basis of such languages as Georgian, Urdu/Hindi and West Greenlandic. The chapter closes with a discussion of ergativity language acquisition (section 6.7), as well as some historical issues (section 6.8).

6.2 The Terminology

In contrast to the well established origins of most case names, e.g., dative, nominative or genitive (chapter 2), the precise origin of the term *ergative* remains uncertain, though some papers have been devoted to this subject (e.g. Seely 1977, Manaster Ramer 1994). In this section, I draw mainly on Manaster Ramer's (1994) collection and organization of the facts.

6.2.1 Torres Straits and the Agentive Nominative

The first documented use of the term 'ergative' was to describe a locative/comitative case in a language referred to as *Miriam* by Ray and Haddon (1873). Miriam is an Eastern Torres Straits language and is now generally known as *Meriam Mir* (where 'mir' means language). As part of a British expedition, Ray and Haddon's job was to record and describe the language and culture of the Torres Straits islanders. Manaster Ramer speculates that the term ergative was coined on the basis of the Latin preposition $erg\bar{a}$ 'against, near', which approximates the locative/comitative case described by Ray and Haddon.

If it had not been for the fact that Meriam Mir also had another case marker which was unusual from the European perspective, then the story might have ended there, and 'ergative' today would simply be another term among a plethora of specialized terms that indicate location or motion. For example, Finnish (famous for having one of the richest morphological case systems of the world) includes 15 cases, among them locational, temporal, and directional cases. Examples of the latter are the *allative* (motion to or toward the referent of the noun) or the *illative* (motion into or direction toward the referent) (see Holmberg and Nikanne 1993 for a collection on Finnish case).

However, Meriam Mir also has a case marker which today would be labelled 'ergative', but which then was called *Nominative of the Agent* by Sidney Ray in 1873 and *Active Instrumental* in 1907 (Ray 1907). This nomenclature was entirely in keeping with the times. New languages and case systems were being discovered and the naming conventions for the newly discovered cases were based on known cases like the nominative, the dative, or the instrumental. Languages like Latin and Greek include only a single case marker for both agentive and non-agentive subjects (i.e., *I pinched the elephant* and *I fell*). This stands in contrast to languages like Basque and West Greenlandic, which have two distinct case markers for agentive and non-agentive subjects. The case marker on the agentive subjects was unexpected from the standard European perspective and some authors tried to pass it off as an instrumental adjunct of a passive sentence. However, this view could not stand up to the actual data, which indicated that this 'extra' case was marking entities that behaved like subjects in several crucial respects.

Because the nominative was seen as the case for subjects, one reasonable procedure for the labelling of this 'extra' agentive subject case was to base the new name on the term *nominative*. Writing in German, Pott (1873), for example, distinguishes between two types of nominatives for Basque and West Greenlandic: *Nominativ des Handelns* 'Agentive Nominative' (today's ergative) vs. *Nominativ des Leidens* 'Nominative of Suffering' or *Nominativ des Neutralen Zustandes* 'Nominative of Neutral State'. The relevant pattern for West Greenlandic is given in (1), where the subject of the transitive, agentive verb 'eat' carries a different case marker than the subject of the intransitive non-agentive verb 'sleep'.[1]

(1) a. Oli-p   neqi   neri-vaa
Oli-Erg meat.Abs eat-IND.TR.3Sg.3Sg
'Oli eats meat.' (Manning 1996:3)   West Greenlandic

b. Oli   sinippoq
Oli.Abs sleep-IND.INTR.3Sg
'Oli sleeps.' (Manning 1996:3)   West Greenlandic

The subject case in (1a) is Pott's agentive nominative and today's ergative. The object in (1a) and the subject in (1b) are both glossed as carrying *absolutive* case. This term is part of a standard nomenclature which labels the unmarked case *absolutive* in languages with an ergative case, and *nominative* in languages without one. The term *absolutive* comes from the literature on Eskimo and was coined to signal an opposition between transitive subjects on the one hand, and objects and intransitive subjects on the other hand. Even though both absolutives and nominatives tend to be phonologically null, the idea was that one needed a special term because the absolutive appears in opposition to the ergative, whereas nominatives appear in opposition to an accusative.

The term absolutive remains well established in work on Eskimo languages (such as West Greenlandic). However, in more recent years, the consensus has moved towards collapsing the terms absolutive and nominative. This is partly because more research into ergative languages has established that the clear ergative-absolutive vs. nominative-accusative distinction does not hold crosslinguistically. In many languages (such as Urdu/Hindi), the direct object does not have to be 'absolutive' or phonologically unmarked, it could also be overtly marked with an accusative case. Furthermore, transitive clauses can contain two phonologically unmarked arguments (see (17)). Calling both of

---

[1] Note that this verb may be classified as agentive in other languages, see section 3.8.

these phonologically unmarked arguments absolutives goes against the definition of an absolutive and so they are generally treated as *double nominatives*.

The approaches which see no reason for a terminological distinction between nominative and absolutive prefer the term *nominative*. Goddard (1982) is an early example of this line of reasoning. He rejects the use of *absolutive* for the analysis of Australian languages, arguing that the case oppositions go beyond the simple ergative-absolutive pattern. He also points out that the name *nominative* derives from the Latin *nomen* 'name', indicating that this is the citation form of the noun. He argues that *nominative* is the most appropriate name for the phonologically unmarked form of a noun, because this is precisely the citation form of the noun. In this book, the terms absolutive and nominative are used interchangeably, with a preference for nominative.

To return to the naming conventions surrounding the ergative, not all authors of the last century followed the 'nominative' naming system. In the South Asian context, for example, Kellogg (1883) uses the term *Agent* for today's Hindi/Urdu ergative. This label is also adopted in Cummings and Bailey's (1912) grammar of Punjabi, where Bailey refers to what would today be called an ergative as the *agent case*.

The original terminology 'agentive nominative' or 'agent case' did not survive into modern times, but was replaced by 'ergative', the term originally coined for a locative/comitative case in Meriam Mir. This modern nomenclature would seem to obscure the strong intuition underlying the older terminology that the extra subject case was to be analysed as a reflex of a semantic parameter of active agency vs. stative being. Before jumping to conclusions, however, let us take a look at how the terminological replacement happened.

6.2.2 A Misunderstanding with Georgian

Dirr (1928) uses the term 'ergative' quite matter-of-factly in his description of Caucasian languages, whereas Schuchardt (1896) had called the same case *Aktivus*, i.e., an active/agentive case. Indeed, the indigenous Caucasian tradition already had a name for this case, but this name did not make it into the linguistic mainstream either. In the indigenous tradition the case was dubbed *mothχrobithi*, a derivative of the verb *mothχroba* 'narrate' (Schuchardt 1896). Harris (1985) uses the term 'narrative case' in a translation of the indigenous name. This name is probably associated with the fact that the narrative/ergative case is associated with a particular aspect, namely, the aorist. The relevant pattern is shown in (2), where the present series is associated with nominative subjects, the aorist with ergative subjects and the perfect series with dative subjects (an example of this was already encountered in section 3.6.2).

(2)

	Present	Aorist	Perfect
Transitives	NOM-DAT	ERG-NOM	DAT-NOM
Unerg. Intrans.	NOM	ERG	DAT
Unacc. Intrans.	NOM	NOM	NOM

Georgian is an extremely complicated language and the interaction between case and aspect is just one difficult part of the system. It is quite usual that languages confine the appearance of the ergative/agentive case to a particular aspect. An example was already encountered with Urdu in chapter 5, where the ergative is associated with perfect morphology. Such languages are called *split ergative* languages (section 6.6). The present, aorist and perfect series in Georgian have distinct verbal morphology. The basic uses of these three tense/aspect series are as in (3).

(3) Present: present, future, imperfect, conditional,
conjunctive present and future
Aorist: aorist, optative
Perfect: present perfect, future perfect

The aorist is the natural expression for narratives. Since the ergative/narrative occurs only in these contexts, the indigenous nomenclature seems reasonable. However, as can be seen from the examples in (4), the distributional pattern of the narrative case in Georgian is in line with the general agentive pattern seen so far for West Greenlandic and Urdu/Hindi (e.g., Butt and King 1991, 2003). The narrative/ergative case appears on the subjects of transitive (4a) verbs, but not on intransitive verbs as in (4b–c), even when the verb has the required aorist morphology. Urdu/Hindi and Georgian differ from West Greenlandic in that they distinguish between two types of intransitive verbs: unaccusatives and unergatives (section 3.7). Unaccusative verbs as in (4b) are not compatible with ergative subjects, while unergative verbs are (4d).

(4) a. nino-m   Ceril-i   daCera.
       Nino-ERG letter-NOM wrote-3SGS;3O
       'Nino wrote a letter.' (Transitive; Aorist)   Georgian

   b. Kar-i   gaiγo.
       door-NOM opened-3SGS
       'The door opened.' (Unaccusative; Aorist)   Georgian

   c. *Kar-ma   gaiγo.
       door-ERG opened-3SGS
       'The door opened.' (Unaccusative; Aorist)   Georgian

   d. nino-m   imγera.
       Nino-ERG sang-3SGS
       'Nino sang.' (Unergative; Aorist)   Georgian

Urdu/Hindi and Georgian differ further in that unergatives can optionally have ergative subjects in Urdu/Hindi, but must obligatorily have ergative subjects in Georgian. Despite these differences, the overall distributional pattern classifies the Georgian narrative case as the same kind of phenomenon as the agentive cases identified in Urdu/Hindi, Basque or West Greenlandic. However, it is not clear why the term 'ergative' rather than something like 'agentive' was adopted by Dirr and the subsequent linguistic tradition.

Manaster Ramer (1994) speculates that faulty communication lies at the root of the matter. The faulty communication seems to have involved Pater Schmidt (1902), who was cited by Trombetti (1903), an Italian scholar who worked on Caucasian languages. Pater Schmidt (1902:88), writing in German, cites the language Meriam Mir as having an ergative case (Casus ergativus), a special case of the subject of transitive verbs:

> Bei den Casus ist zunächst hervorzuheben das Vorkommen eines Casus ergativus, eines besonderen Kasus des Subjekts bei transitiven Verben.
> 'With respect to the cases, one must first mention the occurrence of a Casus ergativus, a special case of the subject for transitive verbs.'

This is clearly a misrepresentation of Ray and Haddon's original description. It seems that Pater Schmidt remembered the curious fact that Meriam Mir had two subject cases along with the term 'ergative', but then mixed up the terminology by attributing the locative/comitative ergative to the agentive nominative subject case. Manaster Ramer assumes that Pater Schmidt associated the term 'ergative' with Greek *ergátes* 'worker', thus inadvertently coining a new word.

This new use of the term was picked up for Caucasian languages, presumably by Trombetti (1903), who attributes the term to Pater Schmidt. By 1907 this term seems to have established itself for specially case marked agentive subjects. One indication is that Ray (1907) dropped the use of the term 'ergative' to describe the comitative/locative use in Meriam Mir.

6.3 Case Systems

At some point during the 20th century, languages came to be classified via the *case system* they exhibit. The most fundamental opposition is often taken to be that between *accusative* and *ergative* type languages. Plank (1979:4) concisely summarizes the basic idea as in (5).

(5) a. A grammatical pattern or process shows ergative alignment if it identifies intransitive subjects (S_i) and transitive direct objects (dO) as opposed to transitive subjects (S_t).

b. It shows accusative alignment if it identifies S_i and S_t as opposed to dO.

The West Greenlandic pattern in (1), for example, displays the basic ergative pattern described in (5). In contrast, Latin, Greek, English and German are accusative languages since they do not distinguish different types of subjects, but do distinguish objects from subjects (subjects are generally nominative, objects are generally accusative).

One standard way of labelling transitive subjects vs. intransitive subjects vs. objects is based on Dixon (1979a, 1994). In (6), 'A' is mnemonic for agent, 'S' stands for intransitive subject and 'O' for object. Since transitive verbs generally have agentive subjects, the 'A' is often used to refer to transitive subjects. However, it can also be used to refer to the single agentive argument in unergatives.

(6)

$$\begin{array}{r} \text{nominative} \left\{ \begin{array}{ll} A & \text{ergative} \\ S & \\ \end{array} \right. \\ \text{accusative} \quad \left. \begin{array}{l} \\ O \end{array} \right\} \text{absolutive} \end{array}$$

Using this terminology, an ergative language is one which singles out the A for special marking, but which groups S and O together by marking them with the same case (often a phonologically null case). The case of S and O is generally absolutive/nominative. In contrast, an accusative language is one which uses the nominative for both A and S and differentiates the O via the accusative case.

The first documented identification of this basic pattern is part of Hans Egede's 1739 manuscript, which formed the basis of Paul Egede's (1760) grammar of Greenlandic (Bobaljik 1993:46). The distinction was also propagated by Uhlenbeck (1916) though with an underlying passive analysis, but hotly disputed by Sapir (1917) on the basis of data from American Indian languages as being too simplistic. The more simplistic view, however, became well established within linguistics and is considered basic textbook knowledge.

The typological variation that is glossed over by this basic distinction is huge. We have already seen that Urdu/Hindi and Georgian, for example, make a distinction between unergative and unaccusative subjects. In Georgian, unergatives require an ergative subject, in Urdu/Hindi, they may appear with one (Davison 1999). Subjects of unaccusatives in both languages are nominative/absolutive. With respect to intransitives, Urdu/Hindi and Georgian thus differ from the basic West Greenlandic pattern. The term *active* has therefore come to be employed for languages like Georgian or Urdu/Hindi (Klimov 1974, 1979, Harris 1995). This extends the basic typology of case systems as shown in (7).

(7)

Clause Type	Language Type		
	Ergative	Accusative	Active
Transitive	Erg-Abs	Nom-Acc	Erg-Abs
Intransitive (Unerg)	Abs	Nom	Erg
Intransitive (Unacc)	Abs	Nom	Abs

However, this extended typology does not suffice to cover the crosslinguistic patterns either. Languages systematically exhibit more possibilities in the marking of subjects and objects. The discussion of Georgian in section 6.2.2 included a mention of dative subjects. As was summarized in (2), the perfect series in Georgian, for example, requires a dative rather than an ergative subject. Some illustrative examples are given in (8).

(8) a. turme   nino-s   Ceril-i   dauCeria.
apparently Nino-DAT letter-NOM wrote-3SGS;3O
'Apparently Nino wrote a letter.' (Transitive; Perfect)   Georgian

b. turme   nino-s   umγeria.
apparently Nino-DAT sang-3SGS
'Apparently Nino sang.' (Unergative; Perfect)   Georgian

c. turme   Kar-i   gaγila.
apparently door-NOM opened-3SGS
'Apparently the door opened.' (Unaccusative; Perfect)   Georgian

Harris (1981) dubs this pattern the 'inversion' construction as part of her RG analysis (cf. section 3.6.2). Although the subject here is dative, Georgian still differentiates between unergatives as in (8b) and unaccusatives as in (8c) in a manner similar to the ergative/active pattern: unaccusative subjects are nominative/absolutive and unergative subjects are dative.

Non-nominative subjects other than the ergative do not tend to figure in the classification of case systems. It is not clear to me why systematic patterns with other types of case such as the dative are not taken into account in typological classifications of languages. However, it is generally acknowledged that the number of case systems go beyond the three listed in (7).

Indeed, Fillmore's (1968) original formulation of Case Grammar (cf. section 3.5) included a recognition of five different types of case systems. Fillmore took just two basic 'cases' to be relevant: A (agentive) and O (objective). Based on these two cases, he made the distinctions in (9) between basic possible clause types.

(9) V+A   intransitive sentences with active 'subjects'
V+O+A transitive sentences with agents
V+O   intransitive sentences with inactive 'subjects'

This basic inventory allowed Fillmore to describe several different types of case systems and he used Sapir's (1917) more complex typological distinctions within American-Indian languages to illustrate his ideas. The system allows for languages like Yana, which treat pronominal As and Os in all sentence types alike: no distinctions whatsoever are made between As and Os in any clause type. It also allows for languages like Paiute, which distinguishes the O in opposition to all others (the classic accusative pattern); Chinook, which distinguishes the A of transitive sentences in opposition to all others (the classic ergative pattern); Dakota, which distinguishes all As from all Os; and Takelma, which has separate forms for almost everything.

More recently, Plank (1995b), for example, discusses six different types of case systems (ergative, accusative, active, neutral, double-oblique, tripartite) and Bittner and Hale (1996b:3) identify the case systems in (10) (also see Blake 2001:118–130 and Kibrik 1997 for a discussion of different types of case systems).

(10)

Case System	Agt-Pt-V	Agt-V	Pat-V	Languages
Accusative	NOM-ACC	NOM	NOM	English, Japanese, etc.
Accusative active	NOM-ACC	NOM	ACC	Acehnese, Eastern Pomo
Ergative	ERG-NOM	NOM	NOM	Dyirbal, Samoan, etc.
Ergative active	ERG-NOM	ERG	NOM	Basque, Georgian
Three-way	ERG-ACC	NOM	NOM	Nez Perce, Pitta-Pitta, etc.

There is no definitive typological classification of case systems to date and as can be seen from (10), even the more complex pictures do not include an account of the systematic appearance of dative subjects, so more work remains to be done on exploring the possible crosslinguistic case marking patterns.

6.4 Syntactic vs. Morphological Ergativity

Another piece of standard linguistic wisdom is that languages may be either *syntactically* or *morphologically* ergative. The difference between the two types of languages has been articulated in terms of *syntactic pivots* by Dixon (1979a, 1994). A syntactic pivot is the relation which syntactic phenomena such as coordination or subordination are sensitive to. This term was first coined by Dixon (1979a) and has since entered the linguistic mainstream. In some frameworks, it has been explicitly adopted as part of the formal terminology (see section 8.1 on Role and Reference Grammar, for example). A syntactic pivot is often identical to the grammatical relation subject, but it need not be. In Tagalog, for example, the syntactic patterns involving voice morphology are best couched in terms of syntactic pivots, rather than in terms of grammatical relations (Kroeger 1993, Schachter 1976, 1977).

Dixon (1979a:121, 1994:154) defines the difference in syntactic pivots between syntactically ergative and accusative languages as shown in (11). A syntactically ergative language is one in which the syntactic pivot revolves around S/O. A syntactically accusative language is one in which the syntactic pivot revolves around S/A (the labels S, A and O are from the classifcation in (6)).

(11) i. S/A pivot — the coreferential NP must be in derived S or A function in each of the clauses being joined;

ii. S/O pivot — the coreferential NP must be in derived S or O function in each of the clauses being joined.

The ergative languages we have seen so far in the book, West Greenlandic, Georgian, Urdu/Hindi, Basque and Wambaya (section 5.8) all group their syntactic pivots in terms of S/A. They are therefore not *syntactically* ergative. The standard test developed by Dixon for the identification of syntactic pivothood revolves around reduced coordination, as shown in (12) and (13) for Urdu and Basque, respectively. In these examples two clauses are coordinated, of which the first is transitive and the second intransitive. The subject of the first clause is an A, the (unexpressed) subject of the second clause is an S.

(12) a. [nadya$_A$ sabina=ko skul c^{h}or-egi] or
Nadya.F.Sg.Nom Sabina.F.Sg=Acc school leave-Fut.Fem.3.Sg and
[—— $_S$ p^{h}ır naha-yegi]
then bathe-Fut.Fem.3.Sg Urdu
'Nadya will leave Sabina at school and [Nadya] will then bathe.'

b. [nadya=ne$_A$ sabina=ko skul c^{h}or-a] or
Nadya.F.Sg=Erg Sabina.F.Sg=Acc school leave-Perf.M.Sg and
[—— $_S$ p^{h}ır naha-ya]
then bathe-Perf.M.Sg
'Nadya left Sabina at school and [Nadya] then bathed.' Urdu

(13) [seme-a eskola-n utzi (zuen)] eta [klase-ra joan zen]
son-Abs school-at leave AUX and class-to go AUX Basque
'S/he left her/his son at school and went to class.' (Manning 1996:9)

The coordination test shows that Urdu and Basque group A and S together as pivots because the A and S in (12) and (13) are coreferential. Accusative languages such as English show the same A/S grouping, as should be evident from the English glosses in (12) and (13). So with respect to the syntactic behaviour of S, A and O, the ergative languages Urdu and Basque behave just like accusative languages. Indeed, the pattern is independent from the appearance of ergative case ((12a) vs. (12b)). It is therefore assumed that languages like Urdu, Basque, Georgian, West Greenlandic, and Wambaya are *morphologically ergative* but *syntactically accusative*. These languages do not differentiate S/O as opposed to A on a deep syntactic level, but distinguish them in terms of morphology.

A syntactically ergative language, in contrast, groups S/O together at the deep syntactic level as well. The only example of such a language to date is Dyirbal. Some relevant data is shown in (14). Here the coordination test shows that the O consistently falls together with the S. This stands in marked contrast to syntactically accusative languages like English or Urdu.

(14) a. [ŋuma$_O$ yabu-ŋgu$_A$ buran] [——$_S$ banagan^{y}u]
father.Abs mother-Erg saw   returned
'Mother saw father and [father] returned.'   Dyirbal
(Dixon 1994:155)

b. [bayi   burrbula$_O$ baŋgul   gubi-ŋgu$_A$ bara-n]
Dem.Abs Burrbula.Abs Dem.Erg gubi-Erg   punch-Nfut

[——$_S$ baji-gu]
      fall.down-Purp
'The gubi punched Burrbula$_i$ and [he$_i$] fell down.'   Dyirbal
(Manning 1996:9)

In some sense, a syntactically ergative language functions 'backwards' in comparison with a syntactically accusative language. The O is the syntactic pivot of the clause, not the A. This syntactic 'inversion' of the usual state of affairs is nicely illustrated by analyses from within GB/MP. Recall that in a syntactically accusative language, the agent argument would normally move up to the SpecIP position (cf. (29) in chapter 4). In a syntactically ergative language, on the other hand, it is the theme argument which moves up to the structural Case position in SpecIP, thus 'inverting' the usual mapping from thematic roles to syntactic function, as shown in (15). This inversion analysis is known as the *syntactic ergativity hypothesis* and was articulated by Marantz (1984). Several linguistic predictions about the behaviour of reflexives and control constructions, as well as the coordination data illustrated in (14) follow from this structure. The correlations were argued to hold for a number of languages, among them Dyirbal. Dyirbal is the only language to date to be regarded as syntactically ergative by common consensus. Levin (1983), for example, conducts a careful examination of Basque, Warlpiri and Dyirbal according to Marantz's criteria: Basque and Warlpiri are identified as morphologically ergative and Dyirbal as syntactically ergative.

The particular analysis in (15) as well as the analyses in (16) for a syntactically ergative language are based on Bittner and Hale (1996a:535). Note that the heads are to the right of the complements in (15), accounting for the head-final (SOV) nature of Dyirbal.

(15) [ŋuma   yabu-ŋgu   buran]
father.Abs mother-Erg saw
'Mother saw father.'   Dyirbal

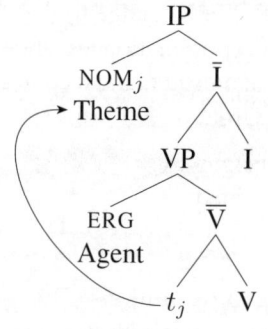

```
                IP
              /    \
         NOM_j      Ī
         Theme    /   \
                VP     I
               /  \
             ERG   V̄
             Agent /  \
                 t_j   V
```

Dyirbal makes no distinction between subjects of unergatives and subjects of unaccusatives, so in both types of clauses the single argument moves up to the structural Case position, as shown in (16).

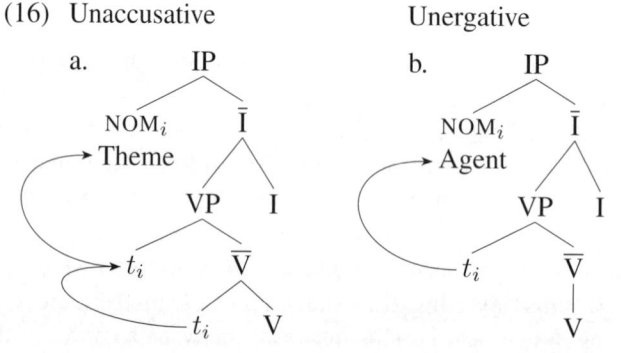

(16) Unaccusative   Unergative
  a.   IP   b.   IP
          /   \   /   \
       NOM_i   Ī   NOM_i   Ī
       Theme /   \   Agent /   \
             VP   I   VP   I
            / \   / \
          t_i   V̄   t_i   V̄
               / \ |
              t_i V   V

As already mentioned, Dyirbal is the only language that qualifies as truly syntactically ergative according to Dixon's (1979a, 1994) definition. There are several possible reasons for this. Either no other language like this exists, or another language like Dyirbal has not been discovered yet. However, if Dyirbal really turned out to be the only representative of its class, then the existence of this class would be in serious doubt.

There is at least one paper arguing that Dyirbal should not be thought of as syntactically ergative (Jake 1978). This paper drew a withering reply from Dixon (1979b), and Manning (1996) resurrects the idea of an 'inverse' alignment of grammatical relations by reexamining the role of syntactic pivots in Inuit, an Eskimo language. He argues that if one 'cuts the pie differently', then one may end up with more syntactically ergative languages than just Dyirbal. Manning (1996) also includes a nice survey of a variety of data and a comprehensive discussion of state-of-the-art approaches to ergativity in different frameworks. Another useful overview is provided by Johns (2000).

6.5 Approaches to Morphological Ergativity

This section presents various possible analyses of morphological ergativity. As already mentioned, one possible analysis is to interpret the ergative NP as an adjunct along the lines of the instrumental adjunct of passive clauses. This was a popular strategy for early analyses of ergativity and continues to be espoused by some scholars even today. This approach is attractive because ergative constructions can simply be analysed as a subtype of normal passivization and thus be brought back into the fold of accusative languages, so to speak. An early example of this type of analysis is Schuchardt (1896).

However, subsequent work on ergative languages has shown that most ergative NPs align themselves with subjects, not with adjuncts. S. Anderson (1976) was the first to propose *subject tests* based on modern syntactic rules like equi-NP deletion, raising, reflexive binding and conjunction formation. This was a very important contribution because up to then nominative case was often equated with verb agreement and subjecthood. Anderson's paper showed that this direct equation is not empirically well founded. Recall that the direct connection between nominative and subjecthood is also not applicable to accusative languages like Icelandic (section 4.8, Zaenen, Maling and Thráinsson 1985). As part of the analysis of any language, a first step should thus always include the establishment of firm subjecthood tests.

In the languages discussed in this section, the ergative NP is always the subject of the clause. However, even if one takes this to be a constant factor underlying any analysis of morphological ergativity, a variety of theoretical options are available. Sample LFG analyses for Urdu (section 5.9) and some Australian languages (section 5.8) have already been presented. The following subsections first present some alternative proposals for an analysis of morphological ergativity within GB/MP. This is followed by a short description of how Kiparsky's linking theory (section 5.5) and LDG (section 5.6) analyse morphological ergativity. A brief discussion of the ergative was already presented as part of the LDG section, however, it is useful to revisit the analysis in the larger context of ergativity.

6.5.1 The Ergative as an Inherent Case

Recall from chapter 4 that GB assumed a basic distinction between inherent and structural Case. Structural Case is equated with nominative and accusative, inherent Case is compatible with all other cases, including the ergative. Mahajan's (1990) treatment of Hindi represents a typical sort of analysis that results from this simple division between structural and inherent Case.

In Hindi/Urdu, the ergative is (mostly) confined to subjects of transitive and unergative verbs carrying perfect morphology.[2] A relevant contrast, based on Mahajan (1990), is shown in (17).

(17) a. ram roṭi kʰa-t-a tʰ-a
 Ram.M.Sg.Nom bread.F.Sg.Nom eat-Impf-M.Sg be.Past-M.Sg
 'Ram used to eat bread.' Hindi

 b. ram=ne roṭi kʰa-yi tʰ-i
 Ram.M.Sg=Erg bread.F.Sg.Nom eat-Perf.F.Sg be.Past-F.Sg
 'Ram had eaten bread.' Hindi

Notice that in (17a) the verb agrees with the nominative subject, whereas it agrees with the nominative object in (17b). In Hindi, the verb only agrees with unmarked (nominative) NPs. Overtly case marked NPs block agreement (this is not true for all South Asian languages). Thus, if the subject is non-nominative and therefore unavailable for agreement, the verb agrees with the nominative object. If there is no nominative object, then the verb shows default masculine singular agreement.

Mahajan (1990) assumes an exploded I(nfl) category in order to be able to deal with both subject and object agreement. In particular, Agr(eement) Phrases are assumed to mediate the perceived relationship between structural Case and verb agreement. Proposals for a complex internal structure of the IP go back to Pollock (1989), who postulated it to account for facts to do with French negation. Chomsky (1995) argues for the abolishment of explicit Agreement Phrases (AgrP), but some sort of complex internal structure of the IP is still assumed, so Mahajan's (1990) analysis of Hindi basic clause structure in terms of AgrP is fairly representative of one type of possible approach. The analyses in (18) and (19) are based on Mahajan (1990), but have been cosmetically altered to make them more consistent with the style of the book.

Like Dyirbal, Hindi is a head-final language, so in (18) the heads are to the right of the specifiers and complements. As was seen in chapter 4 and in (15) above, all of the arguments are assumed to start out VP internally. One reason for arguments to move out of the VP and into the functional projections at the top of the tree is agreement. Another reason is Case. The structure in (18) represents an analysis of the transitive non-perfect clause in (17a).

The exploded IP consists of two AgrPs and a TP. The two AgrPs are responsible for subject and object agreement, respectively (Georgian also has indirect object agreement, and so analyses of Georgian often assume a third agreement phrase). Sandwiched between these two functional agreement projections is a T(ense) phrase (TP) which carries the temporal features of the

---

[2]The ergative can also occur on subjects of certain modal infinitive+auxiliary constructions, see section 7.4.

clause. The auxiliary *tʰa* 'was' starts out as T, but then moves up to Agr_S for purposes of subject agreement. The subject agrees with the verb, so it moves to SpecAgr_S, the functional projection responsible for subject agreement. This projection also licenses structural nominative Case, so *Ram* is correctly analysed as a nominative subject which shows verbal agreement. The object *roṭi* 'bread' does not have to move, because it can be assigned structural accusative Case by virtue of the fact that it is in complement position to the verb. This satisfies the Case Filter and no more need be done. The analysis of (17a) is thus exactly like the analyses of transitive clauses seen before in chapter 4, except that the agreement facts have prompted a more complex functional structure.

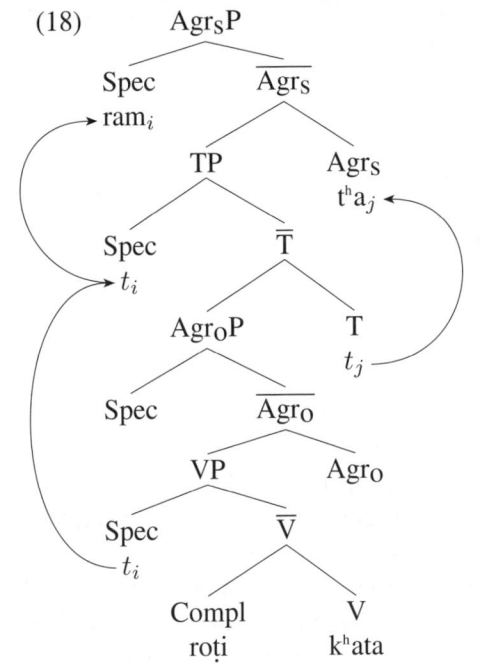

(18)
```
              Agr_S P
             /      \
          Spec      Agr_S
         ram_i     /     \
                  TP      Agr_S
                 /  \     tʰa_j
              Spec   T̄
              t_i   /  \
                Agr_O P   T
                /    \   t_j
             Spec    Agr_O
              t_i    /    \
                    VP    Agr_O
                   /  \
                Spec   V̄
                 t_i  /  \
                   Compl  V
                   roṭi  kʰata
```

The analysis for the ergative variant in (17b) is shown in (19). The basic structure is the same, but the position of the arguments and the way in which Case is assigned is not. SpecAgr_O is responsible for object agreement.

The auxiliary *tʰi* 'was' again starts out as T, but does not move. Instead, it governs verb agreement in Agr_O from within the TP. The object *roṭi* 'bread' moves to SpecTP via SpecAgr_O. This movement ensures that it agrees with the verb and that it receives structural nominative Case. The main verb *kʰayi* 'eat' moves from the V position to Agr_O. The subject Ram does not move from its SpecVP position. In this position it cannot receive structural Case and so must potentially violate the Case Filter. However, Mahajan assumes that perfect participles in Hindi/Urdu such as the *kʰayi* 'eat' in (19) are inherently specified for ergative case in the lexicon. That is, the lexical entry for $k^h ayi$ 'eat' stipulates that its subject receive inherent ergative Case.

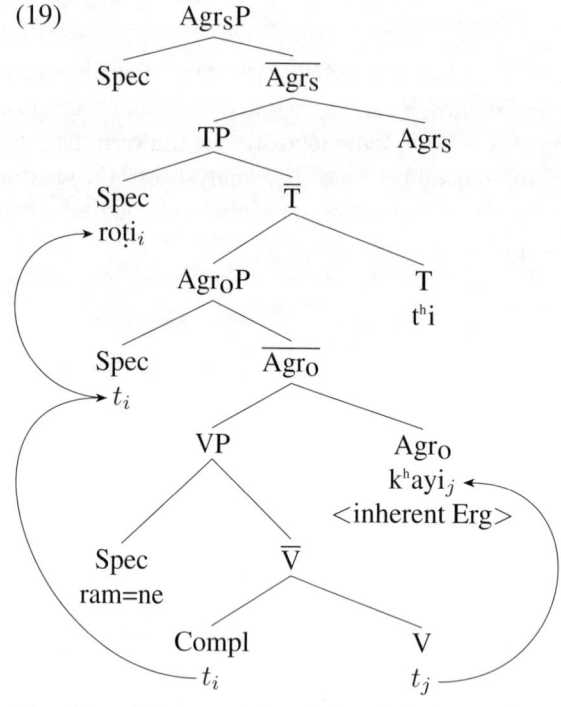

(19)

```
              AgrsP
             /     \
          Spec    Agrs'
                  /    \
                TP     Agrs
               /  \
           Spec    T'
          roti_i  /  \
              AgroP    T
              /   \   t^h i
          Spec   Agro'
          t_i    /    \
               VP     Agro
              /  \   k^h ayi_j
          Spec    V'  <inherent Erg>
         ram=ne  /  \
              Compl  V
               t_i   t_j
```

The Case Filter can thus be satisfied and the analysis works technically. However, there are some drawbacks. For one, the basic order of the arguments does not come out right in (19): the relevant sentence in (17b) has the ergative subject followed by the nominative object, not vice versa. In order to get the arguments in the right order, a reordering mechanism must be assumed at PF (Phonological Form), or further reasons for movement of the ergative NP out of the VP must be postulated. For another, the assignment of inherent ergative Case works out to nothing more than a stipulation. This would be alright if the appearance of ergative subjects were truly idiosyncratic or exceptional. However, ergative case is governed by several regular grammatical principles in Hindi/Urdu. Finally, the number of lexical entries are doubled. There must be two entries for every transitive and unergative verb: one which gives rise to the imperfect, future and other forms, and one which encodes just the perfect form in (20). The analysis is thus not very economical.

Besides these drawbacks, note that if one abstracts away from the details, the analysis of morphological ergativity in (19) bears a close resemblance to the analysis of syntactic ergativity in (15). However, since it has been established quite conclusively that morphologically ergative languages tend to be syntactically accusative (except for Dyirbal), this analytic parallelism points to a fundamental flaw in the approach to ergativity via inherent Case.

6.5.2 The Ergative as a Structural Case

An alternative option is to analyse the ergative as belonging with the structural Cases, rather than with the inherent Cases. For example, Marantz (1991) revisits Burzio's Generalization (chapter 4) from the perspective of ergative languages and proceeds to tease apart some of the factors involved. He identifies morphological case marking as a separate phenomenon from abstract Case. Marantz argues that abstract Case works out to be a licensing condition on arguments. Particularly important is something like a subject condition, which ensures that if there is only one argument, it will surface as a subject (the Extended Projection Principle or EPP). The overt realization of morphological case interacts with this licensing, but is not identical to it, as had been assumed within standard GB.[3]

The ergative along with the accusative is identified as a type of *structural case*, but one which *depends* on the realization of another structural case. Ergative and accusative are classified as *dependent structural cases*. This means that they will only be realized when there is another argument governed by the V+I complex. That is, accusative is only possible if there is also a nominative subject in morphologically accusative languages, and the ergative is only possible if there is also a nominative object in the clause. The ergative as a dependent structural case is illustrated in (20). The verb in (20) is transitive and its two arguments start out VP internally. The agent argument moves into the SpecIP position, where it can receive structural Case, but the realization of morphological ergative case is dependent on the presence of the theme argument.

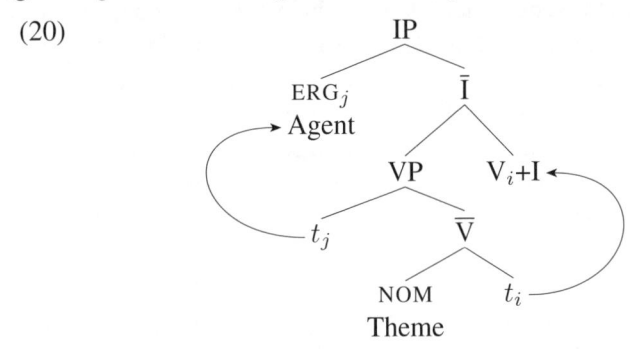

(20)
```
              IP
            /    \
        ERG_j     Ī
        Agent    / \
                VP  V_i+I
               /  \
             t_j   V̄
                  / \
                NOM  t_i
                Theme
```

This type of analysis is much more satisfactory than the inherent or 'quirky' Case approach to ergativity because it recognizes the ergative as a structural subject on a par with nominatives. A quick comparison of (20) with (15) shows

---

[3] It may be instructive to compare Marantz's approach with the basic ideas of RG introduced in section 3.6.

that there is now a clear structural distinction between morphologically and syntactically ergative languages. The syntax of morphologically ergative languages aligns itself with the syntax of syntactically accusative languages like English or German, with the minor difference that the argument in SpecIP is marked morphologically with an ergative case in languages like Urdu, Georgian, West Greenlandic or Basque, but with a nominative case in languages like English or German.

6.5.2.1 Parametrization and Unergatives

The analysis of the ergative as a structural Case has been adopted by a number of differing researchers, among them Bittner (1994), Bittner and Hale (1996a,b), Bobaljik (1992, 1993), Laka (1993), Phillips (1993, 1995) and Davison (1999). Given the analysis of the ergative as a dependent structural Case, it is interesting to see how this approach plays out with respect to unergatives. Unergatives represent a special situation in (at least) two ways. One factor to consider is the optionality of the ergative on unergative verbs in languages such as Urdu/Hindi vs. the obligatory appearance in languages like Georgian. Another factor is that unergatives only have a single argument, so there is no other case marked argument on which the ergative case realization can depend.

Bobaljik (1992), based on an analysis sketched in Chomsky (1995), proposes a parametrization of case assignment in order to account for the differences between case assignment, verb agreement and other asymmetries in accusative vs. ergative languages. The parametrization assumes an exploded IP along the lines of the structures seen for Mahajan's analysis of Hindi: there is an Agr1P which dominates a TP, which in turn dominates an Agr2P. Bobaljik hypothesizes that the ergative/nominative parametrization goes hand in hand with verb agreement in the sense that it matters which of the Agreement Phrases is *active*. This idea is taken up by Laka (1993) for Basque and Davison (1999) for Hindi. Based on later work by Laka, Davison proposes that the relevant functional projection is the Aspectual Phrase (AspP) because the appearance of the ergative in Hindi and in many other languages is partly conditioned by tense/aspect splits (section 6.6). Given this functional projection, the appearance of the ergative case in unergatives is dependent on whether the AspP projection is *active* in the clause. If AspP is active, the ergative case is licensed on subjects. If not, then the subject appears in the nominative. The relevant contrast is shown in (21). In (21a) the AspP is active, thus licensing the morphological ergative case. In (21b), the AspP is inactive and the structural nominative Case is assigned.

(21) a. nadya=ne ro-ya
      Nadya.F.Sg=Erg cry-Perf.M.Sg
      'Nadya cried (on purpose).' Urdu

    b. nadya   ro-yi
       Nadya.F.Sg.Nom cry-Perf.F.Sg
       'Nadya cried.'   Urdu

The various case marking patterns with respect to unergatives can thus be analysed in terms of a parametrization over functional projections such as AgrP or AspP. However, what about the difference between unaccusatives and unergatives? Some languages like West Greenlandic make no distinction between unergatives and unaccusatives, while languages like Georgian, Basque or Urdu/Hindi do make a distinction. One standard solution to the difference between unaccusatives and unergatives is to assume that unergatives are underlyingly *transitive*. That is, while an unergative verb like *dance* in (22) has only one syntactic argument, one assumes the presence of a silent cognate object. According to this analysis, (22a) is really something like (22b) or (22c). The *incorporation* analysis in (22c) (Hale and Keyser 1993, 2002) assumes the presence of a *light verb* like 'do', which incorporates the object and forms a new verb, e.g., 'dance', along the lines of overtly visible noun incorporation documented for a range of languages (Baker 1988).

(22) a. I danced.
       b. I danced [a dance].
       c. I did a dance. →I did+[a dance] →I danced.

Basque provides some evidence for this sort of analysis because there are examples as in (23) which involve the verb 'do' and a noun (Laka 1993). A possible analysis along the lines of (22b) is also supported by data from Basque. Basque has verbal morphology which seems to signal the presence of an extra argument, i.e., a pronoun which stands for a cognate object. Joppen-Hellwig (2001) identifies this verbal morphology as an expletive argument and argues that seemingly intransitive clauses must be recognized as syntactically transitive. An example is given in (24). Further evidence for the idea that unergatives are really underlying transitives comes from verb agreement facts in languages like Yimas (Collins 1993).[4]

(23) Nik lan egin dut
       I.Erg work done have.me
       'I worked.' (Laka 1993:152)   Basque

(24) Kepa-k tarda-tu   d-u
       Kepa-Erg be.late-Perf 3.Acc-have-3.Sg.Erg
       'Kepa was late.' (Joppen-Hellwig 2001:154)   Basque

If unergatives are really underlying transitives, then Marantz's dependent structural Case analysis applies to unergatives as well: the ergative case on the

---

[4]For some comparative data across languages, see Lazard 1998.

single syntactic argument of an unergative verb is licensed because there is another structural argument in the syntactic representation of the clause.

However, this type of analysis does not hold for all languages. Urdu/Hindi, for example, shows no evidence of either an incorporation analysis or of extra verbal morphology which could be interpreted as a second syntactic argument of the clause. Both unergatives and unaccusatives are very clearly syntactically intransitives. Indeed, as Davison (1999) points out, some verbs like 'bark' in (25) simply have no cognate object, so that the incorporation analysis would seem far-fetched, at the very least.

(25) a. kʊtte=ne   bʰõk-a
        dog.M.Sg=Erg bark-Perf.M.Sg
        'The dog barked.'   Urdu

   b. *kʊtte=ne   bʰõk bʰõk-a
        dog.M.Sg=Erg bark bark-Perf.M.Sg
        'The dog barked a bark.'   Urdu

Davison (1999) instead analyses the Hindi/Urdu facts by means of feature checking in which lexical information interacts with structural licensing conditions. Unergative verbs lexically carry an [Erg] feature which must in turn be licensed by a functional projection like AspP. So, the ergative is ultimately licensed structurally, making this a structural Case. However, this structural licensing must be compatible with the lexical specification of the verb.

6.5.2.2 Summary

As should be evident from the above discussion, there is no one coherent approach to ergativity. A number of ideas and standard hypotheses have been formulated over the years which serve as guiding principles for new analyses. However, none of the analyses formulated so far can claim to account for the full range of ergative phenomena. Part of the problem is that not all ergative languages behave alike, as Bittner and Hale (1996b) point out explicitly. There are a myriad of differences with respect to factors such as case realization, verb agreement and verbal morphology, coordination and discourse structure (topic/focus). Only some of these factors have been discussed here — attempting a complete survey of ergativity goes well beyond the scope of this book.

Much remains to be done on exploring the interaction between structural licensing conditions and lexically inherent or stipulated information. This holds for datives as well as ergatives. As discussed in section 6.3, in some languages like Georgian, the dative could be analysed on a par with ergatives as it is also used to mark subjects and also seems to be governed by a combination of structural, semantic and idiosyncratic factors. Some in-depth discussions of the role of structural datives or the related psych-predicates do exist (e.g., Harley 1995, McGinnis 1998a,b,c), but the topic remains comparatively underexplored. McGinnis (1998a) in particular introduces a distinction between *quirky inherent case* and *non-quirky inherent case* in order to be able to account for the regular (non-quirky) properties of the dative in Georgian. This indicates that more distinctions between types of case beyond Marantz's (1991) original proposals may be needed as more data and patterns emerge.

6.5.3 Linking theories revisited and more types of ergativity

Chapter 5 on linking theories saw a gradual introduction of data involving the ergative case. While the ergative figured in discussions of LFG (section 5.7) and LDG (section 5.6), the description of Kiparsky's linking theory avoided all mention of ergativity. This section briefly revisits Wunderlich's LDG and Kiparsky's linking theory in light of the preceding discussion on the ergative.

Within Kiparsky's system, the ergative receives the specification [−LR], as shown in (26), repeated from section 5.5, but now augmented with the ergative.

(26) **Morphosyntactic Case**:
    nominative   [ ]
    accusative   [−HR]
    genitive, ergative [−LR]
    dative   [−HR, −LR]

The ergative bears the same feature specification as the genitive. However, it will not always have the same distribution as the genitive, because not all languages have the same inventory of cases, and because other factors such as verb agreement and structural position play a role as well. Kiparsky sees the ergative as a general sort of default case for obliques. Contrary to what has been asserted so far, the ergative is not just compatible with agents, it can also be used to mark instrumentals (e.g., Australian languages) as well as recipients or directionals (e.g., Kabardian) or locatives (e.g., Ubykh). The latter two types of ergativity are found mainly in Caucasian languages and remain to be studied more closely. For languages like West Greenlandic, where the ergative case is restricted to subjects of transitives, Kiparsky assumes a *restricted ergative* with the feature specification [+HR,−LR]. This ensures that the ergative will only be associated with the highest argument. In other languages, the ergative could be compatible with the highest argument, but it could also be compatible with another one. Some samples of linking patterns are given in (27).

As mentioned previously in section 5.5, no immediate account of unergatives vs. unaccusatives is available under this scenario. This stands in contrast to the closely related LDG, already discussed in section 5.6. LDG deals with differences between unaccusatives and unergatives by either assuming underlying transitivity for languages like Basque, or by assuming that some featural specifications can have semantic connotations such as [+control] and that these featural specifications ([+lr] for control) can be used to guide the association of ergative case with unergative (agentive) verbs. The former strategy is closely related to the analyses discussed above within GB/MP, the latter one is not, but there are some similarities with the association between features and semantic entailments proposed within LFG (section 5.7.7).

(27)

Linking Patterns, Kiparsky						
Valence:	ditransitive			transitive		intransitive
Arguments:	λx	λy	λz	λx	λy	λx
Abstract Case:	[+HR]	[ ]	[+LR]	[+HR]	[+LR]	[+HR] [+LR]
Case Inventory						
Nom/Dat/Acc (German)	[ ] (Nom)	[−LR] [−HR] (Dat)	[−HR] (Acc)	[ ] (Nom)	[−HR] (Acc)	[ ] (Nom)
Erg/Dat/Nom (Warlpiri)	[−LR] (Erg)	[−LR] [−HR] (Dat)	[ ] (Nom)	[−LR] (Erg)	[ ] (Nom)	[ ] (Nom)
Erg/Nom (Kabardian)	[−LR] (Erg)	[−LR] (Erg)	[ ] (Nom)	[−LR] (Erg)	[ ] (Nom)	[ ] (Nom)

The featural specification for case markers assumed within LDG is repeated in (28). In Kiparsky's system, the ergative is specified as [−LR], meaning that it is not the lowest role. In LDG, the featural specification for the ergative is [+lr], which translates to 'there is a lower role'.

(28) **Structural Cases, LDG**
Dative   [+hr, +lr]
Accusative   [+hr]
Ergative   [+lr]
Nominative/Absolutive [ ]

The underlying intuition common to both approaches is that the ergative is associated with the higher thematic roles, that is, arguments which are not deeply embedded. Within the lexical decomposition approach assumed by both LDG and Kiparsky, these arguments would mainly be causers or effectors, i.e. agentive arguments which are probably manipulating another argument. One could therefore argue that Marantz's (1991) notion of the ergative as a dependent structural case shows clear analytic parallels to the classification assumed in these linking theories. However, the definition and use of the featural specification in both Kiparsky's linking theory and Wunderlich's LDG is far more flexible and versatile than the primarily structural approach articulated by Marantz. Kiparsky can account for a greater range of ergatives and LDG allows a reference to semantic factors via the positive features [+lr] (control) and [+hr] (affectedness).

6.6 Split Ergativity

This section introduces yet another complication in the study of ergativity. Most ergative languages are in fact *split ergative*. An example of split ergativity was already encountered in Urdu/Hindi. As already mentioned and as illustrated in (29), the ergative case in Urdu/Hindi is mainly confined to transitive verbs with perfect morphology. This type of tense/aspect split, whereby the ergative aligns itself with perfect/perfective/past morphology, is crosslinguistically very common (see Dixon 1994 for some discussion).

(29) a. ram   gari   cala-ta   hɛ
Ram.M.Sg.Nom car.M.Sg.Nom drive-Impf.M.Sg be.Pres.3.Sg
'Ram drives a car.'   Hindi

b. ram=ne   gari   cala-yi   hɛ
Ram.M.Sg=Erg car.M.Sg.Nom drive-Perf.M.F.Sg be.Pres.3.Sg
'Ram has driven a/the car.'   Hindi

A further common split has been dubbed the *NP-split*. Many languages confine the ergative case to a subset of pronouns or NPs. Silverstein (1976) showed that these splits are not random, but tend to follow a universally relevant person hierarchy in which factors such as number, animacy, and humanness play a role. The hierarchy is implicational and makes complex predictions about the kinds of split ergativity that may develop. A typical NP-split is one in which 3rd person pronoun and NP subjects are ergative, but 1st and 2nd person pronoun subjects are nominative. The examples in (30) from the Pama-Nyungan language Ngawun, based on Blake (1979:292), illustrate this typical pattern.

(30) a. panʸa-ŋka   ṉantu-lpuŋu tʸalaṛu
woman-Erg hold-Pres   baby.Nom
'The woman is holding the baby.'   Ngawun

b. ŋayu   ṭiṇi   ṯaya-lpuŋu
I.Nom tree.Nom cut.Pres
'I'm cutting firewood.'   Ngawun

In Dyirbal, the language that has been analysed as syntactically ergative, the ergative pattern does not extend across the entire system either: pronouns as a class do not take the ergative case and therefore follow the syntax of accusative languages (Silverstein 1976). NP-splits and tense/aspect splits can furthermore interact (see Dixon 1994 for some discussion), leading to complex case marking and agreement systems.

Every theory of ergativity and case must necessarily also deal with split ergativity. Within GB/MP, for example, the analyses tend to involve the interaction of information in AspP, AgrP or similar phrases with other syntactic considerations. The linking theories acknowledge agreement as a possible linker and formulate complex interactions between agreement, prononimal reference and case marking via the linking features. Within OT, *harmonic alignment scales* (Aissen 1999) have been proposed (section 8.2) which determine various optimal case distributions across languages.

6.7 Acquisition Issues

Ergative languages are said to occur less frequently than accusative languages (Dixon 1994). With respect to acquisition, one might therefore wonder if ergative languages are also more difficult to acquire than accusative languages. Work on the first language acquisition of case marking in general remains comparatively underrepresented in the acquisition literature. However, there are a handful of studies which specifically study the acquisition of the ergative. This section briefly presents some of the available evidence to date.

The languages that have been studied in the acquisition literature include some of the languages already discussed, namely, Hindi, Basque and West Greenlandic, as well as some that have not as yet been mentioned, namely K'iche' (a Maya language), Kaluli (spoken in Papua New Guinea) and Samoan.

K'iche' patterns along the lines of West Greenlandic, except that there are two phonologically conditioned versions of the ergative case. Pye (1990) could identify only very few errors with respect to the case marking of subjects. There were only a few instances of children marking either intransitive subjects with the ergative, or transitive subjects with the absolutive. There was no evidence to indicate that the absolutive was acquired before the ergative, and vice versa. The youngest child showed only one error at age 2;1. The evidence suggests that ergative case marking is acquired early and systematically.

Fortescue (1985) examined one West Greenlandic speaking child aged 2;3 and found that the ergative case was always used correctly, again indicating an early and easy acquisition of the ergative. This pattern is confirmed by data from Urdu/Hindi. A small study carried out by myself in 1991 recorded data from 7 children between the ages of 2;6 and 4;5. The results showed vanishingly few errors with the ergative. The order of acquisition seemed to be: first nominative (easy because phonologically unmarked), then the ergative, then the dative/accusative. These preliminary results have recently been broadly confirmed by Narasimhan (2003), who finds that children acquiring Hindi make no 'errors of commission', i.e., producing an ergative where there shouldn't be one. Of the three children she recorded, one produced an ergative only 17% of the time in obligatory contexts between 2;2 and 2;7, but then moved to 100% of the time. Of the other two children, the older one (3;3–3;9) had a perfect score, the younger one was at about 75% from ages 1;7–2;1, but was perfect by 2;3, again indicating an early acquisition of the ergative.

There are two major hypotheses in language acquisition about the nature of the information the child uses to 'bootstrap' its grammar. The *syntactic bootstrapping hypothesis* assumes that the child uses built-in information about universal grammar to get going. The *semantic bootstrapping hypothesis* assumes that the child uses universal semantically based information to organize its grammatical space. Under both the syntactic and the semantic bootstrapping accounts, the ergative case works out to be problematic. From a syntactic point of view, ergative languages are deviant. Syntactically ergative languages 'invert' the more normal correspondences between actor/subject and patient/object (see section 6.4) and it follows from Marantz's (1984) syntactic ergativity hypothesis that acquisition of case in syntactically ergative languages should be harder and therefore take longer. This hypothesis has not been tested, since to my knowledge no acquisition data for a truly syntactically ergative language exists (Marantz 1984 considers West Greenlandic to be syntactically ergative, but Fortescue's study shows that children learning this language acquire the ergative easily and early on).

Pinker's (1984) semantic bootstrapping account also presupposes a correlation between semantic relations such as agent and patient and syntactic relations (subject, object) and under his account children are predisposed to look for languages in which As (transitive subjects) and Ss (intransitive subjects) are grouped together, since the finer distinction between *agents* of transitive verbs and *actors* of intransitive verbs are only attended to later.

Neither one of these basic accounts predicts the early and easy acquisition of ergativity sketched above. Rather, what seems to be true is that children pay attention to what has been articulated as *transitivity* by Hopper and Thompson (1980). Transitivity is proposed as a fundamental human schema which involves situations in which an actor operates upon an object. Transitivity can be expressed in a variety of ways and some fundamental ingredients are volitionality or control over the action, telicity or completion of the action, the affectedness of the object being manipulated, and the focus placed on the actor vs. the object, realis or irrealis mood, and punctuality of the action (compare these factors to Dowty's Proto-Role entailments, section 5.4). Actions are marked as *highly transitive* if a high number of these ingredients are present. If one assumes that children are fundamentally attuned to transitivity, then an early identification and acquisition of the ergative follows immediately (cf. Slobin's 1985 Manipulative Activity Scene).

Indeed, Budwig (1989) in her examination of six English-speaking children between the ages of 1;8 and 2;8 found that some of these children use self-reference pronouns (*my*, *I*, etc.) in a way that expresses the notion of control despite the fact that this distinction is not made in the adult language.

> *My* links up with utterances in which the child attempts to use language to bring about a change in the environment, while *I* appears in utterances where control is not at issue. [Budwig 1989:277]

There are some languages in which the ergative is not acquired as quickly or as easily as described above. However, in these languages, there are some confounding factors which the child must sort through, so that a slightly later acquisition of the ergative patterns would seem reasonable.

Samoan, for example, differs from the usual pattern displayed by split ergative languages in that the appearance of the ergative is grounded in sociolinguistic factors as well as syntactic ones. The more formal register of Samoan requires the ergative on all postverbal transitive subjects. The less formal register allows the ergative not to be expressed at all. Data from six Samoan children between the ages of 1;7 and 2;11 were recorded by Ochs (1985). She found that the ergative is acquired relatively late: children between the ages of 2 and 4 rarely used the ergative. Given that the ergative is only required in the formal register, this data is not surprising.

Kaluli is another example of a language which does not conform to the 'usual' ergative patterns described in this chapter. In Kaluli the appearance of the ergative does not only depend on the transitive/intransitive distinction, it is also related to focus (partly encoded by word order) and the presence of kinship terms. The ergative is furthermore identical in form to the genitive. Consistent use of the ergative takes until 2;8 and there is some indication that children are correlating it with the use of the past tense. This is interesting because it could indicate that the Kaluli children are hypothesizing a tense/aspect split ergative system, which is not found in the adult language.

Returning to an already familiar language, in Basque the acquisition of the ergative turns out to be problematic (Ezeizabarrena and Larrañaga 1996, Larrañaga 2000), not because of any sociolinguistic factors or complications with focus and kinship terms, but because the ergative -*k* marker is identical to the absolutive plural -*k*. However, children do acquire the right verb agreement facts early on. Given that the verb agreement facts reflect the basic ergative structure of the language (transitive and intransitive unergative verbs pattern in opposition to intransitive unaccusative verbs), this indicates that they are attentive early on to the basic ergative pattern, though they may be struggling with the precise form of the case marker on the nouns. In conclusion, even though ergative languages are said to be in the minority, ergativity as such poses no real problems for language acquisition.

6.8 Historical Issues

Another question that can be posed with respect to ergative case systems relates to historical change. How does ergativity arise in the first place? Do ergative languages ever become accusative, and vice versa? This section briefly addresses some of these questions.

Sanskrit was an accusative language, both syntactically and morphologically. Many of its modern descendants, such as Urdu/Hindi, Punjabi, or Marathi are morphologically ergative but syntactically accusative. Others, like Bengali, are morphologically and syntactically accusative. Languages clearly change the way they use case. In part, these changes are often motivated or triggered by the morphophonological erosion of case affixes over time. This loss or change in turn is triggered by a variety of factors, among them changes in the phonological system, or changes in other parts of the morphosyntactic system which need to be adjusted for (e.g., Lahiri 2000, Harris and Campbell 1995). Though there is a huge literature on particular instances of language change, a more complete understanding of the mechanisms and predictable directions of language change remains to be arrived at.

As case marking is lost over time, or becomes difficult to process due to *syncretism*, by which two or more forms fall together,[5] new case markers are generally pressed into the system. These case markers tend to be drawn from the set of adpositions (prepositions or postpositions).

Lehman (1985:304) proposes a cline along the lines in (31) for the development of case markers. Clines are a hallmark of *Grammaticalization Theory* (Hopper and Traugott 1993), which assumes that language change proceeds gradually according to a given path or cline of change (see Meillet 1912 for an early formulation).

(31) relational noun (e.g., top, way, front) >
secondary adposition (e.g., behind, beside) >
primary adposition (e.g., to, by, of) >
morphological case affix

The types of *relational nouns* that commonly lead to case markers are nouns like *top, way, side, foot, head, back, front*, i.e., mainly spatial/locational expressions and nouns denoting body parts. An example of a relational noun developing into a preposition comes from German, where the dative plural of *Weg* 'path' has developed into a preposition meaning 'because': *wegen des Wetters* 'because of the weather' (Hopper and Traugott 1993:107).

Eventually such adpositions can develop into morphological case marking. The basic idea is that relational nouns are *reanalysed* as adpositions, which

---

[5] For example, all of the non-nominative Sanskrit cases eventually fell together. Vestiges of the old system are still evident in modern Urdu as an *-e* morpheme on *oblique* non-nominative nouns.

are then further reanalysed as pieces of the morphology. Reanalysis has been recognized as one of the driving forces of historical change. Another important source of change is language contact, whereby new forms, also new case markers, could be *borrowed* into the language. A third recognized force in language change is *extension*, by which systems can be regularized if they have become too exception ridden due to preceding changes in the language. With respect to case, a typical example of extension might be as shown in (32), where special genitive objects have been absorbed to fit in with the more regular system of accusative objects (Harris and Campbell 1995).

(32)

Verb Type	Old System	New System
Regular Transitive	Nom Acc	Nom Acc
Special Transitive	Nom Gen	Nom Acc

Not all case markers develop exactly according to the cline in (31) and Grammaticalization Theory is not the only theory investigating case and language change. Among more recent work, for example, see Allen (1995) for a detailed study of Old English from a perspective based on LFG, Lightfoot (2002) for a collection of papers from different perspectives, and Harris and Campbell (1995) for an articulation primarily in terms of morphosyntactic reanalysis, borrowing and extension.

The two central factors that have been implicated crosslinguistically in the rise of ergativity are passivization and possessives (e.g., Benveniste 1952, S. Anderson 1977, Plank 1979b, Garrett 1990, Dixon 1994, Harris and Campbell 1995). Ergative case is argued to arise when a former passive participle is reinterpreted as an active verb. Simultaneously, the former oblique agent adjunct (generally an instrumental) is reanalysed as an ergative subject. The basic idea with respect to a reanalysis of former passives is illustrated in (33) with the constructed example from Sanskrit (based on Garrett 1990:263). The adjectival passive participial in Sanskrit is formed with the morpheme *-ta*, the patient is nominative and the agent is instrumental. Over time, this passive or *stative* construction comes to be reanalysed as an active one and the former instrumental is reinterpreted as an ergative.

(33) a. ahi-r indr-eṇa ha-ta-ḥ
serpent-Nom.Sg Indra-Inst.Sg kill-Ptcpl-Nom.Sg
'The serpent has been killed by Indra.'   Sanskrit
Actually: The serpent is one killed by Indra.'
b. **Reanalysed as:**
serpent-Nom.Sg Indra-Erg.Sg kill-Past
'Indra has killed the serpent.'

Reanalysis with respect to possessives works similarly and is illustrated here with data from Old Persian (based on Kent 1953). This pattern is known as the *manā kartam* 'done by me' construction. The participle involved is the same participle as the one implicated in Sanskrit (Proto Indo-European **to*).

(34) a. ima tya   manā   kartam
     that which 1.Sg.Gen do.Ptcpl
     pasāva yaθā xšāyaθiya abavam
     after   when king   become.Past.1.Sg   Old Persian
     'This (is) that (which) was done by me after I became king.'
     Reanalysed as: 'I did that after I became king.'
  b. avaθ=šām   hamaranam kartam
     thus=3.Pl.Gen battle   do.Ptcpl
     'Thus by them battle was done.'   Old Persian
     Reanalysed as: 'Thus they did battle.'

The agent is again realized as an oblique, but this time as a genitive possessive. Again, the idea is that the genitive is reanalysed as an ergative agent, and the participle as an active verb.

The development of an ergative case is assumed to be indicative of a *shift* or *alignment* change between grammatical relations and case marking in the entire case system of the language. This case shift has been proposed for a number of languages. Johns (1992), for example, argues for an analysis of Inuktitut (an Eskimo language) which involves both a passive and a possessive stage. Johns's analysis is interesting and suggestive, but it is based solely on comparative synchronic evidence, because there is no historical record of Eskimo languages. That is, she postulates that the ancestor language was accusative, but she has no direct evidence that the ancestor language was not already ergative as well. This paucity of solid diachronic data plagues the bulk of the research investigating possible accusative to ergative shifts (and vice versa). There are several cases which are generally cited as being solid examples of accusative to ergative shifts (e.g., Dixon 1994, Harris and Campbell 1995), chief among them Polynesian (Chung 1977) and Indo-Iranian.

Under one scenario, the ancestor language of modern Polynesian languages is assumed to be accusative. The modern ergative has been argued to stem from a reanalysis of a passive construction. However, this analysis is controversial, partly because the role of several verbal affixes and their interaction with passivization remains ill understood (see Dixon 1994 for some discussion). The issue remains unresolved in the light of the missing diachronic data and in the absence of new insights or proposals.

The only historically documented case of an accusative to ergative shift is supposed to be Indo-Iranian, featuring the types of examples in (33) and (34).

> In part because the changes are actually attested, the Indo-Iranian languages are among the most discussed and best-understood examples of change in alignment. [Harris and Campbell 1995:263]

Indeed, the literature on an accusative to ergative shift and vice versa in Indo-Iranian and, more broadly, Indo-European is vast. However, again there are substantial problems with the proposal of a passive to ergative reanalysis. For one, the verb forms implicated were adjectival participles, but not standard passive forms. More seriously on the Indo-Aryan side, the Sanskrit instrumental had eroded and fallen together with the dative, accusative, genitive, ablative and locative long before the modern ergative entered the scene (in Hindi/Urdu that was at some point in the 17th century, but the individual case markings had fallen together centuries before then). There is no viable scenario in which the instrumental could have been reanalysed as an ergative for the simple reason that there was no instrumental to reanalyse. Curiously, this was a well known fact in the 19th century (e.g., Beames 1872), but one which did not get picked up by the current linguistic mainstream (see Butt 2001 for a discussion).

Similar problems apply to the analysis of Iranian. The situation there is particularly interesting as one posits an accusative ancestral language that shifted to an ergative language, which then shifted back to an accusative language (modern Persian is morphologically and syntactically accusative).

The best case for an accusative to ergative shift, namely Indo-Iranian, is thus dubious. An alternative proposal could be that the ancestor languages were ergative to begin with, and that the modern languages simply continue this trend. There are solid indications that Middle Indo-Aryan had already moved towards an ergative system, albeit without the presence of an extra ergative case (e.g., Bubenik 1996, Peterson 1998). There are furthermore indications that parts of the Old Indo-Aryan Sanskrit system were ergative already, or P(atient)-oriented as Hock (1986) has dubbed it (see Butt 2001 for a discussion). The precise status of such clues to an ergative system in at least parts of the syntax of a language, but without the presence of an overt ergative case needs to be clarified within linguistic theorizing. Generally, if a language has some ergative properties, it is considered to be ergative, albeit split ergative. However, would one really want to redefine Sanskrit as an underlyingly ergative language?

There are proposals that the even older ancestor language, namely, Proto Indo-European, was ergative to begin with. Bauer (2000) contains a nice discussion of the ergative to accusative vs. accusative to ergative debate with respect to Proto Indo-European. However, if Proto Indo-European was ergative, then the large number of modern Indo-European accusative languages need to be explained. There is quite a bit of data which charts the loss of ergative case marking for a range of languages, which includes Australian languages (see Dixon 1994 for some discussion) and Indo-Iranian (e.g., Bubenik 1989). However, the reasons behind this loss are not well understood.

In conclusion, much more work on the effects of historical change on case systems needs to be done. Butt (2001), for example, attempts to develop an alternative scenario for Indo-Aryan in which it is not the case system that shifts or changes, but the semantics and distribution of individual case markers shift around. As case morphology is lost and as postpositions are being pressed into service as case markers, the syntactic and semantic expression of the case system is redistributed: the case system as a whole remains intact, but the burden of expressing the system is redistributed across individual case markers.

Butt (2001) focused exclusively on the rise of the ergative case in modern Urdu; however, investigations into historical change and case systems should probably be extended to include patterns with other non-nominative subjects such as datives. The origin of the modern Urdu ergative *ne* is obscure, but there are some suggestions (Chatterji 1926) that it is related to a postposition originally meaning 'for the sake of, because of, caused by'. This postpositional meaning is compatible with agency, but also with benefaction. And indeed, *ne* crops up as a dative in some sister languages of Urdu/Hindi. Conversely, the form that encodes the ergative in languages like Nepali (*le*) encodes datives/accusatives in other sister languages. There is thus some indication that the simple ergative-nominative-accusative opposition is too simple: in order to fully understand what is going on, an extended typology of case systems must be recognized and analysed both in synchronic and diachronic terms.

6.9 Summary

This chapter has provided an overview of the major issues with respect to ergativity. Despite formal differences between syntactic theories, most of the approaches discussed accept a fundamental division between accusative languages on the one hand and ergative languages on the other. Most theories also accept the basic division articulated by Dixon (1979) and versions of Marantz's (1984) syntactic ergativity hypothesis, even though there seems to be only one well established case of a syntactically ergative language. It is interesting that Sapir's (1917) and Fillmore's (1968) more complex typology of the relationship between case and grammatical relations has not been adopted into the linguistic mainstream (though there are individual papers pointing out that the typology needs to be more complex). Most investigations of ergativity only take the simple ergative-accusative opposition into account. Some research does investigate a broader spectrum of data. Work on Georgian, for example, tends to include a discussion of the dative construction (in the perfect series, see section 6.2.2). However, more work remains to be done.

A consideration of dative subject constructions tends to involve a more explicit consideration of the semantics involved in case alternations. This and the preceding chapters have implicated semantic factors in the use and function of case, but the primary focus has been on syntactic constraints. The next chapter takes a closer look at some well known case alternations which are primarily semantically governed, including some alternations involving the dative case.

6.10 Exercises

Exercise 1: Basic Concepts
1. Basic Terminology
    (a) How is an ergative language defined?
    (b) How is an accusative language defined?
    (c) What other kinds of systems are there potentially?
2. What kind of ergative languages are there?
3. What kinds of splits do ergative languages show?

Exercise 2 — Punjabi

Punjabi is a North Indian language, spoken mostly in the Punjab (which spans both India and Pakistan). Punjabi is closely related to Urdu/Hindi, but does several things differently.

Punjabi employs the following case clitics.

(1) **Case Clitic**
∅ (Unmarked or zero)
nũ
ne
kolõ
tõ
da/de/di/diã

Exercise 2.1: Case Analysis

Note that none of the clitics in (1) have been identified as to name or function. In fact, there is little information on this topic in either linguistic papers or Punjabi grammars. So, try to use the data presented in the following sections along with the discussion in this chapter to formulate hypotheses about the case system of Punjabi.

1. What labels/names would you give the case clitics?
2. What grammatical relations can these case clitics appear on?

(2) muṇda   tez   doṛ-da   ɛ
    boy.M.Sg fast run-Pres.M.Sg be.Pres.3.Sg
    'The boy runs fast.'   Punjabi

(3) muṇde=ne   kıtab   paṛ-i
    boy.M.Obl=??? book.F.Sg read-Past.F.Sg
    'The boy read a/the book.'   Punjabi

(4) o=ne   mundiã=nũ   mar-ıa
    Pron.Sg=??? boy.M.Pl=??? hit-Past.M.Sg
    'He/She hit the boys.'   Punjabi

(5) admi   gɛa
    man.M.Sg   go.Past.M.Sg
    'A/the man went.'   Punjabi

(6) larki   gɛi
    girl.F.Sg go.Past.F.Sg
    'A/the girl went.'   Punjabi

(7) do tobi   kapre   dʰõge
    two washerman.M.Sg/Pl   clothes.Pl wash.Fut.M.Pl
    'Two washermen will wash clothes.'   Punjabi

(8) do tobi   ram=de   kapre   dʰõge
    two washerman.M.Sg/Pl   Ram.M.Sg=???.M.Pl   clothes.Pl wash.Fut.M.Pl
    'Two washermen will wash Ram's clothes.'   Punjabi

(9) do tobiã=ne   kapre   tote
    two washerman.M.Pl=???   clothes.Pl wash.Past.M.Pl
    'Two washermen washed the clothes.'   Punjabi

(10) munde=kolõ/=tõ   canda   tãg-ã   gɛa
     boy.M.Obl=???/=???   flag.M.Sg   hang-Past.M.Sg   go.Past.M.Sg
     'The flag was hung by the boy.'   Punjabi

(11) ram=tõ   par-ia   nai janda
     Ram.M.Sg=???   read.Past.M.Sg   not go.Pres.M.Sg
     'Ram cannot read.'   Punjabi

(12) tokri=tõ   do amb   dıg pae
     basket.F.Sg=???   two mango.M.Sg/Pl   fall fall.Past.M.Pl
     'Two mangoes dropped out from the basket.'   Punjabi

(13) o   mina=kolõ ɛ
     Pron.3.Sg   Mina=???   be.Pres.3.Sg
     'He/She is with/by Mina.'   Punjabi

(14) ram=di   tokri=tõ   do amb
     Ram.M.Sg=???.F.Sg   basket.F.Sg=???   two mango.M.Sg/Pl
     dıg pae
     fall fall.Past.M.Pl
     'Two mangoes dropped out from Ram's basket.'   Punjabi

(15) sab=ne   tobiã=nũ   inam   dıtta
officer.M.Sg=??? washerman.M.Pl=??? prize.M.Sg give.Past.M.Sg
'The officer gave the washermen a/the prize.'   Punjabi

(16) sab=ne   tobiã=nũ   ram=da
officer.M.Sg=??? washerman.M.Pl=??? Ram.M.Sg=???M.Sg
inam   dıtta
prize.M.Sg give.Past.M.Sg
'The officer gave the washermen Ram's prize.'   Punjabi

Exercise 2.2: Aspect

1. How can the contrast between the sentences in (17a) and (17b) and (18a) and (18b) be explained?
2. What type of a language is Punjabi?

(17) a. ram   muṇḍiã=nũ   mar-da   ɛ
        Ram.M.Sg boy.M.Pl=??? hit-Pres.M.Sg be.Pres.3.Sg
        'Ram is hitting the boys.'   Punjabi

   b. ram=ne   muṇḍiã=nũ   mar-ıa   si
      Ram.M.Sg=??? boy.M.Pl=??? hit-Past.M.Sg be.Past.3.Sg
      'Ram has hit the boys.'   Punjabi

(18) a. larki   muṇḍiã=nũ   mar-di   ɛ
        girl.F.Sg boy.M.Pl=??? hit-Pres.F.Sg be.Pres.3.Sg
        'The girl is hitting the boys.'   Punjabi

   b. larki=ne   muṇḍiã=nũ   mar-ıa   si
      girl.M.Sg=??? boy.M.Pl=??? hit-Past.M.Sg be.Past.3.Sg
      'The girl has hit the boys.'   Punjabi

Exercise 2.3: Agreement

Based on all of the above data, figure out the agreement pattern of Punjabi (ignore the *da/di/de* forms). Note that not all of the sentences will provide you with conclusive evidence, but most of them will.

The following questions should help to guide you towards a generalization.

1. Does the verb always agree with the subject?
2. If the verb does not show subject agreement, then what does it agree with?
3. Does the verb always have to agree with something in the sentence?

Exercise 2.4: Pronouns

Now, in light of the generalization needed to account for the agreement patterns in the above data, evaluate the data given below.

1. The first and second person pronouns look like they do not bear any case marking, in opposition to the third person pronouns.
2. Do the first and second person pronouns behave like other nouns that are not overtly marked for case with respect to agreement?
3. If not, how do they differ?
4. What case would you assign to the first and second person pronouns?

(19) laṛki   gɛi
     girl.F.Sg go.Past.F.Sg
     'A/the girl went.'   Punjabi

(20) mɛ̃   lakṛi   vaḍ-i
     I.F/M wood.F.Sg cut-Past.F.Sg
     'I (male or female) cut the wood.'   Punjabi

(21) tũ   lakṛi   vaḍ-i
     you.F/M wood.F.Sg cut-Past.F.Sg
     'You (male or female) cut the wood.'   Punjabi

(22) tũ   kampuṭar   becʰ-ia
     you.F/M computer.M.Sg sell-Past.M.Sg
     'You (male or female) sold the computer.'   Punjabi

(23) mɛ̃   kampuṭar   becʰ-ia
     I.F/M computer.M.Sg sell-Past.M.Sg
     'I (male or female) sold the computer.'   Punjabi

(24) o=ne   kampuṭar   becʰ-ia
     Pron.3.Sg.F/M=??? computer.M.Sg sell-Past.M.Sg
     'He/She sold the computer.'   Punjabi

7

The Semantics of Case

> It would be an easy map if that were all; but there is also the first day at school, religion, fathers, the round pond, needlework, murders, hangings, verbs that take the dative . . .
> [J.M. Barrie, *Peter Pan*, p.6]

Several examples of *semantically motivated* case alternations have already been encountered in previous chapters. This chapter provides a more coherent discussion of the phenomenon by presenting some further well known semantically based case alternations, and by discussing a variety of approaches, which contain a serious semantic component in their analysis of case.

7.1 Localist Theories

Localist theories of case have already been mentioned at various places in this book. Localist theories attempt to ground patterns of case marking in concrete spatial and locational uses. Abstract or temporal uses of case are argued to be derived from spatial uses. No matter how abstract or structural some case marking may appear, it is argued to be connected to a spatial use.

One generally cited example comes from Latin. In Latin, the accusative marks objects, as in (1a), but it is also used for directional goals as in (1b). Localist theories assume that such *accusatives of direction* are not aberrant parts of the paradigm, but that there are regular principles which connect the abstract structural use in (1a) with the directional use in (1b).

(1)   a. rōmam   vidēre
         Rome.Acc see
         'To see Rome.'   Latin
  b. rōmam   īre
         Rome.Acc go
         'To go to Rome.'   Latin

The idea can perhaps be better illustrated with the English dative *to* in (2a). This is assumed to be directly connected to the directional use in (2b). Because the English *to* is a preposition and not a case morpheme, the parallel between the concrete spatial uses and the abstract use is more obvious.

(2) a. Kim donated books to the library.
    b. Kim walked to her house.

Recall that case morphology is often derived from former prepositions or postpositions via historical change. As such, the connection between concrete spatial uses and abstract case is not far-fetched. However, it is debatable whether the connection is as direct as what is assumed in Localist theories.

Localist theories have a long tradition. The first practitioner was the Byzantine Maximus Planudes, who lived and worked around 1300 CE. In more modern times, well known advocates are Hjelmslev (1935) and J. Anderson (1971). Jakobson's (1936) effort to find coherent semantics for the Russian case system is also classified as an example of a localist analysis. He argued that all of the individual uses of the Russian genitive, for example, should be derivable from one and the same overarching semantics.

The localist perspectives formulated by Gruber (1965) have found their way into much of modern linguistic thought, mostly by way of Jackendoff's (1972, 1976, 1990) subsequent development and formalization of Gruber's initial proposals (cf. section 5.3). That is, most modern generative approaches to case do not explicitly adopt a localist theory. The fundamental ideas have nevertheless 'leaked' into linguistic consciousness to such a degree that they are assumed as basic generalizations about how language works (e.g., see the assumption in section 5.9 that the subjects of psych predicates are abstract goals). Localist theories take these basic generalizations and seek to formalize them in order to drive linguistic explanations.

7.2 Agency vs. Experience

Beyond the clear connection to spatial uses, other factors have recurrently cropped up with respect to case in this book. Two of these are agentivity and affectedness. Wierzbicka (1981) takes a closer look at these factors in a paper entitled 'Case Marking and Human Nature'. In particular, she examines claims based on Silverstein's (1976) person hierarchy (see section 6.6) that humans see themselves as a 'quintessential agent' and that therefore 1st and 2nd persons need to be less marked for agency than other things. With respect to ergativity this view predicts that 1st and 2nd person pronouns will be marked less often with an overt ergative case, than 3rd person pronouns and nouns. This pattern is indeed confirmed by crosslinguistic comparison. The basic idea with respect to case can thus be formulated as in (3).

(3) a. Ergative marks an unexpected agent.

b. Accusative marks an unexpected patient.

Wierzbicka rejects this view and instead argues that what languages pay attention to is 'experiencerhood' or 'patienthood'. That is, rather than seeing themselves as agents, humans instead appear to be more worried about what is happening to them. In support of her theory, she provides ratios of agents to patients in plays and finds the following tendency.

> ... the speaker is more interested in what other people are doing to him than in what he is doing to other people; he is more sensitive to the ways in which other people's actions affect him than to the ways in which his actions affect other people. The speaker regards himself as the quintessential 'victim' or the quintessential experiencer. [Wierzbicka 1981:46]

Wierzbicka goes on to point out that many languages have a special construction for marking experiencers. We have already seen examples of such experiencer constructions: they tend to show up with datives or genitives crosslinguistically. In some languages, the genitives/datives are subjects, in others they are not. An example with a genitive subject is shown for Bengali in (4). Wierzbicka cites the example in (5) for German, which involves the so-called 'free dative'. The basic construction is a simple copula construction 'be good'. In German, a dative argument may be added to this basic predication (and to many others). This dative is an experiencer dative and is not subcategorized for the verb (hence the term 'free dative').

(4) amar tʃa bʰalo lage
I.Gen tea.Nom good be.attached.Pres
'I like tea.' (Klaiman 1980:276)   Bengali

(5) Sei (mir) nur brav!
be.Imp I.Dat only good
'Be good!' (Wierzbicka 1981:48)   German

Wierzbicka goes on to argue that all cases must be seen as having a semantic connection and that there must be a basic meaning for each case, from which a range of meanings can be derived. This echoes Jakobson's (1936) ideas of how to analyse case. In particular, she takes on the structural accusative and argues that even this case must be invested with semantic content (beyond being used to mark patients or themes), because it can participate in semantically determined case alternations. One pertinent example in (6) comes from Russian.

(6) a. Ivan ždet tramvaj.
Ivan.Nom is-waiting-for tram.Acc
'Ivan is waiting for the tram.' (Wierzbicka 1982:56)   Russian

    b. Ivan   ždet   tramvaja.
       Ivan.Nom is-waiting-for tram.Gen
       'Ivan is waiting for a tram.' (Wierzbicka 1982:56)   Russian

In this example, the use of accusative vs. the genitive makes a difference in terms of the definiteness of the object. In (6a), Ivan is waiting for a particular tram, whereas in (6b), some generic tram is being referred to. These kinds of case alternations have already been encountered for Urdu in section 5.9. They turn out to be quite common crosslinguistically, indicating that this is a systematic part of language in need of a good explanation. The next section explores several proposals with respect to such object alternations.

Wierzbicka also implicates *topicality* as playing a role in the appearance of case marking, particularly with respect to the ergative. It is clear that discourse factors do interact with case marking, but as already mentioned in section 5.3, there is little work on this and certainly no 'standard' theory.

7.3 Object Alternations

De Hoop (1996) embeds case alternations as in (6) into a semantic theory of noun phrase interpretation. In particular, she discusses the famous Finnish partitive case alternation shown in (7), and the Turkish alternation shown in (8). Enç (1991) identified the semantic notion of *specificity* as being the relevant factor governing the Turkish alternation. The Finnish alternation involves the use of the *partitive* case, indicating a reference to parts of a whole.

(7) a. Ostin   leipää
       bought.1.Sg bread.Part
       'I bought (some) bread.'   Finnish

     b. Ostin   leivän
       bought.1.Sg bread.Acc
       'I bought the bread.'   Finnish

(8) a. Ali bir piyano kivalamak istiyor.
       A. one piano to.rent   wants
       'Ali wants to rent one (some) piano.' (Enç 1991)   Turkish

     b. Ali bir piyano-yu kivalamak istiyor.
       A. one piano-Acc to.rent   wants
       'Ali wants to rent a certain piano.' (Enç 1991)   Turkish

De Hoop proposes a more general analysis by arguing for a distinction between *weak Case* and *strong Case*. Nouns with weak Case allow nonspecific and partitive readings as in (6b), (7a) and (8a). They are also likely to be *incorporated* into the verb (Baker 1988) and give rise to a modified description of general activities such as hunting or watching. Some examples are *deer-hunting* or *bird-watching*. The particular type of hunting or watching is specified by the noun; however, the noun itself does not refer to a specific deer or bird. The idea is that one could have gone to the forest and not seen or shot a single deer, but one could still come back and claim that one had been 'deer-hunting' for the past few days. In some languages, the noun is incorporated into the verb morphologically, resulting in a single word (e.g., something like *deerhunting*). This does not happen in English, but is a common strategy across languages (Baker 1988).[1]

Noun phrases which have strong Case, in contrast, are compatible with specific and definite readings as in (6a), (7b) and (8b), as well as quantifiers such as *all, every, some*, etc. While de Hoop ostensibly builds on Case Theory as articulated in GB, she implicates case as a crucial factor that must be considered in the formal semantic analysis of a clause. This represents a radical departure from the idea that case on core grammatical relations (i.e., subject and object) is either purely structural (licenses arguments), or is lexically stipulated with no interesting semantic consequences.

Kiparsky (1998) takes issue with de Hoop's (1996) analysis of the Finnish facts. But rather than dismissing the semantic factor, he argues that it has been misunderstood. Kiparsky's (1998) analysis implicates aspectual *boundedness* as formalized by Krifka (1992). Two relevant examples are given in (9).

(9) a. Ammu-i-n   karhu-n
    shoot-Past-1Sg bear-Acc
    'I shot the/a bear.' (Kiparsky 1998:267)   Finnish

b. Ammu-i-n   karhu-a
    shoot-Past-1Sg bear-Part
    'I shot at the/a bear (bear is not dead).'
    (Kiparsky 1998:267)   Finnish

In (9a), the bear has accusative case and the implication is that the bear has been shot and hit and is probably dead. In contrast, the partitive case on (9b) signals that the shot might have missed and that the bear definitely has not been killed. The difference is stated in terms of aspectual boundedness, because an event is considered to be telic or bounded when a change of state in the object has occurred. There is no tangible change of state in the bear in (9b), but there is one in (9a). Prior to (9a), the bear was alive and presumably healthy, but is now wounded or dead.[2]

Ramchand (1997) also discusses the Finnish and Turkish object alternations, but focuses mainly on Scottish Gaelic. Scottish Gaelic is a VSO language and has a syntax that is very different from that of Russian, Turkish, Finnish or Urdu. Nevertheless, the same sort of alternations can be observed. The alterna-

[1] For a recent look at semantic incorporation across languages, see Farkas and de Swart (2003).
[2] For an analysis of the Finnish partitive involving a combination of OT, Kiparsky's linking theory and aspectual boundedness, see Kiparsky (2001).

tion in (10) illustrates the bounded vs. unbounded reading observed for Finnish in (9), and the alternation in (11) allows one to express the difference between wanting something (unbounded) and getting it (bounded).

(10) a. tha   Calum air na craobhan a   ghearradh
         be.Pres Calum Asp the trees.Dir OAgr cut.VN
         'Calum has cut the trees.'   Scottish Gaelic

   b. tha   Calum a'   ghearradh nan craobhan
         be.Pres Calum Asp cut.VN   the trees.Gen   Scottish Gaelic
         'Calum is cutting the trees (no tree has necessarily been cut yet).'

(11) a. tha   mi air am ball   iarraidh
         be.Pres I Asp the ball.Dir want.VN
         'I have acquired the ball.'   Scottish Gaelic

   b. tha   mi ag iarraidh a'bhuill
         be.Pres I Asp want.VN the ball.Gen
         'I want the ball.'   Scottish Gaelic

Ramchand (1997, 1998) argues for a tight interaction between syntactic structures and semantic interpretation. Working within GB, she assumes the presence of an Asp(ectual)P. The head of AspP hosts the various aspectual markers found in Scottish Gaelic. Examples are *ag* or *air* in (10) and (11) above. The distribution of these aspectual particles is correlated with the structural position of objects. In the unbounded interpretations, the object occurs postverbally. In the bounded cases, the object is situated preverbally. Object position, in turn, is correlated with the case marking (direct vs. genitive case).

Ramchand lets the semantic differences in object interpretation follow from an interaction of aspectual semantics (mediated via the AspP) with structural position. Ramchand reifies (but also reinterprets) de Hoop's (1996) strong/weak Case distinction in terms of structural positions. The weak NP is assumed to be directly adjacent to the verb (complement position), whereas the strong NP is licensed in SpecVP (the subject is in SpecAspP). The aspectual semantics are based on a combination of Krifka's (1992) and Verkuyl's (1993) insights.

Sample analyses for (10a) and (10b) are shown in (13) and (12), respectively. In (9b), the form of the aspectual particle *a'* is a version of *ag*. This aspectual particle heads the AspP in (12) and co-occurs with an object in postverbal position. As complement to the verb, this object is in the weak Case position and is interpreted as aspectually unbounded. When the object is in this position, the object does not undergo a change of state. Also, no specificity effects can arise in this position, covering examples like the Turkish example in (8) as well.

In (13), the AspP head is filled by *air*. This aspectual particle co-occurs with an object in preverbal position. Ramchand proposes that the preverbal object is situated in SpecVP and that this position is associated with the semantics of aspectual boundedness (mediated via AspP). In this position, objects can be interpreted as undergoing a change of state, or of measuring out a specific quantity of stuff (giving rise to specificity effects).

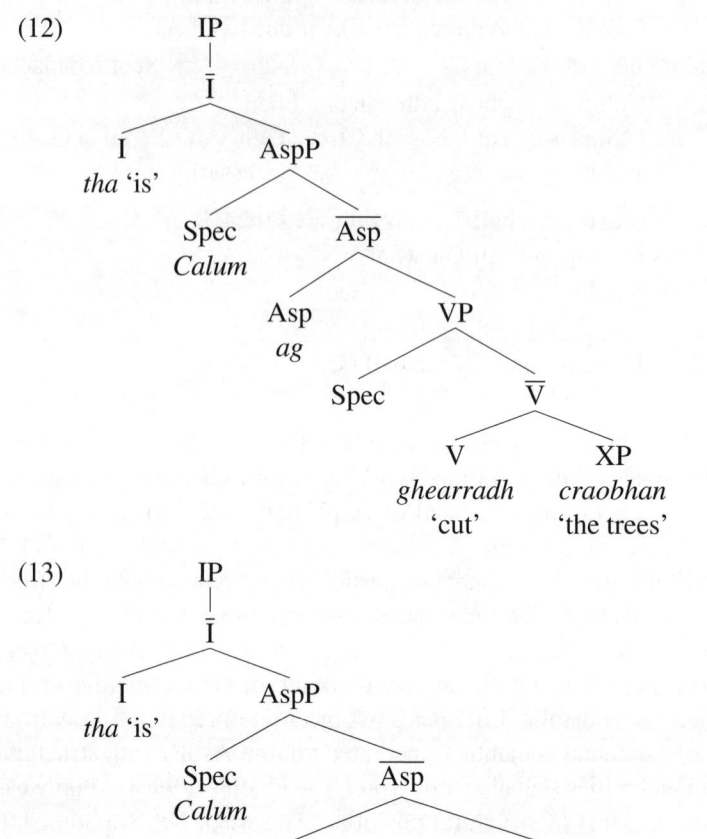

(12)
```
            IP
            |
            Ī
           / \
          I   AspP
       tha 'is' / \
             Spec  Asp̄
             Calum / \
                 Asp   VP
                 ag   / \
                    Spec  V̄
                         / \
                        V   XP
                    ghearradh craobhan
                     'cut'   'the trees'
```

(13)
```
            IP
            |
            Ī
           / \
          I   AspP
       tha 'is' / \
             Spec  Asp̄
             Calum / \
                 Asp      VP
                 air     / \
                      Spec   V̄
                   na craobhan / \
                   'the trees' V   XP
                          ghearradh
                           'cut'
```

The correlations between the differences in word order (VO vs. OV) in Scottish Gaelic suggest that Ramchand's analysis is plausible for that language. But it is not as obvious that there are indeed two different structural object positions in languages like Turkish, Finnish and Urdu. Just going by the surface word order, there would seem to be no difference in the position of the object. However, more subtle tests show that in Urdu and Turkish, the bare or nominative objects are resistant to being separated from the verb. In contrast, the accusative objects can be scrambled away from the verb quite easily for purposes of topicalization, etc. The two types of objects thus behave differently in these languages as well, supporting an analysis like Ramchand's, which posits a tight correlation between structural position and semantic interpretation (but see Kiparsky 2001 for a different take on the Finnish data).

Svenonius (2002) also assumes a tight connection between semantics and syntactic structure. Working within MP, he re-examines Icelandic case. Recall from section 4.8 that data from Icelandic gave rise to the notion of 'quirky' or lexically inherent case. Many analyses therefore assumed (and often still assume) that non-nominative subjects (e.g., datives and accusatives) and non-accusative objects (e.g., datives and genitives) in Icelandic were lexically specified or stipulated by the verb, thus pre-empting structural Case.

Svenonius pays precise attention to the lexical semantics of individual verbs and sorts the verbs into classes, which differ both in terms of their case marking patterns and their semantic entailments. Some of these differences are quite subtle, but robust. For example, verbs involving moving or throwing an object somewhere can have either dative or accusative objects. Svenonius observes that the relevant difference seems to revolve around whether the motion of the object is accompanied or not, i.e., *push a cart* vs. *throw a ball*. Some examples are given in (14) and (15) (Svenonius 2002:211).

(14)
>*kasta* DAT 'throw, fling, hurl'
>*þeyta* DAT 'fling, flow'
>*henda* DAT 'throw away, discard'
>*þrykkja* DAT 'kick or smash'

(15)
>*draga* ACC 'pull, drag, draw'
>*flytja* ACC 'move, transport, carry'
>*færa* ACC 'move, bring'
>*kækka* ACC 'raise'
>*lækka* ACC 'lower'

In order to explain this difference, Svenonius also invokes aspectual notions by assuming the kind of syntactic event decomposition discussed in section 4.10.3. The vP is associated with a causing subevent and the VP is associated with the resulting subevent. These two subevents can stand in different temporal relations to one another: they could overlap completely, so as to be indistinguishable (15), or the temporal relation between the two is looser, allowing a separate identification of each subevent (14).

Unlike Ramchand (1997), Svenonius does not assume an AspP, which steers the aspectual interpretation, but seeks to tie the case features themselves to a temporal interpretation. He proposes that case features are *interpretable*. This stands in direct contrast to standard MP assumptions, by which case features are uninterpretable (Chomsky 1995). As discussed in section 4.10.4, NPs carry uninterpretable case features that must be checked in the course of the derivation. These case features essentially license the appearance of the NP.

Svenonius (2002) builds on Pesetsky and Torrego's (2001) proposal that case features are uninterpretable with respect to the NPs, but interpretable with respect to the functional projection which regulates clausal tense and aspect. In support of their proposal, Pesetsky and Torrego (2001) cite data from Australian languages like that seen from Kayardild in section 1.2.6. In these languages, the case markers explicitly express tense/aspect/mood distinctions. This indicates that case features are interpretable in T(ense)P. Furthermore, because TP (or a projection like TP) is generally responsible for the semantics of tense, aspect, it is also taken to be responsible for expressing the temporal relation (degree of overlap) between the subevents in vP and VP. The case features on the objects (dative vs. accusative) signal different kinds of temporal relations between the subevents in vP and VP. These case features are interpreted in TP and allow for the right semantic distinctions to be made.

Interestingly, Svenonius's findings are in line with Zaenen, Maling and Thráinsson's (1985) original analysis. They assumed that inherent case in Icelandic was stated lexically. However, they also showed that there was a regular correspondence between the type of thematic role and the possible case markings: the Icelandic case system was not entirely random (as one may assume, if non-nominative and non-accusative case is simply stipulated in the lexicon). Svenonius's careful work fleshes out these original findings and builds on further work like that of Maling (2001),[3] which pointed towards a need to examine the underlying lexical semantics more carefully. The work done on Icelandic shows that given an investigation of regular and generalizable interactions between the lexical semantics of certain verb classes, the temporal/aspectual semantics of a clause, and the distribution of case marking, the case system of a language can be understood in a deep way.

Unfortunately, deep and detailed formal semantic analyses, which include a serious treatment of case are still few and far between, but there is increasing evidence that it is needed for a good understanding of case. This is not just true

---

[3]There is a host of literature on Icelandic case, both synchronic and diachronic. This cannot be done justice to in the confines of this book, but see Svenonius (2002) and Maling (2001) for a compendium of references.

for case on objects, but also for case alternations found with subjects, as the next section shows.

7.4 Subject Alternations

Svenonius (2002) analyses non-nominative subjects in Icelandic along the same lines as discussed above. However, there are enough differences between object and subject case alternations to warrant a closer look at non-nominative subjects and possible alternations.

The relevance of agency or control with respect to subject alternations involving ergative subjects has already been discussed in chapter 6. Another large class of non-nominative subjects is found with *experiencer* or *psych* verbs. A typical alternation is illustrated in (16) with an example from Bengali (Klaiman 1980). The verb for 'want' in (16a) in conjunction with a nominative subject expresses a controlled/agentive type of wanting. The same verb 'want' is used in (16b), but here the subject is genitive and the semantic interpretation is that of an uncontrollable need.

(16) a. ami tomake cai
    I.Nom you.Acc wants
    'I want you.' (Klaiman 1980:279)   Bengali

   b. amar tomake cai
    I.Gen you.Acc wants
    'I need you.' (Klaiman 1980:279)   Bengali

Verbs of wanting, needing, feeling are generally called *psych* or *experiencer* verbs because the subject of the clause is not a clear agent, i.e., somebody who acts upon some other entity, but an experiencer who is subjected to a certain *stimulus*. Crosslinguistically, two major types of psych verbs can be identified, the more agentive type as in (16a), and the pure experiencer type as in (16b). Bengali uses the genitive case to differentiate the subjects.

More usual is the appearance of the dative case on experiencer subjects (cf. Verma and Mohanan 1990). An example from Icelandic is given in (17). Note that Icelandic also allows accusative subject experiencers, but that these are currently being encroached upon by the dative in what is known as 'dative sickness'.

(17) Mér batnaði kvefið.
    I.Dat recovered the.cold.Nom
    'I recovered from the cold.' (Svenonius 2002:205)   Icelandic

Other languages, like Italian or English, which have a very impoverished case system, nevertheless make the distinction between these two types of verb classes. Differences can be found in auxiliary selection (Italian), the formation of adjectival participles, passivization, and reflexivization (see Belletti and Rizzi 1988 for a classic discussion, Grimshaw 1990 for a comprehensive overview and discussion).

Aspectual factors have again been implicated to explain the difference between the two types of psych verbs. More precisely, the semantic dimension of *cause* has been argued to play a role in differentiating experiencer oriented psych verbs like *fear* (e.g., *Kim fears snakes*) from causation oriented psych verbs like *frighten* (e.g., *Snakes frighten Kim*) (Grimshaw 1990). As was seen above, the cause component (*v*P in MP) can be seen as interacting with aspectual and temporal information in the clause.

A possible alternative analysis of experiencer subjects involves the notion of prototypical agency (section 5.4). Van Valin's (1991) RRG account (section 8.1) includes a notion of macroroles. Under his analysis of Icelandic, experiencers are neither prototypical actors (agents), nor are they prototypical undergoers (patients). Experiencers represent arguments which are not identifiable via a macrorole. Van Valin proposes that these non-macrorole arguments take the dative as their default case. His account is intended to cover the appearance of the dative on both subjects and objects in Icelandic, as well as 'normal' datives found with ditransitive verbs (see section 8.1.2).

The use of the dative or genitive in subject case alternations does seem to have to do with signalling the presence of a non-prototypical agent, i.e., it stands in opposition to the semantic dimension of *control*.[4] However, there are also some indications that the dative can be used to express a default reading. An example is provided by the Urdu subject alternation in (18), which has already been discussed in section 5.9. Here, an ergative subject appears in opposition to a dative subject. The ergative version in (18a) is more restricted in that it expresses a volitional reading. In contrast, the dative version in (18b) can be interpreted either as describing a situation in which Nadya has to go the zoo (non-volitional), or wants to go to the zoo (volitional) (Bashir 1999).

(18) a. nadya=ne zu ja-na hε
Nadya.F.Sg=Erg zoo.M.Sg.Obl go-Inf.M.Sg be.Pres.3.Sg
'Nadya wants to go to the zoo.' Urdu

b. nadya=ko zu ja-na hε
Nadya.F.Sg=Dat zoo.M.Sg.Obl go-Inf.M.Sg be.Pres.3.Sg
'Nadya has to/wants to go to the zoo.' Urdu

The semantics that are involved here are better characterized in terms of *modality*. That is, the obligation to do something (*deontic* modality) vs. the desire to do something. The dative in conjunction with nonfinite verb forms as in (18) is often used to express semantic modality. The example from Latin in (19) is typical and involves a present participial (gerundive) form.

---

[4]Also recall the nominative/ergative alternation on intransitives in Georgian and Urdu, as discussed in chapter 6. This had to do with a difference in control over the action as well.

(19) haec   caesari   facienda   erant
     this.N.Pl Caesar.Dat do.Gd.N.Pl be.Past.3.Pl
     'These things had to be done by Caesar.'   Latin
     'Caesar had to do these things.'

The example in (20) comes from Sanskrit and again involves participial (gerundive). However, in conjunction with an instrumental NP, this gives rise to a desire reading (parallel to the ergative example in (18a)), rather than an obligational reading.

(20) samprati gan-tavyā   puri   vāraṇasī   mayā
     now   go-Gerund city.Nom.F.Sg Benares.Nom.F.Sg I.Inst
     'now I want to go to the city of Benares' (Speijer 1886§41)   Sanskrit

To my knowledge, there is no work on the semantic effects of subject case alternations or the interaction of dative, genitive, ergative or instrumental case with modality that could rival some of the sophisticated and detailed analyses proposed for object alternations (e.g., the approaches discussed in section 7.3). More work needs to be done with respect to identifying, understanding and analysing these types of phenomena.

7.5 Discussion

Case alternations have mainly been discussed from a morphosyntactic perspective. Semantic factors have often been tied to information about thematic roles (e.g., agents vs. patients vs. experiencers), but there is very little literature which attempts to explore the phenomenon from a primarily semantic point of view. The semantic factors that have been identified are not well understood, though the semantic work on the interpretation of noun phrases in combination with aspectual semantics seems very promising. It is also possible that once a serious exploration of the semantics of case alternations were begun, more factors beyond control, aspect and modality would be identified.

As already mentioned, one relevant factor is connected to the discourse structure of a clause. There are indications that topicality and the focusing of an NP interact systematically with the case system of a language. However, the precise crosslinguistic factors that are involved have not been clearly established and more work needs to be done.

As part of the next chapter, RRG and OT approaches to case are presented. These theories try to do justice to the various factors that have been identified as governing the distribution of case crosslinguistically. Both of these approaches are again primarily syntactically oriented, but do account for an impressive range of data and by assuming a complex interaction between morphosyntactic, semantic, and discoursal factors.

7.6 Exercises

Exercise 1: Dative/Genitive Subjects

Explain the occurrence of dative/genitive subjects in Urdu and Bengali from a localist perspective.

(1) a. nadya=ko   ḍar   lag-a
Nadya.F.Sg=Dat fear.M.Sg.Nom be attached-Perf.M.Sg
'Nadya was afraid.'   Urdu

b. nadya=ko   kɑhani   yad   a-yi
Nadya.F.Sg=Dat story.F.Sg.Nom memory come-Perf.F.Sg
'Nadya remembered the story.'   Urdu

(2) a. taar   ṭhaaṇḍaa laaglo
he.Gen cold   be.attached.Past.3.Sg
'He got chilled.' (Klaiman 1980:279)   Bengali

a. amar ei   kathaa bissaas hay naa
I.Gen this matter belief is   not
'I don't believe this.' (Klaiman 1980:278)   Bengali

Exercise 2: Object Alternations

The Old English and the Vedic data in (3)–(5), respectively, have already been encountered in previous exercises. Allen (1995) actually discusses the Old English examples in order to show that the accusative and genitive objects behaved alike. In GB/MP terms, they should both receive structural Case. This means that genitive case in (4) is not stipulated as part of the lexical entry of 'need', but follows from generalizable syntactic and semantic principles.

Also recall the following observation made by Jamison (1976:131,135) with respect to the Sanskrit data.

> It is probably the case that the alternation between AC [accusative case] and GC [genitive case] with verbs of consumption originally signalled a semantic difference. A food or drink in AC [accusative case] was entirely consumed, while only part of one in the genitive was.

Reconsider your analyses in light of the semantic analyses discussed in this chapter and in light of Allen's and Jamison's argumentation. Provide an alternative analysis of the Old English and Vedic data.

(3) ... swa heo maran læcedom   behofað
     so   it   greater leechcraft.Acc needs
'... so it requires greater medicine' (Allen 1995:135)   Old English
(COE), ÆCHom I, 33 496.30

(4) Micel   wund   behofað micles   læcedomes
    great.Nom wound.Nom needs   great.Gen leechcraft.Gen
    'A great wound requires great medicine.' (Allen 1995:133)
    (COE) Bede 4 26.350.19   Old English

(5) a. pibā   somam
       drink.Imp soma.Acc
       'Drink soma.' (Ṛgveda VIII.36.1)   Vedic

    b. pibā   somasya
       drink.Imp soma.Gen
       'Drink (of) soma.' (Ṛgveda VIII.37.1)   Vedic

8

More Theories Great and Small

> Die flektierende Deklination ist in den Sprachen des romanisch-germanischen Westens bloß durch unbedeutende Relikte vertreten.
>
> 'The inflectional declination of the Romance-Germanic languages of the West is represented only by insignificant relics.'
> [Roman Jakobson, 1936, Beitrag zur allgemeinen Kasuslehre, p.242]

This chapter wraps up the book by discussing some approaches that have not been mentioned as yet. The first half of the chapter introduces Role and Reference Grammar, which is a well articulated theory of syntax with a detailed theory of linking. The second part of the chapter surveys a recent development in syntactic theory, namely the introduction of Optimality Theory.

8.1 Role and Reference Grammar

Like RG and LFG, Role and Reference Grammar (RRG) originated in the 1970s. The founder of the theory, Robert Van Valin, asked himself whether an approach that based itself on core data from Lakhota, Tagalog and Dyirbal, rather than on data from Western European languages (and Hebrew) would differ substantially from the standard Chomskyan derivational/transformational tradition (Foley and Van Valin 1977, Van Valin 1977a,b). The answer to his question is 'yes', as the subsequent development of RRG has shown. RRG today is a theory with many active practitioners, international conferences, and summer schools. Much of the data that is analysed is the result of primary field work. As such, there are several languages for which only RRG analyses exist. Comprehensive discussions of the theory are presented in Van Valin (1993) and Van Valin and LaPolla (1997).

RRG was inspired by Fillmore's Case Grammar and rejects versions of X'-Theory as assumed by GB/MP, LFG and the other linking theories discussed in chapter 5. RRG postulates its own theory of phrase structure in terms of layers of clause structure. The nucleus is represented by the main predicate (e.g., the verb), the core represents the core predication (verb plus arguments), and this is encapsulated in further layers of syntactic structure. The syntactic representations in RRG are therefore very different from the theories discussed so far in this book.

RRG shares some characteristics with LFG in that it assumes a multidimensional architecture. A full-fledged RRG analysis consists of a constituent projection (the basic tree), an operator projection (tense, mood, aspect, etc.), and a focus structure projection for discourse phenomena. These projections interact and none is derived from the other.

On the other hand, RRG differs markedly from LFG and other theories in the generative syntax tradition, because it rejects the universal applicability of grammatical relations such as subject and object. Instead, RRG relies on a relationship between macroroles and the *Privileged Syntactic Argument* (PSA). The PSA functions as the *syntactic pivot* of the clause (cf. section 6.4). It is with reference to the PSA and the macroroles that linguistic generalizations about agreement, control, or the coordinate reduction seen in section 6.4 are stated. In languages like German, for example, 'subject' agreement and the restriction of nominative case to 'subjects' is instead analysed as involving generalizations about the PSA. The inverse alignment of semantic relations in the syntactically ergative language Dyirbal follows from the fact that the Undergoer macrorole, rather than the Actor macrorole as in German, is singled out as the PSA.

The notion of macroroles goes back to Van Valin (1977b). There are just two macroroles: Actor and Undergoer. These two roles generalize over more detailed lexical semantics. Their function is thus very similar to Dowty's Proto-Roles (which were inspired by the previously existing idea of macroroles), see section 5.4.

RRG's theory of the interaction between lexical semantics and syntax owes much to Gruber's (1965) and Jackendoff's (1976) original work (section 5.3). RRG assumes detailed lexical semantic or *Logical Structure* (LS) representations as shown in (1). These representations follow Vendler's (1967) original aktionsart classification and are in line with general assumptions about lexical decomposition (cf. section 4.10.3). The INGR in (1) stands for ingressive, which denotes the beginning of a new event or state. BEC is short for BECOME, which denotes the entry into a new state (change of state). The difference between states and activities is a 'do' component, i.e., whether or not somebody is engaging in an activity, or whether they are simply continuing a given state. States and activities differ from achievements and accomplishments, because the latter have result states (a change of state is achieved or accomplished), and the former do not. The difference between achievements and accomplishments is one of duration: accomplishments are non-punctual.

Vendler's original classification has been discussed and modified in various different ways in the literature, but the basic distinctions assumed by RRG are generally accepted as valid across differing syntactic theories. The LS representations in (1) do not represent an exhaustive list. For a more detailed discussion, see Van Valin and LaPolla (1997).

(1)

Aktionsart	LS Representation	Example
State	**predicate'**(x,y)	**be'**(Pat,[lawyer])
		Pat is a lawyer.
	predicate'(x)	**shattered'**(glass)
		The glass is shattered.
Activity	**do'**(x,[predicate(x)])	**do'**(children,[**cry'**(children)])
		The children cried.
	do'(x,[predicate(x,y)])	**do'**(Dana,[**eat'**(Dana,pizza)]
		Dana ate pizza.
Achievement	INGR **predicate'**(x)	INGR **popped'**(bubble)
		The bubble popped.
	INGR **predicate'**(x,y)	INGR **see'**(Kim,message)
		Kim noticed the message.
Accomplishment	BEC **predicate'**(x)	BEC **melted'**(snow)
		The snow melted.
	BEC **predicate'**(x,y)	BEC **know'**(Leslie,Korean)
		Leslie learned Korean.

As in Jackendoff's (1990) approach, there is no direct representation of thematic roles in RRG: the information that is necessary for the mapping from semantic arguments to syntactic arguments can be read off the detailed LS representations. The mapping or *linking* of semantic arguments to syntactic representations is mediated by the macroroles, as shown in (2).

(2) ACTOR   UNDERGOER
     ──▶
                          ◀──────────────────────────────────────
     Arg. of   1st arg. of   1st arg. of   2nd arg. of   Arg. of state
     DO   **do'**(x,...   **pred'**(x,y)   **pred'**(x,y)   **pred'**(x)

The figure in (2) is referred to as the Actor-Undergoer Hierarchy. The semantic macroroles generalize over the more detailed semantic LS information. The arrows indicate a preference hierarchy: arguments of *do* are preferably interpreted as Actor, arguments of state predicates and second arguments of general predicates are preferably interpreted as Undergoer.

The theory does not admit grammatical relations as part of the syntactic representations. The main linking work in RRG is done between LS and macroroles, as opposed to between thematic roles and grammatical relations, as is assumed by LFG's Mapping Theory, for example. The macroroles do, however, still need to be linked to the PSA (which could be thought of as the single grammatical relation in RRG). In syntactically accusative languages like German, English or Urdu, the PSA is identified as the Actor argument. In syntactically ergative languages (Dyirbal), the Undergoer is selected as the PSA.

The linking algorithm as formulated in Van Valin and LaPolla (1997:427) includes a consideration of case, agreement and word order. Recall that these are the three linkers postulated as part of Kiparsky's linking theory (cf. section 5.5), but RRG and Kiparsky's linking theory differ substantially. The next few sections examine how some of the basic clause types discussed in this book are analysed within RRG. Section 8.1.1 goes through transitives, passives, unaccusatives and unergatives, section 8.1.2 looks at ditransitives and dative subjects, and section 8.1.3 discusses ergativity.

8.1.1 Basic Linking

The basic examples in this section come from German, rather than English. This allows a direct look at how RRG deals with case, as well as subject agreement. It also provides a smooth transition to the next section on ditransitives and datives in general. Consider the basic transitive sentence in (3) from Van Valin and LaPolla (1997:353).

(3) Der　　　　Junge　　　ha-t　　　　　den　　　　　Apfel
 the.M.Sg.Nom boy.M.Sg have-3.Sg.Pres the.M.Sg.Acc apple.M.Sg
 gegessen.
 eat.PastP
 'The boy ate the apple.'　　　　　　　　　　　　　　　　　　German

The verb *essen* 'eat' has the LS representation in (4) as part of its lexical entry. This identifies it as an *activity*. According to (2), the x argument is linked to the Actor macrorole and the y argument is linked to the Undergoer macrorole. German is syntactically accusative, so the Actor is selected as the PSA.

(4) **do**$'(x,$**eat**$'(x,y))$

So far, this is the part of the linking process already described above. Another part of the linking process is 'to assign the core arguments the appropriate case markers/adpositions and assign the predicate in the nucleus the appropriate agreement marking (language specific)' (Van Valin and LaPolla 1997:427).[1]

---
[1] Note that there are actually two sets of linking principles. One links the semantics to the syntax and is the one described here. Another links from the syntax to the semantics. RRG specifies

This is regulated by default assignment rules, which can contain a language specific component. The case and agreement rules are given in (5) and (6), respectively. Interestingly, the rules apply to both German and Icelandic, even though Icelandic allows dative subjects, but German does not. This is discussed in the next section. Also note that the statement of these default rules bears a close resemblance to the original formulations for German and Icelandic proposed by Zaenen, Maling and Thráinsson (1985) (cf. section 5.7.3).

(5) **Case assignment rules for German and Icelandic**
(Van Valin and LaPolla 1997:359)
   a. Assign nominative case to the highest-ranking macrorole argument.
   b. Assign accusative to the other macrorole argument.
   c. Assign dative case to non-macrorole arguments (default).

(6) **Finite verb agreement in German and Icelandic**
(Van Valin and LaPolla 1997:359)
The finite verb agrees with the highest-ranking macrorole argument.

The effect of these rules is that the Actor 'boy' in (3) is assigned nominative case and 'apple' is assigned accusative case as the other macrorole by (5b). By (6), the verb must agree with the Actor (the PSA), which is 'boy', and the linking process is complete.

Now consider the passive version in (7). RRG makes a distinction between *semantic* and *syntactic valence*. The passive is analysed as reducing the syntactic valency by one. Active transitives have a semantic and syntactic valency of two. Passive transitives, in contrast, have a syntactic valency of one, but retain the semantic valency of two. This is because the actor is still part of the semantic predication, even though it cannot be expressed as a syntactic argument. Passives are also thought of in terms of a PSA modulation, since it allows a non-actor to function as syntactic pivot (Van Valin and LaPolla 1997:147,295).

(7) Der   Apfel   wurde-∅   gegessen.
the.M.Sg.Nom apple.M.Sg become.Past-3.Sg eat.PastP
'The apple was eaten.'   German

---

linking principles for both directions because it is concerned with both the *parsing* or *understanding* (syntax to semantics) and the *production* or *generation* (semantics to syntax) of language. This contrasts with GB/MP, which is only concerned with the generation of language. The derivational nature of GB/MP forces unidirectionality: lexical items are put together (merged) to arrive at a clause, but there is no mechanism by which a given sentence could be reliably broken back down into individual lexical items and morphemes. LFG, on the other hand, uses the same grammar for parsing and generation so that nothing special need be said. This is possible because of the explicitly non-derivational nature of LFG, and the mutually constraining and codescriptive nature of the representations (see Butt et al. 1999).

In (7), the syntactic valency has been reduced to one and the Actor macrorole is suppressed. The only remaining macrorole is the Undergoer. This means that it is now the highest ranking one and is assigned nominative case by (5a). It also determines verb agreement by (6).

RRG makes a distinction between unaccusatives and unergatives on the basis of the LS representations associated with the verbs. Besides the Actor-Undergoer Hierarchy in (2), the mapping of semantic LS information to the more general macroroles is regulated by the principles listed in (8). The principles regulate the *number* of macroroles by making sure that the number of macroroles corresponds to the number of semantic LS arguments.[2] The principles also make distinctions as to the *nature* of macroroles.

(8) **Default macrorole assignment principles**
(Van Valin and LaPolla 1997:152)
   a. Number: the number of macroroles a verb takes is less than or equal to the number of arguments in its logical structure
      1. If a verb has two or more arguments in its LS, it will take two macroroles.
      2. If a verb has one argument in its LS, it will take one macrorole.
   b. Nature: for verbs which take one macrorole
      1. If the verb has an activity predicate in its LS, the macrorole is an actor.
      2. If the verb has no activity predicate in its LS, the macrorole is an undergoer.

Verbs without an activity predicate do not contain *doers* or agents. So, these verbs are unaccusative and the corresponding macrorole is an Undergoer. Verbs with an activity predicate, such as 'bark', but with only one macrorole, have doers/agents and therefore the corresponding macrorole is an Actor (unergatives). Case assignment and agreement are regulated by the principles in (5) and (6), just as for transitive clauses. In German, this results in nominative case and agreement of the verb with the single macrorole for both unaccusatives and unergatives (see section 8.1.3 for unergatives in ergative languages).

---

[2] This is like GB's θ-criterion (section 4.7) and LFG's Function-argument Biuniqueness (section 5.7.5) in that it ensures a well defined mapping between semantics and syntax, but it is also very much unlike either of those since the correspondences are between a detailed semantic representation vs. a more general semantic-syntactic interface representation in RRG, but between two essentially syntactic representations in GB and LFG.

8.1.2 Ditransitives and Dative Subjects

Turning to ditransitives, recall the English double object construction, which was discussed in section 4.11, and which is repeated here in (9) with a sketch of the RRG analysis already in place.

(9) a. Pat[Actor] gave the book[Undergoer] to Kim.
    b. Pat[Actor] gave Kim[Undergoer] the book.

RRG posits the LS in (10) for ditransitives such as 'give'. The LS contains three semantic arguments: a doer (x) who causes a situation in which a person or thing (y) ends up being in a state of having another person or thing (z).

(10) *give*   [**do**$'(x,\emptyset)$][CAUSE[BECOME **have**$'(y,z)$]]

The analysis of the English double object construction is very much like Jackendoff's (1990) analysis (section 5.3) in that only one underlying entry for 'give' is assumed, and the alternation follows from different mappings between LS and macroroles. Concretely, according to (2), the z argument is the preferred choice for the Undergoer macrorole. However, the y argument is also possible as a marked option. This marked option can be connected to semantic differences such as affectedness (cf. section 5.3, as the alternation in (11) illustrates: only in (11b) must the students necessarily have been 'affected' by having learnt Pashto; in (11a), no student need have been affected by actually having learned Pashto.

(11) a. The teacher[Actor] taught Pashto[Undergoer] to the students.
     b. The teacher[Actor] taught the students[Undergoer] Pashto.

The dative case on the y argument (corresponding to the English *to* in (9a)) is regulated by (5c). Consider the German ditransitive example in (12). Here 'monkey' is the Actor, 'cake' is the preferred Undergoer and 'dog' receives no macrorole, because there are none left. By (5c), this third argument is assigned default dative case.

(12) Der   Affe   gab   dem   Hund
     the.M.Sg.Nom monkey.M.Sg gave the.M.Sg.Dat dog.M.Sg
     einen   Kuchen.
     a.M.Sg.Acc cake.M.Sg.Acc
     'The monkey gave the dog a cake.'   German

Recall from section 4.8 that Icelandic and German allow for non-accusative objects. In both (13a) and (13b), the object is in the dative. This case pattern follows from the rules and principles already introduced above, in conjunction with another assumption. RRG introduces the notion of *M-transitivity* to deal with situations which appear to violate the default rules in (5).

(13) a. Gabi half dem Hund.
Gaby.F.Sg.Nom help.Past.3.Sg the.M.Sg.Dat dog.M.Sg
'Gaby helped the dog.' German

a. Ég hjálpaði honum.
I helped he.Dat
'I helped him.' Icelandic

M-transitivity is defined in terms of the number of macroroles a verb can take (Van Valin and LaPolla 1997:150,355; Narasimhan 1998). Verbs can lexically carry information about their M-transitivity in cases when it deviates from the semantic transitivity expected on the basis of their LS representations. In German and Icelandic, the verbs for 'help' are assumed to be semantically transitive (two arguments in their LS), but M-intransitive. That is, although there are two semantic arguments, which correspond to two syntactic arguments ('Gaby/I' and 'dog/he'), there is only one macrorole available for linking. In (13), 'Gaby' and 'I' correspond to the Actor macrorole and are assigned nominative by (5a). They also trigger verb agreement by (6). The 'dog' and 'he', in contrast, are left macroroleless and receive dative case by (5c).

Now consider the passive versions in (14). The Actor argument has been suppressed and the 'dog' and 'he' arguments still receive no macrorole. Therefore, both again receive dative case by (5c). But recall that despite the surface similarity of (14a) and (14b), there is a crucial difference between Icelandic and German. The dative argument is a subject in Icelandic, but not in German.

(14) a. Den Hunden wurde geholfen.
the.M.Pl.Dat dog.M.Pl become.Past.3.Sg help.PastP
'The dog was helped.' German

b. Honum var hjálpað.
he.Dat was helped
'He was helped.' Icelandic

This is accounted for by means of PSA selection. In German, the PSA must correspond to a macrorole. Icelandic is more permissive and simply allows the highest-ranking core argument to become the PSA. That is, an argument does not necessarily have to correspond to a macrorole in order to qualify as a PSA in Icelandic. The difference between (14a) and (14b) thus is that dative 'dog' cannot function as the PSA in German, but dative 'he' in Icelandic can. The latter therefore triggers verb agreement, while the former cannot.

This analysis of Icelandic and German goes back to Van Valin (1991) and is interesting because it does not attempt to analyse the differences between the languages directly in terms of the distribution of case and agreement (this has been the GB/MP instinct), but in terms of how picky a language is about what it is willing to admit as a PSA or 'subject'. The analysis also is pleasingly economic, because the same set of rules can account for both dative objects and subjects.

However, a fair amount of the work is done via lexical stipulation of some kind. For one, verbs can specify information about their M-transitivity. For another, verbs can also contribute special information about the precise kind of non-canonical case they require. For example, dative assignment by (5c) is a default specification, which can be overridden by lexically specified information. This is necessary for examples such as in (15), where the subject is accusative rather than dative.

(15) Mig   vantar   nýa skó
     I.Acc need.Pres new shoe.Pl.Acc
     'I need new shoes.' (Svenonius 2002:199)   Icelandic

Similarly, some verbs in German take genitive objects (see (45) in section 4.8) and this must be lexically specified as deviating from the default dative assignment. This type of lexical stipulation is also found as part of GB/MP and the linking theories in chapter 5. It is inevitable that some information about the distribution of case will simply have to be stipulated. But, it is not clear how much should be stipulated. So, one can wonder whether the stipulative nature of M-transitivity is really necessary.

Given the range of variation over possible object case markings and the clear connection to semantic factors established in section 7.3, one might also question the general applicability of (5c). Why should dative be the default case? RRG argues that the dative is the correct default case for non-macrorole arguments, because a host of crosslinguistic data converges on the dative as the most general case for third or 'other' arguments (Van Valin and LaPolla 1997:665).

Another issue to wonder about potentially is why RRG does not assume three macroroles, if there is a general pattern of datives on third arguments. The reason for this is that not all languages have ditransitive verbs. These languages need another piece of morphology (called an *applicative*) or another predicate (resulting in *serial verb constructions*) to license the third argument. RRG seeks to work with a linguistic inventory that is *universally* valid. The postulation of a third macrorole for ditransitives is not an option, because it is not supported by the crosslinguistic data (see Van Valin 2004). In this respect, RRG can be said to be more like GB/MP and less like the linking theories discussed in chapter 5. GB/MP assumes only two core structural Cases, further arguments must be licensed via inherent or quirky case. In contrast, the linking theories assumed up to four structural Cases or arguments.

8.1.3 Ergatives

The case assignment rules discussed so far apply only to accusative languages. Ergative languages require a different set of case assignment and agreement rules. A basic rule set for case assignment is shown in (16).

(16) **Case assignment rules for ergative pattern**
(Van Valin and LaPolla 1997:368)
a. Assign absolutive case to the lowest-ranking macrorole argument.
b. Assign ergative case to the other macrorole argument.
c. Assign dative case to non-macrorole arguments (default).

An application of these rules in combination with the Actor-Undergoer-Hierarchy in (2) to classic ergative patterns as in (17) is straightforward. In (17a), 'Oli' is the Actor and 'meat' is the Undergoer. The Undergoer is the lowest-ranking macrorole and is assigned absolutive case. Ergative case is assigned to the Actor as the other argument by (16b). In (17b), it does not actually matter whether 'Oli' is an Actor or an Undergoer, in either case, this argument is assigned absolutive case by (16a), because there is no other macrorole.

(17) a. Oli-p neqi neri-vaa
Oli-Erg meat.Abs eat-IND.TR.3Sg.3Sg
'Oli eats meat.' (Manning 1996:3)   West Greenlandic

b. Oli sinippoq
Oli.Abs sleep-IND.INTR.3Sg
'Oli sleeps.' (Manning 1996:3)   West Greenlandic

Now consider a more complex situation. Tsova-Tush (Batsbi) is a Caucasian language spoken in Georgia. The distribution of the ergative in Tsova-Tush is broadly similar to that of Urdu and Georgian. Like in Urdu and Georgian, the ergative is not restricted to transitive verbs (as it is in West Greenlandic). Like Urdu and Georgian, Tsova-Tush distinguishes between unergatives and unaccusatives: unergatives have ergative subjects, unaccusatives have nominative subjects. Like Urdu, but unlike Georgian, Tsova-Tush has a class of intransitive verbs which allow variable subject marking, as shown in (18). As in Urdu, this variability is correlated with a semantic reading of volitionality/control.

(18) a. (As) vuiž-n-as
I.Erg fall-Tns-1.Sg.Erg
'I fell down (on purpose).' (Holisky 1987)   Tsova-Tush

b. (So) vuiž-n-as
I.Nom fall-Tns-1.Sg.Nom
'I fell down (accidentally).' (Holisky 1987)   Tsova-Tush

Unlike both Urdu and Georgian, the ergative in Tsova-Tush is confined to first and second person subjects (a classic form of an NP-split, see section

6.6). Van Valin and LaPolla (1997:373) propose the following set of rules for Tsova-Tush.

(19) **Case assignment rules for first- and second-person arguments of intransitive verbs in Tsova-Tush**
    a. Defaults:
        1. Assign ergative case to actors.
        2. Assign nominative case to undergoers.
    b. Utterance-specific options:
        1. Assign nominative case to an actor to block the agentivity implicature.
        2. Assign ergative case to an undergoer to force the agentivity implicature.

These rules apply to (18) as follows. (18b) represents the default under the assumption that 'fall' is an unaccusative verb in Tsova-Tush. In this case, the single macrorole is an Undergoer and the relevant rule is (19a2), yielding a nominative. (18a) illustrates an unaccusative verb that is being used agentively. In this case, the context-related rule in (19b2) becomes relevant: the single Undergoer macrorole is assigned ergative case and this goes hand-in-hand with a forced control/agentivity reading.

As can be seen from (19), the semantic parameters that seem to be relevant for the distribution of ergative case in Tsova-Tush are encoded directly as part of the case assignment rules (for a different RRG take on this basic pattern and dative subjects in Hindi, see Narasimhan 1998). So while there is no explicit and deep semantic analysis of case alternations along the lines sketched in chapter 7, semantic factors enter the picture via a parametrization of case assignment rules as in (19), or by thinking of case assignment in terms of markedness. An example of the latter was seen for the affectedness readings with ditransitives in (11).

This concludes the discussion of RRG. Because RRG analyses exist for a diverse set of languages with rich case morphology, this section represents no more than a brief sketch of the basic RRG approach to case. The next section moves on to present a recent development in syntactic theory, namely Optimality Theory.

8.2 Optimality Theory

The seeds of Optimality Theory (OT) were first formulated in the early 1990s by John McCarthy and Alan Prince. McCarthy and Prince had been working on problems of alignment constraints in prosodic morphology (McCarthy and Prince 1993) and found that the standard phonological apparatus at their disposal was too limited. The problem was that standard linguistic explanations generally rely on a set of *inviolable* rules. These rules distinguish between ungrammatical and grammatical utterances. However, the prosodic alignment constraints examined by McCarthy and Prince seemed to be just that: a set of violable constraints which interacted with one another to produce wellformed utterances. McCarthy and Prince therefore proposed that linguistic explanations should instead be couched in terms of the complex interaction of a set of *violable* constraints. This opened up the possibility of alternative solutions for many problematic phenomena and within a few years of its introduction, OT was flourishing. Within phonology, OT has now become the dominant theory of the field.[3]

The first paper which applied an OT perspective to syntactic questions happened to be on case (Legendre, Raymond and Smolensky 1993) and is discussed in section 8.2.2. The establishment of OT as a serious domain of investigation within syntax is due mainly to landmark articles by Jane Grimshaw (Grimshaw 1997) and Joan Bresnan (Bresnan 1998). Grimshaw's paper formulated ideas about OT syntax on the basis of standard GB/MP assumptions. Bresnan pointed out that this was not a necessary feature of OT, and showed how OT could be used in conjunction with standard LFG.

These initial articles led to an interest and excitement about OT syntax that reached across syntactic theories, so that the same basic OT 'language' is now shared by phonologists, some semanticists, and syntacticians working in various different frameworks. As already mentioned in chapter 5, Kiparsky's linking theory and Wunderlich's LDG assume OT as a basic part of their analyses. Despite this crosstheoretical work, OT remains a minority theory within syntactic thinking. Basic readings on OT include Prince and Smolenksy (1993) and Kager (1999). Important papers for the development of the theory are collected in several edited volumes (Barbosa, Fox, Hagstrom, McGinnis and Pesetsky 1998; Dekkers, van der Leeuw and van de Weijer 2000; Sells 2001; Legendre, Grimshaw and Vikner 2001).

The next section introduces the basic architecture and assumptions of OT. This is followed by the discussion of a number of OT analyses with respect to case. There is a rapidly growing literature on OT analyses of case. This book surveys a subset of the approaches in order to provide a representative sense of the perspectives on case that guide and motivate the newly emerging analyses.

8.2.1 OT Basics

Within OT, the goal is to determine an optimal output (surface form) with respect to a given input. The optimal output is picked from a set of candidates that compete with one another. The competition between the candidates is resolved

---

[3]OT can also be seen as the successor to Harmonic Grammar as first formulated by Paul Smolensky (see Legendre, Sorace and Smolensky 2005).

by an evaluation of constraint violations, as shown in (20) (adapted from Vogel 2001).

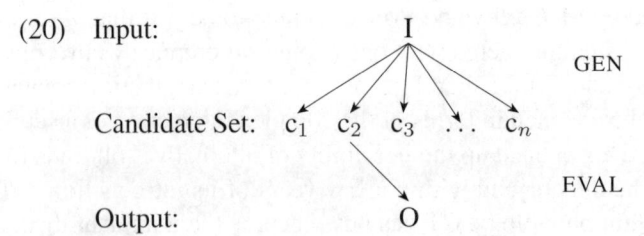

(20) Input: I
              GEN
  Candidate Set: c_1 c_2 c_3 ... c_n

              EVAL
  Output: O

The precise nature of the input is still in need of precise definition in much of OT. Grimshaw's (1997) original paper assumed that the input encompasses the basic argument structure of a predicate, and a specification of tense/aspect. In later work (Grimshaw and Samek-Lodovici 1998), the focus/topic specifications were included as part of the input. A typical input might thus look as in (21), where the argument structure of *give* is specified, along with information about which argument is the topic, and which is in focus.

(21) give(x,y,z), x=topic, z=focus, x=Kim, z=dog, y=bone

This basic assumption generally holds in OT syntax, however, given space constraints and the various different phenomena addressed by OT analyses, the precise form of the input differs from paper to paper. This variation is also evident in the discussion of individual analyses in the next sections.

In OT-LFG (Bresnan 2000, Kuhn 2003), the input is assumed to be an underspecified f-structure in the sense that the grammatical functions are not as yet specified. An example for the transitive verb 'drive' is shown in (22).

(22) $\begin{bmatrix} \text{PRED} & \text{'drive}< \text{GF}_1, \text{GF}_2 >' \\ \text{GF}_1 & [\quad] \\ \text{GF}_2 & [\quad] \\ \text{TENSE} & \text{PAST} \end{bmatrix}$

The inputs, whatever form they may take, are passed on to a function GEN, which generates a set of possible output candidates that could correspond to the input. Within OT-LFG, GEN is assumed to be equivalent to a standard LFG grammar. LFG grammars can be used to both parse and generate, so the idea is that an underspecified input as in (22) is passed on to an existing grammar for English. This searches through its rule space and produces all possible pairings of c-structures and surface strings that could correspond to the input f-structure (Kuhn 2003 shows that this is computationally viable).

Stated more generally, one has a certain amount of information, represented either as in (21), or as in (22), and the goal is to find an optimal candidate surface string for this input. With respect to (21) a possible wellformed English output might be *Kim gave a bone to the dog*. Other candidates competing with this output might be strings like *Kim a bone gave to the dog* or *Kim to the dog a bone gave*. These possible candidates are all produced by the function GEN. In Grimshaw's approach, GEN is guided by the theory of projections and X′-Theory as formulated within GB/MP and generates a set of syntactic (tree) analyses that serve as the set of possible output candidates.

Whichever way they are generated, the output candidates are subject to an evaluation via the EVAL function (cf. (20)). This evaluation examines how many and what kind of *constraints* are violated. The output with the least serious constraint violations is identified as *optimal* for the given input. The nature and content of OT constraints is subject to severe variation from paper to paper. However, there are families of constraints that are assumed by all OT analyses. These constraints constitute a basic part of the OT analyses in phonology and have been adopted within OT syntax. The *Faithfulness* constraints, for example, ensure that the output is as faithful to the input as possible.

All constraints are assumed to be universally applicable. This means that a constraint that requires verbs to be in clause final position, for example, applies to all languages. However, in languages like English, this constraint will be ranked very low in comparison to other constraints. This means that the word order in English can actually work out to SVO due to some other higher ranked constraints, despite the presence of a clause final constraint. Crosslinguistic variation is accounted for by the relative ranking of constraints in each language: constraints are universally applicable, but in some languages they may not be strong enough to ever have an effect.

The evaluation of candidates is represented in terms of a tableau, in which the stronger or higher ranked constraints are listed to the left of lower ranked constraints. Dashed lines between constraints indicate that they are not ranked with respect to one another. The tableau in (23), based on analyses by Woolford (2001), serves to illustrate a simple example with respect to case.

Woolford (2001, 2003) assumes a constraint hierarchy which ranks dative, accusative, ergative and nominative case according to relative markedness as in (23). The '*' in front of the name of a constraint indicates that one should avoid it, i.e., *dative translates to 'avoid dative case'. The idea is that the nominative is the least marked case, and the dative the most marked (cf. RRG's case assignment rules in section 8.1).

(23) *dative ≫ *accusative ≫ *nominative

As can be seen in the sample tableau in (24), the nominative case on unaccusative verbs falls out from the constraint ranking in (23). The input is a verb and an NP argument that is not specified for case. GEN generates several possible candidates, among which there are the three candidates shown in the input column. The first two each violate one of the higher ranked constraints. The '*!' indicates a fatal violation, which means that there is at least one other candidate which violates the constraints less. The optimal candidate (indicated by the '☞') is the winner of the competition and the one which is picked as the optimal output for the given input.

(24)

input: V NP	*dative	*accusative	*nominative
V NPdat	*!		
V NPacc		*!	
☞ V NPnom			*

Due to space constraints, the range of crosslinguistic data taken on by Woolford (2001, 2003) cannot be discussed any further. The next sections instead examine some of the classic work on case and OT.

8.2.2 Structural Case Revisited

Legendre, Raymond and Smolensky (1993) represent the first account of case within an OT setting. Their main concern was to build a model of structural or abstract Case, which could account for a typology of case marking in terms of accusative vs. ergative vs. active systems (see section 6.2.2). They posited a number of universal constraints, shown in (25), which govern case assignment. C_1, C_2 and C_4 stand for abstract cases which are instantiated differently, depending on the case system of the language. In accusative languages, C_1 corresponds to nominative and C_2 corresponds to accusative. In an ergative language, C_1 corresponds to ergative and C_2 corresponds to absolutive. The C_4 functions as the 'other' case, and can be instantiated by datives or other types of non-nominative and non-accusative cases, depending on the language.[4]

(25) **Universal Constraints Governing Abstract Case**
    a. $A \rightarrow C_1$:   Agents receive abstract case C_1
    b. $P \rightarrow C_2$:   Patients receive abstract case C_2
    c. $A \nrightarrow C_2$:   Agents do not receive abstract case C_2
    d. $P \nrightarrow C_1$:   Patients do not receive abstract case C_1
    e. $\alpha \nrightarrow C_4$:   Core arguments (agents and patients) do not receive abstract case C_4
    f. $\alpha \rightarrow C_2$:   Some argument is case-marked C_2
    g. $X \rightarrow C_1$:   High-prominence arguments receive abstract case C_1
    h. $x \nrightarrow C_{12}$:   Low-prominence arguments are not core case-marked (C_1 or C_2)
    i. $[-An] \rightarrow C_2$

---

[4] A C_3 case is absent in this paper, presumably it is being reserved for datives.

The basic perspective on case is thus equivalent to GB: there are two structural Cases which regulate nominative, ergative, accusative and absolutive. All other instances of case are dealt with via the same method (C_4), which could be seen as being essentially equivalent to inherent/quirky Case.

The factors underlying most of these constraints should be familiar by now. By default, agents have either nominative or ergative case, and patients are accusative or absolutive. The constraints in (25c–d) allow for atypical situations in which an agent or patient may be dative, genitive or partitive, for example. The constraints in (25g–h) are not ones we have seen before. These have to do with discourse topicality (a topic is a prominent argument) and have been put in place for those case phenomena which are sensitive to topicality. Finally, the constraint in (25i) brings animacy into the picture so that NPs with low animacy are more likely to receive absolutive and accusative case. This encodes the observation that objects are more likely to be inanimate than animate.

The constraints in (25) are valid for all languages, but are ranked differently from language to language. This approach automatically forces a strong crosslinguistic and typological focus, because the universal applicability of the constraints forces the researcher to consider a wide range of typologies that are predicted by various possible constraint rerankings. Legendre, Raymond and Smolensky's (1993) focus is therefore primarily typological and they show how the variable rankings of their constraints account for a range of case systems. However, the typology of case systems is necessarily restricted, because only core abstract Cases are attended to (cf. section 6.3). The more interesting patterns discussed in chapters 6 and 7 are not taken into account. In terms of providing new theoretical insights on case, the approach is also rather limited. In essence, the GB perspective on case has been transported into a new formalism; but despite the new tools, no new insights seem to have developed.

Legendre, Raymond and Smolensky's (1993) contribution is nevertheless important, because it opened up possible new avenues for an exploration of case. For example, de Hoop (1999) continues the discussion by both problematizing and extending Legendre, Raymond and Smolensky's (1993) original ideas. Recall from section 7.3 that de Hoop (1996) proposed a distinction between *weak* and *strong* Case. This distinction accounts for object alternations like the one shown in (26). The direct case in (26a) is analysed as strong Case, which gives rise to the boundedness reading. The version in (26b), in contrast, does not have a boundedness reading and this correlates with weak Case and a genitive case morphology.

(26) a. tha   Calum air na craobhan a   ghearradh
       be.Pres Calum Asp the trees.Dir OAgr cut.VN
       'Calum has cut the trees.'   Scottish Gaelic

b. tha   Calum a'   ghearradh nan craobhan
   be.Pres Calum Asp cut.VN   the trees.Gen   Scottish Gaelic
   'Calum is cutting the trees (no tree has necessarily been cut yet).'

In order to be able to account for such object alternations, de Hoop (1999) revises Legendre, Raymond and Smolensky (1993) by building on her ideas on weak vs. strong Case. Rather than simply augmenting the system with a few more constraints, de Hoop borrows an intuition from *neural networks* and proposes a hidden level of constraint activation, which serves to bundle together the effects of various constraints, as described below and as shown in (27).

> In the first step, constraint interaction governs the mapping of input arguments to a hidden level in the system where the *strength* of these arguments is determined. Languages may differ in which constraints are crucial here: for example, in some languages, agents will always get the label strong, whereas in other languages only 1st person humans will be labeled strong. ...
> In the second step, the hidden units that represent strong and weak arguments constitute the input for mappings to certain syntactic reflexes in the language, one of them being morphological case assignment. [de Hoop 1999:103]

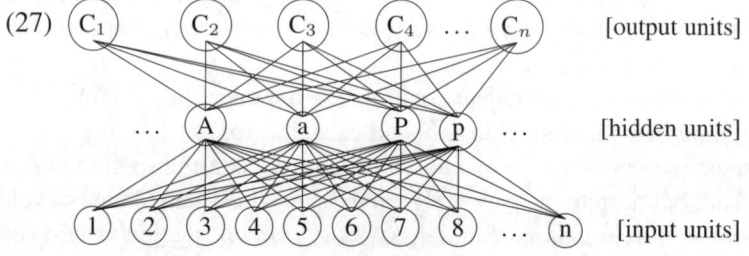

(27) C_1 C_2 C_3 C_4 ... C_n [output units]

... A   a   P   p   ...   [hidden units]

1 2 3 4 5 6 7 8 ... n   [input units]

The lower case nodes in (27) represent weak arguments, the upper case ones are strong arguments. The object 'trees' in (26a), for example, would work out to be a strong argument because of various information from the input about aspectual boundedness, etc. which would have been taken into account. Once the relative strength or weakness of an input has been determined, a set of constraints comes into play that was inspired by Legendre, Raymond and Smolensky (1993). These are shown in (28).

(28) **From Strength to Case Assignment**
   a. X →C_1:   Strong arguments receive C_1
   b. X →C_2:   Strong arguments receive C_2
   c. x →C_1:   Weak arguments receive C_1
   d. x →C_2:   Weak arguments receive C_2
   e. x ↛C_{12}:   Weak arguments don't receive C_1 or C_2

For languages such as Scottish Gaelic, Urdu or Turkish (cf. section 7.3), de Hoop proposes the constraint hierarchy in (29). An application of this constraint hierarchy for the evaluation of possible output candidates with respect to the data in (26) is shown in the tableaux in (30). For the sake of utmost clarity, I have substituted a and p for x and A and P for X in the tableaux.

(29) $x \not\rightarrow C_{12} >> X \rightarrow C_1 >> X/x \rightarrow C_2$

The tableau in (30a) works with an input of two weak arguments.[5] Several output candidates have been generated with GEN for this input. Just two of the possible candidates are shown in (30a). An evaluation of these two candidates identifies the first candidate as optimal. This is because the second candidate violates the constraint that a p argument should not receive nominative (C_1) or accusative (C_2) case. The other candidate violates the lower ranked constraint twice, because neither the p nor the A argument are accusative. But this double low violation is better than a single high violation, so this candidate is optimal.

(30) a.

input: Ag Pt A p	$a \not\rightarrow C_{12}$ $p \not\rightarrow C_{12}$	$A \rightarrow C_1$ $P \rightarrow C_1$	$A/a \rightarrow C_2$ $P/p \rightarrow C_2$
☞ Nom Gen			**
Nom Acc	*!		*

b.

input: Ag Pt A P	$a \not\rightarrow C_{12}$ $p \not\rightarrow C_{12}$	$A \rightarrow C_1$ $P \rightarrow C_1$	$A/a \rightarrow C_2$ $P/p \rightarrow C_2$
Nom Gen		*	**!
☞ Nom Acc		*	*

In contrast, when the input contains a strong object (P), as in (30b), then the second candidate is identified as optimal. Neither candidate violates the most highly ranked constraint for the simple reason that there are no weak arguments in the input. Both the candidates violate the second constraint, because neither one has a nominative P argument. At this point, the two candidates are equally bad. With respect to the third constraint, however, the decision can be made in favour of the second candidate, which only violates this constraint once (the A is not accusative). The second candidate is thus optimal with respect to a strong object (P) and the data in (26) is accounted for.

De Hoop's approach can thus deal with the kind of case alternations discussed in chapter 7 in a way that can do justice to both the semantic and morphosyntactic factors that are involved. The mapping of constraints to a hidden level allows the potential inclusion of a number of different universal or language dependent factors: the system is not rigid, but is very flexible.

[5] These tableaux have been constructed for illustrative purposes and are not part of de Hoop (1999).

However, de Hoop's (1999) proposal is programmatic. It does not spell out the details of her three-layer system and how it can be integrated within a larger OT-based syntactic or semantic framework. De Hoop (1999) also explicitly points out that the Urdu data discussed in section 7.4, which seems to involve modal semantics, remains unaccounted for within her system. De Hoop's programmatic sketch therefore needs to be followed up in further work.

The bulk of the work on case in OT, however, has recently shifted to working with constraints derived from prominence hierarchies via *Harmonic Alignment*, which is able to take into account typological observations about tendencies across languages. The basic ideas behind this proposal are discussed in the next section.

8.2.3 Harmonic Alignment

The discussion in this section is based on Aissen (1999, 2003). Aissen observes that typological work has identified a range of interacting factors governing the distribution of case. A number of these factors have already been discussed here: person hierarchies, agenthood vs. patienthood, specificity/definiteness. These typological observations are often not integrated into standard generative syntactic theories of case. Aissen points out that even when they have been integrated into an analysis, the integration does not do justice to the potentially complex interaction of factors, and also does not situate the analysis within a larger crosslinguistic picture.

Given that there are at least 300 languages for which object case alternations, or *differential object marking*, as it is referred to in Aissen (2003), have been observed (Bossong 1985), Aissen argues that it is high time to formulate a formal analysis that does justice to the phenomenon from a crosslinguistic perspective. She proposes that OT with its constraint based architecture provides just the right tool.

The basic idea is to take the various prominence scales identified so far in the literature, and derive constraints from them. These constraints can then serve to evaluate candidates in an OT competition. For example, Silverstein (1976) established a person and animacy hierarchy with respect to split ergativity (cf. section 6.6). Aissen (1999) distils his and other insights with respect to the factors governing the appearance of ergative subjects into the three *universal prominence scales* shown in (31).

(31) Thematic Role Scale: Agent > Patient
 Relational Scale: Subject > Nonsubject
 Person Scale: Local Person (1st and 2nd) > 3rd Person

These separate scales represent preferentially ordered interacting factors which determine the distribution of case crosslinguistically. Within OT, the elements of these scales can be combined via *Harmonic Alignment* (Prince and

Smolensky 1993), a concept again first motivated with respect to phonological phenomena. Harmonic alignment operates on two scales.[6] Each element of the binary scale is associated with an element of the other scale, going from right to left. The Harmonic Alignment of the Relational and Person scale in (31) is shown in (32) (Aissen 1999:681). The 'x ≻ y' means 'x is less marked than/more harmonic than y'. The 'x ≫ y' means that the x constraint is ranked higher, i.e., is stronger, than the y constraint.

(32)

Scales	Harmonic Alignment	Constraint Alignment
Local > 3	Su/Local ≻ Su/3	*Su/3 ≫ *Su/Local
Su > Non-Su	Non-Su/3 ≻ Non-Su/Local	*Non-Su/Local ≫ *Non-Su/3

The markedness relations arrived at by Harmonic Alignment in (33) state that a 1st person subject is less marked than a 3rd person subject, for example. Under the assumption that case is used to flag those NPs which are marked in some way (see Aissen 1999, 2003 for discussion), this markedness relation correctly predicts that ergative case is more likely to occur on 3rd person subjects, rather than on 1st person subjects (cf. section 6.6).

In order to be able to integrate the universal constraints on relative markedness into an OT analysis, the relations arrived at via Harmonic Alignment need to be massaged a bit further into *violable constraints*. This is done by inverting the order of the scales and interpreting the ranked elements as situations which should be avoided. The result is shown in the third column in (32). The constraint *Su/3, for example, requires that third person subjects should be avoided. This constraint is ranked higher, i.e., makes third person subjects more marked, than 1st and 2nd person subjects, which are legislated against by the constraint *Su/Local.

Aissen (1999, 2003) demonstrates that this general approach allows a linguistically well motivated account of case systems crosslinguistically. Object case alternations as in Turkish or Urdu, for example, fall out from another set of relative prominence constraints. The relevant scales are shown in (33). Definiteness and specificity effects such as that discussed for Urdu and Turkish are related (Enç 1991) and are therefore contained within the same scale.

(33) Relational Scale:　　Subject > Nonsubject
　　　Animacy Scale:　　　Human > Animate > Inanimate
　　　Definiteness Scale:　Pronoun > Proper Name > Definite >
　　　　　　　　　　　　　Indefinite Specific > Nonspecific

Examples of animacy effects have so far not been encountered in this book, but they are reported for a number of languages. The Dravidian language Malayalam, for example, is cited as being sensitive to the relative animacy

---

[6]One of the scales must be binary (contain only two elements), otherwise the combinatory possibilities are uncontrolled.

of the object. In this language, humans are more animate than animals and elephants, for example, are considered to be more animate than mice. Such animacy constraints are not well understood, but they do seem to play a role.

The prominence scales translate into the OT constraints in (34). These constraints state that a non-specific subject, for example, is highly unlikely and therefore marked. The most likely form for a subject is a pronoun. This markedness hierarchy corresponds to the crosslinguistic tendencies identified in the typological literature. Similarly, objects are less likely to be pronouns and are more likely to be non-specific or specific nouns. Since an object pronoun represents a marked situation, this is more likely to bear case marking than a non-specific noun (again, this is borne out by data from language after language).

(34) a. *Su/NSpec ≫ *Su/Spec ≫ *Su/Def ≫ *Su/PN ≫ *Su/Pro
 b. *Obj/Pro ≫ *Obj/PN ≫ *Obj/Def ≫ *Obj/Spec ≫ *Obj/NSpec

Before moving on to an analysis of the Turkish pattern in (35), two more constraints need to be introduced. One is $*\emptyset_C$, which penalizes the absence of case (all NPs are assumed to have a case feature). This is akin to the Case Filter, which ensures that all NPs will have case. There are some differences, however. For one, $*\emptyset_C$ is a violable constraint, unlike the Case Filter. For another, this constraint is about the overt appearance of case, whereas the Case Filter is mainly about abstract/structural Case.

The other constraint is $*Struc_C$, which legislates against the appearance of overt morphological case. This constraint makes unmarked nominatives or absolutives possible. In conjunction with the constraints in (34b), these two constraints allow the analysis of a large number of crosslinguistic object alternations. An analysis for the familiar Turkish alternation in (35) is shown in (36).

(35) a. Ali bir kitab-ı aldı
 A. one book-Acc bought
 'Ali bought a particular book.' (Enç 1991) Turkish
 b. Ali bir kitap aldı
 A. one book bought
 'Ali bought some book or other.' (Enç 1991) Turkish

(36)

input: Patient, Specific	*Obj/Spec & $*\emptyset_C$	$*Struc_C$	*Obj/NSpec & $*\emptyset_C$
☞Object Indef, Spec Acc		*	
Object Indef, Spec (no overt case)	*!		

As can be seen, not all constraints need always be listed in the tableaux. The OT practice is to present only those constraints which are relevant, and to limit the evaluation to the most likely candidates. The input to the evaluation in (36) is just one argument. The evaluation seeks to determine the optimal form for this input, which is a patient that has a specificity reading. The two possibilities listed in (36) are an accusative object with a specific interpretation, and an unmarked object with a specific interpretation. The second candidate violates the requirement that all nouns should have overt case. In comparison, the first candidate does not obey the requirement that nouns should not be overtly case marked. Since it is more important in Turkish that specific nouns be overtly marked, the first candidate wins and is the optimal output.

The set of constraints developed by Aissen to account for such differential object marking is nicely motivated by typological observations. This aspect of the approach is very satisfying, as is the fact that Aissen's account makes interesting predictions as to the kind of variation that should be possible crosslinguistically with respect to object and subject alternations (Aissen 2003). A very interesting part of the proposal is the connection Aissen (2003) draws to language change. Within OT, language change can be expressed as a *re-ranking* of constraints. The constraint *Struc$_C$, for example, could become more or less important in any given language. The more important or highly ranked it is, the less case marking there will be. So, for example, if *Struc$_C$ were ranked above *Obj/PN in (34), then only pronominal objects would be overtly case marked.

Aissen's (1999, 2003) derivation of OT constraints by Harmonic Alignment from typologically established prominence scales has inspired a growing body of work on crosslinguistic case patterns. Some of the data and questions that are explored are extremely interesting; however, there is also a drawback in that the constraints needed to account for any one language tend to become rather specific and therefore take on a stipulative nature. Sharma (2001), needs to stipulate information about perfect vs. non-perfect for an analysis of Kashmiri ergative patterns. Kashmiri is similar to Urdu in that the ergative is restricted to appearing with perfect morphology. This fact simply has to be stated (as in most other approaches), but given the linguistically well-founded nature of the other constraints, this stipulation jars.

To make the point more generally: the set of constraints posed by Aissen (1999, 2003) seems to form a natural and intuitive set. When formulating an analysis for the intricate details of a language's case system, these constraints need to be augmented by other constraints, resulting in a picture that is not quite so satisfyingly beautiful anymore.

Nevertheless, the basic approach presented here has proved to be a fruitful line of research, as the rapidly growing number of works along these lines shows. A representative selection of the work is collected in Sells (2001), other work is currently in the pipeline, e.g., by de Hoop (section 8.2.2). Some work has been done within RRG on OT (Nakamura 1997), and, as already mentioned in section 5.6, work within LDG is now set exclusively in an OT setting that is heavily influenced by the approach presented here (e.g., Stiebels 2000, 2002, Wunderlich and Lakämper 2001, Wunderlich 2003).

Influential though it has proven to be, Aissen's approach is not the only way to incorporate OT into theories of case and linking. Woolford's (2001, 2003) work was already mentioned in section 8.2.1, for example. Kiparsky (2001) has blended OT with his linking theory and Lee (2001) seeks to account for markedness patterns of case with *bidirectional* OT.

Most approaches with OT assume that the constraints evaluate possible alignments between grammatical relations, thematic roles and overt case marking. LDG and Kiparksy's approaches are the only ones that have integrated contraints which operate on the binary linking features (cf chapter 5). Overall, the OT literature is rich in terms of paying attention to all of the guiding themes identified in the beginning of this book: overt case morphology, argument structure and grammatical relations.

8.3 Discussion

This section concludes the book. The material in this book has covered a range of phenomena, attitudes and proposals that have become part of standard knowledge with respect to case. It also sought to bring out some of the approaches and ideas which may not be as standardly acknowledged, but which shed an interesting light on case phenomena, and/or which are representative of an active community of researchers.

There is, of course, much more that has been written and established about case. A single book cannot do justice to the vast literature that exists to date. For example, next to no attention was paid to semantic case on temporal or spatial arguments and adjuncts beyond short discussions in sections 4.9 and 7.1. Much more could have been said, but since there is only a handful of work within syntactic theory on these phenomena, I kept the discussion short.

The book has concentrated on providing a comparative look at case across syntactic theories, seeking to establish how guiding ideas about case, argument structure and grammatical relations were developed and absorbed into current linguistic thinking. A range of ideas and theories have been discussed, but more could have been said. An interesting approach, for example, is Yip, Maling, and Jackendoff's (1987) 'Case in Tiers' approach, which seeks to explain the distribution of case by means of alignment ideas coming out of phonology. A discussion of this may have fitted in with section 8.2 on OT, but the ideas are sufficiently different that a separate section would have been necessary.

Discussions of computationally oriented theories such as Head-Driven Phrase Structure Grammar (HPSG) (Pollard and Sag 1994), Combinatory Categorial

Grammar (Steedman 2001) and Tree-Adjoining Grammar (e.g., Abeillé and Rambow 2000) have also fallen victim to a lack of space. These theories have built serious computational grammars that cover a good range of phenomena. Case is one of the issues that is necessarily dealt with. However, none of these frameworks have developed a theory of case that is non-trivially distinct from the standard GB assumptions discussed in chapter 4. The basic CCG approach to case is briefly discussed in Steedman (2001). Within HPSG, Przepiórkowski (1999) is a recent work on Polish case that also surveys the literature very nicely. For another standard HPSG approach to case, but with respect to German, see Heinz and Matiasek (1994). Interesting ideas about the organization of thematic relations and the integration of a linking theory into HPSG are developed in Davis and Koenig (2000), but they do not treat case per se.

Indeed, in the course of the book, it has emerged that the assumptions of the interaction (or existence) of the three guiding themes of the book, namely overt case morphology, argument structure and grammatical relations, can differ radically. Most modern theories of case have detailed ideas of at least two of the factors, a few contain ideas about all three factors. Some reject the relevance of notions such as grammatical relations altogether, others find the distribution of overt morphological case of less interest than the abstract underlying syntactic relations between predicates and their arguments. But the three guiding themes of the book are implicated over and over again in a variety of theories, indicating that at least these factors are important in understanding the distribution of case. Other factors such as prominence scales or semantic dimensions (e.g., aspectual boundedness) are not implicated across all theories, but are clearly relevant. It can be assumed that there are further factors which have not been identified or properly understood as yet, but which are relevant.

For students new to the field, this book should have provided a first guide to understanding the ideas, motivations and phenomena that have driven the development of theories of case. To my mind, a full understanding of case can only be achieved by a pooling of data and perspectives. For one, more data and patterns need to be identified and understood in synchronic, diachronic and psycholinguistic terms (language acquisition, language processing). There is some work on the processing of case, primarily with respect to datives, but much more could be done. For another, the diverse set of theoretical perspectives on case need to be understood in order to be able to combine the insights of one theory with the insights arrived at by another theory. Given that differing theories work within differing perspectives on the data, not all theories will arrive at the same conclusions about what is important about case. The differences in these conclusions can prove to be interesting and point the way to a deeper understanding of case. The intention behind this book is to provide a first organized look at the perspectives developed by different theories, and the motivations that lie behind the individual proposals.

8.4 Exercises

Exercise 1: Basics

Answer the following questions briefly. They are intended to help you get your bearings with the basic concepts in the theories introduced in this chapter.

RRG

1. How are grammatical relations encoded in RRG?
2. How is morphological (overt) case handled within RRG?
3. What role do thematic roles play in RRG?
4. How are quirky case phenomena dealt with in RRG?

OT

1. What role do the functions GEN and EVAL play in OT?
2. What is the general analytic strategy?
3. How does Harmonic Alignment work in OT?
4. What effects can different constraint rankings have?

Exercise 2: RRG

Provide an RRG analysis for the examples in (1)–(3). Note that 'water' and 'bed' in (1) and (2) are adjuncts and do not need to be dealt with in your analysis.

(1) Der   Affe   ist   ins   Wasser   gefallen.
    the.M.Sg.Nom monkey.M.Sg be.Pres.3.Sg in.the water.N.Sg fall.PastP
    'The monkey fell into the water.'   German

(2) Der   Affe   hat   im   Bett
    the.M.Sg.Nom monkey.M.Sg have.Pres.3.Sg in.the bed.N.Sg
    geniest.
    sneeze.PastP
    'The monkey sneezed in bed.'   German

(3) Dem   Hund wurde   ein   Kuchen gegeben.
    the.M.Sg.Dat dog was.3.Sg a.M.Sg.Nom cake.M. give.PastP
    'The dog was given a cake.'   German

Exercise 3: OT

Provide an OT analysis in terms of Aissen's Harmonic Alignment approach for the nonspecific object reading in (4) (an analysis of the specific object reading was done in section 8.2.3).

(4) Ali bir kitap aldı
   A. one book bought
   'Ali bought some book or other.' (Enç 1991)   Turkish

Harder: Provide an OT analysis in terms of Aissen's Harmonic Alignment approach for the ergative pattern in (5): transitive subjects should turn out to be ergative and intransitives should be absolutive.

Note that the analysis does not follow straightforwardly from the discussion in section 8.2, so you will have to propose your own constraints and rank them.

(5) a. Oli-p   neqi   neri-vaa
       Oli-Erg meat.Abs eat-IND.TR.3Sg.3Sg
       'Oli eats meat.' (Manning 1996:3)   West Greenlandic

   b. Oli   sinippoq
      Oli.Abs sleep-IND.INTR.3Sg
      'Oli sleeps.' (Manning 1996:3)   West Greenlandic

References

Abeillé, Anne, and Owen Rambow (ed.). 2000. *Tree Adjoining Grammars: Formalisms, Linguistic Analysis and Processing*. Stanford: CSLI Publications.

Ackerman, Farrell. 1992. Complex Predicates and Morpholexical Relatedness: Locative Alternation in Hungarian. In *Lexical Matters*, ed. Ivan A. Sag and Anna Szabolcsi. 55–83. Stanford: CSLI Publications.

Ackerman, Farrell, and John Moore. 2001. *Proto-Properties and Grammatical Encoding: A Correspondence Theory of Argument Selection*. Stanford, CA: CSLI Publications.

Adger, David. 2003. *Core Syntax: A Minimalist Approach*. Oxford: Oxford University Press.

Aissen, Judith. 1999. Markedness and Subject Choice in Optimality Theory. *Natural Language and Linguistic Theory* 17(4):673–711.

Aissen, Judith. 2003. Differential Object Marking: Iconicity vs. Economy. *Natural Language and Linguistic Theory* 21:435–483.

Allen, Cynthia L. 1995. *Case Marking and Reanalysis: Grammatical Relations from Old to Early Modern English*. Oxford: Oxford University Press.

Alsina, Alex. 1996. *The Role of Argument Structure in Grammar: Evidence from Romance*. Stanford: CSLI Publications.

Alsina, Alex. 1997. A theory of complex predicates: evidence from causatives in Bantu and Romance. In *Complex Predicates*, ed. Alex Alsina, Joan Bresnan, and Peter Sells. 203–246. Stanford: CSLI Publications.

Alsina, Alex, and Sam Mchombo. 1993. Object Asymmetries and the Chicheŵa Applicative Construction. In *Theoretical Aspects of Bantu Grammar*, ed. Sam Mchombo. 17–45. Stanford: CSLI Publications.

Anderson, John M. 1971a. *The Grammar of Case: Towards a Localistic Theory*. Cambridge: Cambridge University Press.

Anderson, Stephen R. 1971b. On the Role of Deep Structure in Semantic Interpretation. *Foundations of Language* 7:387–396.

Anderson, Stephen R. 1976. On the notion of subject in ergative languages. In *Subject and Topic*, ed. Charles N. Li. 1–23. New York: Academic Press.

Anderson, Stephen R. 1977. On Mechanisms by which Languages become Ergative. In *Mechanisms of Language Change*, ed. Charles Li. 317–363. Austin, TX: University of Texas Press.

Arens, Hans. 1969. *Sprachwissenschaft: Der Gang ihrer Entwicklung von der Antike bis zur Gegenwart*. Freiburg: Verlag Karl Alber.

Arnold, Jennifer, Thomas Wasow, Anthony Losongco, and Ryan Ginstrom. 2000. Heaviness vs. newness: The effects of structural complexity. *Language* 76(1):28–55.

Asudeh, Ash. 2003. A Licensing Theory for Finnish. In *Generative Approaches to Finnic and Saami Linguistics*, ed. Diane C. Nelson and Satu Manninen. Stanford: CSLI Publications.

Auroux, Sylvain, E.F.K. Koerner, Hans-Josef Niederehe, and Kees Versteegh (ed.). 2000. *History of the Language Sciences: An International Handbook on the Evolution of the Study of Language from the Beginnings to the Present*. Berlin: Walter de Gruyter.

Austin, Peter, and Joan Bresnan. 1996. Non-configurationality in Australian Aboriginal languages. *Natural Language and Linguistic Theory* 14(2):215–268.

Baker, Mark. 1983. Objects, Themes, and Lexical Rules in Italian. In *Papers in Lexical-Functional Grammar*, ed. Lori Levin, Malka Rappaport, and Annie Zaenen. Indiana University Linguistics Club.

Baker, Mark. 1988. *Incorporation: A Theory of Grammatical Function Changing*. Chicago: The University of Chicago Press.

Baker, Mark. 1996. On the Structural Position of Themes and Goals. In *Phrase Structure and the Lexicon*, ed. Johan Rooryck and Laurie Zaring. 7–34. Dordrecht: Kluwer.

Barbosa, Pilar, Danny Fox, Paul Hagstrom, Martha McGinnis, and David Pesetsky (ed.). 1998. *Is the Best Good Enough?* Cambridge: The MIT Press.

Bashir, Elena. 1999. The Urdu and Hindi Ergative Postposition *ne*: Its changing role in the Grammar. In *The Yearbook of South Asian Languages and Linguistics*, ed. Rajendra Singh. 11–36. New Delhi: Sage Publications.

Bauer, Brigitte. 2000. *Archaic Syntax in Indo-European: The Spread and Transitivity in Latin and French*. Berlin: Mouton de Gruyter.

Bayer, Josef. 2004. Non-Nominative Subjects in Comparison. In *Non-Nominative Subjects*, ed. Peri Bhaskararao and K.V. Subbarao. 49–76. Amsterdam: John Benjamins.

Bayer, Josef, Markus Bader, and Michael Meng. 2001. Morphological Underspecification Meets Oblique Case: Syntactic and Processing Effects in German. *Lingua* 111:465–514.

Beames, John. 1872–79. *A Comparative Grammar of the Modern Aryan Languages of India*. Delhi: Munshiram Manoharlal. Republished 1966.

Beck, Sigrid, and Kyle Johnson. 2004. Double Objects Again. *Linguistic Inquiry* 35(1):97–124.

Bekkum, Wout van, Jan Houben, Ineke Sluiter, and Kees Versteegh. 1997. *The Emergence of Semantics in Four Linguistic Traditions: Hebrew, Sanskrit, Greek, Arabic*. Amsterdam: John Benjamins Publishing Company.

Belletti, Adriana, and Luigi Rizzi. 1988. Psych-Verbs and θ-Theory. *Natural Language and Linguistic Theory* 6:291–352.

Benveniste, Émile. 1952. La construction passive du parfait transitif. *Bull étin de la Société de Linguistique de Paris* 55.

Berman, Judith. 2003. *Clausal Syntax of German*. Stanford: CSLI Publications.

Bierwisch, Manfred. 1983. Semantische und Konzeptuelle Repräsentation Lexikalischer Einheiten. In *Untersuchungen zur Semantik*, ed. W. Motsch and R. Rüzicka. 61–99. Berlin: Akademie Verlag.

Bierwisch, Manfred. 1986. On the Nature of Semantic Form in Natural Language. In *Human Memory and Cognitive Capabilities*, ed. F. Klix and H. Hangendorf. 765–783. Amsterdam: Elsevier. Part B.

Bierwisch, Manfred, and R. Schreuder. 1992. From Concepts to Lexical Items. *Cognition* 42:23–60.

Bittner, Maria. 1994. *Case, Scope, and Binding*. Dordrecht: Kluwer.

Bittner, Maria, and Kenneth Hale. 1996a. Ergativity: Toward A Theory of a Heterogeneous Class. *Linguistic Inquiry* 27(4):531–604.

Bittner, Maria, and Kenneth Hale. 1996b. The Structural Determination of Case and Agreement. *Linguistic Inquiry* 27(1):1–68.

Blake, Barry. 1979. Degrees of Ergativity in Australia. In *Ergativity: Towards a Theory of Grammatical Relations*, ed. Frans Plank. 291–305. New York: Academic Press.

Blake, Barry. 2001. *Case*. Cambridge: Cambridge University Press. Second Edition.

Bobaljik, Jonathan D. 1992. Nominally absolutive is not absolutely nominative. In *Proceedings of the West Coast Conference on Formal Linguistics (WCCFL)*, 44–60. Stanford Linguistics Association.

Bobaljik, Jonathan D. 1993. On ergativity and ergative unergatives. In *Papers in Case and Agreement II*, ed. Colin Phillips, MIT Working Papers in Linguistics, Vol. 19, 45–88. MIT Department of Linguistics.

Böhtlingk, Otto. 1839–40. *Pāṇinis Grammatik*. Delhi: Motilal Banarsidass. Republished in 1998.

Bok-Bennema, Reineke. 1991. *Case and Agreement in Inuit*. Dordrecht: Foris.

Bolinger, Dwight. 1972. Ambient *it* Is Meaningful Too. *Journal of Linguistics* 9:261–270.

Borer, Hagit. 2003. *Structuring Sense*. Oxford: Oxford University Press. In Press.

Bossong, Georg. 1985. *Differentielle Objektmarkierung in den Neuiranischen Sprachen*. Tübingen: Gunter Narr Verlag.

Bresnan, Joan. 1976. On the Form and Functioning of Transformations. *Linguistic Inquiry* 7(1):3–40.

Bresnan, Joan. 1977. Transformations and Categories in Syntax. In *Basic Problems in Methodology and Linguistics. Part Three of the Proceedings of the Fifth International Congress of Logic, Methodology and Philosophy of Science, London, Ontario, Canada, 1975*, ed. R.E. Butts and J. Hintikka. 261–282. Dordrecht: Reidel.

Bresnan, Joan. 1982a. Control and Complementation. In *The Mental Representation of Grammatical Relations*, ed. Joan Bresnan. 282–390. Cambridge: MIT Press.

Bresnan, Joan (ed.). 1982b. *The Mental Representation of Grammatical Relations*. Cambridge: MIT Press.

Bresnan, Joan. 1982c. The Passive in Lexical Theory. In *The Mental Representation of Grammatical Relations*, ed. J. Bresnan. 3–86. Cambridge: MIT Press.

Bresnan, Joan. 1982d. Polyadicity. In *The Mental Representation of Grammatical Relations*, ed. J. Bresnan. 149–172. Cambridge: MIT Press.

Bresnan, Joan. 1990. Monotonicity and the Theory of Relation-Changes in LFG. *Language Research* 26(4):637–652.

Bresnan, Joan. 1994. Locative Inversion and the architecture of Universal Grammar. *Language* 70(1):72–131.

Bresnan, Joan. 2000. Optimal Syntax. In *Optimality Theory: Phonology, Syntax and Acquisition*, ed. Joost Dekkers, Frank van der Leeuw, and Jeroen van de Weijer. 334–385. Oxford: Oxford University Press.

Bresnan, Joan. 2001. *Lexical-Functional Syntax*. Oxford: Blackwell.

Bresnan, Joan, and Jonni Kanerva. 1989. Locative Inversion in Chicheŵa: A Case Study of Factorization in Grammar. *Linguistic Inquiry* 20:1–50.

Bresnan, Joan, and Lioba Moshi. 1990. Object Asymmetries in Comparative Bantu Syntax. *Linguistic Inquiry* 21:147–185.

Bresnan, Joan, and Annie Zaenen. 1990. Deep Unaccusativity in LFG. In *Grammatical Relations: A Cross-Theoretical Perspective*, ed. Katazyna Dziwirek, Patrick Farrell, and Errapel Mejías-Bikandi. 45–57. Stanford: CSLI Publications.

Bubenik, Vit. 1989. On the Origins and Elimination of Ergativity in Indo-Aryan Languages. *Canadian Journal of Linguistics* 34:377–398.

Bubenik, Vit. 1996. *The Structure and Development of Middle Indo-Aryan Dialects*. Delhi: Motilal Banarsidass.

Budwig, Nancy. 1989. The linguistic marking of agentivity and control in child language. *Journal of Child Language* 16:263–284.

Burzio, Luigi. 1986. *Italian Syntax: A Government Binding Approach*. Dordrecht: Reidel.

Butt, Miriam. 1993. Object specificity and agreement in Hindi/Urdu. In *Papers from the 29th Regional Meeting of the Chicago Linguistic Society*, 80–103.

Butt, Miriam. 1995. *The Structure of Complex Predicates in Urdu*. Stanford: CSLI Publications.

Butt, Miriam. 1998. Constraining Argument Merger through Aspect. In *Complex Predicates in Nonderivational Syntax*, ed. Erhard Hinrichs, Andreas Kathol, and Tsuneko Nakazawa. 73–113. New York: Academic Press. Syntax and Semantics Volume 30.

Butt, Miriam. 2001. A Reexamination of the Accusative to Ergative Shift in Indo-Aryan. In *Time Over Matter: Diachronic Perspectives on Morphosyntax*, ed. Miriam Butt and Tracy Holloway King. 105–141. Stanford: CSLI Publications.

Butt, Miriam, and Wilhelm Geuder (ed.). 1998. *The Projection of Arguments: Lexical and Compositional Factors*. Stanford: CSLI Publications.

Butt, Miriam, and Tracy Holloway King. 1991. Semantic Case in Urdu. In *Papers from the 27th Regional Meeting of the Chicago Linguistic Society*, 31–45.

Butt, Miriam, and Tracy Holloway King. 2003. Case Systems: Beyond Structural Distinctions. In *New Perspectives on Case Theory*, ed. Ellen Brandner and Heike Zinsmeister. 53–87. Stanford: CSLI Publications.

Butt, Miriam, and Tracy Holloway King. 2005. The Status of Case. In *Clause Structure in South Asian Languages*, ed. Veneeta Dayal and Anoop Mahajan. Berlin: Springer Verlag.

Butt, Miriam, Tracy Holloway King, María-Eugenia Niño, and Frédérique Segond. 1999. *A Grammar Writer's Cookbook*. Stanford: CSLI Publications.

Carnie, Andrew. 2002. *Syntax: A Generative Introduction*. Oxford: Blackwell Publishers.

Carter, Richard J. 1977. Some linking regularities. *Recherches Linguistiques* 5-6. Paris: Univ. de Vincennes.

Chatterji, Suniti Kumar. 1926. *The Origin and Development of the Bengali Literature, Volume II*. Calcutta: D. Mehra, Rupa & Co. 1975 edition.

Chomsky, Noam. 1957. *Syntactic Structures*. The Hague: Mouton de Gruyter.

Chomsky, Noam. 1965. *Aspects of the Theory of Syntax*. Cambridge: The MIT Press.

Chomsky, Noam. 1970. Remarks on Nominalization. In *Readings in English Transformational Grammar*, ed. R.A. Jacobs and P.S. Rosenbaum. Waltham: Ginn. Also in N. Chomsky. 1972. *Studies on Semantics in Generative Grammar*. The Hague: Mouton.

Chomsky, Noam. 1981. *Lectures on Government and Binding*. Dordrecht: Foris.

Chomsky, Noam. 1986. *Knowledge of Language, its Nature, Origin, and Use*. New York: Praeger.

Chomsky, Noam. 1988. *Language and Problems of Knowledge: The Managua Lectures*. Cambridge: The MIT Press.

Chomsky, Noam. 1995. *The Minimalist Program*. Cambridge: The MIT Press.

Chomsky, Noam. 2001. Derivation by Phase. In *Kenneth Hale: A Life in Language*, ed. Michael Kenstowicz. 1–52. Cambridge: The MIT Press.

Chung, Sandra. 1977. On the Gradual Nature of Syntactic Change. In *Mechanisms of Syntactic Change*, ed. Charles Li. 3–55. Austin: University of Texas Press.

Cinque, Guglielmo. 1993. A Null Theory of Phrase and Compound Stress. *Linguistic Inquiry* 24(2):239–298.

Cummings, Thomas, and T. Grahame Bailey. 1912. *Panjabi Manual and Grammar: A Guide to the Colloquial Panjabi of the Northern Panjab*. Calcutta: Baptist Mission Press.

Dalrymple, Mary. 1993. *The Syntax of Anaphoric Binding*. Stanford: CSLI Publications.

Dalrymple, Mary (ed.). 1999. *Semantics and Syntax in Lexical Functional Grammar*. Cambridge: The MIT Press.

Dalrymple, Mary. 2001. *Lexical Functional Grammar*. New York: Academic Press.

Dalrymple, Mary, Ronald M. Kaplan, John T. Maxwell III, and Annie Zaenen (ed.). 1995. *Formal Issues in Lexical-Functional Grammar*. Stanford: CSLI Publications.

Dalrymple, Mary, and Helge Lødrup. 2000. The Grammatical Functions of Complement Clauses. In *On-line Proceedings of the LFG'00 Conference*, ed. Miriam Butt and Tracy Holloway King. Berkeley.

Davis, Anthony R., and Jean-Pierre Koenig. 2000. Linking as Constraints on Word Classes in a Hierarchical Lexicon. *Language* 76(1):56–91.

Davison, Alice. 1999. Ergativity: Functional and Formal Issues. In *Functionalism and Formalism in Linguistics, Volume I: General Papers*, ed. Michael Darnell, Edith Moravcsik, Frederick Newmeyer, Michael Noonan, and Kathleen Wheatley. 177–208. Amsterdam: John Benjamins.

Davison, Alice. 2000. 'Dependent structural case' as a consequence of VP structure. *Texas Linguistics Forum* 42(2).

de Hoop, Helen. 1996. *Case Configuration and Noun Phrase Interpretation*. New York: Garland.

de Hoop, Helen. 1999. Optimal Case Assignment. In *Linguistics in the Netherlands, AVT Publications 16*, ed. Renée van Bezooijen and René Kager. 97–109. Amsterdam: John Benjamins Publishing Company.

Dekkers, Joost, Frank van der Leeuw, and Jeroen van de Weijer (ed.). 2000. *Optimality Theory: Phonology, Syntax and Acquisition*. Oxford: Oxford University Press.

Dench, Alan. 1995. *Martuthunira: a Language of the Pilbara Region of Western Australia*. Canberra: Pacific Linguistics.

Dench, Alan, and Nicholas Evans. 1988. Multiple Case-Marking in Australian Languages. *Australian Journal of Linguistics* 8:1–47.

Dirr, Adolf. 1928. *Einführung in das Studium der kaukasischen Sprachen*. Leipzig: Verlag der Asia Major.

Dixon, R. M. W. 1979a. Ergativity. *Language* 55:59–138.

Dixon, R. M. W. 1979b. A Note on Dyirbal Ergativity. In *The Proceedings of the 15th Meeting of the Chicago Linguistic Society*, 90–91.

Dixon, R. M. W. 1994. *Ergativity*. Cambridge: Cambridge University Press.

Dowty, David. 1979. *Word Meaning and Montague Grammar: The Semantics of Verbs and Times in Generative Semantics and in Montague's PTQ*. Dordrecht: Kluwer.

Dowty, David. 1991. Thematic proto-roles and argument selection. *Language* 67(3):547–619.

Egede, Paul. 1760. *Grammatica Groenlandico Danico-Latina*. Copenhagen: ULO.

Enç, Mürvet. 1991. The Semantics of Specificity. *Linguistic Inquiry* 22(1):1–25.

Erteschik-Shir, Nomi. 1979. Discourse Constraints on Dative Movement. In *Discourse and Syntax*, ed. Talmy Givón. 441–467. New York: Academic Press. Syntax and Semantics Volume 12.

Evans, Nicholas. 1995a. *A Grammar of Kayardild: With Historical-Comparative Notes on Tangkic*. Berlin: Mouton de Gruyter.

Evans, Nicholas. 1995b. Multiple case in Kayardild: Anti-iconic suffix ordering and the diachronic filter. In *Double Case: Agreement by Suffixaufnahme*, ed. Frans Plank. 396–428. Oxford: Oxford University Press.

Ezeizabarrena, María José, and María Pilar Larrañaga. 1996. Ergativity in Basque: a problem for language acquisition? *Linguistics* 34:955–991.

Falk, Yehuda. 2001. *Lexical-Functional Grammar: An Introduction to Parallel Constraint-Based Syntax*. Stanford: CSLI Publications.

Fanselow, Gisbert. 1987. *Konfigurationalität*. Tübingen: Narr.

Fanselow, Gisbert. 2000. Optimal Exceptions. In *The Lexicon in Focus*, ed. Barbara Stiebels and Dieter Wunderlich. 173–209. Berlin: Akademie Verlag. Studia Grammatica 45.

Farkas, Donka, and Henriëtte de Swart. 2003. *The Semantics of Incorporation: From Argument Structure to Discourse Transparency*. Stanford: CSLI Publications.

Fillmore, Charles J. 1968. The case for case. In *Universals of Linguistic Theory*, ed. Emmon Bach and Robert T. Harms. 1–88. New York: Holt, Rinehart and Winston.

Fillmore, Charles J. 1977. The case for case reopened. In *Syntax and Semantics: Grammatical Relations, Volume 8*, ed. Peter Cole and Jerald Sadock. 59–91. New York: Academic Press.

Foley, William, and Robert D. Van Valin. 1977. On the viability of the notion 'subject' in Universal Grammar. In *Proceedings of the Third Annual Meeting of the Berkeley Linguistics Society*, 293–320.

Fortescue, Michael. 1985. Learning to speak Greenlandic: A case study of a two-year-old's morphology in a polysynthetic language. *First Language* 5:101–114.

Frank, Anette. 1999. From Parallel Grammar Development towards Machine Translation. In *Proceedings of MT Summit VII "MT in the Great Translation Era"*, 134–142. September 13–17, Kent Ridge Digital Labs, Singapore.

Franks, Steven, and Tracy Holloway King. 2000. *A Handbook of Slavic Clitics*. Oxford: Oxford University Press.

Garrett, Andrew. 1990. The Origin of NP Split Ergativity. *Language* 66:261–296.

Ghomeshi, Jila. 1997. Non-Projecting Nouns and the *Ezafe*: Construction in Persian. *Natural Language and Linguistic Theory* 15(5):729–788.

Givón, Tom. 1984. Direct Object and Dative Shifting: Semantic and Pragmatic Case. In *Objects: Towards a Theory of Grammatical Relations*, ed. Frans Plank. 151–182. New York: Academic Press.

Glassman, Eugene. 1976. *Spoken Urdu*. Lahore: Nirali Kitaben.

Goddard, Cliff. 1982. Case Systems and Case Marking in Australian Languages: A New Interpretation. *Australian Journal of Linguistics* 2:167–196.

Grewendorf, Günter. 1989. *Ergativity in German*. Dordrecht: Foris.

Grimshaw, Jane. 1990. *Argument Structure*. Cambridge: The MIT Press.

Grimshaw, Jane. 1997. Projection, Heads, and Optimality. *Linguistic Inquiry* 28(3):373–422.

Grimshaw, Jane, and Armin Mester. 1988. Light Verbs and Θ-Marking. *Linguistic Inquiry* 19(2):205–232.

Grimshaw, Jane, and Vieri Samek-Lodovici. 1998. Optimal Subjects and Subject Universals. In *Is the Best Good Enough?*, ed. Pilar Barbosa, Danny Fox, Paul Hagstrom, Martha McGinnis, and David Pesetsky. 193–219. Cambridge: The MIT Press.

Gruber, Jeffrey S. 1965. *Studies in Lexical Relations*. Doctoral dissertation, MIT.

Haegeman, Lilliane. 1991. *Introduction to Government and Binding Theory*. Oxford: Blackwell.

Hale, Kenneth. 1993. Warlpiri and the Grammar of Nonconfigurational Languages. *Natural Language and Linguistic Theory* 1:5–47.

Hale, Kenneth, and Samuel J. Keyser. 1993. On Argument Structure and the Lexical Expression of Syntactic Relations. In *The View from Building 20*, ed. Kenneth Hale and Samuel J. Keyser. 53–109. Cambridge: The MIT Press.

Hale, Kenneth, and Samuel J. Keyser. 2002. *Prolegomenon to a Theory of Argument Structure*. Cambridge: The MIT Press.

Halvorsen, Per-Kristian, and Ronald M. Kaplan. 1988. Projections and Semantic Description in Lexical-Functional Grammar. In *Proceedings of the International Conference on Fifth Generation Computer Technology*, 1116–1122. Reprinted 1995 in Dalrymple et al. (eds) *Formal Issues in Lexical-Functional Grammar*.

Harley, Heidi. 1995. *Subjects, Events and Licensing*. Doctoral dissertation, MIT.

Harley, Heidi. 2002. Possession and the Double Object Construction. *Linguistic Variation Yearbook* 2:29–68.

Harris, Alice. 1981. *Georgian Syntax: A Study in Relational Grammar*. Cambridge: Cambridge University Press.

Harris, Alice. 1984. Inversion as a Rule of Universal Grammar: Georgian Evidence. In *Studies in Relational Grammar 2*, ed. David M. Perlmutter and Carol G. Rosen. 259–291. Chicago: The University of Chicago Press.

Harris, Alice. 1985. *Diachronic Syntax: The Kartvelian Case, Syntax and Semantics 18*. New York: Academic Press.

Harris, Alice, and Lyle Campbell. 1995. *Historical Syntax in Cross-Linguistic Perspective*. Cambridge: Cambridge University Press.

Harris, Zellig. 1951. *Structural Linguistics*. Chicago: The University of Chicago Press.

Harris, Zellig. 1957. Co-occurrence and transformations in linguistic structure. *Language* 33:283–340.

Heinz, Wolfgang, and Johannes Matiasek. 1994. Argument Structure and Case Assignment in German. In *German in Head-Driven Phrase Structure Grammar*, ed. John Nerbonne, Klaus Netter, and Carl Pollard. 199–236. Stanford: CSLI Publications.

Hjelmslev, Louis. 1935. *La catégorie des cas*. Aarhus: Universitetsforlaget.

Hock, Hans Henrich. 1986. P-oriented Constructions in Sanskrit. In *South Asian Languages: Structure, Convergence and Diglossia*, ed. Bh. Krishnamurti. Delhi: Motilal Banarsidass.

Holisky, Dee Ann. 1987. The case of the intransitive subject in Tsova-Tush (Batsbi). *Lingua* 71:103–132.

Holmberg, Anders, and Urpo Nikanne (ed.). 1993. *Case and other Functional Categories in Finnish Syntax*. Berlin: Mouton de Gruyter.

Hopper, Paul, and Sandra Thompson. 1980. Transitivity in Grammar and Discourse. *Language* 56:251–299.

Hopper, Paul J., and Elizabeth C. Traugott. 1993. *Grammaticalization*. Cambridge: Cambridge University Press.

Hudson, Richard. 1995. Does English really have case? *Journal of Linguistics* 31:375–392.

Jackendoff, Ray. 1972. *Semantic Interpretation in Generative Grammar*. Cambridge: The MIT Press.

Jackendoff, Ray. 1976. Toward an Explanatory Semantic Representation. *Linguistic Inquiry* 7(1):89–150.

Jackendoff, Ray. 1990. *Semantic Structures*. Cambridge: The MIT Press.

Jake, Janice. 1978. Why Dyirbal isn't Ergative at all. In *The Proceedings of the 14th Meeting of the Chicago Linguistic Society*, 179–192.

Jakobson, Roman. 1936. Beiträge zur Allgemeinen Kasuslehre: Gesamtbedeutungen der russischen Kasus. *Travaux du Cercle Linguistique de Prague* 6:240–288. Reprinted in 1966 in *Readings in Linguistics II*, Eric P. Hamp, Fred W. Householder and Robert Austerlitz (eds.), 51–89. Chicago: The University of Chicago Press.

Jamison, Stephanie. 1976. Functional Ambiguity and Syntactic Change: The Sanskrit Accusative. In *Papers from the Parasession on Diachronic Syntax, 12th Regional Meeting of the Chicago Linguistic Society*, 126–135.

Jelinek, Eloise. 1987. Auxiliaries and Ergative Splits: A Typological Parameter. In *Historical Development of Auxiliaries*, ed. Martin Harris and Paolo Ramat. Berlin: Mouton de Gruyter.

Johns, Alana. 1992. Deriving Ergativity. *Linguistic Inquiry* 23(1):57–87.

Johns, Alana. 2000. Ergativity: A perspective on recent work. In *The First* Glot International *State-of-the-Article Book*, ed. Lisa Cheng and Rint Sybesma. 47–73. Berlin: Mouton de Gruyter.

Joppen, Sandra, and Dieter Wunderlich. 1995. Argument Linking in Basque. *Lingua* 97:123–169.

Joppen-Hellwig, Sandra. 2001. *Verbklassen und Argumentlinking*. Tübingen: Max Niemeyer Verlag.

Kachru, Yamuna. 1978. On Ergativity in Selected South Asian Languages. *Studies in the Linguistic Sciences* 8:111–127.

Kachru, Yamuna. 1987. Ergativity, subjecthood and topicality in Hindi-Urdu. *Lingua* 71:223–238.

Kager, René. 1999. *Optimality Theory*. Cambridge: Cambridge University Press.

Katre, Sumitra M. 1987. *Aṣṭādhyāyī of Pāṇini*. Delhi: Motilal Banarsidass. Republished in 1989.

Katz, Jerrold, and Paul M. Postal. 1964. *An Integrated Theory of Linguistic Descriptions*. Cambridge: The MIT Press.

Kaufmann, Ingrid. 1995a. *Konzeptuelle Grundlagen semantischer Dekompositionsstrukturen: die Kombinatorik lokaler Verben und prädikativer Komplemente*. Tübingen: Max Niemeyer Verlag.

Kaufmann, Ingrid. 1995b. O- and D-predicates: A semantic approach to the unaccusative-unergative-distinction. *Journal of Semantics* 12:377–427.

Kayne, Richard. 1984. *Connectedness and Binary Branching*. Dordrecht: Foris.

Kayne, Richard. 1994. *The Antisymmetry of Syntax*. Cambridge: The MIT Press.

Kelling, Carmen. 2001. Agentivity and Suffix Selection. In *On-Line Proceedings of the LFG'01 Conference*, ed. Miriam Butt and Tracy Holloway King. 147–162. Stanford: CSLI Publications.

Kelling, Carmen. 2003. French Psych Verbs and Derived Nouns. In *Nominals: Inside and Out*, ed. Miriam Butt and Tracy Holloway King. 151–179. Stanford: CSLI Publications.

Kellogg, S. H. 1893. *Grammar of the Hindi Language*. Delhi: Munshiram Manoharlal Publishers Pvt. Ltd. Second Edition, reprinted 1990.

Kent, Roland. 1953. *Old Persian*. New Haven, CT: American Oriental Society.

Kibrik, Aleksander E. 1997. Beyond Subject and Object: Toward a comprehensive relational typology. *Linguistic Typology* 1(3):279–346.

King, Tracy Holloway. 1995. *Configuring Topic and Focus in Russian*. Stanford: CSLI Publications.

Kiparsky, Paul. 1973. 'Elsewhere' in phonology. In *A Festschrift for Morris Halle*, ed. Stephen R. Anderson and Paul Kiparsky. 93–106. New York: Holt, Rinehart and Winston.

Kiparsky, Paul. 1987. Morphology and grammatical relations. Stanford University.

Kiparsky, Paul. 1988. Agreement and Linking Theory. Stanford University.

Kiparsky, Paul. 1997. The Rise of Positional Licensing. In *Parameters of Morphosyntactic Change*, ed. Ans van Kemenade and Nigel Vincent. 460–494. Cambridge: Cambridge University Press.

Kiparsky, Paul. 1998. Partitive Case and Aspect. In *The Projection of Arguments: Lexical and Compositional Factors*, ed. Miriam Butt and Wilhelm Geuder. 265–307. Stanford: CSLI Publications.

Kiparsky, Paul. 2001. Structural Case in Finnish. *Lingua* 111:315–376.

Kiparsky, Paul, and J.F. Staal. 1969. Syntactic and Semantic Relations in Pāṇini. *International Journal of Language and Philosophy* 5:83–117.

Kiss, Katalin É. 1995. *Discourse Configurational Languages*. Oxford: Oxford University Press.

Klaiman, M. H. 1978. Arguments Against a Passive Origin of the IA Ergative. In *The Proceedings of the 14th Meeting of the Chicago Linguistic Society*, 204–216.

Klaiman, M. H. 1980. Bengali Dative Subjects. *Lingua* 51:275–295.

Klimov, Georgij A. 1974. On the Character of Languages of Active Typology. *Linguistics* 131:11–25.

Klimov, Georgij A. 1979. On the Position of the Ergative Type in Typological Classification. In *Ergativity: Towards a Theory of Grammatical Relations*, ed. Frans Plank. New York: Academic Press.

Koopman, Hilda, and Dominique Sportiche. 1991. The Position of Subjects. *Lingua* 85:211–258.

Kratzer, Angelika. 1994. On External Arguments. In *University of Massachusetts Occasional Papers in Linguistics (UMOP)*, ed. E. Benedicto and J. Runner. 103–129. Amherst: GLSA.

Kratzer, Angelika. 1996. Severing the External Argument from its Verb. In *Phrase Structure and the Lexicon*, ed. Johann Rooryck and Laurie Zaring. 108–137. Dordrecht: Kluwer.

Krifka, Manfred. 1992. Thematic relations as links between nominal reference and temporal constitution. In *Lexical Matters*, ed. Ivan Sag and Anna Szabolcsi. 29–53. Stanford: CSLI Publications.

Kroeger, Paul. 1993. *Phrase Structure and Grammatical Relations in Tagalog*. Stanford: CSLI Publications.

Kuhn, Jonas. 2003. *Optimality-Theoretic Syntax—A Declarative Approach*. Stanford: CSLI Publications.

Lahiri, Aditi (ed.). 2000. *Analogy, Leveling and Markedness*. Berlin: Mouton de Gruyter.

Laka, Itziar. 1993. Unergatives that Assign Ergative, Unaccusatives that Assign Accusative. In *Papers on Case and Agreement I*, ed. Jonathan D. Bobaljik and Colin Phillips. MIT Working Papers in Linguistics, Vol. 18, 149–172.

Lakoff, George. 1971. On Generative Semantics. In *Semantics: An Interdisciplinary Reader in Philosophy, Linguistics and Psychology*, ed. Danny D. Steinberg and Leon A. Jakobovits. 232–296. Cambridge: Cambridge University Press.

Lamontagne, Greg, and Lisa de Mena Travis. 1986. The Case Filter and the ECP. *McGill Working Papers in Linguistics* 3(2):51–75.

Larrañaga, María Pilar. 2000. *Ergative Sprachen, akkusative Sprachen*. Frankfurt am Main: Vervuert Verlag.

Larson, Richard. 1988. On the Double Object Construction. *Linguistic Inquiry* 19:335–391.

Lazard, Gilbert. 1998. *Actancy*. Berlin: Mouton de Gruyter.

Lechner, Winfried. 1998. Two Kinds of Reconstruction. *Studia Linguistica* 52(3):276–310.

Legendre, Géraldine. 1989. Unaccusativity in French. *Lingua* 79:95–164.

Legendre, Géraldine, Jane Grimshaw, and Sten Vikner (ed.). 2000. *Optimality-Theoretic Syntax*. Cambridge: The MIT Press.

Legendre, Géraldine, Yoshiro Miyata, and Paul Smolensky. 1989. Can Connectionism Contribute to Syntax? Harmonic Grammar, with an Application. In *Papers from the 26th Regional Meeting of the Chicago Linguistic Society*, 237–252.

Legendre, Géraldine, William Raymond, and Paul Smolensky. 1993. An Optimality-Theoretic Typology of Case and Grammatical Voice Systems. In *Proceedings of the Nineteenth Annual Meeting of the Berkeley Linguistics Society*, ed. Joshua S. Guenter, Barbara A. Kaiser, and Cheryl C. Zoll, 464–478.

Legendre, Géraldine, Antonella Sorace, and Paul Smolensky. 2005. The Optimality Theory—Harmonic Grammar connection. In *The Harmonic Mind: From Neural Computation To Optimality-Theoretic Grammar*, ed. Paul Smolensky and Géraldine Legendre. Cambridge: The MIT Press.

Lehmann, Christian. 1985. Grammaticalization: synchronic variation and diachronic change. *Lingua e Stile* 20:303–318.

Levin, Beth. 1983. *On the Nature of Ergativity*. Doctoral dissertation, MIT.

Levin, Beth, and Malka Rappaport Hovav. 1995. *Unaccusativity: At the Syntax-Lexical Semantics Interface*. Cambridge: The MIT Press.

Levin, Lori. 1987. Toward a Linking Theory of Relation Changing Rules in LFG. Technical Report CSLI-87-115. Stanford.

Levin, Lori. 1988. *Operations on Lexical Forms: Unaccusative Rules in Germanic Languages*. New York: Garland.

Levin, Lori, and Jane Simpson. 1981. Quirky Case and Lexical Representations of Icelandic Verbs. In *Papers from the 17th Regional Meeting of the Chicago Linguistic Society*, 185–196.

Lightfoot, David (ed.). 2002. *Syntactic Effects of Morphological Change*. Oxford: Oxford University Press.

Mahajan, Anoop. 1990. *The A/A-Bar Distinction and Movement Theory*. Doctoral dissertation, MIT.

Maling, Joan. 1989. Adverbials and Structural Case in Korean. In *Harvard Studies in Korean Linguistics III*, ed. Susumu Kuno, Ik-Hwan Lee, John Whitman, Sung-Yun Bak, Young-Se Kang, and Young joo Kim. 297–308. Cambridge: Department of Linguistics, Harvard University. Proceedings of the 1989 Harvard Workshop on Korean Linguistics (Harvard WOKL-1989), July 14–16.

Maling, Joan. 2001. Dative: The Heterogeneity of the Mapping among Morphological Case, Grammatical Functions, and Thematic Roles. *Lingua* 111:419–464. Special Issue *On the Effects of Morphological Case*.

Manaster Ramer, Alexis. 1994. The origin of the term 'ergative'. *Sprachtypologische Universalien Forschung (STUF)* 47(3):211–214.

Manning, Christopher D. 1996. *Ergativity: Argument Structure and Grammatical Relations*. Stanford: CSLI Publications.

Manning, Christopher D., and Avery Andrews. 1999. *Complex Predicates and Information Spreading*. Stanford: CSLI Publications.

Marantz, Alec. 1984. *On the Nature of Grammatical Relations*. Cambridge: The MIT Press.

Marantz, Alec. 1991. Case and Licensing. In *Proceedings of the Eastern States Conference on Linguistics*, 234–253.

Masica, Colin. 1991. *The Indo-Aryan languages*. Cambridge: Cambridge University Press.

Massam, Diane. 1985. *Case Theory and the Projection Principle*. Doctoral dissertation, MIT.

McCarthy, John, and Alan Prince. 1993. Generalized Alignment. In *Yearbook of Morphology 1993*, ed. Gert Booij and Jap van Marle. 79–153. Dordrecht: Kluwer.

McCawley, James D. 1972. A Program for Logic. In *Semantics of Natural Language*, ed. Donald Davidson and Gilbert Harman. 498–544. Dordrecht: Reidel.

McCloskey, James. 1983. A VP in a VSO language. In *Order Concord and Constituency*, ed. Gerald Gazdar, Geoffrey Pullum, and Ivan Sag. 9–55. Dordrecht: Foris.

McGinnis, Martha. 1998a. Case and Locality in L-Syntax: Evidence from Georgian. In *The UPenn/MIT Roundtable on Argument Structure and Aspect*, ed. Heidi Harley. MIT Working Papers in Linguistics, Vol. 32. Cambridge: MIT Department of Linguistics.

McGinnis, Martha. 1998b. Locality and Inert Case. In *Proceedings of NELS 28*, ed. Pius Tamanji and Kiyomi Kusumoto. Amherst: GLSA Publications.

McGinnis, Martha. 1998c. *Locality in A-Movement*. Doctoral dissertation, MIT.

McGregor, R. S. 1972. *Outline of Hindi Grammar: with exercises*. Oxford: Clarendon Press.

Mel'čuk, Igor A. 1986. Toward a Definition of Case. In *Case in Slavic*, ed. Richard D. Brecht and James S. Levine. 35–85. Columbus: Slavica Publisher.

Mohanan, Tara. 1994. *Argument Structure in Hindi*. Stanford: CSLI Publications.

Nakamura, Wataru. 1997. *A Constraint Based Typology of Case Systems*. Doctoral dissertation, University at Buffalo, The State University of New York.

Narasimhan, Bhuvana. 1998. A Lexical Semantic Explanation fo 'Quirky' Case Marking in Hindi. *Studia Linguistica* 52(1):48–76.

Narasimhan, Bhuvana. 2003. Agent Case-Marking in Hindi Child Language. Max Planck Institute for Psycholinguistics, Under Review.

Nordlinger, Rachel. 1998. *Constructive Case: Evidence from Australian Languages*. Stanford: CSLI Publications.

Nordlinger, Rachel. 2000. Australian Case Systems: Towards a Constructive Solution. In *Argument Realization*, ed. Miriam Butt and Tracy Holloway King. 41–72. Stanford: CSLI Publications.

Nordlinger, Rachel, and Louisa Sadler. 2004a. Nominal Tense in Crosslinguistic Perspective. *Language* 80(4):776–806.

Nordlinger, Rachel, and Louisa Sadler. 2004b. Tense Beyond the Verb: Encoding Clausal Tense/Aspect/Mood on Nominal Dependents. *Natural Language and Linguistic Theory* 22:597–641.

Nordlinger, Rachel, and Adam Saulwick. 2002. Infinitives in Polysynthesis: the case of Rembarrnga. In *Problems of Polysynthesis*, ed. Nicholas Evans and Hans-Jürgen Sasse. 185–201. Berlin: Akademie Verlag.

Nunberg, Geoffrey, Ivan Sag, and Thomas Wasow. 1994. Idioms. *Language* 70(3):491–538.

Ochs, Elinor. 1985. Variation and Error: A Sociolinguistic Approach to Language Acquisition in Samoan. In *The Crosslinguistic Study of Language Acquisition, Vol. 1: The Data*, ed. Dan I. Slobin. Hillsday: Lawrence Erlbaum.

Oehrle, Richard. 1976. *The grammatical status of the English dative alternation*. Doctoral dissertation, MIT.

Ostler, Nicholas. 1979. *Case linking: A theory of case and verb diathesis, applied to Classical Sanskrit*. Doctoral dissertation, MIT.

Perlmutter, David M. 1978. Impersonal Passives and the Unaccusative Hypothesis. In *Proceedings of the Fourth Annual Meeting of the Berkeley Linguistics Society*, 157–189.

Perlmutter, David M. 1980. Relational Grammar. In *Syntax and Semantics: Current Approaches to Syntax, Volume 13*, ed. Edith A. Moravcsik and Jessica R. Wirth. New York: Academic Press.

Perlmutter, David M. (ed.). 1983. *Studies in Relational Grammar 1*. Chicago: The University of Chicago Press.

Perlmutter, David M. 1984. The Inadequacy of some Monostratal Theories of Passive. In *Studies in Relational Grammar 2*, ed. David M. Perlmutter and Carol G. Rosen. 3–37. Chicago: The University of Chicago Press.

Perlmutter, David M., and Paul M. Postal. 1983a. Some Proposed Laws of Basic Clause Structure. In *Studies in Relational Grammar 1*, ed. David M. Perlmutter. 81–128. Chicago: The University of Chicago Press.

Perlmutter, David M., and Paul M. Postal. 1983b. Toward a Universal Characterization of Passivization. In *Studies in Relational Grammar 1*, ed. David M. Perlmutter. 3–29. Chicago: The University of Chicago Press.

Perlmutter, David M., and Paul M. Postal. 1984. The 1-Advancement Exclusiveness Law. In *Studies in Relational Grammar 2*, ed. David M. Perlmutter and Carol G. Rosen. 81–125. Chicago: The University of Chicago Press.

Perlmutter, David M., and Carol G. Rosen (ed.). 1984. *Studies in Relational Grammar 2*. Chicago: The University of Chicago Press.

Pesetsky, David. 1995. *Zero Syntax: Experiencers and Cascades*. Cambridge: The MIT Press.

Pesetsky, David, and Esther Torrego. 2001. T-to-C Movement: Causes and Consequences. In *Ken Hale: A Life in Language*, ed. Michael Kenstowicz. Cambridge: The MIT Press.

Pesetsky, David, and Esther Torrego. 2004. Tense, Case, and the Nature of Syntactic Categories. In *The Syntax of Time*, ed. Jacqueline Guéron and Jacqueline Lecarme. Cambridge: The MIT Press.

Peterson, John M. 1998. *Grammatical Relations in Pāli and the Emergence of Ergativity in Indo-Aryan*. München: LINCOM Europa.

Phillips, Colin. 1993. Conditions on Agreement in Yimas. In *Papers on Case and Agreement I*, ed. Jonathan D. Bobaljik and Colin Phillips. MIT Working Papers in Linguistics, Vol. 18, 173–213. MIT Department of Linguistics.

Phillips, Colin. 1995. Ergative Subjects. In *Grammatical Relations: Theoretical Approaches to Empirical Questions*, ed. Clifford Burgess, Katarzyna Dziwirek, and Donna Gerdts. 341–357. Stanford: CSLI Publications.

Pinker, Steven. 1984. *Language Learnability and Language Development*. Cambridge: Harvard University Press.

Pirejko, L. A. 1979. On the Genesis of the Ergative Construction in Indo-Iranian. In *Ergativity: Towards a Theory of Grammatical Relations*, ed. Frans Plank. 481–488. New York: Academic Press.

Plank, Frans. 1979a. Ergativity, Syntactic Typology and Universal Grammar: Some past and present viewpoints. In *Ergativity: Towards a Theory of Grammatical Relations*, ed. Frans Plank. 3–36. New York: Academic Press.

Plank, Frans (ed.). 1979b. *Ergativity: Towards a Theory of Grammatical Relations*. New York: Academic Press.

Plank, Frans. 1995a. (Re-)Introducing Suffixaufnahme. In *Double Case: Agreement by Suffixaufnahme*, ed. Frans Plank. 3–110. Oxford: Oxford University Press.

Plank, Frans. 1995b. Research into Syntactic Change III: Ergativity. In *Syntax: An International Handbook of Contemporary Research*, ed. Joachim Jacobs, Arnim von Stechow, Wolfgang Sternefeld, and Theo Vennenmann. 1184–1199. Berlin: Walter de Gruyter.

Pollard, Carl, and Ivan A. Sag. 1994. *Head-driven Phrase Structure Grammar*. Chicago: University of Chicago Press.

Pollock, Jean-Yves. 1989. Verb movement, UG and the structure of IP. *Linguistic Inquiry* 20:365–424.

Postal, Paul M., and Brian D. Joseph (ed.). 1990. *Studies in Relational Grammar 3*. Chicago: The University of Chicago Press.

Pott, A.F. 1873. Unterschied eines transitiven und intransitiven nominativs. *Beiträge zur vergleichenden Sprachforschung auf dem Gebiete der arischen, celtischen und slawischen Sprachen* 7:71–94.

Pray, Bruce. 1976. From Passive to Ergative in Indo-Aryan. In *The Notion of Subject in South Asian Languages*, 195–211. Madison. University of Wisconsin.

Primus, Beatrice. 1997. The Relative Order of Recipient and Patient in the Languages of Europe. In *Constituent Order in the Languages of Europe*, ed. Anna Siewierska. 421–473. Berlin: Mouton de Gruyter.

Primus, Beatrice. 1999. *Cases and Thematic Roles : Ergative, Accusative and Active*. Tübingen: Niemeyer.

Primus, Beatrice. 2002. Proto-roles and case selection in Optimality Theory. Technical Report 122. SFB 282 "Theorie des Lexicons".

Prince, Alan, and Paul Smolensky. 1993. Optimality Theory: Constraint Interaction in Generative Grammar. Technical Report 2. Rutgers University.

Przepiórkowski, Adam. 1999. *Case Assignment and the Complement-Adjunct Dichotomy: A Non-Configurational Constraint-Based Approach*. Doctoral dissertation, Universität Tübingen.

Pullum, Geoffrey K. 1988. Citation Etiquette beyond Thunderdome. *Natural Language and Linguistic Theory* 6:579–588. Reprinted in Geoffrey Pullum *The Great Eskimo Vocabulary Hoax and other Irreverent Essays on the Study of Language*, 1991, Chicago: The University of Chicago Press.

Pullum, Geoffrey K. 1991. *The Great Eskimo Vocabulary Hoax and other Irreverent Essays on the Study of Language*. Chicago: The University of Chicago Press.

Pye, Clifton. 1990. The Acquisition of Ergative Languages. *Linguistics* 28:1291–1330.

Ramchand, Gillian. 1997. *Aspect and Predication*. Oxford: Oxford University Press.

Ramchand, Gillian. 1998. Deconstructing the Lexicon. In *The Projection of Arguments*, ed. Miriam Butt and Wilhelm Geuder. 65–96. Stanford: CSLI Publications.

Ramchand, Gillian. 2002. Aktionsart, L-syntax, and Selection. In *Perspectives on Aspect*, ed. Henk Verkuyl, 1–15. OTS. Online Proceedings, Utrecht, December, http://www-uilots.let.uu.nl/events/conf.htm.

Rappaport, Malka. 1983. On the Nature of Derived Nominals. In *Papers in Lexical-Functional Grammar*, ed. L. Levin, M. Rappaport, and A. Zaenen. Indiana University Linguistics Club.

Rappaport Hovav, Malka, and Beth Levin. 1998. Building Verb Meanings. In *The Projection of Arguments*, ed. Miriam Butt and Wilhelm Geuder. 97–134. Stanford: CSLI Publications.

Ray, Sidney H. 1907. *Reports of the Cambridge Anthropological Expedition to Torres Straits, Volume II: Linguistics*. Cambridge: Cambridge University Press.

Ray, Sidney H., and Alfred C. Haddon. 1893. A Study of the Languages of Torres Straits with vocabularies and grammatical notes, Part I. *Proceedings of the Royal Irish Academy, Third Series* II:463–616.

Reinhart, Tanya. 1996. Interface Economy — Focus and Markedness. In *The Role of Economy Principles in Linguistic Theory*, ed. Hans-Martin Gärtner Wilder, Chris and Manfred Bierwisch. 146–169. Berlin: Akademie Verlag.

Robins, Robert H. 2000. Greek Linguistics in the Byzantine Period. In *History of the Language Sciences: An International Handbook on the Evolution of the Study of Language from the Beginnings to the Present*, ed. Sylvain Auroux, E.F.K. Koerner, Hans-Josef Niederehe, and Kees Versteegh. 417–423. Berlin: Walter de Gruyter.

Rosen, Carol G. 1984. The Interface between Semantic Roles and Initial Grammatical Relations. In *Studies in Relational Grammar 2*, ed. David M. Perlmutter and Carol G. Rosen. 38–77. Chicago: The University of Chicago Press.

Rouveret, Alain, and Jean Roger Vergnaud. 1980. Specifying Reference to the Subject: French causatives and conditions on representations. *Linguistic Inquiry* 11:97–202.

Ruwet, Nicholas. 1991. *Syntax and Human Experience*. Chicago: University of Chicago Press.

Sadler, Louisa. 2003. Coordination and Asymmetric Agreement in Welsh. In *Nominals: Inside and Out*, ed. Miriam Butt and Tracy Holloway King. 85–117. Stanford: CSLI Publications.

Saksena, Anuradha. 1980. The Affected Agent. *Language* 56(4):812–826.

Sapir, Edward. 1917. Review of C.C. Uhlenbeck, "Het passieve karakter van het verbum transitivum of van het verbum actionis in talen van Noord-Amerika. *International Journal of American Linguistics* 1:82–86.

Schachter, Paul. 1976. The subject in Philippine languages: Topic, actor, actor-topic or none of the above. In *Subject and Topic*, ed. Charles Li, 491–518. New York. Academic Press.

Schachter, Paul. 1977. Reference-related and role-related properties of subjects. In *Grammatical Relations*, ed. Peter Cole and Jerrold M. Sadock, 279–306. New York. Academic Press. Syntax and Semantics Vol. 8.

Schmidt, Pater Wilhelm. 1902. Die sprachlichen Verhältnisse von Deutsch-Neuguinea [pat 6]. *Zeitschrift für afrikanische, ozeanische und ostasiatische Sprachen* 6:1–99.

Schuchardt, Hugo. 1896. Über den passiven Charakter des Transitivs in den kaukasichen Sprachen. *Sitzungsberichte der Kaiserlichen Akademie der Wissenschaften (Wien), Philosophisch-historische Classe* 133(1):1–91.

Seely, Jonathan. 1977. An Ergative Historiography. *Historiographica Linguistica* IV(2):191–206.

Sells, Peter (ed.). 2001. *Formal and Empirical Issues in Optimality Theoretic Syntax*. Stanford: CSLI Publications.

Sen, Subhadra Kumar. 1973. *Proto-New Indo-Aryan*. Calcutta: Eastern Publishers.

Sharma, Devyani. 2001. Kashmiri Case Clitics and Person Hierarchy Effects. In *Formal and Empirical Issues in Optimality Theoretic Syntax*, ed. Peter Sells. 225–256. Stanford: CSLI Publications.

Silverstein, Michael. 1976. Hierarchy of features and ergativity. In *Grammatical Categories in Australian Languages*, ed. R. M. W. Dixon. 112–171. Canberra: Australian Institute of Aboriginal Studies.

Simpson, Jane. 1983. Resultatives. In *Papers in Lexical-Functional Grammar*, ed. L. Levin, M. Rappaport, and A. Zaenen. Indiana University Linguistics Club.

Simpson, Jane. 1991. *Warlpiri Morpho-Syntax*. Dordrecht: Kluwer.

Slobin, Dan I. 1985. Crosslinguistic Evidence for the Language-Making Capacity. In *The Crosslinguistic Study of Language Acquisition, Volume 2: Theoretical Issues*, ed. Dan I. Slobin. Hillsday, NJ: Lawrence Erlbaum.

Speas, Margaret. 1990. *Phrase Structure in Natural Language*. Dordrecht: Kluwer.

Speijer, J. S. 1886. *Sanskrit Syntax*. Delhi: Motilal Banarsidass. Republished 1973.

Steedman, Mark. 2001. *The Syntactic Process*. Cambridge: The MIT Press.

Stiebels, Barbara. 2000. Linker Inventories, Linking Splits and Lexical Economy. In *Lexicon in Focus*, ed. Barbara Stiebels and Dieter Wunderlich. 211–245. Berlin: Akademie Verlag. Studia Grammatica 45.

Stiebels, Barbara. 2002. *Typologie des Argumentlinkings: Ökonomie und Expressivität*. Berlin: Akademie Verlag. Studia Grammatica 54.

Stowell, Tim. 1981. *Origins of Phrase Structure*. Doctoral dissertation, MIT.

Subbarao, K.V. 2001. Agreement in South Asian Languages and Minimalist Inquiries: The Framework. In *The Yearbook of South Asian Languages and Linguistics*, ed. Peri Bhaskararao and K.V. Subbarao. 457–492. New Delhi: Sage Publications. Tokyo Symposium on South Asian Languages: Contact, Convergence and Typology.

Svenonius, Peter. 2002. Icelandic Case and the Structure of Events. *Journal of Comparative Germanic Linguistics* 5:197–225.

Tesnière, Lucien. 1959. *Éléments de Syntaxe Structurale*. Paris: Klincksieck.

Thompson, Sandra. 1995. The Iconicity of 'Dative Shift' in English. In *Syntactic Iconicity and Linguistic Freezes*, ed. Marge E. Landsberg. 155–175. Berlin: Mouton de Gruyter.

Trask, R. L. 1979. On the Origins of Ergativity. In *Ergativity: Towards a Theory of Grammatical Relations*, ed. Frans Plank, 385–404. New York. Academic Press.

Trombetti, Alfredo. 1903. Delle relazioni delle lingue caucasiche, Part II. *Giornale delle Società asiatica italiana* 16:145–175.

Uhlenbeck, C. Cornelis. 1916. Het passieve karakter van het verbum transitivum of van het verbum actionis in talen von Noord-Amerika. *Verslagen en mededeelingen der Koninklijke Akademie van Wetenschappen. Afd. Letteren* 187–216. 5e reeks.

Van Valin, Robert D. 1977a. *Aspects of Lakhota Syntax*. Doctoral dissertation, University of California, Berkeley.

Van Valin, Robert D. 1977b. Ergativity and the Universality of Subjects. In *Papers from the Thirteenth Regional Meeting of the Chicago Linguistic Society*, 689–706.

Van Valin, Robert D. 1991. Another Look at Icelandic Case Marking and Grammatical Relations. *Natural Language and Linguistic Theory* 9:145–194.

Van Valin, Robert D. 1993. A Synopsis of Role and Reference Grammar. In *Advances in Role and Reference Grammar*, ed. Robert D. Van Valin. 1–164. Amsterdam: John Benjamins.

Van Valin, Robert D. 2004. Semantic macroroles in Role and Reference Grammar. In *Semantische Rollen*, ed. Rolf Kailuweit and Martin Hummel. 62–82. Tübingen: Narr.

Van Valin, Robert D., and Randy J. La Polla. 1997. *Syntax: Structure, Meaning and Form*. Cambridge: Cambridge University Press.

Vendler, Zeno. 1967. *Linguistics in Philosophy*. Cornell University Press.

Verkuyl, Henk. 1993. *A Theory of Aspectuality*. Cambridge: Cambridge University Press.

Verma, M. K., and K.P. Mohanan (ed.). 1990. *Experiencer Subjects in South Asian Languages*. Stanford: CSLI Publications.

Versteegh, Kess. 1997. *Landmarks in Linguistic Thought III: The Arabic Linguistic Tradition*. London: Routledge.

Vogel, Ralf. 2001. Case Conflict in German Free Relative Constructions: An Optimality Theoretic Treatment. In *Competition in Syntax*, ed. Gereon Müller and Wolfgang Sternefeld. 341–375. Berlin: Mouton de Gruyter.

Vogel, Ralf und Marksu Steinbach. 1998. The Dative — an Oblique Case. *Linguistische Berichte* 65–90.

Wegener, Heide. 1991. Der Dativ — ein struktureller Kasus? In *Merkmale und Strukturen syntaktischer Kategorien*, ed. Gisbert Fanselow and Sascha Felix. 70–103. Tübingen: Narr.

Wheelock, Frederic M. 1963. *Latin: An Introductory Course Based on Ancient Authors*. New York: Barnes and Noble.

Wierzbicka, Anna. 1981. Case Marking and Human Nature. *Australian Journal of Linguistics* 1:43–80.

Williams, Edwin. 1981. Argument Structure and Morphology. *The Linguistic Review* 1(1):81–114.

Woolford, Ellen. 2001. Case Patterns. In *Optimality-Theoretic Syntax*, ed. Géraldine Legendre, Jane Grimshaw, and Sten Vikner. 509–543. Cambridge: The MIT Press.

Woolford, Ellen. 2003. Burzio's Generalization, Markedness and Locality Constraints on Nominative Objects. In *New Perspectives on Case Theory*, ed. Ellen Brandner and Heike Zinsmeister. 301–329. Stanford: CSLI Publications.

Wunderlich, Dieter. 1996. A Minimalist Model of Inflectional Morphology. In *The Role of Economy Principles in Linguistic Theory*, ed. Hans-Martin Gärtner Wilder, Chris and Manfred Bierwisch. 267–298. Berlin: Akademie Verlag.

Wunderlich, Dieter. 1997. Cause and the Structure of Verbs. *Linguistic Inquiry* 28(1):27–68.

Wunderlich, Dieter. 2003. Optimal Case Patterns: German and Icelandic Compared. In *New Perspectives on Case Theory*, ed. Ellen Brandner and Heike Zinsmeister. 331–367. Stanford: CSLI Publications.

Wunderlich, Dieter, and Renate Lakämper. 2001. On the Interaction of Structural and Semantic Case. *Lingua* 111:377–418. Special Issue *On the Effects of Morphological Case*.

Yip, Moira, Joan Maling, and Ray Jackendoff. 1987. Case in Tiers. *Language* 63(2):217–250.

Zaenen, Annie. 1993. Unaccusativity in Dutch: Integrating Syntax and Lexical Semantics. In *Semantics and the Lexicon*, ed. J. Pustejovsky. 129–161. Dordrecht: Kluwer.

Zaenen, Annie, and Joan Maling. 1983. Passive and Oblique Case. In *Papers in Lexical-Functional Grammar*, ed. L. Levin, M. Rappaport, and A. Zaenen. Indiana University Linguistics Club.

Zaenen, Annie, Joan Maling, and Höskuldur Thráinsson. 1985. Case and grammatical functions: The Icelandic passive. *Natural Language and Linguistic Theory* 3:441–483. Reprinted in Joan Maling and Annie Zaenen (Eds.) *Syntax and Semantics 24: Modern Icelandic Syntax*, 95–164. New York: Academic Press. 1990.

Zakharyin, Boris. 1979. On the Formation of Ergativity in Indo-Aryan and Dardic. *Osmania Papers in Linguistics* 5:50–71.

Zubizarreta, Maria Luisa. 1998. *Prosody, Focus and Word Order*. Cambridge: The MIT Press.

Zwicky, Arnold. 1975. Settling on an underlying form: the English inflexional endings. In *Testing Linguistic Hypotheses*, ed. D. Cohen and J.R. Wirth. Washington: Hemisphere.

Language Index

American Indian, 160
Arabic, 2, 18–20, 22, 25, 26, 54
Australian, 9–11, 108, 139–142

Bantu, 83, 122, 123, 132, 136
Basque, 115, 155, 156, 159, 163, 164, 171, 172, 174, 177, 179
Batsbi, *see* Tsova-Tush
Bengali, 180, 191, 198, 201
Bulgarian, 5

Chicheŵa, 132–134, 136
Chinese, 13, 108, 109, 111
Chinook, 162
Choctaw, 43, 100

Dakota, 162
Dutch, 42, 66, 100, 110, 124, 136
Dyirbal, 164, 165, 167, 170, 176, 203, 204, 206

English, 4, 5, 8, 11, 25, 26, 30–32, 38, 47, 52–55, 58, 63, 66, 67, 69, 77, 83, 85, 88, 93–96, 99, 102, 105, 108–111, 113, 115, 119–123, 127, 128, 133, 134, 139, 141, 146, 152, 160, 163, 164, 171, 178, 190, 193, 198, 206, 209, 215, 216
  Old, 45, 90, 181, 201

Finnish, 10, 107, 112, 155, 192–194, 196

French, 4, 9, 47, 55, 67, 133–136, 138, 167

Georgian, 36–38, 45, 77, 145, 155, 158–161, 163, 164, 167, 171–174, 185, 199, 212
German, 7, 11, 26, 27, 32, 40, 42, 44, 58, 63, 67–70, 87, 105, 106, 108–113, 115–117, 122, 127, 128, 151, 154, 156, 159, 160, 171, 180, 191, 204, 206–211, 226
Greek, 1, 2, 101, 140, 155, 159, 160
  ancient, 12–14

Hebrew, 13, 203
Hindi, 70, 91, 111, 121, 134, 148, 155–160, 163, 166–169, 171–173, 176, 177, 180, 183–185

Icelandic, 4, 5, 9, 107, 108, 115–117, 122, 124, 126, 128, 130, 132, 135, 166, 196–199, 207, 209, 210
Indo-Iranian, 182
Inuit, 165
Inuktitut, 182
Irish, 53, 54, 58, 94
Italian, 4, 40–43, 66, 67, 100, 110, 115, 198

Japanese, 8, 108, 109, 111

K'iche', 177
Kabardian, 174

Kaluli, 177, 179
Kashmiri, 224
Kayardild, 10, 139, 197
Korean, 7

Lakhota, 203
Latin, 1, 3–5, 7, 9, 11, 12, 14, 15, 21, 26, 38, 58, 59, 67, 87, 140, 141, 155, 157, 160, 189, 200

Malagasy, 26, 76, 77
Malayalam, 223
Marathi, 134, 180
Martuthunira, 139, 142
Meriam Mir, 155

Navajo, 5

Paiute, 162
Persian, 6, 183
  Old, 181
Polynesian, 182
Punjabi, 157, 180, 185, 187

Romance, 134–136, 138
Russian, 9, 145, 146, 190, 191, 193

Samoan, 179
Sanskrit, 2, 12–15, 94, 104, 140, 152, 154, 180–183, 200, 201
Scottish Gaelic, 193–195, 218
Slavic, 141
South Asian, 55
Spanish, 4

Tagalog, 162, 203
Takelma, 162
Tsova-Tush, 212, 213
Turkish, 26, 144, 192–194, 196, 220, 222–224

Ubykh, 174
Urdu, 7–9, 11, 22, 40, 67, 103, 107, 110, 115, 116, 120, 126, 130, 133–136, 143–145, 147, 148, 150, 152, 153, 155–160, 163, 164, 166–169, 171–173, 176, 177, 180, 183–185, 192, 193, 196, 199, 201, 206, 212, 220–222, 224

Vedic, 152, 201

Wambaya, 141, 142, 163, 164
Warlpiri, 141, 142, 164
Welsh, 53, 54
West Greenlandic, 212
West Greenlandic, 27, 30, 156, 158–160, 164, 171, 172, 174, 177, 178

Yana, 162
Yimas, 172

Subject Index

ϕ projection, 119
$\pm$HR, 103
$\pm$LR, 103
$\pm$hr, 112
$\pm$lr, 112
$\pm$o, 126, 128
$\pm$r, 126, 128
θ-Criterion, 130
θ-assignment, 60
θ-criterion, 32, 57, 208
θ-role, 32, 49, 56, 57, 60, 62, 63, 65, 67–69, 76, 77
θ-theory, 49, 55
vP, 76
ezafe construction, 6
ne-cliticization, 40
suru, 8
1-Advancement Exclusiveness Law, 34

syntactic ergativity hypothesis, 164

a-structure, 122
Aṣṭādhyāyī, 15
Abstract Case, 103
accusative
  language, 32, 159
Action Tier, 95
Actor-Undergoer Hierarchy, 205
adjunct, 7
advancement, 34
adverbial
  case, 6
  duration, 7
AFF, 95
affectedness, 96, 116, 134, 135, 146, 190
agent, 16, 17
  quintessential, 190
agreement, 53–56, 64, 166–168, 171–174, 176, 177, 179, 187, 204, 206–208, 210, 212
  and case, 55
  linking, 107, 115
  subject, 109, 110, 132
AgrP, 88, 167
aktionsart
  Vendler, 204
Al-Kitāb, 18
alternations, 132
  object, 144, 192
  semantically motivated, 189
  subject, 144, 198
animacy hierarchy, 176, 221
applicative, 83, 211
arcs, 33
argument
  alternation, 49
  demotion, 35, 65, 109, 125
  external, 62, 76, 79
  highest, 49, 76
  roles, 49
  selection, 98
  thematic, 102

252

Argument Fusion, 130, 134
argument linking, *see* linking
Argument Selection Principle, 99
argument structure, 49, 51, 58, 86, 88, 91–94, 102, 104–106, 109, 114–116, 122, 126, 135, 138, 143
Aristarchos of Samothrake, 13
Ars Grammatica, 13
aspectual boundedness, 193
AspP, 86, 171, 197
attribute-value matrix, 118
auxiliary selection, 40, 66, 110, 115, 136, 138
Auxiliary Selection Principle, 138
AVM, 118

beneficiary, 21
bootstrapping
  semantic, 178
  syntactic, 178
Burzio's Generalization, 62

c-structure, 118
Case
  absorption, 65
  abstract, *see* Case (structural)
  accusative, 58, 59, 62, 63, 66, 67, 81, 87
  inherent, 67–70, 87, 89
    dative, 69
  nominative, 55, 57, 59, 60, 67–69, 71, 84, 87
  semantic, 71
  strong, 192, 218
  structural, 58, 70, 75, 87, 89, 95, 217
  weak, 192, 218
case
  rafʻ, 19
  absolutive, 27, 32, 156, 157, 160, 161, 177, 179
  absolutive vs. nominative, 157
  abstract vs. morphosyntactic, 103
  accusative, 4, 7, 8, 17, 19, 21, 25, 26, 30, 32, 37, 40, 43, 45
  accusative of direction, 15, 21, 189

active instrumental, 155
adverbial, 6
agent, 157
agentive nominative, 156
allative, 155
assignment rules, 207
dative, 8, 9, 11, 14, 15, 21, 31, 36–38, 45, 67
  free, 191
dative of location, 15
default, 17, 130, 147
default association principles, 126
dependent structural case, 170
ergative, 27, 30, 40
  restricted, 174
ergative assignment rules, 212
genitive, 8, 18, 45
genitive of origin, 15
illative, 155
inherent, non-quirky, 174
instrumental, 17, 67
interpretable, 197
inventory, 106, 112
jarr, 19
morphosyntactic, 106, 174
naṣb, 19
narrative, 157
nominal, 8
nominative, 4, 8, 9, 18, 25, 26, 32, 36–38, 43, 45, 53–56, 58, 59, 63, 70, 87, 156
nominative of the agent, 155
non-canonical, 211
origin, 180
overt marking, 13
partitive, 192
positional, 146
quirky, *see* quirky case, 147
role, 49, 50
semantic, 6, 71
structural, 112, 146
terminology, 12
TMA, 10
verbal, 8
vocative, 13, 14

case alternation, 36
case and agreement, 55
case features, 81, 103
   uninterpretable, 75
Case Filter, 58, 60–62, 71, 80, 147, 168, 169, 223
case frames, 29, 32
Case Grammar, 29, 161, 203
case paradigm
   Latin, 3, 4
   Sanskrit, 16
case relationships, 30
   Agentive, 30
   Dative, 30
   Factitive, 30
   Instrumental, 30
   Locative, 30
   Objective, 30, 50
   Predicative, 50
Case Resistance Principle, 7
case role, 29, 51
case stacking, 10, 139
case system, 159
   active, 160
   typology, 161
case sytem
   typology, 162
Case Theory, 29, 47, 71, 72
causative, 20, 133, 134, 136, 145, 153
   alternation, 133
chômeur, 33–35, 37, 38, 45
clitic, 11
Combinatory Categorical Grammar (CCG), 226
complement, 51, 52, 56–59, 61–63, 66, 68, 69, 78, 80, 81, 84–86, 90
complementizing oblique, 10
complex predicate
   noun-verb, 8, 149
constraint
   *$\emptyset_C$, 223
   *Struc$_C$, 223
   activation, 219
   re-ranking, 224
   violable, 214
constructive case, 141, 145
control, 72
control (agency), 198–200
copy-theory of movement, 77

dative, 107
dative alternation, 45, 67, 83, 86, 92, 96, 97, 99, 104, 133, 134, 152, 209
dative inversion, 36
dative sickness, 198
De Lingua Latina, 14
Deep Structure, 47
deep structure, 30, 31, 51, 92
default case, 145, 147
definiteness, 144
Dependency Grammar, 29
dependent, 4, 7
   marking, 5
derivation, 24
differential object marking, 144, 221
differential subject marking, 144
Dionysios Thrax, 13
discontinuous constituent, 141
discourse configuration, 5
ditransitive, 31, 38, 67, 90
double nominative, 120
double object
   English, 83, 209

ECM, 55, 71
Elsewhere Case, 147
Elsewhere Condition, 13
Elsewhere Principle, 104
English, 22
EPP, 63, 76, 170
ergative
   inherent vs. structural Case, 166
   language, 32, 159
   origin of term, 155
   system, 154, 179, 183
   verb
      German, 40
      unaccusative, 40
ergativity, 154

acquisition, 177
  ergative shift, 182
  historical change, 180
  passivization, 181
  possessives, 181
  split, *see* split ergativity
  syntactic
    tests, 164
  syntactic vs. morphological, 162
EVAL, 216
evidential marking, 36
Exceptional-Case-Marking, *see* ECM
experiencer, 191
  subject, 149
experiencer verb, *see* psych verb
expletive, 71, 102, 115
Extended Projection Principle, *see* EPP

f-structure, 118
feature
  checking, 75
  interpretable, 75
  interpretable case, 197
  lexical assignment, 116
  linking, 126
  strong, 75
  unification, 103
  uninterpretable, 75
Final 1 Law, 35, 63
Function-argument biuniqueness, 130
Function-argument biuniqueness, 208
functional category, 53
  Asp, 54
  I, 56
  T, 56
functional equation, 119
functional projection, 74
  AspP, 86
  IP, 62
  TP, 55, 81

GB, 26, 29, 46, 47, 58, 62, 64–66, 69, 71, 74, 77, 80, 87, 89
GEN, 215
Generative Semantics, 78

genitive, 201
genitive 's, 52
gerundive, 200
goal/beneficiary, 48, 67
governed, 19
Government-Binding, *see* GB
government theory, 20
governor, 19
grammaticalization cline, 180
Grammaticalization Theory, 180
grammatical functions, 93, 121, 124, 127, 128, 130, 131, 136, 138, 139, 146, 148
  classification, 129
  semantically restricted, 127
  semantically unrestricted, 127
grammatical relations, 2, 11, 13, 27, 28, 38, 42, 44, 87
  hierarchy, 33
  inverse alignment, 165
  non-term, 33
  term, 33

Harmonic Alignment, 221
Harmonic Grammar, 214
head, 4–7, 9
Head-driven Phrase Structure Grammar, *see* HPSG
head marking, 5
HPSG, 120, 226

Icelandic Association Principles, 124
iconicity principle, 140
idioms, 123
impersonal, 102
  passive, 40, 63, 70
indirect object, 27–29, 33, 35–37
infinitive, 8
  narrative, 9
inside-out functional uncertainty, 142
intransitive, 30, 38–41
inverse alignment, 204
Inversion, 37, 45
inversion construction, 161
IP, 53, 62

Kāraka Roles, 17
Kāraka Theory, 16
karman, 16
Katz-Postal Hypothesis, 50
kernel, 23, 24

lambda abstraction, 101
LCS, 77, 94–97
LDG, 111, 151–153, 225
Lexical-Functional Grammar, see LFG
Lexical Conceptual Structure, see LCS
lexical decomposition, 15, 78, 91, 94, 100
 two-tiered, 101
Lexical Decomposition Grammar, see LDG
Lexical Mapping Theory, see LMT
LFG, 91, 93, 94, 100, 111, 117
linking, 91, 94, 205
 algorithm, 206
 by agreement, 108
 by case, 108
 by position, 108
 features, 126
 Kiparsky's theory, 100
 patterns, 175
 principles, 146
 rules, 127
 space, 131
LMT, 136
localist theory, 14, 15, 189
locative inversion, 132
Logical Form (LF), 47
Logical Structure, 204

M-transitivity, 209
macrorole
 Actor, 204
 Undergoer, 204
macroroles, 199
 default assignment principles, 208
 number vs. nature, 208
Mapping Principles, 129
Mapping Theory, 91, 122, 126, 128

markedness, 106, 113
 hierarchy, 130
Maximus Planudes, 15, 190
merge, 74
middle, 102
Minimalist Program, see MP
modal, 149
 ablative, 10
 oblique, 10
 proprietive, 10
Move-α, 60
movement
 featural trigger, 75
MP, 46, 73–75, 77, 79, 83, 85, 87
multistratal, 35

narrative infinitive, 9
neural networks, 219
nominalization, 8, 48, 51, 59, 92–94
nominative
 double, 120
nonconfigurationality, 141
NP-movement, 54

object, 25, 27–30, 32–37, 40, 45
 genitive, 68, 194, 201
Optimality Theory, see OT
OT, 117, 150, 213
 bidirectional, 225
OT-LFG, 215

Pāṇini, 13, 15, 16
participial, 200
passive, 20, 24–27, 34, 35, 38, 44, 45, 64, 82, 102, 109, 113, 114, 125, 130, 131, 151, 207, 210
 dative, 69
 impersonal, 40
 properties, 64
patient, 16–18, 191
phases, 73
Phonological Form, 47
pivot
 syntactic, 162, 204, 207
Polish, 226
polyadicity, 94

positional case, 146
predicate-argument, 91, 92, 94, 123, 146
Privileged Syntactic Argument, *see* PSA
PRO, 71
Projection Principle, 56
prominence scale, 221
pronouns, 176, 179, 188
proposition, 92
Proto-Agent, 98–100, 137, 138
Proto-Patient, 98–100, 137
proto-roles, 31, 91, 98, 100, 137, 139, 151, 178
   entailments, 98
proto roles, 199
PSA, 204
   modulation, 207
   selection, 210
psych verb, 88, 138, 149, 198

quirky case, 60, 70, 71, 116, 124–126, 145, 147, 149, 151, 170, 196
   inherent, 174

receiver, 21
reflexive, 41
Relational Grammar, *see* RG
Relational Network, 33
Remarks on Nominalization, 48
Remmius Palaemon, 13
resultatives, 94
RG, 26, 33, 48, 63–66, 89, 90, 161
Role and Reference Grammar, *see* RRG
RRG, 203
rule ordering, 15

Sībawaihi, 18
semantic case, 144, 147
Semantic Form, *see* SF
semantic primitives, 94
semantic projection, 122
semantic roles, *see* thematic roles
SF, 101–103, 105, 111, 112
small clause, 83

SpecCP, 70
specificity, 144, 148, 150, 192, 194, 195
Specificity Principle, 104, 106
specifier, 51–54, 56–59, 61, 75, 85
SpecIP, 60
SpecVP, 60
spell-out, 73
split ergativity, 176
   NP-split, 176, 212
   tense/aspect, 176
split Infl hypothesis, 167
spray/load alternation, 96
Stoics, 14
Stratal Uniqueness Law, 35
stratum, 34, 35
structural case, 146
subject, 25, 27, 28, 30, 31, 33–38, 40, 43, 45
   active, 30, 39
   dative, 201, 211
   inactive, 30, 39
   quirky, 9
   tests, 70, 166
Subject Condition, 130
subject requirement, 35
Suffixaufnahme, 10
Surface Structure, 47
syncretism, 180
syntactic pivot, 162
Syntactic Structures, 24, 46

T-model, 47
Tékhnē, 13, 15
TAG, 74, 226
telicity, 42, 137
term relation, 33
TG, 20, 24, 25, 28, 31, 46
thematic argument, 102
thematic hierarchy, 31, 96, 101, 123, 145
   evidence for, 123
thematic relation, *see* thematic roles
thematic roles, 4, 11, 13, 14, 31–33, 36, 38, 42, 44, 49, 56–58, 85
   agent, *see* agent

beneficiary, 21
classification, 129
experiencer, 58
Kāraka Roles, 17
Kāraka Theory, 16
karman, 16
kartr, 16
patient, *see* patient
receiver, 21
stimulus, 58
theme, 58
types, 31
Thematic Tier, 95
topicality, 192, 218
TP, 55, 81, 167, 197
trace, 60
Transformational Grammar, *see* TG
transformations, 23, 24, 48, 50, 52, 60, 73
  passive, 25
transitive, 30, 32, 33, 38, 40, 42, 81
transitivity, 95, 174, 178
Tree-Adjoining Grammar, *see* TAG

unaccusative, 39–41, 43, 57, 60, 81, 94, 100, 109, 110, 115, 126, 130, 132, 139, 152, 154, 160, 161, 179, 208, 213, 216
  definition, 39
  terminology, 39
Unaccusative Hypothesis, 33, 38, 39, 60
unergative, 39–43, 60, 80, 100, 110, 130–132, 138, 148, 152, 158, 160, 161, 167, 169, 172, 173, 175, 179, 208, 212
  definition, 39
  incorporation analysis, 172
  terminology, 39
unergative/unaccusative distinction, 43
unification, 119
Unification Principle, 104
Uniformity of Theta Assignment Hypothesis, *see* UTAH

Uniqueness Constraint, 113
Uniqueness Principle, 104
UTAH, 44, 57, 85

valence
  semantic, 207
  syntactic, 207
Varro, 13
verb
  affective, 45
verbal noun, 8
voice, 18, 76
volitional, 199
VP-internal subject hypothesis, 53, 55
VP-shell, 77, 83
VSO, 19, 53, 54

word order, 5
  and morphology, 108
  freedom, 5

X′-syntax, 51
X′-theory, 26, 118
Xena, 58

Zeno of Citium, 14